THE BUSINESS OF FASHION

THE BUSINESS OF FASHION

Designing, Manufacturing, and Marketing

FIFTH EDITION

Leslie Davis Burns, Kathy K. Mullet, and Nancy O. Bryant

Fairchild Books
An imprint of Bloomsbury Publishing Inc

B L O O M S B U R Y
NEW YORK · LONDON · OXFORD · NEW DELHI · SYDNEY

Fairchild Books

An imprint of Bloomsbury Publishing Inc

1385 Broadway	50 Bedford Square
New York	London
NY 10018	WC1B 3DP
USA	UK

www.bloomsbury.com

**FAIRCHILD BOOKS, BLOOMSBURY and the Diana logo
are trademarks of Bloomsbury Publishing Plc**

First published 1997
This edition first published 2016
© Bloomsbury Publishing Inc, 2016

Library of Congress Cataloging-in-Publication Data
Names: Burns, Leslie Davis. | Mullet, Kathy K., 1958- | Bryant, Nancy O.
Title: The business of fashion: designing, manufacturing, and marketing / Leslie Davis Burns,
Kathy K. Mullet, and Nancy O. Bryant.
Description: Fifth edition. | New York, NY, USA : Fairchild Books, an imprint
of Bloomsbury Publishing Inc., 2016.
Identifiers: LCCN 2016009229 | ISBN 9781501315213 (paperback)
Subjects: LCSH: Clothing trade—United States. | Fashion—Economic aspects. |
Fashion design. | Fashion merchandising. | BISAC: BUSINESS & ECONOMICS /
Industries / Fashion & Textile Industry.
Classification: LCC TT496.U6 B87 2016 | DDC 338.4/76870973—dc23
LC record available at http://lccn.loc.gov/2016009229

ISBN: PB: 978-1-5013-1521-3
         ePDF: 978-1-5013-1522-0

Typeset by Lachina
Printed and bound in the United States of America

contents

extended contents

PART III
PRODUCTION AND DISTRIBUTION
OF FASHION BRANDS

10 Preproduction Processes 229

11 Sourcing Decisions and
Production Centers 254

preface

Since the publication of the fourth edition of *The Business of Fashion: Designing, Manufacturing, and Marketing*, the global textile, apparel, accessories, home fashions, and retailing industries have continued to undergo tremendous change. Supply chain management, product life cycle management, mass customization, and fast fashion continue to evolve. International trade agreements continue to affect sourcing options, and strategies around responsible design, production, and marketing within the global industry have emerged. Omnichannel distribution strategies integrate bricks-and-mortar and non-store retailing strategies to create seamless experiences for the consumer. The fifth edition of this book attempts to capture the dynamics of the current fashion industry by emphasizing corporate social responsibility, technological changes, and changes in the global dimensions of its various components.

The Business of Fashion focuses on the organization and operation of the fashion industry—how fashion apparel and accessories and home fashions are designed, manufactured, marketed, and distributed—within the global economy. As we investigate this ever-changing industry, it is important to place current strategies within their historical context. Thus, Chapter 1 begins with a history of the textile, apparel, and accessories industries—from its inception in the late 1700s to the development and implementation of supply chain management strategies, globalization, fast fashion, e-commerce, and corporate social responsibility strategies. After setting the historical context, we turn to the global fashion supply/value chain and current organizational structures and forms of competition among companies within the fashion industry.

Chapter 2 discusses types of marketing channels within the global fashion industry, brand management, and fashion brand licensing. Because of the prevalence of licensing, this chapter discusses licensing contracts and examines the advantages and disadvantages of licensing. Marketing channels within the industry (i.e., direct, limited, and extended), as well as marketing channel integration, are outlined and explained. Chapter 3 discusses company ownership within the fashion business, including sole proprietorships, partnerships, corporations, and limited liability companies. Because of the increased interest in entrepreneurship, the chapter includes a discussion of starting a business. Chapter 3 ends with an overview of the laws affecting the textile, apparel, accessory, and home fashions industries, including international trade agreements, laws protecting inventions and designs, and laws related to business practices.

Chapter 4 outlines the organization and operation of the global materials industry—that is, the designing, manufacturing, and marketing of fibers and fabrics used in producing apparel, accessories, and home fashions. Leathers and fur are materials used for apparel and accessories and follow much of the same processing and marketing steps as other fabrics. We follow textile production from color forecasting and fiber processing through the marketing of seasonal lines of fabrics. Recent developments and issues within the industry, such as technological advancements and environmental and sustainability issues, provide a basis for understanding future trends in the global materials industry.

Chapter 5 focuses on the general classifications and organizational structures of fashion brand companies that produce men's, women's, and children's apparel and accessories and home fashions. Comparisons between ready-to-wear and couture, as well as among types of producers, classifications of brand names, and price zones, reinforce appreciation of the complexities of fashion industries. The chapter also introduces merchandising philosophies and major divisions within fashion brand companies (research and merchandising, design and product development, operations, sales/marketing, advertising/sales promotion, and finance and information technology). Trade associations and trade publications also are described in this chapter.

Chapter 6 begins a four-chapter sequence on creating and marketing fashion brand merchandise. This sequence follows a fashion line/collection through the various stages of research, design, style selection, and marketing. In this chapter we focus on the various forms of research conducted before developing the line/collection: consumer research, product research, market analysis, brand position, and fashion research. Chapter 7 highlights the creation and use of a design brief. Components of the design brief include target customer analysis; color, fabric, and style considerations; materials, fabrics, and trims; and technical drawings of each item. The role of the design team and their review process are also examined in this chapter. The creation of a fashion line continues in Chapter 8, which discusses design development and style selection, including the development of first patterns, creation of prototypes, initial cost estimates, and selection of styles for the final line. This chapter also outlines the process of writing an effective garment/product specification sheet. Similarities and differences in developing national brands and private label brands are discussed. The chapter concludes at the stage when the final line is marketed to retail buyers.

Chapter 9 describes locations of, and roles played by, marts and trade shows in facilitating the marketing of fashion brands. Next, it discusses how merchandise is sold through corporate selling and sales representatives. The chapter ends with an overview of marketing strategies used by fashion brand companies when distributing and promoting their lines. Throughout this sequence of events in creating and marketing fashion brands, the chapters highlight new technological developments, including product life cycle management, Web-based communications including social media, global perspectives, and organizational changes in the industry.

Chapter 10 begins a four-chapter treatment of the production and distribution of fashion brand merchandise. This chapter describes preproduction processes, including determining production orders, factoring, ordering production fabrics/materials, pattern finalization, pattern grading, making the production marker, and production cutting. Chapter 11 outlines the sourcing options for producing fashion brand merchandise and the criteria companies use in making sourcing decisions. The chapter also describes global patterns of production and applications of corporate social responsibility in assessing the advantages and disadvantages of domestic and foreign production. Chapter 12 explores the various production methods used for fashion brand merchandise. After first describing production sewing systems and technological developments, the chapter then provides an overview of quality assurance strategies and auxiliary production agents. Chapter 12 ends with a summary of product finishing and the creation of floor-ready merchandise. Once produced, the merchandise is distributed to retailers, often through distribution centers. Chapter 13 summarizes distribution strategies and processes used by fashion brand companies. A description of the various types of store and non-store retailers and omnichannel distribution strategies ends this chapter.

In introducing students to this dynamic, multifaceted business, the book incorporates real-world examples from its component industries. To give readers a sampling of the many career options throughout the fashion industry, lists of selected career opportunities are included at the end of each chapter. We also include case studies at the end of each chapter, so that students can apply what they have learned to a real-world situation. Other end-of-chapter features that help students prepare for their own entry into the fashion business include chapter summaries, lists of key terms, discussion questions, class activities, and references.

STUDENT RESOURCES

The Business of Fashion STUDIO:
- Study smarter with self-quizzes featuring scored results and personalized study tips.
- Review concepts with flashcards of terms and definitions.

INSTRUCTOR RESOURCES
- Instructor's Guide includes projects, case studies, and test questions connected to the knowledge and skill guidelines in the Association to Advance Collegiate Schools of Business (AACSB) standards.
- PowerPoint presentations include images from the book and provide a framework for lecture and discussion.

Fairchild Books offers STUDIO access free with new book purchases (order ISBN 9781501315282); this resource is also sold separately through Bloomsbury Fashion Central (www.BloomsburyFashionCentral.com).

acknowledgments

Many people have assisted with the development of this book, and we are grateful for their time, effort, and support. Leslie Davis Burns thanks her former students and wonderful colleagues at numerous companies and universities, who shared their ideas and resources in the development of the book. Leslie particularly thanks her coauthor, Kathy Mullet, whose valuable expertise in technical design, production, and industry trends is highlighted in this fifth edition. Kathy Mullet expresses her appreciation to Leslie Burns for the opportunity to work with her on the fifth edition of this book. Kathy also thanks her former students for their continual sharing of information about the apparel industry. Many other professional contacts in the apparel industry also most willingly shared their expertise.

We also thank the many readers and reviewers of the current and previous editions of this book. Their excellent input is reflected throughout. We owe our deepest appreciation to Amanda Breccia, Kiley Kudrna, Edie Weinberg, and Rona Tuccillo at Fairchild Books for their patience, professional attention to details, and invaluable assistance with this book. Thank you!

Leslie Davis Burns
  Responsible Global Fashion LLC
Kathy K. Mullet
  Associate Professor

PART I
Organization of the Global Fashion Industries

Historical Perspective of the Fashion Industry

IN THIS CHAPTER, YOU WILL LEARN
THE FOLLOWING:

- what the fashion industry is and how the textile and apparel industry fits within this context

- the history of the transition of the fashion industry from a craft industry to a factory-based industry to an information-based global industry

- the historical basis for the emergence of supply chain management, corporate responsibility, technological applications, and consumer focus

- the forms of interindustry cooperation and technologies needed for the success of global supply chain management

- current strategies in the fashion and retailing industries

The fashion industry consists of large and small companies that design, produce, and market fibers, textiles, apparel, and related fashions for consumers around the world. The fashion industry contributes to the economies of communities throughout the world. How did it all begin? How did these industries develop and grow into the dynamic industries they are today? To fully understand the modern textile, apparel, and related fashions industries, a brief review of how they began, grew, and changed since the industrial revolution of the 1800s is important.

WHAT IS FASHION?

According to Merriam-Webster's dictionary, **fashion** is defined as the prevailing style (as in dress) during a particular time (2016). More specifically, Sproles and Burns (1994, p. 4) defined fashion as a "style of consumer product or way of behaving that is temporarily adopted by a discernible proportion of members of a social group because that chosen style or behavior is perceived to be socially appropriate for time and situation."

Therefore, fashion can be seen in products from cars to shoes and interiors. In this text, we use this broad term, *fashion*, to relate more specifically to the apparel, footwear, accessories, and home fashion industries and any associated industries that contribute to the manufacture and selling of fashion products.

Because *fashion* is a broad term and is the prevailing style, fashion is studied by those involved with the design, production, and distribution of fashion products. Fashion forecasting firms are research businesses that track trends and attitudes in consumers to determine what will evolve as the next prevailing style. Because fashion is evolutionary and not revolutionary in its development, understanding the history of fashion enables researchers to predict the prevailing style.

FASHION INDUSTRY

Before the industrial revolution, in the mid-1700s, the upper class ruled fashion. Sumptuary laws have been used throughout history to dictate what type of clothing could be worn and by whom. Often, the higher social classes dictated fashion. Dressmakers or tailors were producing styles that were worn by the wealthy. In fashion history, we usually relate the prevailing style in an era to a prominent ruler and not to a specific designer or company. Not until the rise of the middle class during the industrial revolution do we see the influence of technology and need for ready-to-wear (RTW) fashion.

1789–1890: Mechanization of Production

For thousands of years, the spinning and weaving of fabrics were labor-intensive hand processes. Then, in England, in the mid-1700s, the spinning of yarn and weaving of cloth began to be mechanized. At that time, England's cotton and wool textile industries were the most technologically developed in the Western world. In response to a growing demand for textiles both in England and abroad, a series of advances in the spinning and weaving of fabrics by English inventors brought the British industry to world prominence. These inventions included the following:

- the flying shuttle loom invented by John Kay in 1733
- the spinning machine or "jenny" invented by James Hargreaves in 1764
- the water-powered spinning machine invented by Sir Richard Arkwright in 1769
- the mechanized power loom invented by Reverend Edmund Cartwright in 1785–1787

The process for printing fabrics was also mechanized. England was protective of its technological developments, and levied severe penalties on people attempting to take blueprints and/or machines or their parts out of the country. Even the mechanics themselves were restricted from leaving the country. At the time, the England's textile factory system was one of the most productive—but it was also one of the most dehumanizing and unhealthy for its workers. England's labor reform movement in the mid-1800s was a call for reform in the textile industry (Yafa 2005).

In the United States, a fledgling cotton industry was taking root, but America lacked England's advanced technology for spinning and weaving cotton fibers. Then, in 1789, Samuel Slater, a skilled mechanic, brought English textile technology to the United States by memorizing the blueprints of the Arkwright water-powered spinning machine. Slater set up a spinning mill similar to the one shown in Figure 1.1. This mill, which opened in 1791, sparked the textile industry in the United States. Within a few years, spinning mills had sprung up all over New England. By the mid-1800s, towns such as Waltham, Lowell, Lawrence, and New Bedford, Massachusetts, as well as Biddeford, Maine, became centers of the newly emerging textile industry. These factories still relied on British inventions; any technological changes were based on reproducing and improving textile machinery used in England.

Figure 1.1
Early spinning mills, as introduced by Samuel Slater, included carding, drawing, roving, and spinning. Universal History Archive/UIG via Getty Images.

Figure 1.2
The Whitney Cotton Gin, patented by Eli Whitney, increased the speed and quality of the cotton cleaning process. Archive Photos/Getty Images.

Although the spinning process was becoming mechanized, the weaving process continued to be contracted out to individual hand weavers. In 1813, Francis Cabot Lowell originated a functional power loom. He set the stage for vertical integration within the industry; his factory was the first in the United States to perform mechanically all processes from spinning yarn to producing finished cloth under one roof. As early as 1817, power looms were being installed in textile mills all over New England. Despite the technological developments in weaving, however, the contracting out of the weaving process to hand weavers for complex fabrics continued until the late 1800s.

The mechanization of spinning and weaving made these processes so much faster, and fiber producers were pressured to supply a greater amount of cotton and wool. However, cotton growers in the South were limited by the time needed to handpick seeds from cotton. In 1794, Eli Whitney patented the cotton gin (*gin* stood for "engine"), which could clean as much cotton in one day as fifty men (Figure 1.2). Thanks to this invention, the cotton growers soon were able to supply New England's spinning and weaving mills' increased demands for fiber.

To be closer to this important source of cotton, manufacturers built textile mills in the southern states. The Northeast continued to be a primary producer of wool fabrics. By 1847, more people were employed in textile mills than in any other industry in the United States. Unfortunately, the squalor of the textile factory towns in England was also found in textile factory towns in the northeastern and southeastern United States. It took many years for unions and labor reforms to improve the pay and factory working conditions for those in the textile industry. In the meantime, consumer demand for cotton increased, and, by the late 1890s, three-quarters of the clothing in Europe and the United States was made from cotton (Yafa 2005).

The **ready-to-wear (RTW)** industry had its beginnings in the early eighteenth century. To meet the demand for ready-made clothing, tailors would make less expensive clothes from scrap material left over from sewing custom-made suits. Sailors, miners, and slaves were the primary target market for these early ready-made clothes, which were cut in "slop shops" and sewn by women at home. The term **slops** later became a standard word for cheap, ready-made clothing.

In 1858, Charles Fredrick Worth established the first fashion House in Paris. "Haute couture" was the name instituted by the government for the fashion houses that met industry standards. These fashion houses had to adhere to standards such as keeping at least twenty employees engaged in making the clothes, showing two collections per year at fashion shows, and presenting a certain number of patterns to customers. Worth was the first to commercialize his designs. Clients reviewed and ordered dresses from his showroom. He used live models to present his designs, included labels in his gowns, and became a successful brand that women sought. Though Worth did not mass-produce his designs, his promotion of fashions influenced how apparel went from a craft industry to a factory industry.

In the early nineteenth century, the demand for RTW clothing grew. The expanding number of middle-class consumers wanted good-quality apparel but did not want to pay the high prices associated with custom-made clothing. But RTW clothing did not become available to most consumers until the sewing process of apparel production became mechanized . Sewing machine inventions by Walter Hunt 1832), Elias Howe (1845), and Isaac Singer (1846) made it possible for apparel to be produced by machine, thereby speeding up the manufacturing process. From 1842 to 1895, there were 7,339 patents for sewing machines and accessories issued in the United States. The advertisement in Figure 1.3 shows how competitive the business had become. The sewing machine allowed relatively unskilled immigrant workers to sew garments in their homes. In addition, sewing factories were established, and some of the first men's clothing factories appeared as early as 1831. In fact, Singer's sewing machine, patented in 1851, was designed for factory use.

In the United States, men's RTW developed first. Children's RTW followed, first for boys and then for girls. The last to develop was RTW apparel for women. Men's RTW came first because the styling of men's apparel was less complicated than that of women's. By 1860, a variety of ready-made men's clothing was available. Indeed, between 1822 and 1860, the RTW segment of the menswear tailoring industry grew larger than the custom-made segment. Because of this increased demand, the number of sewing factories also grew.

A number of other advances contributed to the growth of the industry at this time. During the late 1800s, inventors developed motorized cutting knives and pressing equipment. Paper patterns also simplified the mass production of apparel. Ebenezer Butterick started a pattern business in 1863; James McCall started a similar one in 1870. Thus, by the end of the nineteenth century, mechanization of the textile and apparel production processes resulted in a growing number of companies. Table 1.1 summarizes the supply and demand needs of U.S. textile and apparel industries.

Figure 1.3
Sewing machine inventions provided increased speed in the production of apparel. Jay Paull/Getty Images.

Table 1.1 Supply and Demand Needs for the Emergence and Growth of Fashion Industries in the United States
Supply

• The need for plenty of fabric that could be produced quickly and the means to sew it quickly was achieved by the following inventions:
  – spinning machine (1764)
  – power loom (1785–87)
  – cotton gin (1794)
  – sewing machine (1832, 1845, 1846)
• The need for a ready supply of labor was achieved by immigrant workers who
  – began production sewing in their homes
  – were employed by sewing factories

Demand

• The need for customers and consumer demand for mass-produced apparel was achieved by the following:
  – sailors, miners, and slaves who needed inexpensive, ready-made clothing (slops)
  – an expanding number of middle-class consumers who wanted good-quality apparel at reasonable prices
• The need for a distribution system for mass-produced apparel, accessories, and home fashions was achieved by the following:
  – mail-order catalogs
  – general stores in rural areas
  – department stores (mid-1800s) in cities

Table 1.2	Historical Events 1789–1890: Mechanization of Spinning, Weaving, and Sewing
1791	Samuel Slater, who came to the United States in 1788, opens the first U.S. spinning mill.
1793	Hannah Slater, Samuel's wife, invents the 2-ply cotton sewing thread.
1794	Eli Whitney's cotton gin is patented.
1818	Brooks Brothers opens in New York City.
1851	Isaac Singer patents the sewing machine for factory use.
1853	Levi Strauss joins the family business founded by his brother-in-law, David Stern, which will come to be known as Levi Strauss & Co.
	Mid-1800s to late 1890s: Dry goods stores (forerunners of today's department stores) are opened: 1826–Lord & Taylor 1852–Marshall Field's 1857–R. H. Macy & Co. 1867–Rich's 1872–Bloomingdale Brothers, Inc. 1898–Burdines
1854	The first U.S. trade association, Hampden County Cotton Manufacturers Association, starts in Hampden County, Massachusetts.
1865	William Carter begins knitting cardigan jackets in the kitchen of his house in Needham Heights, Massachusetts. The William Carter Co. will grow to be one of the nation's largest children's companies.

With the availability of ready-made clothing, distribution outlets to consumers in cities increased. Brooks Brothers, one of the first well-known men's apparel stores, opened in New York City in 1818 and catered primarily to sailors and working-class men who could not afford custom-tailored clothing. In the mid-1800s, cities saw the development of dry goods stores that later became department stores.

For consumers unable to shop in the cities, illustrated catalogs were offering a wide variety of goods by the latter part of the nineteenth century. With the expansion of the U.S. postal service due to the introduction of parcel post in 1913, the continued development of railroads, and the introduction of rural free delivery (RFD) in 1893, such companies as Montgomery Ward (established in 1872) and Sears, Roebuck & Co. (established in 1886) created a growing mail-order business for ready-made clothing. Table 1.2 presents a timeline of other significant historical events during this period.

1890–1950: Growth of the Ready-to-Wear Industry

Although most men's apparel was available ready-made by the mid-nineteenth century, the women's RTW industry did not expand until the late nineteenth century (Figures 1.4, 1.5, and 1.6). The first types of RTW apparel produced for women were outerwear capes, cloaks, and coats. Because these garments fit more loosely than fashionable dresses, sizing was not a critical problem. Women also accepted manufactured corsets, petticoats, and other underwear items, perhaps because this type of clothing was hidden from public view. By the beginning of the twentieth century, RTW skirts and shirtwaists (blouses) were offered for sale. The popularity of the shirtwaist, made fashionable by Charles Dana Gibson's "Gibson girl," shifted women's apparel production from a craft industry to a factory-based industry. The emerging women's RTW industry was based on the shirtwaist and the popularity of separates—coats, blouses (shirtwaists), and skirts worn by young working women in the cities.

Production of RTW apparel was labor intensive. A ready supply of immigrant workers spurred the growth of the mass production of apparel. By 1900, approximately 500 shops in New York City were producing shirtwaists. The contracting system of production grew in popularity because it was esti-mated that an investment of only $50 was enough to start a business with a few workers and a bundle of cut garments obtained from a manufacturer or wholesaler. Production was divided into two segments:

1. a large number of sewing operations located in the homes of immigrants producing lower-priced garments
2. a relatively small number of large, modern sewing factories engaged in the production of better-quality garments

These sewing factories, primarily on the Lower East Side of New York City, were notorious for their poor working conditions. The term **sweatshop** origi-nally referred to the system of contractors and subcontractors whereby work was "sweated off." Later, the term became associated with the long hours, unclean and unsafe working conditions, and low pay of contract sewing factories, as well as with the dismal conditions of home factories, where contract workers sewed clothing.

In an effort to improve working conditions for industry employees, most of whom were young immigrant women, the International Ladies' Garment

Figure 1.4
Gibson Girl, illustration by Charles Dana Gibson, 1899. Hulton Archive/Getty Images.

Figure 1.5
By the 1890s, most men's apparel and some women's apparel were available ready-to-wear. Hulton Archive/Getty Images.

Figure 1.6
Ready-to-wear children's apparel was available for purchase by the 1890s. Lewis WickesHine/Buyenlarge/Getty Images.

Workers' Union (ILGWU) was formed in 1900 at a convention in New York City. The tragic fire at the Triangle Shirtwaist Co. factory on March 25, 1911, in which 146 young women died, brought public attention to the horrid working conditions while increasing support for the ILGWU. It is now the Textile, Manufacturing, and Distribution Division of the union UNITE HERE, which represents workers in the hospitality, food service, textile, apparel, and retailing industries.

In the 1920s, the women's fashion industry in New York moved from the Lower East Side to Seventh Avenue. This area of midtown Manhattan became known as New York's garment district, and it has remained the hub of women's fashion. The manufacturing of menswear was less centralized—Chicago, Baltimore, and New York emerged as manufacturing centers.

At the beginning of the twentieth century, most RTW clothing was made from cotton and wool. Silk fabric, imported from France and Italy, was highly desired for its luxurious qualities. However, it was very expensive, and the supply was limited. Thus, when synthetic substitutes for natural fibers were initially explored, "artificial silk" (rayon, made from wood pulp) was the first to be developed and patented in the United States. The first American rayon plant was opened in 1910. Synthetic dyestuffs for textile dyeing were developed and available by the beginning of the twentieth century.

Other inventions made during this time became staples in the RTW industry. An invention called the "locker" was demonstrated at the Chicago World's Fair in 1893. It was renamed the "zipper" in 1926 and had a major impact on the apparel industry. First used to fasten boots, the zipper was not generally used in fashion apparel until the 1930s.

Fashion magazines, beginning with *Vogue*, were first published in 1892. These magazines provided consumers with up-to-date fashion information and helped spur the desire for new fashions (Figure 1.7). Between 1910 and 1920, a variety of communication channels helped unite the fledgling RTW industry. Trade publications, such as the *Daily Trade Record* (menswear), established in 1892, and *Women's Wear Daily*, established in 1910, provided a great impetus to the RTW industry.

Another step in the development of the RTW industry was the result of wartime manufacturing. The First World War spurred the need for the manufacture of military uniforms, and, in turn, helped streamline apparel production methods. The closing of French and British fashion houses during the war was also important to U.S. textile and apparel industries; it allowed American fashion to develop from 1914 to 1918.

Although most items of women's clothing were available ready-made by the early 1900s, growth in the garment industry came about with the simplification of garment styles in the 1920s (Figure 1.8). The simpler styles may have spurred the growth of the industry, but industry methods also affected the styles of apparel that could be produced for, and thus adopted by, consumers. By the 1920s, mass-produced clothing was available to many people. The era of inexpensive fashion had begun. Most consumers valued new styles

Figure 1.7
Vogue is one of the oldest fashion magazines.
Conde Nast via Getty Images.

and variety more than costly one-of-a-kind apparel. Retail stores increased their inventory ratio of moderately priced clothing in proportion to more expensive goods.

A new development in retailing during this decade was the country's first outdoor shopping mall. The Country Club Plaza was built in 1922 in Kansas City, Missouri. It remains a gem among shopping areas, with its Spanish-style architecture and fountains reminiscent of Seville, Spain.

In the United States, New York City remained the center of the women's fashion industry, and Seventh Avenue was becoming synonymous with women's fashion. By 1923, New York City was producing nearly 80 percent of U.S. women's apparel in the city's growing garment district. Also during the 1920s, specialized sewing machines were developed, such as overlockers (sergers) and power-driven cutting equipment.

The U.S. stock market crash in 1929 devastated all aspects of the American economy. Repercussions were felt in Paris, as U.S. retail stores and private clients canceled orders overnight. The Great Depression of the 1930s, which resulted from the 1929 stock market crash, was a severe blow to the textile and apparel industries. These and other industries did not recover until the start of the Second World War. In 1929, it was estimated that New York had 3,500 dress companies; by 1933, there were only 2,300.

However, the 1930s brought about the development of the first synthetic fibers synthesized entirely from chemicals. Because most manufactured fibers were developed as substitutes for natural fibers, their properties were intended to emulate those of silk, wool, and cotton. Nylon, the first synthetic fiber, was conceptualized by E. I. du Pont de Nemours and Company in 1928, successfully synthesized in 1935, marketed in 1938, and introduced in nylon stockings in 1939. However, nylon production for consumer use was interrupted by the war, so its widespread popularity did not come until later.

It also became more common for manufacturers to use other companies, known as **contractors** and **subcontractors**, for some of their sewing operations. Some contractors specialized in specific processes, such as fabric pleating. For example, the manufacturer would ship the needed quantity of yard goods to the contractor for pleating. The contractor would return the pleated goods to the apparel manufacturer. Then the manufacturer would proceed with cutting and sewing operations.

During the 1930s, a large number of dress and sportswear companies emerged and grew in New York. In addition, the sportswear industry in California and other western states began to expand. The California sportswear industry actually began in the 1850s, when Levi Strauss & Co. began production of work trousers. It was not until the 1930s that sportswear made by other companies, such as White Stag, Jantzen, Cole of California, Pendleton Woolen Mills, and Catalina, became popular (see Figure 1.9). The sportswear trend was further legitimized by American designers, such as Claire McCardell and Vera Maxwell. These designers introduced informal, casual designer clothing in the late 1930s.

Several fashion magazines also debuted in the 1930s, each catering to a particular segment of consumers. *Mademoiselle*, established in 1935, and *Glamour*, first

Figure 1.8
Fashions with simplified designs and the "feeling of Paris couture." George Hoyningen-Huene/Conde Nast via Getty Images.

Figure 1.9
The 1930s brought a growth in the sportswear industry and the influence of sports on fashion. H. Armstrong Roberts/Retrofile /Getty Images.

published in 1939 as *Glamour of Hollywood*, catered to fashionable college coeds and young working women. *Esquire*, first published in 1933, was designed to enlighten men about the world of fashion and elegance. Movies of the era also served as a source of fashion inspiration for consumers, and movie stars became the fashion leaders of the day.

Brand names of manufacturers gained strong consumer recognition during the 1930s. One of the first to gain national recognition was the Arrow shirt. Launched in 1905, the Arrow shirt advertising campaign continued for many years. The ads featured color fashion illustrations of a sophisticated male, wearing an Arrow shirt, engaged in a variety of activities suitable to a man of taste and leisure. These ads remain classic examples of lifestyle advertising.

A number of changes in the 1940s profoundly influenced the U.S. apparel industry. Although the Second World War devastated the fashion industry in France,

Paris emerged once again after the war as a prominent player in the international fashion industry. However, the war allowed American designers such as Claire McCardell to become well known among consumers. The United States became known as the sportswear capital, and it held on to this title even after the Paris fashion houses reopened.

By the 1940s, the production of RTW clothing was located primarily in modern factories. Thanks to rising costs in New York City, factories had been built in New Jersey, Connecticut, and upstate New York. Apparel manufacturing factories were also springing up in other parts of the country. The apparel industry in California, centered in Los Angeles, emerged as the hub for the growing active and casual sportswear industry in the West. Dallas, Texas, also gained prominence in apparel manufacturing. Table 1.3 presents a timeline of other significant historical events during this period.

Table 1.3 Historical Events 1890–1950: Growth of the Ready-to-Wear Industry	
1892	American *Vogue* magazine begins publication.
1892	*Daily Trade Record*, the trade newspaper for the RTW menswear industry, begins publication; became *Daily News Record* in 1916.
1900	The International Ladies' Garment Workers' Union (ILGWU) is founded.
1901	Walin & Nordstrom Shoe Store opens in downtown Seattle.
1902	James Cash Penney, age 26, opens a dry goods and clothing store in Kemmerer, Wyoming.
1904	New York seamstress Lena Bryant introduces ready-to-wear (RTW) maternity wear. Her company, named Lane Bryant, becomes the first plus-size RTW producer.
1907	Herbert Marcus Sr., his sister Carrie, and brother-in-law, A. L. Neiman, start Neiman Marcus department store in Dallas.
1908	Filene's opens its "automatic bargain basement" in Boston. Merchandise in the upstairs store is automatically marked down 25 percent every week for three weeks, then sent to the basement. This practice marks the beginnings of the off-price store.
1910	*Women's Wear Daily*, trade newspaper for the women's wear industry, begins publication.
1911	146 garment workers die in a fire at the Triangle Shirtwaist Co. factory in New York's garment district. The tragedy stimulates a movement to end sweatshop conditions.
1914	The Amalgamated Clothing Workers of America (ACWA) union is formed as the primary union for the men's wear industry.
1922	Country Club Plaza, the country's first outdoor shopping mall, opens in Kansas City, Kansas.
1925	The first Sears Roebuck & Co. store opens in Chicago.
1926	J. M. Haggar starts his own men's wear company in Dallas, Texas, using assembly lines to manufacture men's trousers.
1939	Nylon stockings are introduced.
1941	Employment in the textile industry peaks at approximately 1.4 million.
1949	Bloomingdale's opens its first branch store in Fresh Meadows, New York.

Figure 1.10
Ozzie and Harriet Nelson, with sons Ricky and David. Spurred by the popularity of television and pop music, teenage fashion became a separate category in the 1950s. Al Pucci/NY Daily News Archive via Getty Images.

1950–1980: Diversification and Incorporation

The 1950s saw a general growth in consumer demand for apparel as well as a shift in the product mix demanded by consumers. Because of lifestyle changes, casual clothing and sportswear were an expanding segment of the fashion industry. In fact, between 1947 and 1961, wholesale shipments of casual apparel and sportswear increased approximately 160 percent. During the same period, suit sales decreased by approximately 40 percent.

Teenage fashion developed as a special category during the 1950s (Figure 1.10). It reached its peak during the youth explosion of the 1960s, when **mass fashion** became affordable to most of the population. Mass fashion focused on simplified styling and sizing, mass-production sewing in large factories, and distribution through retail chain stores. In 1965, half the U.S. population was under 25, and teenagers spent $3.5 million annually on apparel.

Spurred by increased orders from the military in the early 1950s, the textile industry also grew. In 1950, Burlington ranked as the largest Fortune 500 textile manufacturer with annual sales just over $1 billion. By the early 1950s, acrylic and polyester (both developed in the 1940s) were available to the U.S. market. Triacetate was introduced in 1954, and it provided a less heat-sensitive alternative to acetate, a previously developed synthetic fiber. Apparel made with synthetic fibers offered consumers easy-care, wrinkle-free, and drip-dry clothing that freed them from the high demands of caring for cotton and woolen clothing. These new fibers provided lower-cost and lighter-weight alternatives. Fashion trends and technological developments in textiles became intertwined. Textile mills developed new texturizing processes that made possible such innovations as stretch yarn. Nylon stretch socks became available in 1952. Later in the decade, nylon stretch pants became a fashion sensation.

In the 1960s, synthetic fibers began to overtake natural fibers in popularity. Apparel designers, such as Pierre Cardin, experimented with space-age materials. Plastic was used extensively, and heat-fusing techniques were developed. The natural fiber industry fought back with strong organizations such as the Cotton Council and the International Wool Secretariat. Eventually, natural fibers would again gain public favor, but not until after the 1970s—the decade of consumers' love affair with polyester.

After the Second World War came Christian Dior's New Look, and consumer attention turned again to Paris. During the 1950s and 1960s, Parisian haute couture continued to set fashion trends worldwide. However, increased productivity in mass-produced clothing allowed designer fashions to be copied and reproduced at a fraction of the cost of haute couture (Figure 1.11). During this period, RTW fashions became the standard worldwide, and Chanel suits, which were less expensive copies of the originals, were available to everyone. Since the 1970s, haute couture has been overshadowed by mass market apparel.

Figure 1.11
Ready-to-wear apparel of the 1950s copied the haute couture designs of the time. AGIP/RDA /Getty Images.

One of the most obvious changes in the apparel industry during the late 1950s and throughout the 1960s was the increase in large, publicly owned apparel corporations. In 1959, only 22 public apparel companies existed; by the end of the 1960s, more than 100 apparel companies had become publicly owned corporations. Some companies that went public early on were Jonathan Logan, Bobbie Brooks, and Leslie Fay.

Thanks to the growth of suburbia in the United States, fewer people lived in cities, and consumers wanted shopping outlets closer to their new homes. Thus, the shopping mall emerged. In 1956, Southdale Center, the first enclosed shopping mall, was built in a suburb of Minneapolis. During the 1960s, shopping malls appeared in virtually every suburb. Typically, regional or national department stores served as anchors.

However, rising labor costs in the United States led to increased prices of apparel for consumers. To keep costs down, retailers explored the idea of low overhead, self-service, and high-volume stores for apparel and other products. The strategy was successful, and retailers such as Kmart (Figure 1.12), Target, Walmart, and Woolco—known as discounters—flourished. In addition, as labor costs continued to rise, fashion brand companies searched for a cheaper workforce. Their search began within the United States, particularly in the Southeast. Then, it was expanded outside the United States, particularly in Hong Kong and

Figure 1.12
Discount retailers grew from retail strategies to keep merchandise costs to consumers as low as possible. Justin Sullivan/Getty Images.

Southeast Asia. Textile technology, once the domain of American companies, was increasingly imported from abroad. In 1967, for the first time in its history, the United States ran a trade deficit in textile machinery.

The 1970s saw the beginning of trends in which companies became vertically integrated, and large, publicly owned conglomerates bought apparel companies. For example, during this time, General Mills acquired Izod, David Crystal, and Monet jewelers; Consolidated Foods purchased Hanes hosiery and Aris gloves; and Gulf & Western bought Kayser-Roth.

Technological advances in the textile industry included a new generation of photographic printing and dyeing processes. Computer technology entered the textile and apparel manufacturing areas. The popularity of polyester double knit and denim fabrics sparked sales in the textile industry. However, increased competition from textile companies outside the United States cut into profits, and textile imports rose 581 percent between 1961 and 1976. Table 1.4 presents a timeline of other significant historical events during this period.

1980–1995: Imports and Quick Response

The 1980s and 1990s saw an increase in vertical integration among manufacturing and retailers. **Vertical integration** is a business strategy whereby companies control several steps of the design, production, marketing, and/or distribution of products. Strategies included the following:

- fashion brands (e.g., Nike, Tommy Hilfiger, Ralph Lauren) opening or expanding retail store operations
- department and specialty stores entering into partnerships with manufacturers and contractors to produce private label merchandise for their stores
- retail stores (e.g., The Limited, Gap, Banana Republic, Old Navy, Victoria's Secret) adopting a **store brand** concept, whereby the store offers only merchandise with the store name as its brand (These would become known as SPAs—specialty store retailers of private label apparel.)

Table 1.4 Historical Events 1950–1980: Diversification and Incorporation

1952	Orlon® acrylic is introduced; by 1956, over 70 million Orlon sweaters are sold.
1955	Mary Quant opens her boutique, Bazaar, in London.
1956	Southdale Center, the first enclosed shopping mall, is built in a Minneapolis suburb to serve shoppers. Dayton's serves as an anchor department store.
1958–59	To the benefit of intimate apparel, hosiery, and swimwear companies, DuPont introduces its first spandex fiber.
1960	Hanes-Millis Sales Corp. becomes the first national sock manufacturer to distribute its products through wholesalers.
1960	American Apparel Manufacturers Association (AAMA) is founded.
1962	Dayton's opens its discount store chain, Target.
1962	Sam Walton opened the first Walmart discount store; the company incorporates as Wal-Mart Stores Inc. in 1969.
1969	The Gap opens in San Francisco, selling records, cassettes, and Levi's. The store draws its name from the "generation gap."
1969	Target opens its first distribution center in Fridley, Minnesota.
1972	Nike brand footwear debuts.
1975	John T. Molloy's book, *Dress for Success*, is published.
1975	The first Zara store opens in Coruña, Spain.
1976	Liz Claiborne, Inc. is created and later grows to be one of the largest U.S. women's apparel companies.
1976	The nation's first major warehouse retailer, Price Club, opens in San Diego.
1976	The Amalgamated Clothing Workers of America union merges with the Textile Workers of America and the United Shoe Workers of America unions to form the Amalgamated Clothing and Textile Workers Union (ACTWU).

During the early 1980s, certain segments of the industry were affected by the continued growth of textile and apparel imports. Companies such as Liz Claiborne, founded in 1976, and Nike, Inc. founded in 1972, were producing merchandise worldwide to obtain the best labor price for production. Concern about rising labor costs in the United States and the continued surge of imports led industry executives to join forces in examining ways to improve the productivity of U.S. fashion industries.

In 1984–1985, the Crafted with Pride in U.S.A. Council engaged Kurt Salmon Associates, textile and apparel industry analysts, to analyze industry inefficiencies. This project developed the idea of **Quick Response (QR)** to describe a philosophy that promoted potential ways to increase efficiencies. Quick Response was a change from the **push system** of the past, in which supply-side strategies were used to push the products produced on the consumer. In contrast, QR was **a pull system** of demand-side strategies based on the flow from consumers to the manufacturers of timely and accurate information about consumers' wants and needs.

The following year, the Crafted with Pride in U.S.A. Council sponsored pilot projects linking fabric producers, apparel manufacturers, and retailers to determine if QR was feasible and to identify obstacles and difficulties in implementing

Table 1.5	Historical Events 1980–1995: Imports and Quick Response
1980	[TC]² begins operation to research and demonstrate new computer technology in the textile and apparel industries.
1984	Crafted with Pride in U.S.A. Council is formed.
1986	May Department Stores acquires Associated Dry Goods.
1988	Target becomes the first mass merchandiser to introduce UPC scanning in all Target stores and Distribution Centers.
1990	Nike introduces "Reuse-A-Shoe" program, whereby consumers can drop off worn athletic shoes that Nike grinds up and uses for new sports surfaces.
1990	Walmart becomes the nation's number one retailer.
1992	Macy's files for protection under Chapter 11.
1992	Levi Strauss & Co. establishes a code of conduct for hired contractors worldwide.
1994	The North American Free Trade Agreement (NAFTA) goes into effect.
1994	Federated Department Stores acquires Macy's.

QR strategies. Results from these pilot projects were positive in terms of increases in sales, stock turnover (the number of times during a specific period that the average inventory on hand has been sold), and return on investment (relationship between company profits and investment in capital items).

In general, these strategies included the following:

- increased speed of design and production through the use of computers
- increased efficiency with which companies communicate and conduct business with one another
- reduced amount of time goods are in warehouses or in transit
- decreased amount of time needed to replenish stock on the retail floor

It soon became apparent that the key barrier to implementing QR was the variety of computer systems used by manufacturers and retailers and the lack of standards within the industry. Thus, in the mid-1980s, interindustry councils were formed to establish voluntary communications standards. Once these standards were instituted and adopted, companies that had embraced QR saw growth in sales and market share. By the late 1990s, virtually all successful firms had implemented some QR strategies. Table 1.5 presents a timeline of other significant historical events during this period.

1995–2005: Supply Chain Management and Globalization

By the late 1990s, QR strategies had been adopted by large and small companies alike. Three types of apparel companies made up the supply chain for soft goods:

- companies that performed almost all of their own manufacturing, from yarn or fabric to finished garments or other textile products

- companies that had a particular niche within the industry, performing specific manufacturing operations such as manufacturing yarns or fabrics, finishing fabrics, or performing sewing operations
- companies that were involved in the design, marketing, and distribution of apparel but contracted sewing operations to other companies, either domestically or in other countries

For each type of company, QR highlighted the importance of and need for additional partnerships among companies throughout the soft goods pipeline. With advances in information technology, the ways companies designed, manufactured, and distributed soft goods were affected. This philosophy of sharing and coordinating information across all segments of the soft goods industry was termed **supply chain management (SCM)**. Supply chain management comprises the "collection of actions required to coordinate and manage all activities necessary to bring a product to market, including procuring raw materials, producing goods, transporting and distributing those goods, and managing the selling process" (Abend 1998, p. 48).

Similar to QR, the goals of SCM are to reduce inventory, shorten the time for raw material to become a finished product in the hands of a consumer, and provide better service to the consumer. Collaboration, trust, and dependability are the cornerstones to making both the QR and the SCM processes effective. However, SCM goes beyond QR in that SCM companies share forecasting, point-of-sale data, inventory information, and information about unforeseen changes in supply or demand for materials or products.

By 2002, large companies such as VF Corporation invested in the information technology infrastructure to make SCM a reality. As **business-to-business (B2B)** web-based technologies emerged, both smaller and larger companies have implemented effective supply chain management strategies for information sharing. Through the use of password-protected websites, businesses can share information and conduct business transactions effectively and efficiently.

As supply chain management strategies brought increased efficiencies to companies, new technologies continued to provide companies with tools for communication and integration.

Globalization

Globalization is the process whereby nations' economies become intertwined and interdependent. Although the fashion industries have been an integral part of the process of globalization for decades, the end of the twentieth century and the beginning of the twenty-first century brought increased attention to how the industries would adapt to and reflect the evolving global economy. Trade among countries for fibers, fabrics, apparel, accessories, and the machinery needed to produce these products has contributed to globalization. From its inception, the fashion industries have offered countries opportunities for increased employment and economic growth. Regulation of international trade has evolved over the centuries as countries have set up trade incentives and barriers to improve their economies or protect domestic industries.

In 1995, the World Trade Organization (WTO) was created as a vehicle for member countries to negotiate trade agreements with an overall goal of enhancing international trade. As compared to **bilateral trade agreements** between two countries, the WTO contributes to the creation of **multilateral trade agreements** or trade agreements among multiple countries. Through the WTO, many of the barriers to trading textiles and apparel were removed over a 10-year period (1995–2004). Thus, countries such as the United States that protected their domestic production of textiles and apparel through the use of quotas (numerical limits on imports) and tariffs (taxes on imports) were required to lower or eliminate these barriers to trade. The work of the WTO to increase opportunities for trade among member countries brought about dramatic shifts in the design, marketing, and production of apparel worldwide. These new rules resulted in countries redefining their roles to maximize their competitive advantages within the global economy:

- Countries such as the United States and France focused primarily on design and marketing.
- Countries such as China and India focused primarily on production.
- Other countries have found appropriate niches for their expertise and infrastructure. For example, Japan and Taiwan are producers of high-tech textiles.

Through globalization, developing countries are becoming emerging markets. Just as we saw in the United States in the late 1890s, the rise of the middle class and desire for fashion merchandise resulted in companies seeking to supply fashion to consumers from all over the world.

2005–Present: Fast Fashion, E-Commerce, and Corporate Social Responsibility

Fast Fashion

Within this context of globalization and supply chain management, international companies have expanded their capabilities of vertical integration across countries. At the same time, consumers are demanding high-quality and fashion-forward products at reasonable prices. This ultrafast supply chain that focuses on consumer demand is known as **fast fashion**. Fast-fashion companies continuously introduce new products in small quantities with little or no replenishment. One of the most successful fast-fashion companies is Zara (Figure 1.13), a member of the Inditex Group, a vertically integrated group of more than one hundred companies. Zara is headquartered in Spain and has over 1,400 stores in 76 countries and more than 400 cities in Europe, the Americas, Asia, and Africa. Its success has depended on these factors:

- vertical integration (controlling many stages of the supply chain)
- designers working alongside production planners and market specialists
- making design and production decisions based on consumer demand
- offering consumers limited quantities of multiple styles of merchandise
- the ability to produce merchandise in weeks instead of months

Indeed, Zara can design and produce a garment and distribute it to a retailer in just 15 days. Swedish company H&M, and U.S. companies such as Bebe, Forever 21, and Charlotte Russe, have also implemented fast-fashion philosophies.

Fast fashion relies on constant communication among all elements of a

Figure 1.13
Zara is an example of a successful global fast-fashion company. Cameron Spencer /Getty Images.

company's supply chain—from customers to store personnel, from store managers to designers and merchandisers, from designers to buyers and sourcing agents, from buyers to contractors, from contractors to warehouse managers and distributors. Fast fashion has created an expectation among consumers of always seeing something new in stores and on the internet. Although not all companies may be able—or even want—to focus on all elements of fast fashion, large and small companies worldwide are copying strategies such as producing merchandise closer to the time the ultimate customer buys it.

E-Commerce

With the introduction of **e-commerce** in the mid-1990s, many companies began experimenting with online business. At that time, the idea of **multichannel retailing** meant that a bricks-and-mortar store might also have a seasonal catalog. A number of issues needed to be resolved before online retailing would become readily accepted by consumers, and retailers struggled with the relationship between traditional stores and online extensions. Both retailers and consumers were skeptical about the security of ordering merchandise online.

By the beginning of the twenty-first century, online retailing had become an important component of many retailers' multichannel approach. Today, new technological developments in website design include online tools that mimic the tactile experiences consumers have in bricks-and-mortar apparel and accessories stores. In addition, consumers now expect true **omnichannel retailing** that seamlessly integrates bricks-and-mortar and online operations.

Many companies have become internet retailers only. Companies such as Amazon and Zappos have no bricks-and-mortar stores and sell strictly online. Additional developments in online retailing have included the rise of **peer-to-peer (P2P)** commerce, such as Etsy, which provides a platform for individual crafters to sell their product without the expense of maintaining their own website or store. Just as we saw with the mail order catalog in the early 1900s, shopping online allows the consumer to shop 24/7 and have the product delivered directly to their door.

Corporate Social Responsibility

As the twentieth century drew to a close, reflections of the industries 100 years earlier revealed that the same inhumane conditions of the early textile factory towns in England and the United States were occurring again in factories around the world. A combination of public outcry, student activists, and media attention brought these issues to the forefront of government. In 1996, President Clinton created the Apparel Industry Partnership, a voluntary partnership of apparel and shoe manufacturers, trade unions, and consumer and human rights organizations, to create a standardized code of conduct for apparel companies. The Fair Labor Association was formed in 1998, and the Workers' Rights Consortium was formed in 1999. Since then, most companies have implemented codes of conduct, and they routinely monitor factories.

Companies have incorporated socially responsible business practices throughout the supply chain in many ways. In general, **corporate social responsibility (CSR)** refers to business practices that contribute positively to society. Companies that engage in corporate social responsibility ask the question: How do we design, produce, and distribute the highest quality and the most environmentally sustainable products under the best factory and business conditions in a profitable manner? Indeed, in today's business environment, manufacturers, marketers, and retailers must offer consumers competitively priced merchandise that is designed, manufactured, and distributed in responsible ways that foster sustainability from both environmental and business perspectives (Figure 1.14).

Corporate social responsibility in the fashion industries is evidenced throughout the supply chain. **Socially responsible supply chain management** is achieved through design, sourcing, and distribution decisions that positively affect social, environmental, and economic systems:

- **Socially responsible design** includes practices that enable designers to influence the social, environmental, and economic systems through design solutions. This is achieved through inclusive design, environmentally responsible design, health-related design, and design that promotes fair trade.
- **Socially responsible production** is achieved through safe and healthy working conditions, environmentally responsible production, fair wages, and production that promotes fair trade.
- **Socially responsible marketing** considers consumers' desire to purchase goods and services that have been produced and distributed with sustainability in mind and in safe and humane conditions by individuals who are paid a fair or living wage.
- **Socially responsible distribution** is achieved through safe and sustainable practices for getting products to the ultimate consumer.

As a framework for the business of fashion, corporate social responsibility is discussed throughout the book in relation to the policies, practices, and business

REIMAGINE

REDUCE
WE make useful gear that lasts a long time   YOU don't buy what you don't need

REPAIR
WE help you repair your Patagonia gear   YOU pledge to fix it if it's broken

REUSE
WE help find a home for Patagonia gear you no longer need   YOU sell or pass it on to someone who needs it

RECYCLE
WE will take back your Patagonia gear that is worn out   YOU pledge to keep your stuff out of landfills

REIMAGINE
TOGETHER
we reimagine the world where we take only what our planet can replace

Figure 1.14
Patagonia's Common Threads campaign highlights trends in apparel production focusing on environmental responsibility. Courtesy Patagonia.

decisions described in each chapter. To be sustainable into the next decade, the business of fashion must reflect a global value system of social responsibility. Table 1.6 presents a timeline of other significant historical events during this period.

Table 1.6 Historical Events 1995–Present: Globalization, Internet, and Fast Fashion	
1995	Amazon.com goes online.
1995	eBay starts as online auction site.
1995	The World Trade Organization (WTO) begins as an international organization for negotiating trade agreements.
1996	President Clinton creates the Apparel Industry Partnership to develop a plan to eliminate sweatshops.
1996	www.macys.com is launched.
1996	Patagonia uses only 100% organic cotton for all its cotton garments.
1997	Google is registered as a domain.
1997	Walmart becomes the largest private employer in the United States, with 680,000 U.S. associates and another 115,000 international associates.
1998	[TC]^2 makes a 3-D body measurement system commercially available.
1998	Liz Claiborne, Inc. launches lizclaiborne.com as a branding/information website. It is relaunched in 2000 as an e-commerce website.
2000	Dayton Hudson Corporation is renamed Target Corporation; 2004 Associated Merchandising Corporation is renamed Target Sourcing Services.
2000–06	Liz Claiborne expands to 40 brands, with $4.85 billion in sales; acquisitions include Monet (2000), Mexx (2001), Ellen Tracy (2002), Juicy Couture (2003), Enyce (2003), and Mac & Jac (2006).
2002	PayPal became a wholly owned subsidiary of eBay.
2003	Target launches its exclusive licensing agreement with Isaac Mizrahi.
2004	Facebook is launched from a dorm room at Harvard University.
2005	Quotas on textiles and apparel imported from World Trade Organization (WTO) members are phased out.
2005	Federated Department Stores acquires May Department Stores, realigning stores into eight operating divisions: one Bloomingdale's and seven Macy's.
2005	Term "CyberMonday" is first used for the Monday after Thanksgiving's "Black Friday."
2006	Twitter is launched, allowing users to post microblogs.
2007	Kohl's launches its exclusive licensing agreement with Vera Wang, introducing Simply Vera Vera.
2007	Federated Department Stores changes its name to Macy's, Inc.
2007	Apple introduces its first iPhone.
2008	Nike launches its Nike Considered Design, a collection of footwear that combines sustainability principles with sport innovations.
2009	Macy's and Bloomingdale's launch social media programs to reach customers.
2015	Amazon surpassed Walmart as the most valuable retailer in the United States by market capitalization.

SUMMARY

Fashion is evolutionary. Historically, the fashion industry has evolved based on changing technology and changing consumer demand. Starting with the industrial revolution and the mechanization of spinning, weaving, and sewing processes, the textile and apparel industries moved from craft industries to factory-based industries. Immigrants provided the necessary labor force for these growing industries and became major consumers of the products.

By the 1920s, ready-made apparel was available to most consumers. Two types of apparel production were developed—modern, large factories, and small contractors who sewed piecework at home. The textile and apparel industries emerged from the Great Depression of the 1930s with the need to address growing and changing demands from consumers. Technological advancements in synthetic fibers provided a new source of materials for apparel. However, it was not until after the Second World War that these easy-care fibers hit the American market.

The 1950s saw growth and expansion of apparel companies, many of them becoming large, publicly owned corporations. This growth continued through the 1960s. However, as labor costs in the United States increased and consumer demand for lower-cost clothing also increased, companies began moving production outside the United States.

As imports of textiles and apparel surged, the American industry examined how it could increase productivity and global competitiveness. The result of this analysis was the development of the Quick Response (QR) system, an industry-wide program involving a number of strategies to shorten the production time from raw fiber to the sale of a finished product to the ultimate consumer. QR strategies are seen in all segments of the textile, apparel, and retailing industries.

Enhanced information technology has allowed for increased partnerships throughout the soft goods pipeline. Supply chain management (SCM) encompasses these information sharing processes to improve the efficiency and effectiveness of the textile and apparel industries. Since the beginning of the twenty-first century, the textile and apparel industries have been adapting to new rules associated with international trade and consumer demand for high-quality, fashionable, and reasonably priced goods. Strategies such as fast fashion and e-commerce tap the industries' capabilities for effective integration and communication.

The textile and apparel industries will continue to be integral industries for globalization and economic growth. With globalization comes the integration of corporate social responsibility throughout the textile and apparel supply chain, including socially responsible design, production, marketing, and distribution.

KEY TERMS

bilateral trade agreement
business-to-business (B2B)
contractor
corporate social responsibility (CSR)
e-commerce
fashion
fast fashion
globalization
mass fashion

multichannel retailing
multilateral trade agreement
omnichannel retailing
peer-to-peer (P2P)
pull system
push system
Quick Response (QR)
ready-to-wear (RTW)
slops
socially responsible design

socially responsible distribution
socially responsible marketing
socially responsible production
socially responsible supply chain management
store brand
subcontractor
supply chain management (SCM)
sweatshop
vertical integration

DISCUSSION QUESTIONS AND ACTIVITIES

1. Look in a historic costume book, and select a fashion from at least 15 years ago. What social and technological developments were necessary for the production and distribution of the fashion?

2. In your own words, define *supply chain management*. Why would a textile or apparel manufacturer want to adopt SCM strategies? What technological developments have led to supply chain management?

3. What are the disadvantages and advantages of fast fashion for textile and apparel companies? What are the advantages and disadvantages of fast fashion for consumers?

4. Go to your favorite apparel and/or accessory website. What characteristics of the website do you find helpful in making selections and purchases? How might the website be improved?

5. In your own words, define *corporate social responsibility* in the textile, apparel, home fashions, and retailing industries. What business practices and decisions are instrumental for effective corporate social responsibility?

CASE STUDY

Historical Context of Fashion Brands

To be successful over time, fashion brands must continually adapt to changes in interrelated aspects of society: technologies, consumer demands, government regulations, and social parameters. Thus, an in-depth analysis of how a particular fashion brand changed over time can reveal the importance of understanding the historical context of fashion brands. Historical analysis includes the use of *primary sources* of information. A primary or original source is one that was created at the time being studied. In fashion history, primary or original sources include artifacts (actual articles of clothing or accessories); documented photographs of individuals at the time; newspaper or magazine articles and/or advertisements; video recordings; and interviews, journals, or diaries of people who lived at the time. Typically, when conducting historical analysis, several primary sources are used to validate the accuracy of the analysis. In this case study, you will use at least three primary sources to conduct a historical analysis of a fashion brand that has been in operation at least 40 years.

Historical Analysis

1. Select a fashion brand that has been in operation for at least 40 years. Examples include Levi Strauss & Company, Brooks Brothers, Woolrich, Pringle of Scotland, Adidas, Calvin Klein, Nike, Gucci, Tiffany, Pendleton Woolen Mills, and Burberry.

2. Using at least three primary or original sources, conduct a historical analysis of the brand, including a historical overview of the brand; the major changes in technologies, consumer demands, government regulations, and social parameters that affected the fashion brand; and how the fashion brand adapted to these changes. Note: You may also use valid and reliable secondary sources (e.g., books written about the time period, published research about the time period), but at least three of your references must be primary sources.

   - Provide an overview of the history of the brand, including when and where it started and by whom, major changes or milestones in the fashion brand over time, and its current organization and operation. Include and cite at least five images of the fashion brand over time that effectively represent the changes that occurred with the brand.

- Describe major changes in technologies, consumer demands, government regulations, and social parameters that affected the fashion brand over time, and explain how the fashion brand adapted to these changes.

3. Given this historical analysis, why do you believe the brand has remained popular for such a long time? Provide at least three reasons and a justification/rationale for these reasons.

4. Cite primary and secondary resources used in your analysis.

REFERENCES

Abend, Jules. (1998). "SCM Is Putting a Buzz in Industry Ears." *Bobbin*, May, pp. 48–54.

Sproles, George B., and Leslie Davis Burns. (1994). *Changing Appearances: Understanding Dress in Contemporary Society*. New York: Fairchild Publications.

Merriam-Webster Dictionary. (2016) http://www.merriam-webster.com/dictionary (accessed March 31, 2016).

Global Fashion Supply/Value Chain

IN THIS CHAPTER, YOU WILL LEARN THE FOLLOWING:

- the importance of effective supply chain networks and logistics in the success of fashion brand companies.

- the characteristics of the predominant marketing channels in the fashion industries and how merchandise, ownership of merchandise, information, payments, and promotions flow through these channels.

- marketing channel integration strategies including conventional, vertical, and multichannel and omnichannel distribution strategies.

- definitions of brand, brand identity, brand positioning, and brand image.

- classifications of successful fashion brands.

- the importance of licensing in the fashion industries and strategies for successful licensing.

THE MATERIAL–BRAND–RETAIL SUPPLY/VALUE CHAIN

Before exploring the design, development, manufacturing, marketing, and distribution of fashion merchandise in greater detail, we must first describe the overall business operations involved in the global supply/value chain for fashion. **Supply chain networks** include all of the interconnected individuals, businesses, and processes that are necessary to get a product to the ultimate consumer.

Throughout these supply chain networks are processes that add value to the product for each of the customers along the way. As with other industries, the fashion industries rely on supply and value chain networks to take the product from material (e.g., fibers, fabrics) to fashion brands sold through one or more of many types of retail venues to the ultimate consumer of the fashion. In today's global economy, effective coordination of the purchasing and movement of materials and components to factories and from factories to distribution centers and to the retailer is central to the company's success. **Logistics** is the term used to describe the processes of coordinating these interconnected activities. Imagine the challenges of assuring that fabrics, thread, zippers, production patterns in multiple sizes, construction instructions, and skilled labor are all in place at the same time at a factory to meet retailers' deadlines for the merchandise.

Fashion companies often compete based on how efficient and effective their supply chain networks are. Thus **supply chain management** is an important element in successful fashion companies' operations. For example, according to industry analysts, a key aspect of turning around the profitability of lifestyle brand Billabong was to reorganize the brand's global sourcing organization, reduce the number of vendors with which the brand was working, and overhaul the brand's logistics systems to achieve quality improvements and price reductions (Barrie 2015).

MARKETING CHANNELS

Within the supply chain networks are **marketing channels** or routes that products follow to get to the ultimate user. They consist of businesses that perform manufacturing, wholesaling, and retailing functions in order to get merchandise to the consumer. Marketing channels have several structural systems, including the following (see also Table 2.1):

- direct marketing channel
- limited marketing channel
- extended marketing channel

With the **direct marketing channel**, fashion companies sell directly to consumers. For example, consumers may purchase goods directly from the fashion company through catalogs or over the internet. With the growth of fashion brand companies selling merchandise directly to the consumer, direct marketing channels have become more prevalent in the fashion industries. However, consumers do not have the resources to deal directly with fashion companies for all of their fashion purchases, nor do all fashion companies have the resources to deal directly

Table 2.1 Marketing Channels

Direct Marketing Channel						
Manufacturer ⟶	Consumer					
Limited Marketing Channel						
Manufacturer ⟶	Retailer ⟶	Consumer				
Extended Marketing Channels						
Manufacturer ⟶	Wholesaler ⟶	Retailer ⟶	Consumer			
Manufacturer ⟶	Wholesaler ⟶	Jobber ⟶	Retailer ⟶	Consumer		

with individual consumers. Therefore, consumers must rely on retailers to search for and screen fashion brands and products for them.

In a **limited marketing channel**, retailers survey the various fashion brand companies and select (i.e., buy) merchandise that they believe their customers will want. Retailers also serve as gatekeepers by narrowing the choices for consumers and providing them with access (through retail outlets) to the merchandise, thus performing an important service to consumers. Retailers may also arrange for the production of specific goods (private label merchandise) that they then make available to their customers. In some cases, fashion brand companies sell merchandise through their own retail stores (e.g., Ralph Lauren, Nike, Eileen Fisher). Because a retail store is used in the process, this form of distribution is considered a limited marketing channel rather than a direct marketing channel, even though the product is sold by the fashion brand company. The limited marketing channel is the most typical marketing channel for fashion brands.

Extended marketing channels involve one of the following:

- Wholesalers acquire products from manufacturers and make them readily available to buyers, usually retailers.
- Intermediaries buy products from wholesalers at special rates and make them available to retailers. Intermediaries are sometimes referred to as jobbers in this segment of the industry.

Extended marketing channels are used in the distribution of many basic items, such as T-shirts, underwear, and hosiery. For example, a company may produce white T-shirt "blanks" and sell them to wholesalers. The wholesalers sell the T-shirts to manufacturers that will have designs screen-printed on the shirts, using a textile converter for the screen printing process. The shirts are then sold to retailers. However, because of the increased time involved, this type of marketing channel is seldom used for fashion goods that companies want to get to the consumer as quickly as possible.

Marketing Channel Integration

Marketing channel integration is the process of connecting the various levels of marketing channels so that they work together to provide the right products to consumers in the right quantities, in the right place, and at the right time.

Integration can be created through conventional marketing channels or through vertical marketing channels.

Conventional marketing channels consist of independent companies that separately perform the designing, manufacturing, and retailing functions. For example, KEEN Inc. with headquarters in Portland, Oregon, designs outdoor footwear that is manufactured by contractors and sold through a variety of bricks-and-mortar and online retailers. Each of these segments represents separate companies. **Vertical marketing channels** (also called **vertical integration**) consist of companies that work as a united group to design, produce, market, and distribute merchandise. Examples of vertical marketing channels include the following:

- An apparel manufacturer sells merchandise only through its own (or franchised) retail stores.
- A textile producer also manufactures and distributes finished textile products (e.g., hosiery, sheets, towels) to retail stores.
- Private label (e.g., JCPenney's Arizona brand, Nordstrom's Caslon brand) and **specialty store retailer of private label apparel (SPA)**/store brand merchandise (e.g., Crate and Barrel, The Limited, Gap, Old Navy) are produced specifically for a retailer.

The hosiery/legwear industry is dominated by large firms (e.g., Kayser-Roth, Gold Toe Brands, HanesBrands, Inc.) that are often part of vertically integrated companies that produce knitted fabrics as well as the finished hosiery and legwear products. For example, Courtaulds Socks, a part of Sara Lee Courtaulds, is a leading vertically integrated sock supplier to British retail giant Marks & Spencer, as well as other department stores and supermarkets in the UK. Through advanced technologies in design and production in a vertically integrated context, these hosiery companies take advantage of enhanced supply chain management opportunities for their efficiencies and cost savings.

In some cases, fashion brand companies will sell their merchandise through their own stores as well as through other retailers. This distribution strategy is known as **dual distribution**. Many manufacturers, such as Tommy Hilfiger, Ralph Lauren, Pendleton, Eileen Fisher, and Nike, distribute merchandise through both their own retail outlets and through the outlets of other retailers. Thus they are engaged in dual distribution. Some brands will also develop separate brand assortments for their different retail clients. For example, Nike develops different assortments for Foot Locker, JCPenney, and their own Niketown stores.

With the growth of non-store retailing, including web-based and mobile retail formats, many fashion companies have moved to a **multichannel distribution** approach. In multichannel distribution, companies offer merchandise through varying retail venues: bricks-and-mortar stores, catalogs, and/or websites. For example, J. Jill offers merchandise through bricks-and-mortar stores, catalogs, and a website. More recently, fashion brand companies have taken on an **omnichannel distribution** approach. With omnichannel distribution, retail formats are integrated to create a seamless shopping experience for the consumer. For example, a consumer may research a fashion using a smartphone, purchase the fashion through the company website using a laptop, and pick up the merchandise at the company's bricks-and-mortar store. Multichannel and omnichannel retailing are discussed in greater detail in Chapter 13.

Marketing Channel Flows

A marketing channel connects the companies within it in several streams, including ones for physical flow, ownership flow (or title flow), information flow, payment flow, and promotion flow. Each stream relates to specific functions that companies perform throughout the marketing channel.

- *Physical flow:* This is the tracking of fashion merchandise from the factory to the retailer or ultimate consumer. It includes warehousing (or storing), handling, and transporting merchandise so that it is available to consumers at the right time, at the right place, and in the right quantity.
- *Ownership flow or title flow:* This is the transfer of ownership or title from one company to the next. For example, does the retailer own the merchandise when it leaves the factory, or the manufacturer's distribution center, or when the retailer actually receives the merchandise? The manufacturer and retailer negotiate when the title is to be transferred.
- *Information flow:* This is communication among companies within the marketing channel pipeline. Increased information flow between manu- facturers and retailers has resulted from many supply chain management strategies.
- *Payment flow:* This is the transfer of monies among companies as payment for merchandise or services rendered. This includes both the methods used for payment and the company to whom payments are made.
- *Promotion flow:* This is the flow of communications designed to promote the merchandise either to other companies (trade promotions) or to consumers (consumer promotions) in order to influence sales.

Figure 2.1
A successful fashion brand, such as H&M, has a strong brand identity and brand position. Mathias Kniepeiss/Getty Images for H&M.

FASHION BRAND STRATEGIES

What Is a Brand?

We can all think of famous fashion brands—Chanel, Ralph Lauren, Levis, Nike, H&M, and Zara. These brand names create images in the minds of consumers—images that influ- ence their decision to purchase the brand. As such, effective brand management strategies are important for the success of fashion brand companies. A **brand** is "an entity with a distinctive idea expressed in a set of functional and experiential features with a promise of a value reward relevant to its end user and in economic return to its producers (through the building of equity). A successful brand has a strong identity (mentally and physically), is innovative, consistent, competitively positioned, and holds a matching positive image in the consumer's mind" (Hameide 2011, pp. 5–6). Key aspects identified by Hameide (2011) in this definition include brand distinction, promise of a value, brand identity, innovation, consistency, positioning, and image. Think of your favorite **fashion brand**. How does this brand name reflect these key aspects (Figure 2.1)?

Brand Identity, Brand Positioning, Brand Image

Brands have meanings to the consumer that include both functional and experiential aspects of the product carrying the brand (Davis, 2009; Hancock, 2009). Fashion companies strive to create a positive and strong **brand identity** through marketing and advertising efforts. Brand identity is controlled by the fashion brand company and includes all means by which a company portrays the brand and communications with the consumer. This brand identity is determined through the process of **brand positioning**, or how the company positions its brand on key characteristics as compared to its competitors. Merchandisers for fashion brand companies will use brand positioning processes to analyze how their brand compares with competitors—and more importantly, how their brand is different from competitors on characteristics important to the target customer. **Brand differentiation** results in creating distinct brand images in the minds of consumers. For example, Figure 2.2 shows a brand position map of women's swimwear.

Consumers create a **brand image** in their minds based on their experiences with the brand and their attention and interpretation of the company's marketing and advertising efforts. Thus brand identity and brand image are not necessarily the same thing. Think again about your favorite fashion brand. What is the brand image for this brand? How do you think this brand differentiates itself from its competitors?

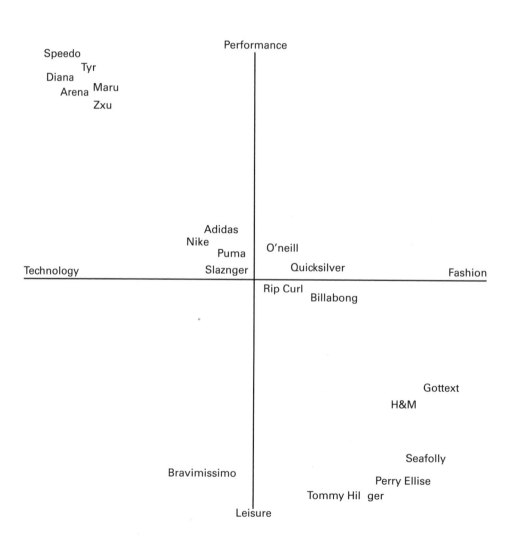

Figure 2.2
Example of a brand positioning map for women's swimwear.

Fashion Brand Classifications

Fashion brands fall into one or more of the following categories. These categories are not mutually exclusive. That is, a luxury brand may also be considered a lifestyle brand.

- *International designer or luxury brands:* Some designers have international recognition and sell their licensed merchandise through boutiques or other high-end retail venues (e.g., Armani, Chanel, Louis Vuitton, Dolce & Gabanna). In addition, a number of brands have positioned themselves along with designer brands at the luxury level (e.g., Burberry, Tiffany). **Designer brands** and other **luxury brands** are associated with high prices, high quality, and distinct prestige. Numerous lists of top luxury brands exist. However, these lists consistently include the following brands: Louis Vuitton, Hermès, Gucci, Chanel, Prada, Burberry, Tiffany & Co, Dolce & Gabbana, Armani, and Fendi.

- *National/local designer or luxury brands:* Some designers have more local or national recognition and sell their merchandise through boutiques in their community or country. These brands are also associated with high prices and high quality but may not have the international reputation as the international designer or luxury brands. For example, the luxury brand Michelle Lesniak, named for the winner of Season 11 of *Project Runway*, is well known in the Portland, Oregon, area where this designer's studio and boutique are located.

- *International name brands:* Some companies have established international recognition as a brand name. Examples include companies such as Nike, Adidas, Roots, and Timberland.

- *Private label brands:* A **private label brand** is specific to a particular retailer that oversees the design and marketing of the brand.
  - *Department store private label brands:* Examples include JCPenney's Worthington label and Nordstrom's Classiques Entier and Treasure&Bond brands.
  - *Exclusive licensing brands:* Examples include
    - Jaclyn Smith's line of apparel licensed to Kmart.
    - Vera Wang's Simply Vera Vera Wang exclusive brand for Kohl's.
    - Target's GO International program that has featured exclusive licenses. with designers including Luella Bartley, Tracy Feith, and Zac Posen.
    - Shaun White shoes and clothing available through an exclusive license with Target.
  - *SPA retail brands:* One type of private label brand is the SPA retail brand. SPA stands for "specialty store retailer of private label apparel." In these cases, the retailer and the brand are one and the same and so are sometimes referred to as **store brands**. Examples include Gap, Banana Republic, Victoria's Secret, and A&F.
  - *Fast fashion retail brands:* One type of SPA retail brand is the **fast fashion retail brand**. Fast fashion companies are characterized by their low prices, fashion trends, and short time from concept to retail. Examples include Uniqlo, Zara, H&M, and Forever 21 Table 2.2 presents a comparison of three fast fashion SPA brands (Figure 2.3).

Table 2.2 Comparison of the Top Three Fast Fashion SPA Brands

Brand	Zara	Uniqlo	H&M
Company	Inditex	Fast Retailing Company, Ltd.	H&M Hennes & Maruitz AB
Headquarters (Founding Year)	Spain (1975)	Japan (1984)	Sweden (1947)
Stores	Over 2,000 stores across 88 countries	1,486 (2014) stores across 16 countries	3,700 stores across 61 countries
Design and Product Development	Over 200 design professionals focus on trend analysis and customer feedback	Research and design teams analyze trends, customer feedback, and focus on new materials	In house design teams focus on trends, quality, price and sustainability
Supply Chain Management	• Secure fabrics in advance • 14 company-owned factories	• Secure fabrics in advance • No company-owned factories	• Partner companies secure fabrics • No company-owned factories

Adapted from Yuntak Cha (2013, September 6). "The Big 3: Fast Fashion (SPA) Brands and Strategies". Maeil Business Newspaper (www.mk.co.kr)

Figure 2.3
Fast fashion brands, such as Zara, focus on low prices, fashion trends, and short time from concept to retail. Stephen Ehlers/Getty Images.

- *Lifestyle brands*: A **lifestyle brand** is a term used to describe brands that are associated with a particular target customer's activities and way of life. Tommy Bahama is a good example of a lifestyle brand as the merchandise is associated with the lifestyle of people who live or vacation in tropical locations. Ralph Lauren is also a lifestyle brand that exemplifies upper-class sensibilities and activities.
- *All other brands:* In addition to these brands, licensed merchandise and specialized brands exist. Examples include Wilson, Mickey & Co., and Looney Tunes/Warner Bros.

Table 2.3 presents the apparel brands with the highest value based on corporate earnings, potential for future earnings, and characteristics associated with brand image (Millward Brown & WPP 2015).

FASHION BRAND LICENSING

One method that fashion companies use to create a perceived difference in their product is **licensing**. Because of the widespread use of licensing within the fashion industries, an understanding of the role it plays in the creation of fashion brands is important. Licensing is the selling by the owner (*licensor*) of the right to use a particular name, image, or design to another party (*licensee*), typically a manufacturer, for payment of royalties. The licensee buys the right to use the name, image, or design, referred to as the *property*, on merchandise to add value to the merchandise. Licensing has grown dramatically as companies recognize the value of established brand names, characters, and **brand extensions**. Here are some examples of licensed products:

Brand	Brand Value (2015) US$M
1. Nike	29,717
2. Zara	22,036
3. H&M	13,827
4. Uniqlo	8,074
5. Next	5,973
6. Ralph Lauren	5,643
7. Adidas	4,615
8. Hugo Boss	4,320
9. Lululemon	2,898
10. Tommy Hilfiger	2,580

Table 2.3 Apparel Brands with the Highest Value Based on Corporate Earnings

- Licensing agreement between Cherokee Global Brands (licensor) and 5 Horizons (licensee) to produce Everyday California brand backpacks, bags, and luggage and with NTD Apparel (licensee) for certain apparel and accessory categories for distribution throughout the United States and Canada
- Licensing agreement between Perry Ellis International (licensor) and Itochu Prominent USA (licensee) to produce Perry Ellis and Original Penguin brands men's dress shirts for distribution through U.S. department stores
- Licensing agreement between Sean John (licensor) and Evy of California, Inc. (licensee) to produce Sean John children's sportswear and outerwear. Evy of California also holds licenses for children's wear for Hello Kitty, My Little Pony, Transformers, DC Comics, and Peanuts.
- Licensing agreement between Authentic Brands Group (licensor) and Global Brands Group to design, produce, and distribute Jones New York brand women's wear, menswear, children's wear, accessories, and footwear.
- Licensing agreement between Richloom Fabrics Group, a home furnishings and fabric converter company, and Christie Brinkley to produce the Christie Brinkley Home collection of home decorative fabrics.

Some companies' products are entirely licensed (e.g., Hang Ten); other companies license only certain product lines (e.g., Vera Wang fragrances, Donna Karan sunglasses, Polo by Ralph Lauren boys' wear). Many designer/luxury brands that started in apparel use licensing agreements to expand their offerings into accessories including belts, hosiery, footwear, and eyewear. Similarly, designer/luxury brands that started in accessories have used licensing agreements to expand their offerings. For example, Kenneth Cole has successfully licensed a broad range of merchandise, including all of the company's non-footwear products except handbags. Many name brands use licensing agreements to expand their production and distribution in other countries. For example, Hong Kong–based brand Esprit (licensor) recently signed a licensing agreement with retailer Groupe Zannier (licensee) to develop, produce, and distribute Esprit Kids in Europe and the Middle East.

Types of Licensed Names, Images, and Designs

The types of names, images, and designs that are licensed vary widely, although most of them fall into the following categories:

- *Celebrity name licensing*: As noted by Teri Agins in *Hijacking the Runway: How Celebrities Are Stealing the Spotlight from Fashion Designers*, "a celebrity's name on a label effectively fast-tracks a new fashion brand—shaving off as much as ten years to develop widespread recognition." Celebrity name licensing includes
  - Camuto Group licensing agreements with Jessica Simpson and Tory Burch for brands of footwear bearing the celebrities' names.
  - Lancaster Group (a division of Coty Inc.) licensing agreements for fragrances with Sarah Jessica Parker and Jennifer Lopez; Coty Beauty (another division of Coty Inc.) licensing agreements for fragrances with Celine Dion and Isabella Rossellini.
  - A range of licensing agreements between Kathy Ireland and companies including Martin Furniture (kathy ireland Home), Root Candle Company (kathy ireland Home candles), The RFA Group (kathy ireland footwear), Alok (kathy ireland Home bed linens and bath towels).
- *Designer name licensing*: Designers—including Chanel, Christian Dior, Yves Saint Laurent, Ralph Lauren, Calvin Klein, Giorgio Armani, Vera Wang, Donna Karan, and many others—license their names as brand names for products including scarves, jewelry, fragrances, cosmetics, home fashions, and shoes. For example, the Camuto Group has a licensing agreement with Tory Burch for footwear.
- *Exclusive licensing for a retailer*: Retailers often team up with celebrities and designers to create merchandise sold exclusively at a particular retailer, creating a unique form of private label merchandise. Whether it is Alexander Wang's exclusive collection for H&M, Missoni's exclusive collections for Target, or the Kate Moss collection for British retailer Topshop, exclusive licensing programs can contribute to the brand identity of retailers.
- *Character and entertainment licensing*: Such images as cartoon characters, movie or television characters, and fictional characters are often licensed to appear on a range of merchandise, from sleepwear to backpacks to sheets and towels. Examples include Disney characters, Marvel comic book and movie characters, and South Park cartoon characters.

  In recent years, licensed merchandise relating to movies and movie characters has been extremely popular, particularly for infant and children's clothing and other children's merchandise.
- *Corporate licensing*: Licensing of brand names and trademarks of corporations such as IBM, Harley-Davidson, or Coca-Cola is also common. This type of brand extension licensing extends a brand that is well known in a

particular product area to a different product area. Examples include Porsche sunglasses, Moet & Chandon iPhone cover, Coca-Cola stuffed-toy polar bears, and Harley-Davidson armchairs.

- *Nostalgia licensing:* Manufacturers license the names and images of legends, such as Marilyn Monroe, James Dean, and Babe Ruth, as well as old-time movies and radio and TV shows, such as *The Lone Ranger*, *Superman*, and *King Kong*.
- *Sports and collegiate licensing*: Professional sports team and university logos are licensed to appear on sport-related merchandise, such as sweatshirts with the Green Bay Packers logo, jackets with the Boston Red Sox logo, hoodies with the FC Barcelona logo, and caps with the University of Michigan logo. Athletic footwear companies often have unique licensing agreements with professional and collegiate sports leagues (e.g., Major League Baseball) or individual teams. In these agreements, footwear companies pay the leagues or teams for the right to sell merchandise with the league or team logo. They may also purchase the right to outfit the team with athletic footwear and/or uniforms bearing the company's logo (Figure 2.4).
- *Event and festival licensing*: Names or logos of events including the Kentucky Derby, the Indianapolis 500, Wimbledon, the Olympics, the World Cup, and the Masters golf tournment are also licensed for use on products.
- *Art licensing*: Manufacturers license great works of art to be reproduced on their merchandise.

The success of licensing depends on consumers' desire for goods with a perceived difference based on brand name, trademark, or image. The diversity of licensed goods proves their effectiveness in creating a favorable difference in consumers' minds.

Figure 2.4
Licensing of collegiate and professional sports is a growing trend worldwide. Doug Pensinger/Getty Images.

Development of Licensed Products

To succeed, any licensed product must have a well-established, visually oriented property (an image or design). When such a property exists, the following stages are involved in developing the licensed product:

1. The image or design, commonly referred to as the *property*, is created. For example, the red, white, and blue logo of Tommy Hilfiger is established.
2. Consumers are exposed to the property through the media. The Tommy Hilfiger name and trademark are used in advertising, hangtags, publications, and so on.
3. The property is marketed by the licensor to build name or image recognition. Tommy Hilfiger builds a reputation among consumers for trendy fashion, quality, and value. The name and trademark are associated with these characteristics in consumers' minds.
4. Merchandise with the property added is produced by a variety of manufacturers. Tommy Hilfiger licenses the name and trademark to several manufacturers of apparel, accessories, and fragrances.
5. Merchandise is distributed by retailers. Retailers who have been successful with Tommy Hilfiger sportswear will also want to carry licensed Tommy Hilfiger merchandise, such as accessories and fragrances.
6. Merchandise is demanded by consumers. Consumers identify with the Tommy Hilfiger name and perceive the licensed products as having an added value because the Tommy Hilfiger name and trademark are attached to the merchandise.

The Licensing Contract

The terms of the agreement between the licensee and licensor are outlined in a contract. Typically, a licensing agreement includes the following elements:

- *Time limit:* For many licensed products, timing is everything. For example, the contract for the image of a currently popular movie character may be for a shorter time than for a classic designer name.
- *Royalty payment:* Typically, the licensee pays the licensor royalties of 7 to 14 percent of the wholesale price of the goods sold.
- *Image:* Contract clauses specify how the image will appear, giving the licensor control over graphics, colors, and other design details. For example, Ocean Pacific (OP) controls the design of all graphics on its licensed merchandise.
- *Marketing and distribution:* Licensors often want to control the marketing consistency of their licensed merchandise. Also, many designers do not want their licensed merchandise distributed through discount or off-price retailers, and they put clauses in their contracts to prevent it.
- *Quality:* Clauses about the materials and manufacture of merchandise and the submission of samples of merchandise for approval by the licensor give the licensor control over product quality.
- *Advances:* Contract clauses set the amount of advance money that will be paid up front and then deducted from the royalty payments.
- *Guarantees:* Contracts often guarantee that the licensee will be paid a minimum dollar amount, even if royalties fall below this amount.

- *Notification of agreements to customs department:* If goods are being manufactured offshore, or outside the United States, this notification is needed so the goods will clear customs and not be confiscated as counterfeit goods. Contract clauses assure licensees that the licensor will provide notification if needed.

Advantages of Licensing

Licensing agreements have some advantages for both the licensee and licensor. For the licensee, the value added to the merchandise by a licensed name, image, or design comes in many interrelated forms. The licensee gets automatic brand identification (Figure 2.5). For example, a youth T-shirt with a picture of characters from the 2015 movie *Star Wars: The Force Awakens* received automatic recognition from children and parent-consumers.

In many instances, the licensed product is trusted for qualities that stem from the licensor—a designer name attached to a handbag adds fashion credibility to the handbag. For manufacturers, a licensed product can also be a marketing shortcut for launching new products. By purchasing the rights to a designer or celebrity name, a fragrance company can launch a new fragrance with immediate brand name recognition.

Figure 2.5
Licensed products create immediate brand identification in the consumers' minds. Ethan Miller/Getty Images.

The licensor also gains from licensing agreements. Licensing allows for brands to extend into other categories of merchandise without revealing to consumers that the licensor is not manufacturing the merchandise. Such arrangements allow companies to expand their product lines by taking advantage of the manufacturing and distribution expertise and facilities of other companies.

For example, when Nike decided to expand its product line into women's swimwear, rather than spending the resources to develop the expertise in this area, it licensed its name to Jantzen, one of the world's largest women's swimwear manufacturers. That agreement allowed Nike to take advantage of the expertise at Jantzen, and it gave Jantzen the opportunity to expand its business by producing a new line of women's swimwear for a new target market.

As another example of this cooperation between corporations in licensing, Hartmarx, a well-known and well-respected producer of men's tailored clothing, is one of Tommy Hilfiger's licensees. Hartmarx handles both tailored and business-casual clothing and slacks for Tommy Hilfiger (owned by Phillips–Van Heusen). Hilfiger controls the design, distribution, and visual presentation of the products, and Hartmarx handles the production. Designer–manufacturer licensing collaborations are common in intimate apparel and legwear. For example, over the past 25 years, Calvin Klein hosiery has been licensed by Kayser-Roth Corporation. HanesBrands Inc. holds the license for Donna Karan and DKNY hosiery. For well-established names or images, licensing arrangements can also be lucrative. Designers such as Calvin Klein and Ralph Lauren likely make millions of dollars each year in royalties from licensed merchandise.

Disadvantages of Licensing

Licensing also has some disadvantages for the licensor and licensee. For the licensor, overuse of licensing arrangements may result in saturation of the property in the marketplace. This can lead consumers not perceiving a distinct image with the property. For example, thanks to hundreds of licensing agreements, Pierre Cardin's name can be seen on everything from luggage to cookware to children's apparel. Because of this, the name has lost some of its prestige.

When a licensed product sells well, the licensor must rely on the licensee's ability to react by producing goods quickly. Depending on the licensing contract, licensors also risk losing control over quality or distribution of licensed merchandise. To assure consistent quality, the licensor must arrange for constant monitoring of production quality by inspecting samples or production facilities.

A tragic example of the risk involved in losing control of a licensed name is that of the designer Halston. In the 1960s and 1970s, Halston became a well-known designer of expensive apparel worn by celebrities. In 1973, Halston sold the exclusive rights to his name to Norton Simon Industries (NSI). In 1982, NSI asked Halston to design a line of affordable mass-merchandised clothing for JCPenney. After Halston introduced this line, high-end retailers dropped his designer-priced collection. Although Halston received some royalties until his death in 1990, he never regained control over the use of the Halston name, which changed ownership at least eight times during its almost forty-year history. Today the Halston name is regaining prestige after the Halston Heritage brand was launched in 2011 and its flagship store opened in New York City in 2013.

For licensees, the major disadvantage of licensing is the risk associated with predicting the popularity of the licensed name or image. Timing is extremely important for the success of many licensed products, and licensees must be experts in understanding and predicting consumer demand. Sometimes, however, the license does not turn out as anticipated. This often happens when big-budget movies flop.

Licensees also bear the expense of controlling channels of distribution and trying to prevent counterfeiting of the licensed goods. They are responsible for additional costs related to the manufacture of licensed products according to the licensor's rules and regulations. For example, many licensors have rules governing where a product may be manufactured, which may make production more expensive than it otherwise might be. Despite these disadvantages, licensing will continue to be an important business strategy for many fashion companies.

SUMMARY

Supply chain networks within the fashion industries include all the interconnected individuals, businesses, and processes necessary to get a fashion product to the ultimate consumer. Because the success of fashion companies often depends on the effectiveness of supply chain networks, effective and efficient logistics and supply chain management are essential. Within these supply chain networks are marketing channels or routes that products follow in getting to the ultimate consumers.

In the fashion industries, direct marketing channels, limited marketing channels, and extended marketing channels are used. Limited marketing channels are the most common for fashion merchandise. With conventional marketing channel integration, fashion companies will separately preform functions within the marketing channel. However, fashion companies may also engage in vertical integration of marketing channels by performing more than one function. In addition, fashion companies may engage in dual or multichannel distribution strategies, leading to omnichannel strategies whereby the multiple distribution strategies appear seamless to the consumer.

Fashion brands are entities with a set of functional and experiential features that create distinct images in the minds of consumers. Fashion brand companies strive to create a positive and unique brand identity through the process of brand positioning. Through a variety of company-controlled communication strategies and experiences with the brand, consumers develop a brand image. Fashion brands can be classified by type of brand (e.g., designer brand, luxury brand, international name brand, private label brand, lifestyle brand).

Through fashion brand licensing strategies, licensors (owners of the property) sell the rights to use the brand, image, or design to the licensee (typically a manufacturer) for the payment of royalties. Licensing agreements in the fashion industries are common and include celebrity name licensing, designer name licensing, exclusive licensing agreements with retailers, character and entertainment licensing, corporate licensing, nostalgia licensing, sports and collegiate licensing, event licensing, and art licensing. Licensing agreements or contracts involve a number of elements including the time limit, royalty payment, image control, marketing and distribution control, quality standards, royalty advances, and royalty guarantees. To use these strategies successfully, fashion brand companies must thoroughly analyze the advantages and disadvantages of licensing.

KEY TERMS

brand	extended marketing channel	multichannel distribution
brand differentiation	fashion brand	omnichannel distribution
brand extension	fast fashion retail brand	private label brand
brand identity	licensing	SPA
brand image	lifestyle brand	store brands
brand positioning	limited marketing channel	supply chain management
conventional marketing channel	logistics	supply chain networks
designer brand	luxury brand	vertical integration
direct marketing channel	marketing channel	vertical marketing channel
dual distribution	marketing channel integration	

DISCUSSION QUESTIONS AND ACTIVITIES

1. Select a fashion item currently in your closet. What is the brand name of the product? Look at the label; in what country was it produced? Describe the supply/value chain for this product, including material, brand, and retail aspects.

2. Think of your three favorite fashion brands. What category of brand are they? How does the fashion brand company convey a brand identity for each of them? What is the brand image for each?

3. What are some examples of licensed fashion products that you own? In which category of licensed goods does each product fall? What characteristics of the property or product were appealing to you as a consumer? Why?

CASE STUDY

Brand Positioning: Tomboy Style Brands

Over the past five years, a number of tomboy style brands have emerged on the market as lifestyle brands. Wildfang, a tomboy style brand based in Portland, Oregon, is expanding its product lines and has added a bricks-and-mortar store. It is now time for Wildfang to analyze its brand position.

Background information:
9 Androgynous Clothing Labels You Should Know by Lily Hiott-Millis
http://www.buzzfeed.com/lilyhiottmillis/9-androgynous-clothing-labels-you-should-know#.wemNklqyA
10 Tomboy Clothing Companies You Didn't Know Existed
http://askatomboy.blogspot.com/2014/10/10-tomboy-clothing-companies-you-didnt.html
Tomboy Style Brands
Wildfang http://www.Wildfang.com
TomboyX http://tomboyx.com
TomboyBKLYN http://tomboybklyn.com
All Saints http://www.us.allsaints.com
OAK NYC http://www.oaknyc.com
VEER NYC http://veernyc.com

1. Select six tomboy style brands to analyze for this brand positioning case study. One of the brands must be Wildfang. Go to the websites of the brands to answer the following questions about each brand:
   - Name of brand
   - Retail organization—web, bricks-and-mortar, and/or other?
   - Private label brands only or a mix of private label and other brands?
   - Price range/price point of the merchandise?
   - Stated/inferred target customer?
   - Look at the merchandise offered—what is the brand image? (What words or phrases come to mind when you look at the merchandise, website, and/or store?)

2. Define *brand differentiation*. Why is brand differentiation important for these tomboy style brands?

3. Construct a *brand positioning map* to illustrate each brand/retailer's positioning. (Tip: Use the categories related to how the brands differentiate themselves.)

4. What challenges in differentiating their brand do the six tomboy style brand identities face? That is, what are the similarities and differences among brands? How do the brands attempt to differentiate themselves from other similar brands (e.g., style, price, sizing, service, product assortment, etc.)?

5. How does Wildfang compare to the other brands in its brand positioning? Based on this analysis, how might Wildfang become more competitive?

In other words, what does this brand need to do in the next three years to set itself apart from the other brands? Identify at least three strategies that Wildfang might take to differentiate itself, and detail the advantages and disadvantages of each approach.

6. What course of action would you recommend Wildfang take to strengthen its competitive advantage? Why?

7. Cite resources/references you use in this case study, and include a reference list.

CAREER OPPORTUNITIES

Careers in creating and managing fashion brands include these opportunities:

- Brand manager
- Marketing researcher with focus on brand image and brand positioning
- Marketing professional with focus on brand identity communications
- Graphic designer with focus on visual brand communications
- Licensing agent

REFERENCES

Agins, Teri. (2014). *Hijacking the Runway: How Celebrities Are Stealing the Spotlight from Fashion Designers*. New York: Penguin Group.

Barrie, Leonie. (2015, September 2). "Supply Chain Improvements to Save Billabong $30m." http://www.just-style.com/analysis/supply-chain-improvements-to-save-billabong-30m_id126107.aspx (accessed September 8, 2015).

Davis, Mellissa. (2009). *The Fundamentals of Branding*. Lausanne, Switzerland: AVA Publishing SA.

Hameide, Kaled K. (2011). *Fashion Branding Unraveled*. New York: Fairchild Books.

Hancock, Joseph. (2009). *Brand Story*. New York: Fairchild Books.

Millward Brown & WPP (2015). *BrandZ Top 100 Most Valuable Global Brands 2015*. http://www.millwardbrown.com/BrandZ/2015/Global/2015_BrandZ_Top100_Report.pdf (accessed September 10, 2015).

CHAPTER 3

Business and Legal Framework of Companies in the Fashion Industries

IN THIS CHAPTER, YOU WILL LEARN THE FOLLOWING:

- the ways in which a business can be owned and operated in the United States—sole proprietorships, partnerships, limited liability companies, and corporations

- terminology related to business ownership and company expansion and diversification

- the ways in which businesses within the fashion industries compete

- the U.S. federal laws that can affect fashion brand companies

BUSINESS ORGANIZATION AND COMPANY OWNERSHIP

Companies in the fashion industries—textiles, apparel, footwear, home fashions—come in all sizes and types. Some are large corporations that employ thousands of people; others are small companies with one or two employees. Regardless of size and organizational structure, every company in the fashion industries supply chain is in business to make a profit by providing customers with the products and services they desire and need. Because many people planning careers in these industries hope to own their own businesses someday, understanding of the various types of business organizations is an important starting point before going on to examine how these companies operate. In addition, information about business organizations is important for planning careers and assessing companies in terms of employment and advancement opportunities. Depending on their objectives, needs, and size, companies in the fashion industries can be owned and organized in a number of ways. The four most common legal forms of business ownership in the United States are sole proprietorships, partnerships, limited liability companies, and corporations (Table 3.1). Each of these forms of business can be found among companies in the fashion industries. This chapter focuses on U.S. business ownership.

Sole Proprietorships

The **sole proprietorship** is a common form of business ownership in which an individual, the sole proprietor, owns the business and its property. Indeed, from a legal perspective, the sole proprietor or owner is indistinguishable from the company itself. The sole proprietor typically runs the company's overall day-to-day operations but may have employees to help with specific aspects of the business. Employees may be full-time, part-time, or hired to conduct certain tasks. Any profit from the business is considered personal income of the sole proprietor and taxed accordingly; the owner is personally liable for any debt the business may incur.

Advantages of Sole Proprietorships

A sole proprietorship has a number of advantages. For one thing, processes for applying for and/or obtaining needed business licenses are fairly easy. For example, to open an apparel manufacturing business (including contractors) in Los Angeles, a sole proprietor requires federal government licenses (e.g., federal employer identification number—EIN), licenses from the State of California (e.g., state EIN, resale certificate, garment registration certificate), licenses from Los Angeles County (e.g., Los Angeles County Business License, public health license), and a license from the City of Los Angeles (e.g., Los Angeles Business Tax Certificate).

Sole proprietorships are also easy to dissolve. When the sole proprietor decides to stop doing business, the sole proprietorship is essentially ended. Another advantage of a sole proprietorship is the control and flexibility given the sole proprietor, who often finds personal satisfaction in being the boss and making the decisions regarding the direction the business will take. This personal satisfaction is the characteristic of this form of business ownership that individuals most often desire.

Table 3.1 Comparisons among Sole Proprietorships, Partnerships, and Corporations

Business Organization Form	Sole Proprietorship	Partnership	Corporation	Limited Liability Company
Ease of formation	Easy to form Business licenses required	Easy to form Business licenses required Written contract advisable	Difficult to form Charter required Registration with the SEC required for publicly held corporations	Easy to form Business licenses required Operating Agreement required
Operational strategies	Owner also runs the business	Partners can bring range of expertise to running the business	Board hires individuals with specific expertise to run the business	Owner "members" can bring a range of expertise tor running the business
Liability	Unlimited personal liability	Unlimited personal liability for each partner	Limited liability; stockholders not personally liable for corporate debt	Limited liability for members
Tax considerations	Sole proprietor's income taxed as personal income	Partners' income taxed as personal income	Double taxation (corporation's income taxed, and dividends taxed as personal income)	May be taxed as a sole proprietorship, partnership or corporation depending on operating agreement
Potential for employee advancement	Limited, depending upon size of company	Some incentive for employees to become partners	Employees can move up through the ranks	Some incentive for employees to become members
Examples	Small companies Freelance designer Independent sales representative	Small or medium-size companies Designer and marketer who join forces to form a fashion company	Large companies May be private or publicly held Some may be multinational	Small, medium, and large-size companies

Disadvantages of Sole Proprietorships

A sole proprietorship also has some disadvantages. The biggest one is that sole proprietors are personally liable for any business debts. This means that if the business owes money, creditors can take all business and personal assets (such as the owner's home) to pay the debts of the business. This **unlimited liability** is one of the largest risks a sole proprietor takes in starting the business.

Another disadvantage of a sole proprietorship is that because there are no partners, the sole proprietor needs to have expertise in all areas of running the business. For example, an apparel designer who wants to start his or her own business must do the following:

- handle the design aspect of the business
- work with fabric suppliers, contractors, and retailers
- deal with accounting

- manage personnel
- market the product to potential buyers

The difficulty in running all aspects of the business is often overwhelming for a new sole proprietor. In some cases, a sole proprietor will hire employees who have expertise in specific areas that the owner is not familiar with. For example, a designer may hire an accountant to manage the financial aspects of the business.

In a sole proprietorship, raising **capital** (funds or resources) for starting or expanding the business can be difficult. Access to such capital may be obtained in the following ways:

- tapping the owner's personal funds
- purchasing goods and services on credit
- borrowing money from banks, friends, family members, or other investors

A well-written business plan is essential for a sole proprietor to garner funds from banks and other investors. As with other forms of business ownership, sole proprietorships must keep books of account for federal, state, and municipal income tax and other regulatory purposes. Profits are taxed as personal income.

Examples of Sole Proprietorships

Sole proprietorships tend to be small companies whose resources and complexities can be handled by one owner. Individuals may start companies as sole proprietorships and then, as the company grows, change the form of ownership to a partnership or corporation. Examples of sole proprietorships within textile, apparel, and home fashions industries might include

- a freelance textile or apparel designer who sells his or her work to larger textile or apparel companies
- an independent sales representative who sells apparel lines to retailers
- an apparel retailer who owns a small specialty store

The Bureau of Labor Statistics estimates that more than one out of every four fashion designers is self-employed (U.S. Department of Labor, 2015).

Partnerships

At times, two or more people want to join forces in owning a business. In these cases, a **partnership** may be formed. According to the Uniform Partnership Act (UPA), a partnership is an "association of two or more persons to carry on as co-owners of a business for profit" (National Conference of Commissioners on Uniform State Laws, 1997). A partnership may be formed between two individuals or among three or more individuals through written contracts called **articles of partnership**. Although contracts will vary, they typically include

- the partnership's name
- the partners' and officers' names
- the intentions or purposes of the partnership
- the amount and form of contributions (e.g., money and real estate) from each partner
- the length of the partnership

- procedures to add and eliminate partners
- how profits or losses will be divided among the partners
- the degree of management authority each partner will have
- the designation of which partners, if any, are entitled to salaries
- how partnership affairs will be handled if a partner dies or is disabled

Profits are shared among the partners, known as **general partners**, according to the conditions laid out in the partnership contract. Profit from a partnership is taxed as part of each partner's personal income. Similar to sole proprietors, partners have unlimited liability. This means that, together, they are liable for the entire debt of the partnership as outlined in the partnership contract. Dissolution of a partnership can result from the following:

- a partner's withdrawal
- the entry of new partners
- a partner's death
- a partner's bankruptcy
- a partner's incapacity or misconduct
- the business goals becoming obsolete

Limited Partnerships

Sometimes individuals want to join or invest in a partnership, but they do not want to have the unlimited liability for partnership debt that may be larger than their investment. This can be achieved through a **limited partnership**. In this type of partnership, a limited partner has **limited liability**—he or she is liable only for the amount of capital that he or she invested in the business. Any profits are shared according to the conditions of the limited partnership contract. Establishing limited partnerships can be an attractive way for general partners to raise capital to initiate or expand their business. Typically, the limited partner does not take an active role in managing the business, which is handled by the general partners.

Advantages of Partnerships

Partnerships have some advantages over sole proprietorships. Similar to sole proprietorships, partnerships are relatively easy to establish; the same business licenses are required to start a partnership as a sole proprietorship. Unlike sole proprietorships, where only one person owns the business, partners can pool their range of expertise and resources to run the company. For example, one partner in an apparel company may have expertise in design, and another partner may have expertise in business and accounting.

Raising capital for partnerships is also somewhat easier than for sole proprietors because the resources of more than one person can be tapped, and the combined resources of partners can be used as collateral when borrowing money. Through the use of limited partnerships, resources can also be raised for starting or expanding the business. As with sole proprietorships, a quality business plan is needed for partnerships to secure funding from investors.

Another advantage of partnerships over sole proprietorships is that advancement opportunities for employees are greater: Employees may be given the opportunity to become partners in the business. This can be a valuable incentive when recruiting and hiring employees.

Disadvantages of Partnerships

Partnerships also have disadvantages. As with sole proprietorships, the primary disadvantage of partnerships is liability exposure. This means that each partner is personally liable for any debt of the partnership, regardless of which partner was responsible for incurring the debt. In addition to books of account, the UPA also requires that partnerships keep minutes of meetings and business records.

Another disadvantage of a partnership is the potential for disagreement among partners in running the business or setting the future direction of the business. Partnerships often dissolve because of such disagreements. As with sole proprietorships, a partnership is dependent on its owners, and dissolution is presumed when a partner leaves the partnership. Although ease of dissolution of a partnership can be viewed as an advantage, it can also lead to a lack of continuity in the business operations.

Examples of Partnerships

Partnerships are typically small to medium-size companies that require a combination of specialized skills to be successful. For example, two or more individuals may start an apparel company, each bringing unique skills (e.g., design, marketing, operations) to the business. Brands including Calvin Klein, Esprit de Corp., and Liz Claiborne started as partnerships.

- Calvin Klein borrowed money from his friend Barry Schwartz to start his design company, and the two remained partners in the business until it was sold to PVH Corp in 2003.
- In the 1960s and 1970s, Doug Tompkins, Susie Tompkins, and Jane Tise owned an apparel company called Plain Jane. In 1979, the Tompkins bought out Tise and renamed the company Esprit de Corp.; it is now known as Esprit. The Tompkinses divorced in the early 1990s, and the company is now owned by Hong Kong investors. With headquarters in Hong Kong and Germany, Esprit has been listed on the Hong Kong Stock Exchange since 1993.
- Elisabeth "Liz" Claiborne started her business in 1976 with her husband, Arthur Ortenberg, and a manufacturing expert, Leonard Boxer, as partners. Later, Jerome Chazen joined as a partner. Within a year, the company was making a profit, and in 1981 it became a publicly traded corporation, Liz Claiborne, Inc. Liz Claiborne, Inc. was renamed Fifth & Pacific in 2012 and then renamed Kate Spade & Company in 2014. The Liz Claiborne brand is currently sold exclusively by JCPenney.

Corporations

The **corporation** is the most complex form of business ownership because corporations are considered legal entities that exist regardless of who owns them. Corporations are created by filing **articles of incorporation** (also referred to as articles of organization or articles of association) with the state or federal government. General requirements of articles of incorporation include

- name of corporation
- purpose and power of the corporation

- time frame or period of existence
- authorized number of shares/owners
- types of shares
- other conditions of operation

Typically, corporations are designated by the words *Corporation*, *Corp.*, or *Inc.* Although assets owned by the corporation, such as buildings or equipment, are tangible, the corporation itself is considered intangible.

Unlike a sole proprietorship or partnership, ownership of a corporation is held by **stockholders** (or shareholders), who own shares of stock in the corporation. Each share of stock represents a percentage of the company: If someone owns 50 percent of the stock in a company, he or she owns 50 percent of the company. Stockholders in a corporation are liable only for the amount they paid for their stock. Thus, if the company fails, stockholders are not liable for the corporation's debts beyond their investments in the company's stock.

The stockholders elect the corporation's **board of directors**. In electing the board, each stockholder has a percentage of votes that reflects the percentage of stock he or she owns. The board of directors is the chief governing body of the corporation. It plans the direction the company will take and sets policy for the corporation. The board also hires the corporate officers (e.g., president, chief executive officer, chief financial officer), who run the business. Stockholders may participate in managing the business, but many stockholders in corporations have little or no participation in day-to-day operations.

Profits are paid out to stockholders in the form of **dividends**, which are taxed as personal income. Stockholders may also receive dividends in the form of additional stock in the company.

Types of Corporations

C Corporations, S Corporations, and B Corporations

The most common type of corporation is the **C corporation**, or **regular corporation**. This type of corporation distributes profits to shareholders through dividends. Therefore, earnings of the corporation are taxed twice—once at the corporate level, and again at the individual level. This is known as **double taxation**. For small domestic corporations with a limited number of domestic individual shareholders, **S corporations** are becoming more common. The Internal Revenue Service gives S corporations special status: Earnings are taxed only at the individual level, thus eliminating double taxation. **B corporations**, or benefit corporations, include a purpose of general public benefit such as social or environmental benefit. B corporations operate as traditional corporations except that their goals include social and environmental performance in addition to financial performance. Patagonia is an excellent example of a B corporation in the apparel industry. Headquartered in Ventura, California, USA, Patagonia is a major contributor to a number of environmental causes and organizations.

Publicly Traded and Privately Held Corporations

Differences between publicly traded and privately held corporations are primarily seen in the ownership and transferability of shares of stock. In publicly traded corporations, (or **publicly held corporations**), the general public owns at least some of the shares of stock. **Publicly traded corporations** usually have a large number of stockholders who buy and sell their stock on the public market, either through an exchange (e.g., in the United States, the New York Stock Exchange, American Stock Exchange, or National Association of Securities Dealers Automatic Quotation System [NASDAQ]) or through brokers "over the counter." Publicly traded corporations must submit financial information to the Securities and Exchange Commission (SEC), which regulates the securities markets. Table 3.2 presents selected publicly traded corporations in the fiber and textile industries. Table 3.3 presents selected publicly traded corporations in the apparel, accessory, and home fashion industries. Table 3.4 presents selected publicly traded corporations in the fashion retail industry.

Privately held corporations (also called **private corporations**, **closely held corporations**, or **close corporations**) are those in which a small number of individuals own the shares; that is, the stock is not available in public markets and has not been issued for public purchase. Typically, the stockholders of a private corporation are highly involved in the company operations. Examples of privately held corporations in the fashion industries include WL Gore & Associates (maker of GORE-TEX®), Nine West Holdings, Inc., New Balance, Forever 21, J.Crew, Sports Authority, L.L. Bean, Inc., Pendleton Woolen Mills, and Retail Brand Alliance (owner of Brooks Brothers).

Multinational corporations are either private or publicly traded corporations that operate in several countries. In today's global economy—with increased world production and trade of apparel, accessories, and home fashions—multinational corporations have grown in number and

Table 3.2 Examples of U.S. Publicly Held Fiber and Textile Corporations	
Celanese Corporation	(NYSE: CE)
Culp, Inc.	(NYSE: CFI)
E. I. du Pont de Nemours & Co.	(NYSE: DD)
International Textile Group	(OTC US: ITXN)
The Dixie Group	(NASDAQ: DXYN)
Unifi, Inc.	(NYSE: UFI)

Table 3.3 Examples of U.S. Publicly Held Fashion Brands and Home Fashion Corporations	
Carter's, Inc.	(NYSE: CRI)
Cherokee, Inc.	(NASDAQ GS: CHKE)
Coach Inc.	(NYSE: COH)
Columbia Sportswear Company	(NASDAQ GS: COLM)
Decker's Outdoor Corp.	(NYSE: DECK)
Ethan Allen Interiors, Inc.	(NYSE: ETH)
Fossil Group Inc.	(NASDAQ GS: FOSL)
G-III Apparel Group Ltd.	(NASDAQ GS: GIII)
Guess? Inc.	(NYSE: GES)
Hanesbrands, Inc.	(NYSE: HBI)
Kate Spade & Co.	(NYSE: KATE)
La-Z-Boy Inc.	(NYSE: LZB)
Michael Kors Holdings Ltd	(NYSE: KORS)
Mohawk Industries Inc.	(NYSE: MHK)
Nike, Inc.	(NYSE: NKE)
Oxford Industries, Inc.	(NYSE: OXM)
Perry Ellis International Inc.	(NASDAQ GS: PERY)
PVH Corp.	(NYSE: PVH)
Ralph Lauren Corp	(NYSE: RL)
Tiffany & Co.	(NYSE: TIF)
Under Armour, Inc.	(NYSE: UA)
VF Corporation	(NYSE: VFC)

Table 3.4 Examples of Publicly Held SPA, Specialty, Discount, and Department Stores	
American Eagle Outfitters	(NYSE: AEO)
Buckle	(NYSE: BKE)
Chico's FAS Inc.	(NYSE: CHS)
Dillards Inc.	(NYSE: DDS)
Foot Locker Inc.	(NYSE: FL)
Gap Inc.	(NYSE: GPS)
JCPenney Co Inc.	(NYSE: JCP)
Kohl's Corp	(NYSE: KSS)
L Brands Inc.	(NYSE: LB)
Macy's Inc.	(NYSE: M)
Nordstrom Inc.	(NYSE: JWN)
Target Corp.	(NYSE: TGT)
TJX Companies Inc.	(NYSE: TJX)
Wal-Mart Stores Inc.	(NYSE: WMT)

importance. Multinational corporations can be set up in the following ways:

- in horizontally integrated corporations, operations throughout the world are involved in producing the same or similar products
- in vertically integrated corporations, operations throughout the world are involved in specific aspects of production across the supply chain
- diversified corporations include some aspects of both horizontal and vertical integration

Examples of multinational corporations include Nike, Inc. and Walmart (Figure 3.1).

Advantages of Corporations

Corporations have some advantages over other forms of business ownership. The main advantage of incorporation is the limited liability of the owners (stockholders). If the corporation fails, creditors cannot seize the stockholders' personal assets to pay the corporate debt. This is the primary reason two or more

Figure 3.1
Walmart is an example of a multinational corporation. Justin Sullivan/Getty Images.

individuals may decide to create a private corporation rather than a partnership when beginning a business.

Another advantage corporations have is the flexibility and ease of transferring ownership. Unlike a sole proprietorship or partnership, a corporation does not cease to exist if one of its owners withdraws or dies. Shares are simply transferred to heirs or sold. In most cases, stockholders are free to sell their stock at any time. Because transferring ownership is this easy, corporations seldom dissolve because of ownership issues.

Unlike managing a sole proprietorship or partnership, management of a corporation does not depend on ownership. The management group runs the day-to-day operations of the company regardless of who owns the business that day. This structure allows the board of directors to hire the best-qualified individuals to manage specialized areas of the company.

In addition, large corporations offer great potential for employee advancement in the organization. Employees may work in specialized areas of the company and advance through the ranks—such potential for advancement can serve as employee incentive.

For publicly traded corporations, the act of going public, or becoming a publicly traded corporation, can be a benefit to businesses in raising capital to expand or diversify. When a corporation goes public, investors buy shares of stock based upon how well they believe the company will perform in the future. These investments can then be used to expand or improve the company.

Disadvantages of Corporations

With all these advantages, why are not all businesses structured as corporations? Despite their apparent advantages, corporations have a number of disadvantages. It is much more complicated to establish a corporation than a sole proprietorship or partnership. As noted earlier, a corporation is organized around a legal charter or articles of incorporation that outline its scope and activity. Because of this, legal fees and other costs involved in incorporation are higher than for other forms of business ownership. This is especially true if a company wants to become a publicly traded corporation or go public through the selling of shares to public investors. It is estimated that the costs of an **initial public offering (IPO)** can be up to 25 percent of the company's equity (the difference between the company's assets and its liabilities).

The corporation's articles of incorporation also restrict the type of business it can perform. In other words, the board of directors or officers of a publicly traded apparel company cannot shift from producing apparel to producing automobiles without filing new articles of incorporation.

Corporations are organized under the laws of specific states, and each state has statutes that govern corporations. There are also federal laws (i.e., Securities Act of 1933, Securities Exchange Act of 1934) that regulate publicly held corporations in the issuing and selling of their shares of stock. Other federal laws that govern businesses, including corporations, are described later in this chapter.

Another disadvantage to corporations are corporate taxes. Because they are legal entities, corporations are taxed on their income at a tax rate higher than that on personal income. In addition, for C corporations, dividends paid to stockholders are considered personal income; therefore, they are subject to personal income tax.

Corporations are often large companies that can have thousands of employees. This may cause some employees to view corporations as impersonal and bureaucratic. In addition, unlike other forms of business ownership, owners of corporations—especially publicly traded corporations—might not be involved in the day-to-day operations of the business. Employees who are not stockholders may not have the same commitment to the corporation that owners of sole proprietorships or partnerships may have.

Despite these disadvantages, the limited liability associated with corporations and the ease of transferring ownership make them attractive for investors who want to own part of specific companies. Thus, privately held and publicly traded corporations are the most powerful forms of business in the fashion industries.

Limited Liability Companies

First authorized in 1977 and then expanded in 1988, **limited liability companies (LLC)** provide business owners with tax advantages (as with partnerships) along with limited liability (as with corporations). All limited liability companies are required to have either the abbreviation *LLC* or the words *limited liability company* in their name. These companies can be owned by a single individual or a few members who all participate in managing the company. Owners of an LLC, called members, create an operating agreement that outlines how the LLC will be considered for tax purposes, how the company will operate, and the outcome of the company if a member leaves the company.

Examples of LLCs include small companies such as PFW Productions, LLC, the production company for Portland (Oregon) Fashion Week, and Sweetface Fashion Company LLC—a joint venture with Jennifer Lopez that designs and markets women's contemporary fashions—as well as large companies such as Stuart Weitzman Holdings LLC (luxury footwear and handbags), Maidenform Brands LLC (intimate apparel), and Eddie Bauer LLC.

Advantages of Limited Liability Companies

As indicated by the name *limited liability company*, LLCs provide members with limited liability, thus offering business owners a financially safer option over sole proprietorships or partnerships. Also, the U.S. Internal Revenue Service (IRS) does not consider LLCs distinct entities for tax purposes. Therefore, depending on how the LLC is established, it may be taxed like a sole proprietorship, partnership, or corporation. Moreover, the number of members in an LLC is unlimited—it may have one member or a hundred members. LLCs also have less paperwork and formality than corporations because they do not require a board of directors, annual meetings, and accounting requirements.

Disadvantages of Limited Liability Companies

As noted earlier, an operating agreement is an important aspect of creating an LLC. Without an operating agreement, operations of the LLC may be ambiguous. In addition, fees to establish an LLC may be higher than a sole proprietorship, and adding members to an LLC requires additional paperwork. Lastly, rules around LLCs vary by state, and expansion of the business to other states may require other forms of ownership.

Terms Associated with Company Expansion and Diversification

As you read trade and consumer literature about companies' organizations and operations, you will come across a number of terms (e.g., *merger*, *acquisition*, *takeover*, and *conglomerate*) related to the company's organization. To interpret the meaning of literature, it is important to have a basic understanding of these terms.

Mergers and acquisitions are often spoken of in the same breath and may be viewed as synonymous, although their meanings are slightly different. A **merger** is the blending of one company into another company. If company A and company B merge, the result will be a larger company C. Mergers typically take place between companies that are of approximately equal size. On the other hand, an **acquisition** is when company A purchases company B and assumes ownership of company B's assets and liability for all of company B's debts. A **takeover** results when one company or individual gains control of another company by buying a large enough portion of its shares. Takeovers can be either mergers or acquisitions; they are friendly when the company that is taken over agrees to the association, or hostile when the company that is taken over does not agree to the association.

In the fashion industries, mergers, acquisitions, and takeovers are relatively frequent as large companies often acquire a number of brands. For example, PVH acquired Calvin Klein in 2003, Tommy Hilfiger in 2010, and The Warnaco Group in 2013. Through acquisitions and takeovers, Louis Vuitton Moet Hennessey (LVMH) owns brands including Louis Vuitton, Givenchy, DKNY, Christian Dior, Kenzo, Fendi, and Céline. Kerring/PPR owns GUCCI, Saint Laurent, Alexander McQueen, Stella McCartney, Balenciaga, Bottega Veneta, and PUMA. The Japanese company Fast Retailing owns Uniqlo, Helmut Lang, and Theory; and the Spanish company Inditex owns Zara, Zara Home, Massimo Dutti, Oysho, and Bershka.

Conglomerates are diversified companies (typically corporations) that are involved with significantly different lines of business. The biggest advantage for conglomerates is their ability to realign assets among companies to increase efficiencies, support expansions, and minimize the impact of losses. For example, LVMH is a conglomerate including companies focusing on wine and spirits (e.g., Moët & Chandon champagne), fashion and leather goods (e.g., Louis Vuitton, Céline, Givenchy, Fendi), perfumes and cosmetics (e.g., Guerlain, Parfums Christian Dior, Benefit cosmetics), watches and jewelry (e.g., TAG Heuer, Zenith, De Beers, Fred), and retailing (e.g., DFS, Franck et Fils, Sephora).

ENTREPRENEURSHIP—STARTING YOUR OWN BUSINESS

Some people with careers in the fashion industries want to own their business someday—as a researcher, designer, manufacturer, or retailer. That is, they want to become an **entrepreneur**. According to dictionary.com, an entrepreneur is "a person who organizes and manages any enterprise, especially a business, usually with considerable initiative and risk." As such, entrepreneurs often create a new business as either a sole proprietorship, partnership, or an LLC, depending on the number of people involved in creating the business and the financial risks assumed by the owners. Because of the personal satisfaction and potential, entrepreneurship is a coveted endeavor. In general, entrepreneurs possess the following characteristics: passion for their business, perseverance and patience, resourcefulness, open-mindedness, and spongelike absorption in learning (Resnick 2014).

Many websites, books, courses, and higher education degree programs are available to assist entrepreneurs in creating, finding investors for, and building a business from the ground up. In the apparel industry, Maker's Row (makers row.com) assists brands and designers in starting their own business, finding U.S. contractors throughout the supply chain, and showcasing U.S.-made products.

FORMS OF COMPETITION

The goal of every sole proprietorship, partnership, corporation, and LLC in the fashion industries is to earn a profit by providing products and/or services that are desired by the ultimate consumer. However, many companies are vying for the consumer's dollar. Thus companies compete with one another, whether they are sole proprietorships, partnerships, or corporations. Companies that successfully compete will make a profit that will either be reinvested in the company or paid to the company's owners or stockholders.

Competitive Strategies

Companies compete in a number of ways that, in part, determine their business strategies. Companies typically compete on any of the following bases:

- the *price* of the merchandise to the retailer or consumer
- the *quality* of the design, fabrics, and construction
- *innovation*—how unique or fashionable the merchandise is
- *services* offered to the business customer or ultimate consumer
- *social benefit of the merchandise*—how the company or brand creates a lasting benefit to the environment or society through the design, production, and/or distribution of the merchandise
- a combination of these factors

One company that produces children's wear may have lower prices than its competition; another may provide better-quality merchandise; another may produce children's wear that is more innovative; another may offer services to accept and donate slightly worn children's apparel merchandise; and still another may offer consumers free shipping or other services. Thus, a company's business practices are based on competitive strategies.

For example, Hanna Andersson, a children's apparel brand and multichannel retailer headquartered in Portland, Oregon, is known for its innovative and quality merchandise as well as its socially responsible business practices (Figure 3.2). Here is the company mission statement:

> To share our passion for outstanding quality and our care for children by providing uniquely styled, long lasting, and comfortable clothing that lets kids be kids and is inspired by our Swedish heritage and socially responsible business practices.

Figure 3.2
One of Hanna Andersson's competitive advantages is to focus on the quality, functionality, durability, and environmental responsibility of its designs. Alamy © NetPhotos/Alamy.

This corporate philosophy is demonstrated in various ways. Organically grown cotton is used for sleepers, long johns, and T-shirts; garments are also tested for harmful substances. The Hanna Helps program gives grants to a variety of employee-selected nonprofit organizations that focus on children's lives. The Hanna-Me-Downs program collects clothing and books in stores across the country for contribution to local groups assisting children. Such corporate practices are one way Hanna Andersson separates itself from its competition and appeals to the company's customers.

Competitive Situations or Market Forms

Five primary competitive situations or market forms exist among U.S. companies:

1. monopoly
2. oligopoly
3. oligopsony
4. pure or perfect competition
5. monopolistic competition

In a **monopoly**, one company typically dominates the market and thus can price its goods and/or services at whatever level it wishes. Because a monopoly essentially eliminates or drastically reduces competition, federal laws prohibit companies from buying out their competition and, in effect, becoming a monopoly. Only essential services, such as utilities, can legally operate as monopolies in today's market, and the prices they charge are heavily regulated by the government.

In an **oligopoly**, a few companies dominate and essentially have control of the market, thereby making it difficult for other companies to enter. The dominant companies compete among themselves through product and service differentiation and advertising. Although oligopolies are not illegal, the dominant companies are not permitted to set artificial prices among themselves. In many ways, the athletic footwear industry can be considered an oligopoly because it is dominated by a few companies. For example, Nike (including Jordan brand and Converse) and Adidas Group (including Reebok), account for the largest share of athletic footwear worldwide. Thus, these companies have some control over the price they charge for their goods.

Oligopsony exists when there are a small number of buyers for goods and services offered by a large number of sellers. This type of competition is most often found in agricultural products (e.g., cocoa) when numerous growers sell to a limited number of buyers worldwide.

In **pure competition**, or **perfect competition**, there are many producers and consumers of similar products, so price is determined by market demand. The market for agricultural commodities, such as cotton or wool, is the closest to pure competition that can be found in the textile and apparel industries. In these cases, the price for the product—raw cotton or wool—is determined by supply and demand of the commodity. For example, supply and demand for cotton are estimated two years in advance. Cotton supplies can be affected by weather conditions, production yield, trade negotiations, legislation, and other factors that affect how many bales of cotton are produced. When supplies are high and demand is stable or low, prices of cotton can decrease. When supplies are low and demand high, prices of cotton can increase.

The most common form of competition in the fashion industries is **monopolistic competition**, in which many companies compete in a certain product type, but the specific products of any one company are perceived as unique by consumers. For example, many companies produce brands of denim jeans, including Levi's®, Lee, Wrangler, 7 for All Mankind®, Nudie Jeans, Joe's, Gap, True Religion, and AG. However, through product differentiation, advertising, distribution strategy, and pricing, each company has created a unique image. By creating this unique image in consumers' minds, each company has, in some respect, a monopoly in its specific product and, therefore, has some control over price. A consumer who wants only 7 for All Mankind® jeans and seeks out that particular brand may be willing to pay a premium for that brand.

In monopolistic competition, each company must create a perceived difference between its product and the competition's products. This difference can be achieved in the following ways:

- The product is differentiated by design characteristics.
- The company uses advertising to create public awareness of its brand name or trademark (Figure 3.3).
- The company buys the use of a well-established brand name, trademark, or other image through licensing programs.
- A retailer creates **private label brand** merchandise that is unique to its store. Examples of private label brands are Arizona (JCPenney), Classiques Entier and Halogen (Nordstrom), and Charter Club and INC International (Macy's).

Figure 3.3
Fashion brands strive to create unique brand images to gain competitive advantage. WWD/© Conde Nast.

- A specialty store offers only private label merchandise, thus becoming a **specialty store retailer of private label apparel (SPA)**. Examples of SPAs are Abercrombie and Fitch, Gap, Banana Republic, Uniqlo, Zara, H&M, and Ann Taylor.
- A manufacturer may expand its services to consumers, as when it opens retail stores (e.g., Polo Ralph Lauren, Nike, Adidas, Calvin Klein, Timberland) or offers merchandise through websites, catalogs, and other non-store venues.

In these ways, consumers associate a company's goods with a particular unique image.

LAWS AFFECTING COMPANIES IN THE FASHION INDUSTRIES

This section briefly reviews a number of U.S. federal laws and international treaties that affect companies in the global fashion industries. Obviously, not all of these laws will affect all companies, but it is important to note the variety of areas covered by U.S. federal laws and international treaties—everything from protecting personal property to protecting consumers to protecting fair trade. In addition to these U.S. federal laws, various state and municipal laws may apply to companies. Professionals in the industries must be aware of and abide by these laws, the details of which can be found in federal, state, and municipal government documents. It is beyond the scope of this book to cover the laws of every country; however, whenever a company has operations or has contracts with companies in other countries, its success depends on knowing—and following—the laws of those particular countries.

Laws Protecting Fashion Inventions and Designs

Many companies in fashion industries are involved in creating, inventing, or designing new processes and products. Laws related to patents, trademarks, copyrights, and trade secrets were established to protect **intellectual property (IP)** such as inventions and creations (Jimenez and Kolsun 2010).

Laws protecting original garment designs vary from one country to another. Unlike designs created in European countries, in the United States, specific apparel designs are not protected. The United States has generally held a philosophy that laws protecting industrial design (including apparel) would impede design innovation. Inventions, textile print designs, and logos are protected under patent, trademark, and copyright laws, respectively; however, apparel designs are not protected by U.S. law. Some believe this lack of design protection in the United States inhibits apparel design innovation in the United States and has resulted in many U.S. designers working instead in Europe (Keyder 1999). The laws in Europe do provide more design protection than do current U.S. laws. As noted by Virginia Brown Keyder (1999), an attorney who specializes in design law:

> European design law, though widely divergent in terms of detail at the national level, continues to afford stronger protection to the designer and is fast becoming harmonized across Europe. In addition, EU [European Union] design law is increasingly being used as a model of legal reform throughout the world.

Figure 3.4
Patents allow companies such as Nike the exclusive right to use, make, or sell a product innovation. LOC.

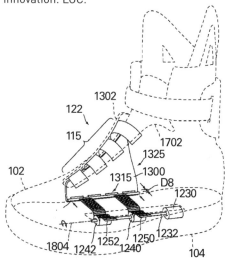

Patents

According to the U.S. Patent and Trademark Office (2015), a **patent** grants property rights to an inventor, including "the right to exclude others from making, using, offering for sale, or selling the invention in the United States or importing the invention into the United States." A patent allows the inventor or producer the exclusive right to use, make, or sell a product for a period of 20 years. From a legal perspective, products must be new inventions or technological advancements in product design. In the textile, apparel, and home fashions industries, patents can be acquired for technological advancements in textile processing, apparel production, or in products themselves. For example, Nike was granted 544 new patents in 2013 and 541 in 2014 (of these, 43 were for apparel innovations and 281 were for footwear innovations). These patents grant Nike the sole use of these innovations (Figure 3.4). If another company uses a patented product or process, the patent owner has the right to sue the party for patent infringement.

Trademarks and Service Marks

A **trademark** or **trade name** is a "word, phrase, symbol, or design, or a combination of words, phrases, symbols, or designs, that identifies and distinguishes the source of the goods of one party from those of others" (U.S. Patent and Trademark Office 2015). **Service marks** are similar to trademarks but refer to identifications for services rather than for products. The Lanham Act (Federal Trademark Act) provides for federal registration and protection of trademarks. Although any company can claim rights to a trademark or service mark by using the TM or SM designators, trademarks can be registered through the U.S. Patent and Trademark Office or through the Secretary of State in a state for products that are not in interstate commerce. Federal trademarks are effective for as long as they are used and registrations are updated. Once the trademarks has been registered, the ® symbol is used, and others cannot use it without permission. Legal assignment (permission to use) of trademarks or service marks can be accomplished through licensing contracts. In this case, royalties are paid to the owner of the trademark or service mark. If merchandise is produced and sold without acquiring legal assignment of the trademark or service mark, the entity producing or selling the merchandise can be sued for trademark infringement. Trademark and patent searches are conducted by attorneys who specialize in ensuring that a trademark, trade name, patent, or business name is available for use.

Trademarks and trade names may not be generic terms such as *wonderful* or *exciting*, or, in the apparel industry, such generic terms as *trouser* or *dress*. In the early 1990s, Fruit of the Loom claimed to have ownership of the word *fruit* and sued another company for trademark infringement for using the word *fruit* as a trademark on apparel goods. Fruit of the Loom did not win the case. On the other hand, in 2013 the surfer lifestyle brand, Quiksilver, lost a trademark infringement lawsuit over its VSTR brand, which was found to infringe on World Marketing's *Visitor* trademark brand. In the fashion industries, registered trademarks and trade names are widespread and include the following:

- trade names of manufactured fibers used for apparel and home fashions (e.g., Dacron® polyester, Lycra® spandex)
- trade names of natural fiber associations and companies (e.g., Cotton Incorporated's cotton symbol, Wool Company's Woolmark symbol)
- fashion brand names (e.g., Levi's Dockers®, 7 for all Mankind®, WestPoint Stevens Vellux®)
- trademarks of fashion brands (e.g., Nike's swoosh, the stitching on the back pocket of Levi's jeans, Burberry's distinctive plaid)

Well-known and well-respected trade names and trademarks take years to establish through concentrated efforts in designing goods that meet the needs of consumers, quality control, and advertising. Consumers become confident that goods with a well-known trade name or trademark will meet certain standards of quality and/or image (Figure 3.5).

Consumers' desire for fashion merchandise with well-known and visible trade names and trademarks has led to many **trademark infringements** and a proliferation of **counterfeit goods** (goods bearing unauthorized registered trade names or trademarks). Typically, counterfeit goods are of much lower quality than the

authentic merchandise and are sold at a fraction of the price of genuine merchandise. Counterfeiters exploit consumer awareness and trust of a brand image by producing low-quality merchandise, and they do not pay royalties to the companies that may have spent millions creating that awareness and trust.

To establish trademark infringement in court, the plaintiff must prove the following:

1. Its trademark has achieved a secondary meaning (i.e., the consumer associates the trademark with the company or product).
2. The trademark is nonfunctional (i.e., the trademark is ornamental or does not contribute to the function of the product).
3. There is likelihood of confusion by the consumer for "famous" trademarks, or the trademark has been weakened by the association with the infringing product.

According to *World Trademark Review* (Elings, Keith, and Wukoson 2013), counterfeit fashions represent a US$500–US$600 billion global market. The growth of electronic commerce (e.g., auction websites, business-to-consumer websites, business-to-business websites) and social media has created opportunities for anyone to engage in the selling of counterfeit merchandise. In addition to counterfeit luxury brands, counterfeit merchandise is also sold under international name brands such as Nike, The North Face, and Polo Ralph Lauren.

Given the prevalence of counterfeiters worldwide, enforcement of anti-counterfeit laws is difficult. However, holders of trade names in the fashion industries are using the Lanham Act (including the Trademark Counterfeiting Act of 1984 and the Anticounterfeiting Consumer Protection Act of 1996) in the U.S. courts to curb online selling of counterfeit merchandise. Several non-legislative initiatives have been created to assist companies. These include the International

AntiCounterfeiting Coalition, a nonprofit organization whose mission is to "combat counterfeiting and piracy by promoting laws, regulations, directives, and relationships designed to render the theft of intellectual property undesirable and unprofitable" (IACC, 2015). In addition, the Ads Integrity Alliance of 2012 is a joint initiative of Google, AOL, Facebook, and Twitter to disable paid-for ads that promote counterfeit goods.

Companies also discourage trademark infringement in the following ways:

- Including strict security standards in their contracts with factories using UV yarns, UV inks, holographic labels, holographic yarns, watermarks, and QR codes to distinguish authentic goods from counterfeits.
- Working with the Department of Homeland Security—U.S. Customs and Border Protection to stop the flow of imported counterfeit goods into the United States. In 2014, U.S. Homeland Security seized over US$880 million worth of counterfeit watches, jewelry, handbags, apparel, and footwear that accounted for 72 percent of the seizures.

Trade dress is a subset of trademark law, only instead of protecting the identifying words or logos, the law of trade dress protects the overall look or image of a product itself or the packaging of a product, provided that the overall look or combination of features has come to identify the manufacturer of the product. Governed primarily by the Lanham Act, in 2000, the U.S. Supreme Court weighed in on trade dress, creating two categories: protection for product packaging and protection for product design. Product packaging includes classic examples such as the Coca-Cola bottle and the turquoise packaging of merchandise purchased at Tiffany & Co. In each of these examples, the packaging itself has acquired secondary meaning. Protection of product design requires that the design itself has secondary meaning and that consumers associate the design with the brand. Providing evidence to protect product design is difficult in the fashion industry. However, in 2012 U.S. courts ruled that French footwear designer Christian Louboutin's distinctive red-soled shoes had come to represent the brand in consumers' minds and therefore were appropriately protected under trade dress law.

Copyrights

Copyrights protect a number of written, pictorial, and performed works, including literature, music, films, television shows, artworks, dramatic works, and advertisements. Under the Copyright Act of 1976 (with periodic amendments), the copyright holder has the exclusive right to use, perform, or reproduce the material for life of the author plus 70 years—or, if the work is of corporate authorship (e.g., Disney characters), for 95 years from publication or 120 years from creation, whichever expires first. All works published before 1923 are considered to be in the public domain. Under the *fair use* doctrine, works protected by copyright can be used on a limited basis for educational or research purposes. Reproduction of material protected by copyright without permission is considered infringement.

In the U.S. fashion industries, although garment or product style is not protected by copyright, original textile prints and graphic designs are protected, even when incorporated into a garment or home fashions item. To collect damages when a copyright is infringed, the copyright must be registered with the Copyright Office of the U.S. Library of Congress. A textile designer may also print a copyright notice (©) in the selvage of the fabric, although this notice is not necessary. A designer owns the copyright unless she or he is a salaried employee of a company; then the employer holds the copyright. Any unauthorized reproduction of the textile print or design protected by copyright is considered copyright infringement, and once the copyright is registered, the copyright holder can take the infringer to court. Following are some examples of copyright infringement in the textile industry:

- dishonest textile converters who buy apparel or home fashions at retail in order to copy the textile print
- unscrupulous apparel or home fashions manufacturers that work with one converter to develop new prints and then take the samples to another converter to have them reproduced more cheaply
- fraudulent retailers that copy textile prints for use in their private label merchandise

U.S. copyrights are partially protected in the international market under the Berne Convention, an international treaty designed to help fight infringement across national borders.

Federal Laws Related to Business Practices and International Trade

Many federal laws relate to how a company must run its business, including requirements concerning fair competition, international trade, environmental practices, consumer protection, and employment practices.

Fair Competition

A number of federal laws have been established to assure fair competition. Table 3.5 reviews the primary laws that prohibit monopolies and unfair or deceptive practices in interstate commerce. Any fashion brand company that distributes products or services across state lines is governed by these laws. These laws are all administered by the Federal Trade Commission (FTC).

International Trade

International trade laws are constantly changing, and it is essential for apparel companies and retailers to stay up to date on trade issues. International organizations, laws, and treaties exist for countries and companies with international trade of products, including fashion merchandise (Table 3.6). The primary objective of these laws and treaties is to establish fair trade among countries. Because of shifts in international relations, these laws and treaties are reviewed and amended regularly. Any fashion brand companies that import or export goods are affected by these laws and treaties.

World Trade Organization

Established in 1995, the World Trade Organization (WTO) is a global trade organization that deals with the rules of trade among member countries. As of 2015, 161 countries are members. The WTO's Agreement on Textiles and Clothing phased

Table 3.5 Federal Laws Related to Competition

Federal Laws	Effects on Competition
Sherman Antitrust Act (1890)	Outlawed monopolies and attempts to form monopolies
Clayton Act (1914)	Amended the Sherman Antitrust Act by — forbidding a seller from discriminating in price between and among different purchases of the same commodity — outlawing exclusive dealing and tie-in arrangements — forbidding corporate asset or stock mergers where the effect may be to create a monopoly — forbidding persons from serving on boards of directors of competing corporations
Federal Trade Commission Act (1914)	Declared unlawful unfair methods of competition in or affecting commerce and unfair or deceptive acts or practices in interstate commerce. The FTC's Bureau of Competition investigates potential law violations and serves as a resource for policy makers regarding competition (http://www.ftc.gov)
Robinson-Patman Act (1936)	Amended the Clayton Act by preventing large firms from exerting excessive economic power to drive out small competitors in local markets
Cellar-Kefauver Act (1950)	Made it illegal to create a monopoly by eliminating competition through company mergers and acquisitions
Wheeler-Lea Act (1938)	Amended the Federal Trade Commission Act by allowing the FTC to stop unfair competition, even if a competitor is not shown to be harmed by a business practice when a consumer is injured by deceptive acts or practices

out quotas established by the Multi-Fiber Arrangement (MFA) and reduced tariffs on textiles and apparel over a 10-year period between 1995 and 2005. The quota phaseout (quotas remained for a few product categories after 2005 for China, Russia, Ukraine, and Vietnam) gave countries more open access to consumer markets. The WTO administers WTO trade agreements, serves as a forum for trade negotiations, monitors trade policies, and resolves any trade disputes. It also assists developing countries in building their international trade capacity.

United State Trade Policies and Agreements

In the United States, trade policies are set by the executive branch of the government and carried out by the U.S. Trade Representative. The trade laws are implemented and administered by several departments, including the following:

- The U.S. Department of Commerce oversees the Committee for the Implementation of Textile Agreements (CITA) and the Office of Textiles (OTEXA).
- The U.S. Customs and Border Protection (of the Department of Homeland Security) oversees the physical control of imports and the collection of tariffs (taxes on imports), and prevents counterfeit goods from entering the country.

The United States has negotiated a number of **free trade agreements (FTA)** with specific countries or world regions. The goals of these FTAs have been to

Table 3.6 Laws, Agreements, and Organizations Related to International Trade Practices

Laws, Agreements, and Organizations	Effects on Trade Practices
General Agreement on Tariffs and Trade (GATT, 1947)	A multinational agreement regarding global trade policies. In international trade of textiles and apparel, GATT allowed for the use of tariffs (taxes on imports) to protect domestic industries and for quantitative limits (quotas) on certain textile and apparel merchandise entering the United States from specified countries during a specified period of time.
Multifiber Arrangement (MFA I: 1947–1977, MFA II: 1977–1981, MFA III: 1981–1986, MFA IV: 1986–1991, extensions to MFA IV: 1991, 1992, 1993)	A general framework for international textile trade that operated under the authority of GATT and allowed for the establishment of bilateral agreements between trading partners. The MFA was phased out in 2005 when international trade for textile, apparel, and home fashions industries came under the jurisdiction of the World Trade Organization.
World Trade Organization (WTO, 1995)	The WTO Agreement on Textiles and Clothing (ATC) provided for the reduction and phasing out of quotas on textiles and apparel imported from WTO member countries in three stages between 1995 and 2005. The ATC was approved as part of the Uruguay Round Agreements Act by the U.S. Congress in December 1994 and went into effect on January 1, 1995. In 2015, the WTO had 162 member countries.
United States Free Trade Agreements and implementation dates	Australia (2005) Bahrain (2006) Central America–Dominican Republic–United States Free Trade Agreement (CAFTA-DR, 2005): Costa Rica, El Salvador, Guatemala, Honduras, Nicaragua, the Dominican Republic, and the United States Chile (2004) Israel (1985) Jordan (2001) KORUS (2012) Morocco (2006) North American Free Trade Agreement (NAFTA, 1994) United States, Canada, and Mexico Oman (1985) Peru (2009) Singapore (2004) Transatlantic Trade and Investment Partnership (T-TIP) (in negotiations) Trans-Pacific Partnership (TPP) (as of 2015, approved but not yet ratified)

reduce trade barriers among the countries, encourage economic development, and foster business relationships. These goals have been achieved through

- elimination or reduction of tariff rates
- improvement of intellectual property regulations
- opening of government purchasing opportunities, and
- easing of investment rules

See Table 3.6 for a complete listing of U.S. FTAs.

The United States has also enacted several **Trade and Investment Framework Agreements (TIFAs)** that provide a forum for dialogue on trade and investment issues between the United States and other governments. In addition, **trade preference programs** have been enacted to enhance opportunities for trade and economic development with specific regions of the world. For example, The African Growth and Opportunity Act (AGOA) supports thirty-nine eligible nations in sub-Saharan Africa. This program allows for tariff/duty-free and quota-free treatment for a number of eligible apparel products including apparel made of U.S. yarns and fabric (yarn forward rule), apparel made of yarns and fabrics made in sub-Saharan Africa or not produced commercially in the United States, and certain handmade or folklore products.

Environmental Practices

Federal environmental laws regulate business practices related to environmental pollution. The goal of these laws is to protect the environment from toxic pollutants. In the fashion industries, these laws particularly affect chemical companies that manufacture fibers. These companies' processes often produce or require the use of toxic substances, and their factories may emit toxic substances that are considered pollutants. Table 3.7 outlines the primary environmental laws, which are administered by the Environmental Protection Agency (EPA).

Table 3.7 Federal Laws Related to Practices to Protect the Environment	
Federal Laws	**Effects on the Environment**
National Environmental Policy Act of 1969	Established the national charter for the protection of the environment
Clean Air Act (1970)	Controls air pollution through air quality standards to protect public health
Endangered Species Act (1973)	Provides for the conservation of threatened or endangered plants and animals and the habitats where they are found
Resource Conservation and Recovery Act of 1976	Controls the management of solid waste products and encourages resource conservation and recovery
Toxic Substances Control Act (1976)	Allows regulation of the manufacturing, use, and disposal of toxic substances
Clean Water Act (1977)	Controls water pollution by keeping pollutants out of lakes, rivers, and streams
Pollution Prevention Act (1990)	Focused on reducing pollution through cost-effective changes in production, operations, and use of raw materials

Consumer Protection

Beginning in the 1930s and 1940s, a number of laws were enacted to protect the health and safety of consumers (Table 3.8). Over the years since then, many additional protections have been added. These laws require companies to label the fiber content and care procedures of products truthfully and to prohibit companies from selling flammable products. They are administered by either the Federal Trade Commission or the Consumer Product Safety Commission (CPSC).

Table 3.8 Federal Laws Associated with Practices for Consumer Protection	
Federal Laws	**Effects on Consumer Protection**
Wool Products Labeling Act (1939), Fur Products Labeling Act (1952), the Textile Fiber Products Identification Act (1958, effective 1960, last amended 2006)	Require specified information to be on textile and fur product labels; require the advertising of country of origin in mail-order catalogs and promotional materials; administered by the FTC
Enforcement Policy Statement on U.S. Origins Claims (1997)	Provides guidelines for labeling products as Made in the U.S. to be "all or virtually all" made in the United States
Flammable Fabrics Act (1953, last amended 1990)	Regulates the manufacturing of wearing apparel and fabrics (including carpets, rugs, and mattresses) that are so highly flammable as to be dangerous when worn. Sets standards of flammability and test methods. Sets standards for flammability of children's sleepwear. Originally administered by the FTC; administration transferred to the CPSC in 1972
Consumer Products Safety Act (1972)	Established the Consumer Products Safety Commission (CPSC) to reduce or eliminate risk of injury associated with selected consumer products
Care Labeling of Textile Wearing Apparel and Certain Piece Goods Act (1971, last amended 2000)	Requires that care labels be affixed to most apparel and be attached to retail piece goods. Administered by the FTC
Federal Hazardous Substance Act (1960; last amended 1995)	Addresses issue of choking, ingestion, aspiration of small items by children, and hazards from sharp points and edges on articles intended for use by children by requiring that decorative buttons or other decorative items on children's clothing pass use and abuse testing procedures. Prohibits the use of lead paint on children's articles, including clothing. Administered by the CPSC.

Employment Practices

To assure fair hiring and employment practices among companies, laws have been enacted to regulate child labor and homework (piecework contracted to individuals who do the work in their homes) and to prohibit discrimination based on such characteristics as race, sex, age, or physical disability. Any company with employees is regulated by these laws (Table 3.9).

Table 3.9 Federal Laws Related to Employment Practices

Federal Laws	Effects on Employment Practices
Fair Labor Standards Act of 1938 (last amended 2004)	Guarantees fair employment status by establishing minimum wage standards, child labor restrictions, and other employment regulations
Equal Pay Act of 1963	Amends the Fair Labor Standards Act by requiring employers to provide equal pay to men and women for doing equal work
Age Discrimination in Employment Act (1967)	Prohibits an employer from discriminating in hiring or other aspects of employment because of age. Administered by the Equal Employment Opportunity Commission (EEOC)
Occupational Safety and Health Act of 1970 (last amended 2004)	Created the Occupational Safety and Health Administration (OSHA); assures safe and healthful working conditions for employees by setting general occupational safety and health standards, and requiring that employers prepare and maintain records of occupational injuries and illnesses. Administered by the Department of Labor/OSHA.
Equal Employment Opportunity Act of 1972	Prohibits discrimination by employers in hiring, promotions, discharge, and conditions of employment if such discrimination is based on race, color, religion, sex, or national origin
Americans with Disabilities Act (ADA) of 1990	Prohibits discrimination against qualified individuals with disabilities in all aspects of employment; prohibits discrimination on the basis of disability by requiring that public accommodations and commercial facilities be designed, constructed, and altered in compliance with accessibility standards. Administered by the Office of the ADA, Department of Justice
Family and Medical Leave Act of 1993	Grants eligible employees up to a total of 12 work weeks of unpaid leave for one or more family and medical reasons (e.g., birth of a child, care of an immediate family member)
Immigration and Nationality Act (last amended 2000)	Establishes conditions for temporary employment in the United States by non-U.S. citizens
Trade Adjustment Assistance Reauthorization Act of 2015	Reauthorized the Trade Adjustment Assistance Program (first established in 1974), which provides aid to workers whose employment is negatively affected by international trade

SUMMARY

Depending on the objectives, needs, and size of fashion brand companies, they are owned as sole proprietorships, partnerships, corporations, or limited liability companies (LLC). The advantages and disadvantages of each form of business ownership are related to the ease of formation and dissolution (an advantage of sole proprietorship and partnership and a disadvantage of corporations), the degree of liability that owners have for business debts (an advantage of corporations and a disadvantage of sole proprietorship and partnerships), and operational strategies (some advantages and disadvantages for each form of ownership).

Each company—whether a sole proprietorship, partnership, corporation, or LLC—competes with other companies based on price, quality, innovation, service, social benefit of merchandise, or a combination of these factors. In the fashion industries, competitive strategies include monopolies, oligopolies (e.g., athletic shoe industry), oligopsonies, pure competition (e.g., textile commodities), and monopolistic competition—the most common of the five. In monopolistic competition, although companies compete in a product type (denim jeans), the specific product attributes of any one company (7 for All Mankind® jeans) are perceived as different from the product attributes of other companies (Levi's® jeans, Gap jeans). Companies create this perceived difference through product differentiation, advertising, licensing programs, private label merchandise, or services offered. In the fashion industries mergers, acquisitions, and takeovers are relatively frequent as large companies often acquire brands through these strategies.

A number of U.S. federal laws affect businesses in the textile, apparel, and home fashions industries. Laws related to patents, trademarks, and copyrights protect the identity, inventions, and designs of designers and companies. For example, a textile designer's fabric design is protected by the copyright law so that others cannot legally copy it. Laws have also been established that relate to how companies must run their businesses, including requirements as to competition, international trade, protecting consumers, protecting the environment, and employment practices.

KEY TERMS

acquisition
articles of incorporation
articles of partnership
B corporation
board of directors
C corporation
capital
close corporation
closely held corporation
conglomerate
copyright
corporation
counterfeit goods
dividend
double taxation
entrepreneur
general partner

initial public offering (IPO)
intellectual property (IP)
limited liability
limited liability company (LLC)
limited partnership
merger
monopolistic competition
monopoly
multinational corporation
oligopoly
oligopsony
partnership
patent
perfect competition
private corporation
private label brand
privately held corporation

publicly held corporation
publicly traded corporation
pure competition
regular corporation
S corporation
service mark
sole proprietorship
specialty store retailer of private
    label apparel (SPA)
stockholder
takeover
trade dress
trademark
trade name
trademark infringement
unlimited liability

DISCUSSION QUESTIONS AND ACTIVITIES

1. Interview a small-business owner in your community. Find out whether the business is a sole proprietorship, partnership, LLC, or corporation. Ask the owner why this form of business ownership was chosen, and what he or she views as the primary advantages and disadvantages to the ownership form. Find out what business licenses were required of the owner to start the company. Compare this information with information that others in class receive.

2. Suppose you wanted to invest (buy stock) in a publicly traded corporation. Where can you find information about the corporation? Select a publicly traded corporation in the textile, apparel, and home fashions industries, and find information about the company.

3. Currently, textile designs and prints are protected by copyright from illegal copying, but apparel designs (designs of the garment itself) are not protected in the United States. Do you think that apparel designs should also be covered under copyright law? Why or why not? Justify your response.

CASE STUDY

Protecting Intellectual Property in Fashion Design

According to industry analysts, the global market for children's apparel, footwear, and accessories is expected to continue to grow over the next five years. One recent trend in children's wear is adapting high-performance materials and construction techniques used in making men's and women's high-performance sportswear to the children's sportswear industry. Both large and small companies have been exploring new sportswear technologies and how they may be adapted for their children's wear lines.

Maria Rodriguez was recently hired as an apparel designer by a small children's wear company in the United States to design technologically innovative children's sportswear. Maria's background in material science and apparel design made her an ideal employee for this company, and her work has combined innovative use of high-performance fabrics with the functionality needed for quality children's sportswear. As the company is moving forward with producing these designs, they are eager to ensure that their intellectual property inherent in the designs is protected.

1. Outline various strategies that this company can use to protect the intellectual property inherent in Maria's designs.

2. What are the advantages and disadvantages of each of these strategies?

3. If you were the decision maker for this company, which strategy would you employ, and why?

CAREER OPPORTUNITIES

Career opportunities associated with ownership and legal aspects of the global fashion industry include

- Sole proprietor (e.g., freelance designer, independent sales representative)
- Partnership (e.g., designer and merchandiser who together start a new company)
- Legal professional for a fashion brand
- Legal professional for a law firm that focuses on the global fashion industry

REFERENCES

Committee for the Implementation of Textile Agreements (CITA), U.S. Department of Commerce. (2015). http://otexa.trade.gov/ (accessed March 21, 2016).

Elings, Roxanne, Lisa D. Keith, and George P. Wukoson. (2013). "Anti-counterfeiting in the Fashion and Luxury Sectors: Trends and Strategies." http://www.worldtrademarkreview.com/Intelligence/Anti-Counterfeiting/2013/Industry-insight/Anti-counterfeiting-in-the-fashion-and-luxury-sectors-trends-and-strategies (accessed March 2, 2016).

Fisher, Bruce D., and Marianne M. Jennings. (1991). *Law for Business* (2nd ed.). St. Paul, MN: West Publishing Co.

International AntiCounterfeiting Coalition (IACC). (2015). "History & Mission." http://www.iacc.org/about/history-mission (accessed March 2, 2016).

Jimenez, Guillermo C., and Barbara Kolsun. (2010). *Fashion Law: A Guide for Designers, Fashion Executives, and Attorneys*. New York: Fairchild Books.

Keyder, Virginia Brown. (1999, November 12). *Design Law in Europe and the U.S.* Presentation at the Annual Meeting of the International Textile and Apparel Association, Santa Fe, NM.

National Conference of Commissioners on Uniform State Laws (1997). Uniform Partnership Act (1997). http://www.uniformlaws.org/shared/docs/partnership/upa_final_97.pdf (accessed March 21, 2016).

Office of Textiles and Apparel (OTEXA), U.S. Department of Commerce. (2015). Trade Agreements. http://otexa.trade.gov/ (accessed March 21, 2016).

Resnick, Nathan. (2014, April 22). "5 Key Characteristics Every Entrepreneur Should Have." http://www.entrepreneur.com/article/232991 (accessed March 2, 2016).

U.S. Department of Homeland Security. (2014). "Intellectual Property Rights Seizure Statistics: Fiscal Year 2014." http://www.cbp.gov/sites/default/files/documents/2014%20IPR%20Stats.pdf (accessed March 2, 2016).

U.S. Department of Labor. (2015). Bureau of Labor Statistics, *Occupational Outlook Handbook*. http://www.bls.gov/ooh/ (accessed March 2, 2016).

U.S. Patent and Trademark Office. (2015). U.S. Department of Commerce. http://www.uspto.gov/ (accessed March 2, 2016).

World Trade Organization. (2015). "About WTO." http://www.wto.org/ (accessed March 2, 2016).

Global Materials Industry

IN THIS CHAPTER, YOU WILL LEARN
THE FOLLOWING:

- the importance of materials knowledge for the successful design, production, and marketing of fashion goods

- terms used in describing textiles and textile manufacturing

- the organization and operation of the textile industry

- procedures followed in the processing and marketing of natural and manufactured fibers, yarns, and fabrics

- current developments in the textile and material industry, including responses to environmental issues and new material and production innovations

The materials used to produce fashion products are developed and used all over the world. Understanding the design, production, and distribution of these materials is important. Because textiles and other materials are the foundation of the fashion industries, all professionals require an understanding of the organization and operation of the textile. This chapter describes such organization and operation as well as the marketing of fibers, fabrics, and other materials. The chapter concludes with a discussion of future trends and materials.

TERMINOLOGY

Anyone who is engaged in the business of producing or selling fashion goods needs to understand the terms used in the textile and materials industries. This terminology forms the basis for an understanding of the materials used in fashion products. First, what are **textiles**? The term *textile* is used to describe any product made from fibers. There are four basic components of textile production:

- fiber processing
- yarn spinning
- fabric production or fabrication
- fabric finishing

Fibers comprise the basic unit used in making textile yarns and fabrics. Fibers are classified into **generic families** according to their chemical composition and can be divided into two primary divisions:

- natural fibers
- manufactured (man-made) fibers

Natural fibers include those made from natural protein fibers of animal origin (e.g., wool, cashmere, camel, mohair, angora, and silk) and natural cellulose fibers of plant origin (e.g., cotton, flax, jute, bamboo, and sisal). Leather and fur are considered natural fiber products created from the **pelts**, **skins**, and **hides** of various animals. Leather and fur are unique textiles in that the fibers are not spun into yarns and then constructed into fabrics. Instead, the pelts are tanned to create supple and durable fabrics.

Although natural fibers have been used in making textiles for thousands of years, manufactured fibers have been around for only about 120 years. In the mid-1800s, scientists became interested in duplicating natural fibers.

- In 1891, "artificial silk," made from a solution of cellulose, was commercially produced in France.
- In 1924, the name of this fiber was changed to rayon.
- In 1939, nylon, the first fiber to be synthesized entirely from chemicals (synthetic), was introduced by E. I. du Pont de Nemours and Company.

Since then, many more manufactured fibers have been developed, including the following:

- cellulose-based fibers (e.g., lyocell, acetate)
- synthetic fibers (e.g., acrylic, aramid, modacrylic, olefin, polyester, and spandex)
- mineral-based fibers (e.g., glass, gold)

Yarns are the collection of fibers or filaments laid or twisted together to form a continuous strand strong enough for use in fabrics. Yarns are classified as **spun yarns** made from shorter staple fibers, or **filament yarns** made from long continuous fibers. Filament yarns can be either plain or textured. The type of yarn selected affects the fabric performance, tactile qualities, and appearance.

Fabric construction or **fabrication** processes include the following methods used to make fabrics:

- from solutions (e.g., films, foam)
- directly from fibers (e.g., felt, nonwoven fabrics)
- from yarns (e.g., braid, knitted fabrics, woven fabrics, and lace)

The fabric construction process used often determines the name of the fabric (e.g., satin, jersey, lace, felt). Note that the fiber name is not interchangeable with the fabric name.

Dyeing and finishing the fabric are the final steps in the textile production process. **Finishing** refers to "any process that is done to fiber, yarn, or fabric either before or after fabrication to change the *appearance* (what is seen), the *hand* (what is felt), or the *performance* (what the fabric does)" (Kadolph and Langford 2002, p. 270). **Greige goods** (also referred to as *grey, gray,* or *loom state goods*) are fabrics that have not received finishing treatments, such as bleaching, shearing, brushing, embossing, or dyeing. Once finished, the fabrics are then referred to as **converted goods**, or **finished goods**. Finishes can be classified in the following ways:

- *general* or *functional*
- *mechanical* or *chemical*
- *durable* (permanent) or *renewable* (impermanent)

Both greige goods and finished fabrics are used in a variety of end uses: apparel, home fashions, other sewn products such as sleeping bags and flags, and industrial uses such as liners for highways and hoses.

ORGANIZATION OF THE TEXTILE INDUSTRY

Companies in the textile industry take part in one or more of the four basic components of textile production: fiber processing, yarn spinning, fabric production, and fabric finishing. Figure 4.1 illustrates the structure of the textile industry. Some companies specialize in certain aspects of textile production, as shown in the following examples:

- **Throwsters** modify filament yarns for specific end uses, such as increasing luster or texture by altering the yarn.
- **Textile mills** concentrate on the fabric construction stage of production (e.g., weaving, knitting, nonwoven fabric, lace).
- Companies that specialize in finishing fabrics are called **textile converters**.
- Finished fabrics are sold to apparel and home fashions manufacturers, retailers that sell fabrics, or jobbers that sell surplus goods.
- Retailers that sell private label merchandise may also work directly with converters and/or textile mills.

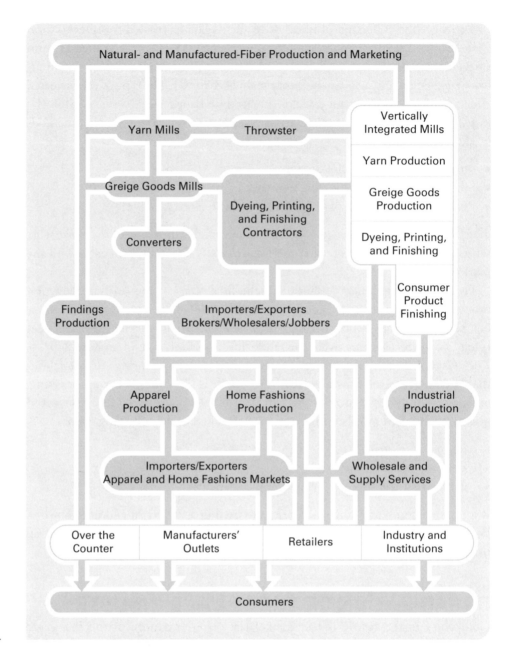

Figure 4.1
This flowchart depicts the structure of the textile industry.

The textile industry includes a number of large corporations that operate through a vertically integrated marketing channel. Each corporation handles all four steps—from processing the fiber to finishing the fabric—within its own organization. Some vertically integrated companies are also involved in making end-use products, such as towels, sheets, or hosiery. Vertically integrated companies include companies that produce textile products made from both natural and manufactured fibers. Although vertically integrated companies may process fibers, they might not actually produce their own fibers. For example, a vertically integrated company that produces cotton knit fabrics might not be involved in growing the cotton. Instead, it might purchase raw cotton from cotton growers. Some companies are partially integrated, in that they focus on several steps of production. For example, some knitting operations (e.g., hosiery, sweaters) not only knit, dye, and cut the fabrics but also construct the knitted garments to be sold to retailers.

One of the oldest vertically integrated textile companies in the United States is Pendleton Woolen Mills, headquartered in Portland, Oregon. Pendleton was started by Clarence and Roy Bishop in Pendleton, Oregon, in 1909. Led by a fourth generation of Bishops, the company now manufactures woolen menswear, women's wear, and blankets; non-woolen apparel; and over-the-counter fabrics. It is involved with the following:

- selection and processing of wool
- designing and weaving of fabrics
- development of garments
- shipment and sale of garments, over-the-counter piece goods, and blankets

Such vertical integration allows for coordination among all production steps and increased control of quality throughout the production of the textiles and end-use products. For example, Pendleton textile designers work closely with the apparel designers in engineering the plaid fabrics that will work best for pleated skirt designs.

FIBER PROCESSING AND YARN SPINNING

The development and marketing of natural fibers versus manufactured fibers varies greatly. In general, natural fibers, as part of the larger agricultural industry, are the product of a crop that is grown and harvested or of an animal that is raised. Manufactured fibers, on the other hand, are created by large nonagricultural corporations through research and development efforts.

Natural-Fiber Processing

Of the natural fibers produced in the United States, cotton has the largest production and wool the second-largest production. **Cotton** is obtained from the fibers surrounding the seeds of the cotton plant. The plant is grown most satisfactorily in warm climates where irrigation water is available. Worldwide, China, the United States, India, and Pakistan are the four largest producers of cotton; these four countries account for approximately two-thirds of all cotton.

The cotton industry has implemented a number of "environmentally cleaner" processes. These include naturally colored cotton, organic cotton, cleaner dyeing methods, and reduced water use. For example, one cotton producer, Sally Fox, developed naturally colored cotton in various shades of green, brown, and red. Natural colors had been bred out of modern cotton because the colored fibers were too short and weak for automated textile manufacturing. Fox began crossing the longer, stronger white cotton fibers with colored cotton to create Foxfibre cotton, the first naturally colored cotton that could be processed with modern textile equipment (Foxfiber.com 2013). The natural colors did more than eliminate the need for dyeing the cotton; instead of fading, naturally colored cotton actually deepens in color when washed. In addition, Foxfibre cotton has a silky feel and a wool-like elasticity. Foxfibre, Colour-by-Nature, and Colorganic are all registered trademarks for naturally colored cottons.

Fox is also committed to organic cotton production, in which synthetic chemical fertilizers and pesticides are used minimally or not at all. Fox is not the only cotton producer interested in organic cotton. According to the Organic Trade Association, sales of organic cotton have been steadily rising over the past five years, and it will continue to grow an estimated 15 percent per year over the next few years. Organic cotton fibers are now included in end-use products, ranging from cotton puffs and ear swabs to sheets and blankets to diapers to fashion apparel. The challenge for companies is finding enough quality organic cotton. Some companies use only organic cotton (e.g., Patagonia), whereas others use a blend of organic and regular cotton.

In conventionally grown cotton, synthetic fertilizers, insecticides, herbicides, fungicides, and defoliants are used. The significant amounts of chemical pesticides and fertilizers—as well as water—used in production have led to criticism of the industry. Organic cotton has emerged as an environmentally responsible approach to growing cotton. Rather than using synthetic chemical fertilizers and pesticides, cotton growers use the following organic techniques:

- Natural fertilizers, such as manure, are used because these fertilizers biodegrade.
- Fields are weeded by hand, or cover crops are planted to control weeds.
- Crops are rotated for disease control.
- Beneficial insects that consume destructive insects are introduced.
- Once harvested, certified organic cotton is stored without the use of chemical rodenticides and fungicides.

According to the Organic Trade Association (2015), organic cotton is produced worldwide. The top ten producer countries are led by India, followed by (in rank order) China, Turkey, Tanzania, the United States, Burkina Faso, Egypt, Mali, Uganda, and Peru. Thanks to consumer interest, many fashion brands (e.g., Nike, Patagonia) have organic cotton programs, thus increasing the demand for certified organic cotton. The United States Department of Agriculture (USDA) sets standards and certifies cotton (and other organic agricultural products). The USDA Organic Certification is used in advertising end-use products to the consumer. In traditional cotton production, after the cotton is picked, a cotton gin is used to separate the fiber, called cotton lint, from the seeds. (The seeds, a valuable by-product of the cotton industry, are used to produce cattle feed and cottonseed oil.) The cotton lint is then packed into large bales and shipped to yarn and textile mills. The spinning process of cotton yarns is highly automated; cotton fibers are cleaned, carded, and combed and then drawn and spun to create yarns. For blended yarns, other fibers, such as polyester, nylon, or wool, are blended with the cotton during the spinning process. Figure 4.2 shows a cotton processing plant.

Wool fibers are derived from the fleece of sheep, goats, alpacas, and llamas. Worldwide, the largest producers of wool are Australia, New Zealand, and the United Kingdom. China and Italy are the world's largest wool buyers. Although wool production occurs in every state and has a long history in the United States, currently it plays a minor role in U.S. textile production.

Most wool comes from specific breeds of sheep, including Delaine-Merino, Rambouillet, Hampshire, and Suffolk. Some breeds of sheep can graze in areas of the country with extreme climates that are unsuitable for other livestock. Farm flock production (animals raised in a more confined area) is best suited for other

Figure 4.2
Cotton yarn production includes multiple steps, from carding and combing cotton fibers to drawing and spinning yarns. WWD/© Conde Nast.

breeds of sheep. Because wool growers often produce small amounts of wool, wool co-ops or pools and warehousing operations are common.

Wool fabrics are often processed by the same company that processes the fiber. Wool, like other fibers, can be dyed at one of the following stages in the production process:

- immediately after it is washed and blended (stock dyed or vat dyed)
- after it has been spun into yarns (yarn dyed)
- after it has been woven or knitted into fabric (piece dyed)

Wool absorbs many different dyes uniformly. Some wool producers market wools that, rather than being dyed, are sorted and sold in natural sheep colors, ranging from cream to a broad spectrum of browns, blacks, and grays.

Mohair comes from the wool of the Angora goat. Almost all of the raw mohair fiber produced in the United States is exported for processing, primarily to China. This is because most U.S. textile mills have equipment designed to process cotton and wool—which are much larger industries in the United States than is mohair. Cotton and wool fibers measure two inches or less, whereas mohair fibers are often four to six inches long. Therefore, machinery designed to process cotton and wool cannot be used for mohair. Worldwide production has also declined as other luxury fibers have gained favor.

Cashmere comes from the undercoat wool of the Cashmere or Kashmir goat. Most of the world's cashmere comes from China, Mongolia, and Tibet. China, Italy, and the United Kingdom are the world's largest buyers of cashmere. Cashmere is considered a luxury fiber because of its cost and is often blended with other, less-expensive wools. However, demand for cashmere has grown in recent years as high-end designers (e.g., Burberry, Gucci, Armani) have included cashmere products in their collections and consumer desire for the soft fibers has increased.

Leather Production

Leather is obtained from the skins and hides of cattle, goats, and sheep, as well as from a variety of reptiles, fish, and birds. Most skins and hides are by-products of animals raised primarily for their meat or fiber. Thus the leather industry is a bridge between the meat industry, from which the hide is a by-product, and the manufacture of basic raw material into nondurable goods such as shoes and wearing apparel. Pelts are categorized according to the following weights:

- The term *skins* refers to pelts weighing 15 pounds or less when shipped to the **regular tannery**.
- The term kips refers to pelts weighing from 15 to 25 pounds.
- The term hides refers to pelts weighing more than 25 pounds.

Animal pelts go through a number of processes that transform them into leather. They are first cleaned to remove hair. Then they are tanned, colored or dyed, and finished (e.g., glazed, embossed, napped, or buffed).

Tanning is the process used to make skins and hides pliable and water resistant. The tanning process can use a number of agents, including vegetable materials, oils, chemicals, and minerals, or a combination of more than one type of agent. With vegetable tanning, natural tannic acids found in extracts from tree bark are used. Because vegetable tanning is extremely slow and labor intensive, it is seldom used in commercial tanning. Oil tanning uses fish oil (usually codfish) as a tanning agent. Oil tanning is used to make chamois, doeskin, and buckskin. One of the quickest tanning methods is to use chemicals, typically formaldehyde.

Two tanning methods use minerals—alum tanning and chrome tanning. Alum tanning is rarely used today. Chrome tanning, the least expensive and most commonly used method, requires the use of heavy metals and acids, which are toxic. The chrome tanning process also produces acidic wastewater with a pH of 4.5 to 5.0 (acidic). Thus, this industry is heavily regulated by the Environmental Protection Agency (EPA) and must meet its waste standards for air, liquid, and solid wastes. This explains why there are few leather tanneries and finishers in the United States and a growth of tanneries in developing countries where labor costs are less and environmental standards are not as strict. However, tanning systems that include recycling chromium have been developed and have allowed U.S. companies to reduce the amount of chromium found in waste.

Compared to other textiles, leather production is a relatively slow process. Because of the longer production lead time needed in going from hide to finished product, leather producers often must make styling and color decisions before other textile producers. Therefore, they are keenly involved with trend forecasting and market research.

Fur Production

Fur fibers are considered luxury products that come from animals valued for their pelts, such as mink, rabbit, beaver, and muskrat. Pelts are the unshorn skins of these and other animals. Fur is divided into two categories: farm-raised and wild fur. Farm-raised fur is derived from reproducing, rearing, and harvesting domestic fur-bearing animals in captivity. Mink and fox are the most popular pelts produced on fur farms. In addition, chinchilla, fitch, nutria, and other furbearers are raised in smaller numbers, while some countries produce large quantities of pelts from sheep, goats, and rabbits as a valuable by-product of meat production. Wild fur is derived from the selective and regulated harvesting of surplus fur-bearing animals that are not endangered or threatened species and that do not live in captivity. Fur pelts are sold at fur auctions to fur processors. Major fur auction houses are located in Copenhagen, Frankfurt, Helsinki, Hong Kong, Leipzig, New York, Seattle, St. Petersburg, Toronto, and Vancouver.

The tanning process for fur, known as **tawning**, differs from the tanning of hides for leather. The tanning of fur pelts requires salt, water, alum, soda ash, sawdust, cornstarch, and lanolin. Each ingredient is natural and nontoxic, and the tawning process produces neutral wastewater with a pH of 7 (neutral—neither acidic nor alkaline). Many furs are also bleached or dyed to improve their natural color or to give them a nonnatural color (e.g., blue, green). Pelts are also glazed to add beauty and luster to the fur.

Fur production and the wearing of fur have been politically charged topics for many years. In the 1970s, efforts of animal rights and other organizations (e.g., World Wildlife Fund, Fur Conservation Institute of America) pushed for the enactment of the Endangered Species Conservation Act of 1973, which protected endangered animal species in eighty countries worldwide. More recently, animal rights groups have organized anti-fur campaigns, creating an intense and widespread debate over the humane treatment of animals used for fur production and environmental claims of the fur industry. The Fur Commission USA (2016) certifies fur farmers who are committed to humane treatment in all aspects of fur farming, including "attention to nutritional needs; clean, safe and appropriate housing; prompt veterinary care; consideration for the animals' disposition and reproductive needs; and elimination of outside stress." However, even with such assurances, anti-fur activists continue to campaign against the killing of animals for the production of luxury goods.

Manufactured-Fiber Processing

Since the first synthetic fiber (nylon) was introduced in 1939, the demand for synthetics has steadily increased. The Asia–Pacific region, particularly China and India, will continue to be the largest producer of manufactured fibers. In 2015, China accounted for 69 percent of all polyester fiber produced worldwide; India and Southeast Asia accounted for an additional 17 percent.

The largest synthetic textile company in the United States is INVISTA, a multinational company and the world's largest producer of nylon and spandex. Originally the textiles and interiors division of DuPont, it was renamed INVISTA in 2004. INVISTA produces and markets fiber brand names such as Lycra spandex and Antron nylon carpet fiber. Table 4.1 lists selected U.S. manufactured-fiber producers. Many of these companies are said to be **horizontally integrated**, in that they produce several fibers or variations of fibers that are at the same stage in the process (i.e., fiber processing). For example, INVISTA produces several types of nylon.

Table 4.1 Selected Manufactured-Fiber Producers and Fiber Trade Names	
American Fibers and Yarns Co. • Impressa Olefin • Innova Olefin **Celanese Corporation** • Celanese Acetate • Celstar Acetate **DAK Americas** • Dacron Plus Polyester **DuPont Performance Materials** • Kevlar Aramid • Nomex Aramid • Tyvek Olefin **FiberVisions, Inc.** • Herculon Olefin **Honeywell Nylon, Inc.** • Anso Nylon 6 • Caprolan Nylon 6 • Zeftron Nylon 6 **Honeywell International** • Spectra Olefin **INVISTA, Inc.** • Antron Nylon 6.6 • Cordura Nylon 6.6 • TACTEL Nylon 6.6 • Lycra Spandex	**Lenzing Group** • Tencel Lyocell **Nylstar, Inc.** • Meryl Nylon **Solutia, Inc.** • Acrilan Acrylic • Duraspun Acrylic • SEF Modacrylic • Ultron Nylon 6.6 **Sterling Fibers, Inc.** • Creslan Acrylic • Creslite Acrylic • Cresloft Acrylic **Wellman, Inc.** • Wellon Nylon • Fortrel Polyester • ComFortrel Polyester • Ultra Polyester

New manufactured fibers are developed through research efforts that take up to five years before the fiber is available on the market. According to the Textile Products Identification Act, when a fiber belonging to a new generic family is invented, the U.S. Federal Trade Commission (FTC) assigns it a new generic name. Currently, more than twenty-five generic fibers are recognized by the FTC; see Table 4.2 for a listing of these fibers.

Manufactured fibers can be modified in terms of shape (cross section), molecular structure, chemical additives, or spinning procedures to create better-quality or more versatile fibers and yarns. Generic fibers are also combined within a single fiber or yarn to take advantage of specific fiber characteristics. Yarn variations include monofilament and multifilament yarns, stretch yarns, textured yarns, and spun yarns. Companies continue to invest in research to create fiber and yarn innovations to meet consumer demand.

A number of manufactured-fiber companies developed more environmentally responsible production processes, including recycling. For example, in 1988, Courtalds Fibres UK developed lyocell, a cellulosic fiber made from harvested wood pulp (and therefore a subcategory of rayon) that is processed with recycled nontoxic solvents. In its production, virtually all the dissolving agent is recycled. In addition,

Table 4.2 Names of Generic Fibers

acetate	olefin (polypropylene)
acrylic	PBI (polybenzimidazole)
anidex	PBO (polyphenylenebenzobisozazole)
aramid	PEN (polyethylene naphthalate)
azlon	PLA (polylactic acid fiber)
elastoester	polyester
glass	rayon
lyocell (subcategory of rayon)	saran
melamine	spandex
metallic	sulfar or PPS (polyphenylene sulfide)
modacrylic	triacetate
nylon	vinal
nytril	vinyon

waste emissions (air and wastewater) are lower than for other manufactured-fiber production. The resulting fiber is machine washable and stronger than cotton or wool—as well as having a silkier touch. Currently, the only company manufacturing lyocell in the United States is Lenzing, Inc. (headquartered in Austria) under the TENCEL trade name. Fabrics made from 100 percent lyocell or in a variety of blends are used for apparel, accessories, and home fashions.

In addition to lyocell, some companies are making rayon from bamboo fibers. Because of its fast growth rate, renewability, and ability to take in greenhouse gases, bamboo is being promoted by environmentalists. Rayon made from bamboo fibers has a silk-like hand, making it popular for apparel and home fashions. Linda Loudermilk's Luxury eco collection combines fabrics made from bamboo and other renewable plants in high-fashion collections shown on New York City runways.

Polyester staple fibers are also being recycled from plastic soda bottles, which are made of polyethylene teraphthalate, or PET. The process of making recycled polyester fibers includes these steps:

1. All caps, labels, and bases made of other materials are removed from the bottles.
2. The bottles are sorted by color (clear and green).
3. The bottles are chopped.
4. The pieces are washed and dried.
5. The pieces are heated, purified, and formed into pellets.
6. The purified polyester is extruded as fine fibers that can be spun into thread, yarn, or other materials.

It takes an average of 25 plastic soda bottles to make one garment. Foss Manufacturing LLC produces Fortrel Ecospun®, a polyester that contains 100 percent recycled fiber and is used by dozens of apparel companies (see Figure 4.3). It is estimated that 2.4 billion bottles are kept out of landfills per year through the manufacturing of Fortrel Ecospun® fibers.

Figure 4.3
Fortrel Ecospun® is made of 100 percent recycled plastic bottles and is used in a variety of end products. TIMOTHY CLARY /AFP/Getty Images.

Several companies are also recycling scrap yarns and fabric as a means of reducing the amount of scrap materials ending up in landfill. Recycled scrap denim is being used in a variety of products, including fabrics, pencils, and paper. Milliken Floor Covering promises to recover all carpets returned to them by renewing the products, donating them to charities, recycling them, or using them in energy cogeneration (an environmentally responsible means of producing power). According to Milliken's website, since 1999, the company's carpet manufacturing plants have not sent any waste to landfill.

As Martin Bide stated in his article "Fiber Sustainability: Green Is Not Black + White," the development or use of sustainable fibers is not clear-cut (AATCC Review 2009). Everything comes with some environmental advantage or disadvantage. Bide does foresee that the consumer of the future will be more of a realist and will have a longer view of sustainability. This consumer will buy fewer clothes, avoid cotton/polyester blends, wash in cold water with less water, line-dry the clothes, and recycle the fabric at the end of the garment's wearing cycle.

FIBER MARKETING AND DISTRIBUTION

Marketing Natural Fibers

Natural fibers are considered commodities; they are bought and sold on global markets at prices based on market demand. For example, in the mid-1990s, cotton prices soared as consumer demand went up and cotton supplies dwindled because of devastating weather and insect-related crop failures in China (the world's largest producer of cotton) and other major producing countries, such as India and Pakistan. The largest commodity markets for cotton in the United States are Dallas, Houston, Memphis, and New Orleans; for wool, Boston; and for mohair, a warehouse system throughout Texas. These natural fibers are sold to mills for yarn spinning and fabric production. Furs are sold at public auction.

It was not until the late 1940s and early 1950s, when the popularity of manufactured fibers was growing, that marketing efforts for natural fibers were initiated by each trade association that represents a specific fiber. These trade associations—such as Cotton Incorporated, the American Wool Council, the Mohair Council of America, and the Cashmere and Camel Hair Manufacturers Institute (CCMI)—are supported by natural-fiber producers and promote the use of the natural fibers through activities such as research, educational programs, and advertising on television and in trade and consumer publications. Through these activities, natural-fiber trade associations have become an important support arm for the fashion industries, and strong relationships have developed between the trade associations and the companies that use natural fibers.

Founded in 1961, Cotton Incorporated is a research and promotional organization supported by U.S. cotton growers and importers of cotton products. Cotton Incorporated's members receive technical services, color and trend forecasting services, and promotional services. In 2000, Cotton Incorporated opened a new research and development headquarters in Cary, North Carolina. The research facility includes **textile testing**, product care, and color labs. Cotton Incorporated's

Seal of Cotton trademark (Figure 4.4) is used on hangtags and in advertisements, along with the association's slogan "The Fabric of Our Lives." In recent years, Cotton Incorporated has sponsored collections of new designers during the spring fashion shows in New York City. Cotton Incorporated is also involved in market research. Research results are published as print and Web reports in the *Lifestyle Monitor*. This report includes consumer segment profiles, retail patronage profiles, summaries of consumers' attitudes, and forecasts.

Trade associations focusing on wool fall into the following two categories:

- those that focus on wool production (e.g., California Wool Growers Association, Montana Wool Growers Association)
- those that focus on product development, marketing, and education (e.g., American Wool Council and Australian Wool Innovation Limited)

Established in 1955, the American Wool Council is a division of the American Sheep Industry Association. Its programs are involved in all aspects of wool marketing, from raw wool marketing and product development to registered trademark programs, advertising, and publicity. The American Wool Council has been involved in standardizing quality levels of wool and promoting wool applications with spinners, weavers, knitters, designers, manufacturers, and retailers.

The Woolmark Company was established in 1937 as the International Wool Secretariat (IWS) and is now a subsidiary of Australian Wool Innovation Limited. In 1964, the Woolmark program, with its well-known Woolmark symbol (Figure 4.5), was created to identify quality products made from new wool. The Woolmark Blend symbol was introduced in 1971 to identify products made from at least 50 percent new wool. Its services include trend and color forecasting, textile testing, licensing the Woolmark symbols, and global market analyses.

Established in 1966, the Mohair Council of America is "dedicated to promoting the general welfare of the mohair industry" (Mohair Council of America 2015). The council's programs focus on market surveys, research, and development activities, including advertising, workshops, and seminars. Because most of the mohair produced in the United States is exported, the council conducts foreign as well as domestic market research and promotion. The council's trademark is shown in Figure 4.6. Other trade associations focusing on natural fibers include the Cashmere and Camel Hair Manufacturers Institute, International Linen Promotion Commission, National Cotton Council, and International Silk Association.

Trade associations also play an important part in marketing leather and fur. Associations such as the Leather Industries of America and the Fur Information Council of America are involved with promotion, including advertising and consumer education programs. The mink industry also has a number of breeder associations, such as the Fur Commission USA and the Canada Mink Breeders Association, that are involved in promotion efforts.

The trade associations just discussed concentrate their efforts on specific segments of the natural-fiber industry (Figure 4.7). The National Council of Textile Organizations (NCTO) has a broader mission: It represents the entire spectrum of the textile sector, including fiber producers, textile mills, and other textile suppliers. The NCTO is highly involved with lobbying efforts in Washington, D.C., on the behalf of the U.S. textile industry. As its website states: "NCTO is

Figure 4.4
Cotton Incorporated's trademark for products made of 100 percent (upland) cotton. Cotton, Inc.

PURE NEW WOOL
WOOLMARK

Figure 4.5
The Woolmark, a registered trademark of The Woolmark Company, is used on hangtags and in advertising. Woolmark.

Figure 4.6
Registered trademark of the Mohair Council of America. Mohair USA.

Figure 4.7
Natural fiber trade associations promote the use of natural fibers through advertising. Cotton Inc.

also mobilizing global resources in its efforts to preserve the U.S. textile industry. Through new powerful international alliances, our voice is heard and has an impact from Washington, DC, to Geneva, to Beijing." (National Council of Textile Organizations 2015). Table 4.3 lists selected trade associations in the textile industry.

Marketing Manufactured Fibers

Manufactured fibers are most often produced by **vertically integrated** companies. Prices are set primarily by the cost of developing and producing the fibers. Manufactured fibers are sold either as commodity fibers or brand name fibers.

- *Commodity fibers* are generic manufactured fibers (parent fibers) sold without

Table 4.3 Selected Textile Trade Associations

American Association of Textile Chemists and Colorists (AATCC)

P.O. Box 12215
Research Triangle Park, NC 27709
Tel: (919) 549-8141
Fax: (919) 549-8933
www.aatcc.org

American Fiber Manufacturers Association (AFMA)

1530 Wilson Blvd.
Suite 690
Arlington, VA 22209
Tel: (703) 875-0432
Fax: (703) 875-0907
www.afma.org

American Wool Council c/o American Sheep Industry Association

9785 Maroon Circle
Suite 360
Centennial, CO 80112
Tel: (303) 771-3500
Fax: (303) 771-8200
www.sheepusa.org

Australian Wool Innovation Limited (Woolmark Company)

1120 Avenue of the Americas, Suite 4107
New York, NY 10036 USA
Tel: (212) 626- 6744
www.wool.com

Cotton Incorporated

6399 Weston Parkway
Cary, NC 27513
Tel: (919) 678-2220
Fax: (919) 678-2230
www.cottoninc.com

Fur Information Council of America (FICA)

8424 A Santa Monica Blvd. #860
West Hollywood, CA 90069
Tel: (323) 848-7940
Fax: (323) 848-2931
www.fur.org

Industrial Fabrics Association International

1801 County Road B W
Roseville, MN 55113-4061
Tel: (651) 222-2508
Fax: (651) 631- 9334
www.ifai.com

Leather Industries of America

3050 K Street, NW, Suite 400
Washington, DC 20007
Tel: (202) 342-8086
Fax: (202) 342-8583
www.leatherusa.com

National Council of Textile Organizations

910 17th Street NW, Suite 1020
Washington, DC 20006
Tel: (202) 822-8028
Fax: (202) 822-8029
www.ncto.org

Synthetic Yarn and Fiber Association

737 Park Trail Lane
Clover, SC 29710
Tel: (704)-589-5895
Fax: (803)746-5566
www.thesyfa.org

a brand name attached. For example, a carpet labeled "100 percent" nylon is probably manufactured with commodity nylon fibers.

- Manufactured fibers are also sold under **brand names** (or **trade names**) given to the fibers by manufacturers. Brand names distinguish one fiber from another in the same generic family. Modified manufactured fibers with special characteristics are typically sold under brand names (see Table 4.3). Examples include the following:
  - Lycra spandex (INVISTA)
  - TENCEL Lyocell (Lenzing Fibers)
  - Dacron polyester (INVISTA)
  - Fortrel polyester (Wellman, Inc.)

- Ascend nylon (Solutia, Inc.)
- Antron nylon carpet fiber (INVISTA)

To establish consumer recognition of brand name fibers, promotion activities focus on the company, brand name, and specific qualities of the fiber (Figure 4.8). Companies spend a great deal of money establishing brand name identification among consumers, and brand name fibers are generally higher in price than commodity fibers. Advertisements also connect brand name fibers with specific end uses. Therefore, cooperative advertising between manufactured fiber companies and apparel and home fashions manufacturers is common.

Licensed brand name programs, or **controlled brand name programs**, set minimum standards of fabric performance for the trademarked fibers. Determined through regular textile testing, these standards are established as a form of quality assurance and relate to a specific end use. The following examples illustrate minimum standards for trademarked fibers:

- The Wear-Dated brand of nylon carpet fibers produced by Solutia, Inc. has minimum standards for wear and soil resistance, stain resistance, color and light fastness, and tuft bind (adhesion to carpet backing).
- The Trevira polyester program (Trevira is a company in the Reliance Group) establishes minimum standards for fabric quality for specific end uses.
- Coolmax is a registered trademark of INVISTA. It certifies high-perfomance fabrics that include INVISTA and, in some cases, other companies' fibers.

The standards set through these programs can especially benefit apparel and home fashions manufacturers in quality assurance and marketing end-use products.

Fiber producers also design and create **concept garments** to promote their

Figure 4.8
Brand name manufactured fibers are advertised to increase name recognition among customers. Neilson Barnard/Getty Images for Mercedes-Benz Fashion Week/Getty Images.

new fibers to textile mills. For example, when Solutia, Inc. has a new product to show textile mills, it often shows the new product in garment form. When creating concept garments, fiber companies either create fabrics and the garment on their own machinery, or work with a textile mill and manufacturer that will produce small runs of the concept garment. For example, as part of its marketing program, INVISTA shows samples of Coolmax fabrics made into actual performance garments.

As with natural fibers, **trade associations** are also important to the manufactured-fiber industry. The American Fiber Manufacturers Association (AFMA) began in 1933, first as the Rayon Institute and then as the Man-Made Fiber Producers Association. The current name was adopted in 1988. The AFMA focuses on domestic production of synthetic and cellulosic manufactured fibers. Programs include government relations, international trade policy, the environment, technical issues, and education services. AFMA's statistics division, the Fiber Economics Bureau, collects and publishes data on production and trade of manufactured fibers.

COLOR FORECASTING IN THE TEXTILE INDUSTRY

Color is an important criterion used by consumers in the selection of textile products, including apparel and home fashions. Therefore, an understanding of consumers' color preferences is crucial to successfully marketing a particular textile product. Whereas some classic colors remain popular over many years, fashion colors have a shorter fashion life cycle. Because color is typically applied at the textile production stage, textile companies are often involved in determining the colors selected for end-use products. Through the process of **color forecasting**, color palettes or color stories are selected and translated into fabrics produced by a company for a specific fashion season. Manufacturers also conduct color forecasting.

The Color Association of the United States (CAUS) is a nonprofit service organization that has been involved in color forecasting since 1915. More than 700 companies, including fiber producers, textile companies, apparel manufacturers, and home fashions producers, belong to CAUS. A committee of volunteers from these companies determines general color palettes for the coming 18 to 24 months. Twice a year (in March and September), swatch cards (Figure 4.9) are sent to member companies for use in determining color palettes for their own products.

The International Colour Authority (ICA) is an international **color forecasting service**. Teams of representatives from member companies and color experts meet biannually to determine general color palettes approximately 22 to 24 months before the products they make are available to the consumer. ICA services provide some of the earliest predictions in the industry. Separate palettes are created

Figure 4.9
Swatch cards from color forecasting services assist textile companies in their color decisions. Color Association of America.

for menswear, women's wear, leather, home fashions, and paints. ICA then sends the forecasts to member companies for their use.

Other color forecasting services also sell color forecasts to companies. These forecasts may be specific to a particular target market and product (e.g., women's apparel, children's apparel). Often the services will also include style and fabrication forecasting. "The color box" provides subscribers with four-color and design forecasts per year for menswear, children's wear, and women's wear. Color forecasting services include the following:

- Trendstop.com is a highly regarded online global color and trend forecasting service that provides subscribers with current research on a variety of international fashion trends.
- Headquartered in Paris, Promostyl is an international color, fabric, and style forecasting service that provides trend analyses for men's, women's, and children's apparel 12 to 18 months ahead of the fashion season.
- Peclers Paris also offers color and trend forecasts for fashion, industrial design, and home fashions.
- Color forecasts may also be conducted by trade associations for their member companies. For example, Cotton Incorporated provides color forecasting services to its members.

Fashion companies also conduct their own color forecasting, which is more specific to their product and target market than the information provided by color forecasting services. This type of color forecasting is accomplished in several ways:

- reviewing color predictions from color forecasting services
- tracking color trends by examining the colors that were the best and worst selling from previous seasons
- observing general trends that may affect color preferences of the target market
- looking at what colors have been missing from the color palettes in order to select colors that may be viewed as new

FABRIC PRODUCTION

Textile Mills

Textile mills focus on the fabric construction or fabrication stage of textiles. According to North American Industry Classification System (NAICS, 2015) definitions, Sector 313 Textile Mills are companies "that transform a basic fiber (natural or synthetic) into a product, such as yarn or fabric, that is further manufactured into usable items, such as apparel, sheets, towels, and textile bags for individual or industrial consumption." The two most common fabric construction methods are weaving and knitting. Except for vertically integrated companies that produce both woven and knitted goods, textile mills typically specialize in producing one type of fabric. In addition to fabric production, woven textile mills often spin their own yarn (Figure 4.10), whereas knit producers typically purchase their

Figure 4.10
Fabric production is highly automated. These machines are used for carding fibers, spinning them into yarn, and weaving fabric. Cultura RF/Getty Images.

yarn. All textile mills sell greige goods. Greige goods may be used as is or bought by converters who finish the goods. In addition to selling greige goods, vertically integrated companies finish the goods themselves and may make end-use products, such as home textiles (e.g., sheets and towels).

Mills sell staple and/or specialty (novelty) fabrics. Staple fabrics, such as denim or tricot, are produced continually each year with little change in construction or finish. Novelty fabrics have special design features (e.g., surface texture, specialty weave) that are fashion based and, therefore, change with fashion cycles. Because of this, fashion fabrics require shorter production runs and greater flexibility.

The knitting industry has two main divisions:

- the knitted products industry, which manufactures end-use products such as T-shirts, hosiery, and sweaters
- the knitted fabrics industry, which manufactures knitted yard goods sold to apparel and home fashions manufacturers and retailers

Textile mills are found throughout the world. Eastern Asian countries (China, Taiwan, Japan) and India account for most of the world's textiles. Many multi-national companies have textile mills in a variety of countries. For example, the International Textile Group (ITG)—headquartered in Greensboro, North Carolina—comprises six companies: Cone Denim, Burlington Worldwide Apparel, Cone Decorative Fabrics, Narricot, Safety Components, and Carlisle Finishing. ITG has global operations in China, Hong Kong, Vietnam, Mexico, and Nicaragua. Similarly, Springs Global, which is a merger of Springs Industries of the United States and Coteminas of Brazil, has operations in Argentina, Brazil, Canada, Mexico, Turkey, India, China, Vietnam, and the United States.

Textile Design

Textile design involves interrelationships among the following processes:

- color (e.g., dyeing, printing)
- fabric structure (e.g., woven or knitted fabric)
- finishes (e.g., napping, embossing)

In addition to knowing about color and fabric structure, textile designers must have expertise in computer-aided design or graphics software and an understanding of the technology used in producing textiles. The use of computer-aided design or graphics software allows textile designers to experiment with color and fabric construction, and then to print and prepare exact instructions to replicate the fabric design (Figure 4.11).

Textile designers specialize according to printing method and fabric structure; they may be freelance designers or work for textile design studios, textile mills, or converters. For example, one textile designer may work for a textile mill and specialize in direct roller-printing processes; another may be a freelance designer of graphics for T-shirts and specialize in screen printing processes. The term **textile stylist** is currently used to designate individuals who have expertise in the design and manufacturing of textiles, as well as an understanding of the textile market. The stylist's combination of design, technical, and consumer/business expertise is particularly important in reflecting consumer preferences in the textiles being

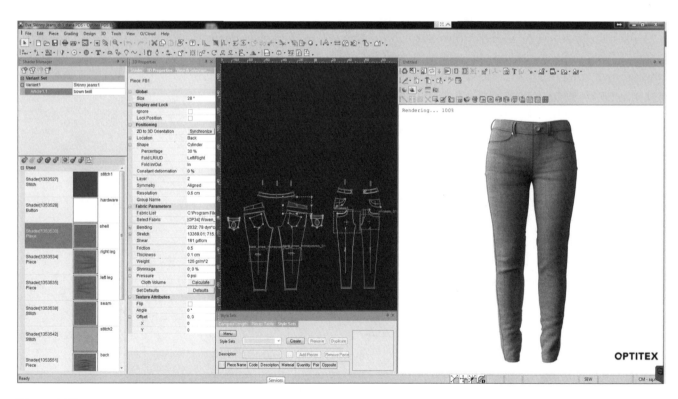

Figure 4.11
Computer-aided design helps a designer see how a new fabric or design will look in a garment. Optitex.

designed. Designers and stylists may work directly with apparel and home fashions manufacturers to create special prints, or with retailers to create prints to be used for private label merchandise.

Textile Converters

Textile converters buy greige goods from mills; have the fabrics dyed, printed, or finished; and then sell the finished fabrics. Textile converters focus on the following:

- aesthetic finishes (e.g., glazing, crinkling)
- performance finishes (e.g., colorfast, stain resistant, water resistant, durable pressed)
- dyeing or printing fabrics

Textile converters are experts in color forecasting and understand consumer preferences in fiber content, fabric construction, and various aesthetic and performance fabric finishes. Often textile converters will contract with dyers, printers, and finishers to create fabrics that they market to apparel and home fashions manufacturers, jobbers, and retailers. Some converters specialize in a certain type of fabric; others may design several types of fabrics. Most converters that print fabrics use rotary printing presses. **Digital printing** with ink-jet printers is becoming more widespread. Because the fabric is finished close to the time when consumers will be purchasing the end-use product, converters play an important role in analyzing and responding to changing consumer preferences.

Although converters do most of the fabric finishing, they do not do all of it. Woolen and worsted wool fabrics are seldom sold through converters, but rather are generally sold finished by mills. In addition, industrial fabrics are typically sold directly from mills because they are made to meet buyer specifications and may require special performance tests. Also, converters are seldom used in the manufacturing of sweaters and other knitwear, which are typically knitted and then constructed into garments by the same company.

Other Fabric Resources

Textile jobbers and fabric retail stores buy and sell fabric without any involvement in producing or finishing the fabric. Textile jobbers buy from textile mills, converters, and large manufacturers and then sell to smaller manufacturers and retailers. Typically, jobbers will buy mill overruns (fabrics the textile mill produces beyond what was ordered) or discontinued fabric colors or prints. For example, a textile jobber may buy extra or discontinued fabric from a textile mill and sell it to a small apparel manufacturer that does not need a large volume of fabric. Retail fabric stores sell over-the-counter piece goods primarily to home sewers. Fabric stores may purchase their bolt yardage from fabric wholesalers that have purchased large rolls from textile mills.

Textile brokers serve as liaisons between textile sellers and textile buyers. For example, a broker may connect a small textile mill wanting to sell greige goods to a small converter that wants to buy them. Textile brokers differ from jobbers in that brokers never own the fabric.

Textile Testing and Quality Assurance

The textile industry is highly involved in quality assurance programs and textile testing. Textile testing involves inspecting and measuring textile characteristics (e.g., strength, flammability, abrasion resistance, colorfastness) throughout the production and finishing of the textile. Standard test methods developed by the American Society for Testing and Materials (ASTM) and the American Association of Textile Chemists and Colorists (AATCC) are used by companies in testing the quality and specific performance requirements of the textile materials they use.

Although the terms **quality control** and **quality assurance** are sometimes used interchangeably, they have different meanings:

- *Quality control* involves inspecting finished textiles to make sure they adhere to specific quality standards as measured by a variety of textile-testing methods (Figure 4.12).
- *Quality assurance* is a broader concept, covering not only the fabric's general functional performance (quality), but also how well it satisfies consumer needs for a specific end use. For example, a textile to be used in children's

Figure 4.12
Fabrics are inspected by trained experts to ensure that they meet quality standards. Cultura RF/Getty Images.

apparel must not only meet minimum standards of functional performance but also specifications such as colorfastness that are important to the consumer of children's apparel. Whereas a textile mill may test for general functional performance of the fabric, often the apparel or home fashions manufacturer or retailer must determine if the fabric meets the specifications of importance to its consumers. This is why the testing of fabrics is often conducted by the following:

- apparel and home fashions manufacturers (e.g., Nike, Pendleton Woolen Mills)
- retailers (e.g., JCPenney, Target) of these goods
- independent textile testing companies contracted by manufacturers or retailers

MARKETING AND DISTRIBUTION OF FABRICS

Marketing Seasonal Lines

Fiber producers, textile mills, and converters take part in the marketing of textile fabrics. Most manufactured-fiber producers have showrooms that exhibit fabrics and end-use products made from their fibers. Textile showrooms are located in most major U.S. cities (e.g., Los Angeles, Dallas, Atlanta, Chicago), although New York is the primary market center for textile mills, converters, and textile product manufacturers. Internationally, textile showrooms are prevalent in the major cities of countries with large numbers of textile mills, as well as large marketing headquarters (e.g., Paris, Milan, Taipei, Hong Kong, Shanghai, Tokyo). Showrooms house the fabric samples to be marketed by textile mills or converters to designers and apparel or home fashions manufacturers.

Textile mills and converters market their textile fabrics as Fall/Winter and Spring/Summer seasonal lines. Each fabric line includes a grouping of fabrics with a similar theme or **color story**. It is the responsibility of the merchandising or marketing staff of textile companies to show fabric samples to prospective buyers in their showrooms or at textile trade shows. Samples of Fall/Winter lines of fabrics are shown to prospective fabric buyers in October or November, approximately nine to twelve months before the end-use product (e.g., apparel) hits the stores. Spring/Summer lines of fabrics are shown in March or April. During these shows, apparel and home fashions companies will purchase yardage for their samples. Some large manufacturers may order their end-use fabrics at this time, but most will wait until their own orders from retailers are known. For large accounts, fabric samples can be confined, which means that the textile company will not sell the fabric to other end-use companies.

Fabric companies also promote their lines through sites on the Internet and through other online services. Such online marketing of fabrics offers an efficient method for companies to advertise their products to prospective fabric buyers. A number of Internet companies focus on connecting fabric/textile sellers with fabric/textile buyers in the apparel industry.

Textile Trade Shows

Textile **trade shows** exhibit textile mills' newest fabrics for the coming fashion seasons. Typically held twice per year, in spring (March) and fall (October /November), textile trade shows offer visitors a look at general trends in color, textures, prints, and fabrications (see Figure 4.13). For example, a textile trade show held in March 2016 would exhibit Spring/Summer 2017 fabrics.

Because every apparel line or collection begins with fabrics, textile shows provide designers and manufacturers with inspirations for their next line or collection. Trade shows become an important venue to source out new materials. Below is a listing of selected textile trade shows:

- Direction, an international textile design show held in New York City, focuses on trendsetting textiles from around the world.
- Sourcing at MAGIC, held in Las Vegas in association with MAGIC Marketplace, connects apparel and accessory manufacturers with fabric and trim suppliers from around the world.

Figure 4.13
Textile trade shows provide opportunities for textile companies to promote their lines to manufacturers.
Sardella/WWD/© Conde Nast.

- Interstoff, managed by Messe Frankfurt, is one of the largest textile trade show organizations in the world. Interstoff includes the following:
  - Interstoff Asia (Hong Kong)
  - Interstoff Rossija (Moscow)
  - Intertextile Beijing
  - Intertextile Shanghai
  - Source It (Hong Kong)
  - Texworld (Paris)
  - Texworld India (Mumbai)
  - Texworld USA (New York City)
  - Yarn Expo
- Première Vision, held in Villepinte, near Paris, focuses on high-quality and innovative fabrics. Designers often get inspirations for apparel designs from the textiles shown at Première Vision. Première Vision has expanded worldwide to include the following:
  - Première Vision Shanghai
  - Première Vision New York
  - Première Vision Moscow
  - Première Vision Tokyo
- Material World New York, sponsored by the American Apparel and Footwear Association, is a growing textile trade show in the United States.
- Ideacomo, held in Como, Italy (near Milan), was created in 1975 by silk apparel producers near Como. It now focuses on medium- to high-market luxury and innovative fabric collections of member companies.
- L.A. International Textile Show, held at the California Market Center and sponsored by the Textile Association of L.A., is one of the largest textile trade shows in the United States. It focuses on creative domestic and European designer fabric and trim collections and other textile resources.
- Taipei Innovative Textile Application Show (TITAS) focuses on high-tech and innovative textiles (primarily from Asian countries) and their applications for a variety of end uses.

Leather producers also use biannual trade shows to market their products. Some of the best known are LE CUIR A PARIS, China International Leather Fair, Moscow International Fur Trade Fair, and Fur and Fashion Frankfurt Fair.

DEVELOPMENTS IN MATERIALS AND TEXTILE INDUSTRY

Technological Advances

In order to compete successfully in a global economy, the textile industry has invested in new technology to increase productivity in textile mills and improve communication among textile mills, their suppliers, and their customers. These investments in technology are part of supply chain management and product life cycle management.

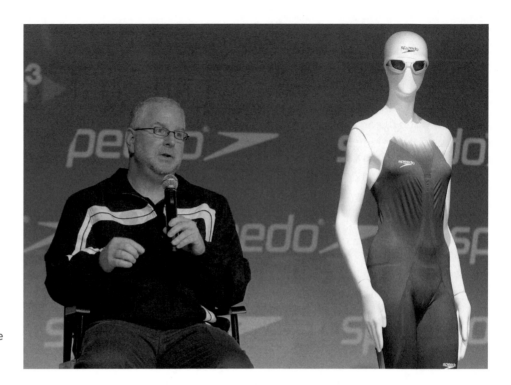

Figure 4.14
Speedo's Fastskin is an example of a smart textile. Mike Stobe /Getty Images for Speedo.

Supply chain management shortens the time from fiber production to sale to the ultimate consumer by enhancing the communications and partnerships among industry sectors. In the material industry, supply chain management strategies include computer-aided textile design, computerized knitting machines, and computer-controlled robots. Enhanced communication links between textile companies, their suppliers, and their customers have also contributed to effective supply chain management strategies.

More importantly, changes in how apparel is made and what it is capable of is changing the way people view their clothing and accessories. According to "Smart Textiles Market Size, Market Share, Application Analysis, Regional Outlook, Growth Trends, Competitive Scenario and Segment Forecasts 2015 to 2022" (2014), smart textiles market growth is due to the launching of textile fibers and conductive materials that can be easily integrated with electronics. Optical fibers with integrated electronics have been developed, allowing fibers that can sense, process, and store data to be woven into fabric. Initial applications for these **smart or** intelligent materials include military uniforms, medical devices, protective garments for extreme environments, and performance athletic wear (Figure 4.14). These smart textiles have become a major segment globally thanks to several advantages, including functional requirement, health and safety, cost effectiveness, durability, high strength, and so on. Sensing, monitoring, computing, communications, and heat and energy management are expected to be the main functions for the intelligent textile products of the future (Sinclair 2014, p. 374).

The textile industry has also played an important role in the research, development, and implementation of new strategies to increase productivity and competitiveness. Examples of investment in technologically advanced equipment and processes include digital textile printing, which has reshaped the process of creating fabric designs. Ink is a promising area for technical innovation because it has the ability to get better fiber penetration and print on more types of fabric. The overall printing industry across the globe is estimated to be US$1 trillion, of which textiles represent about 15 percent of total value (Fashionatingworld.com 2016).

Along with digital printing is 3D printing. Designers are looking at new ways to incorporate this technology, which allows for custom made and sized garments. Van Herpen developed an innovative new textile called TPU 92A-1, which is being billed as the first printable material that is flexible, durable enough to be worn, and can be put in the washing machine (Rietveld 2013). This textile represents a massive step forward in usability and has great potential for the fashion industry.

Environmental and Sustainability Issues

Demand for environmentally responsible products, once limited to younger consumers and consumers with a sense of social responsibility, has become mainstream. Companies, including textile producers, are working to improve environmental conditions and show that they are environmentally conscious. They are incorporating environmentally responsible processes, including

- manufacturing products that include organic or recycled materials
- using less-toxic materials, such as low-impact dyes
- using less water in production

Apparel manufacturers are also pressuring textile producers to supply environmentally responsible textiles. Therefore, a number of environmentally responsible textile manufacturing processes have been implemented, including organically grown cotton, cleaner dyeing and finishing processes, and waste reduction.

Each year, textile companies spend billions of dollars to ensure that their processes are environmentally responsible through efforts in conserving water, energy, and electricity and in recycling products (e.g., paper and plastic) and natural resources (e.g., water and energy). Plants are built or adapted with environmental impact in mind.

Significant innovations in sustainability include reducing water and energy consumption, which are vital developments that benefit the environment and reduce costs. Environmental and economic considerations go hand in hand and have been a driving force even in areas such as finishing, where water consumption and pollution have been particular issues (Fashionatingworld.com 2015). The rise of digital printing, which does not require water, is an environmentally friendly technology and also offers opportunities for reshoring because it can produce small lots of printed fabrics.

SUMMARY

The textile industry includes companies that contribute to the four basic stages of textile production: fiber processing, yarn spinning, fabric production or fabrication, and fabric finishing. Some companies specialize in one or more of the production processes; vertically integrated companies handle all four. Both natural and manufactured fibers are processed in the United States.

Natural fibers produced in the United States include cotton, wool, mohair, and other specialty fibers. Leather and fur, also produced in the United States, are considered natural-fiber products. Natural fibers are commodities bought and sold on international markets and are generally promoted by trade associations that focus on specific fibers. These trade associations encourage the use of the various natural fibers through activities such as market research, advertising, and consumer education programs.

Manufactured fibers are typically produced by large, vertically integrated companies. They are marketed either as commodity fibers or brand name (trademarked) fibers, such as Lycra spandex fiber or Dacron polyester fiber. Brand name fibers are advertised by companies to create consumer awareness and preference for the specific fibers. Trade associations are also involved in promoting manufactured fibers.

Textile companies are often involved in determining the colors to be selected for end-use products. Through the process of color forecasting, color palettes are selected and translated into fabrics produced by a company for a specific fashion season. Color forecasts are available from nonprofit service organizations, such as the Color Association of the United States, or from color forecasting services. Companies may also conduct their own color forecasting.

Textile mills focus on fabric production and sell greige goods; some textile mills will finish the fabric as well. Textile design involves the interrelationships among color (e.g., dyeing, printing), fabric structure (e.g., woven, knitted), and finishes (e.g., napping, embossing). Textile converters specialize in fabric finishing. They buy greige goods and finish the fabric according to specifications from textile mills, apparel manufacturers, or retailers. Other fabric resources include textile jobbers, textile brokers, and fabric retail stores. Through quality assurance programs, textile mills, apparel manufacturers, and retailers test textiles according to standards for end-use products. Textile mills and converters market their textile fabrics as Fall/Winter and Spring/Summer seasonal lines in showrooms and at textile trade shows throughout the world.

To compete successfully in a global economy, the U.S. textile industry continues to invest in new technology and environmentally responsible practices designed to increase the productivity of textile mills and improve communication among textile mills, their suppliers, and their customers. These investments in technology are part of supply chain management strategies, designed to shorten the time from fiber to finished product. The textile industry is addressing environmental concerns through manufacturing and by making available to consumers new products that incorporate environmentally responsible processes.

KEY TERMS

brand name
cashmere
color forecasting
color forecasting service
color story
concept garment
controlled brand name program
converted goods
cotton
digital printing
fabric construction
fabrication
fiber
filament yarn
finished goods
finishing

generic family
greige goods
hide
horizontally integrated
intelligent textile
kip
licensed brand name program
mohair
pelt
quality assurance
quality control
regular tannery
skin
smart textile
spun yarn
tanning

tawning
textile
textile converter
textile jobber
textile mill
textile stylist
textile testing
throwster
trade association
trade name
trade show
vertically integrated
wool
yarn

DISCUSSION QUESTIONS AND ACTIVITIES

1. What are the advantages and disadvantages to a textile company of being horizontally integrated? Vertically integrated? How are the advantages and disadvantages of each type of integration related to the types of textile companies that are horizontally and vertically integrated?

2. What are the differences between the production and marketing of natural fibers and manufactured fibers? Why do these differences exist?

3. What roles do trade associations play in the promotion of natural and manufactured fibers? Give examples of the activities performed by trade associations. Bring in examples of cooperative advertising between trade associations and end-use producers.

4. Select an item of clothing, such as a jacket or coat. How many different textiles and fibers are used to make the garment?

5. Form groups to debate whether cotton is environmentally more or less harmful to the ecosystem than polyester; or whether disposable or cloth diapers are better when balancing production costs, water and energy use, and disposal.

Fabric Choices for Brooks Brothers' Made-to-Measure Dress Shirts

Brooks Brothers was one of the earliest ready-to-wear apparel retailers in the United States; the first store opened in New York in 1818. In 1896, the company introduced a ready-to-wear men's shirt with a button-down collar, and since then it has introduced classic men's and women's apparel through retail stores and a website. One of the distinct services offered by Brooks Brothers is its Made-to-Measure program. This program enables clients to select a design from a portfolio of suits, sport coats, and dress shirts; select a material from a catalog of fabrics; and order a custom-made garment in one of the unique fits offered by Brooks Brothers. Brooks Brothers Made-to-Measure dress shirts continue to be popular items among those wanting classic dress shirt designs with customized details. Currently, Brooks Brothers offers fibers/fabrics for these dress shirts: 100% cotton, 100% linen, 100% cotton finished with a wrinkle-free finish, and BrooksCool®, a 100% cotton fabric treated to enhance breathability.

A team of designers and merchandisers at Brooks Brothers is evaluating these fiber and fabric options and will be deciding whether to add any additional fiber/fabric choices to the offerings for the Made-to-Measure program for dress shirts. The team of designers and merchandisers is considering adding fabrics made from the following fibers to the options available to their Made-to-Measure clients: 100% silk, 100% Tencel® lyocell.

1. Go to the Brooks Brothers website and review the styles, fabrics, and prices of Brooks Brothers dress shirts. How would you describe the primary target customer for Brooks Brothers dress shirts?

2. List at least three advantages and three disadvantages of each of the fiber options currently being used by Brooks Brothers; also list three advantages and three disadvantages of the two additional fiber options the company is considering. You will need to research each of the fibers/fabrics and their characteristics and then evaluate how and why these characteristics may be considered an advantage, disadvantage, or both.

3. From a merchandising perspective, the team of designers and merchandisers has determined that they will offer only four fiber/fabric options to their clients for the Made-to-Measure program. Of the fiber/fabric options you evaluated, which four fiber/fabric options would you recommend being offered? Why did you recommend these four options? Why did you decide to not recommend the other options?

Source: http://www.brooksbrothers.com/ (accessed March 3, 2016).

CAREER OPPORTUNITIES

Careers in the global materials industry include the following opportunities:

- Textile designer
- Textile stylist
- Textile-testing professional for a fashion brand or an independent or government testing facility
- Material librarian for a fashion brand or independent materials library
- Material/fabric sales representative
- Materials/fabric buyer or sourcing analyst

REFERENCES

Bide, Martin. (2009). "Fiber Sustainability: Green Is Not Black + White." *AATCC Review* 9 (7): 34–37.

Foxfiber.com (2013) http://foxfibre.sites.musicwell.org/about/ (accessed March 31, 2016).

Fur Commission USA. (2016). http://www.furcommission.com (accessed March 31, 2016).

Kadolph, Sara J., and Anna L. Langford. (2002). *Textiles* (9th ed.). New York: Fairchild Publications.

Mohair Council of America. (2015). http://www.mohairusa.com (accessed March 3, 2016).

National Cotton Council of America. (2015). "World of Cotton." http://www.cotton.org/econ/world/detail.cfm (accessed March 3, 2016).

National Council of Textile Organizations. (2015). "About NCTO." http://www.ncto.org (accessed March 3, 2016).

North American Industry Classification System. (2015). "Definitions: 313 Textile Mills." https://www.osha.gov/pls/imis/sic_manual.display?id=15&tab=group (accessed March 28, 2016).

"Opportunities: New Innovations, Technologies to Drive Industry in 2016." (2016, January 6). http://fashionatingworld.com/new1-2/item/4490-new-innovations,-technologies-to-drive-industry-in-2016.html (accessed March 3, 2016).

Organic Trade Association. (2015). http://www.ota.com/organic/environment/wool.html (accessed March 3, 2016).

Rietveld, Fira. (2013). "3D Printing: The Face of Future Fashion?" http://tedx.amsterdam/2013/07/3d-printing-the-face-of-future-fashion (accessed March 3, 2016).

Sinclair, Rose. (2014). *Textiles and Fashion: Materials, Design and Technology*. Cambridge, MA: Elsevier Science.

"Smart Textiles Market Size, Market Share, Application Analysis, Regional Outlook, Growth Trends, Competitive Scenario and Segment Forecasts 2015 to 2022." (February 2014). http://www.hexaresearch.com/research-report/smart-textiles-industry/ (accessed March 3, 2016).

"Sustainability: Global Business to Continue Focus on Green Initiatives." (2015, December 31). http://Fashionatingworld.com/new1-2/item/4445-trendspotting-2016 (accessed March 3, 2016).

CHAPTER 5

Fashion Brands: Company Organization

IN THIS CHAPTER, YOU WILL LEARN THE FOLLOWING:

- the difference between the ready-to-wear industry and haute couture

- the various types of fashion brand companies

- the organizational structure of fashion brand companies

- the merchandising philosophies of fashion brand companies

- the primary trade associations and trade publications in the fashion industry

As discussed in previous chapters, fashion brand companies come in all sizes and ownership models. However, all of these companies have something in common—they design, produce, and sell ready-to-wear (RTW) apparel, and accessories or home fashions ready for use by the consumer. In this chapter we will explore the characteristics, organization and merchandising philosophies of RTW and home fashion companies.

READY-TO-WEAR: WHAT DOES IT MEAN?

Most of the apparel and accessories produced and sold is called **ready-to-wear (RTW)**. As the term implies, the merchandise is completely made and ready to be worn (except for finishing details, such as pants hemming in tailored clothing) at the time it is purchased. In the United Kingdom, this merchandise is called off-the-peg; in France, it is called **prêt-à-porter**; and in Italy, it is called moda pronto. RTW fashion brand merchandise is made in large quantities using mass-manufacturing processes that require little or no hand sewing.

Many fashion companies produce seasonal lines or collections of merchandise. Lines or collections are groups of styles designed for a particular **fashion season**. The primary difference between a line and a collection is the cost of the merchandise—the term **collection** typically refers to more expensive merchandise. Often name designers will create and offer collections; other apparel companies will offer **lines**.

Fashion brand companies typically produce four to six new collections or lines per year, corresponding to the fashion seasons: Spring, Summer, Fall I (Pre-Fall), Fall II, Holiday, and Resort or Cruise. These fashion seasons coincide with the times consumers would most likely wear the merchandise, not with when companies design or manufacture the merchandise or when the merchandise is delivered to stores. For example, a company may start to design a Fall season line in September, market the line in March, actually manufacture it from March through April, and deliver the merchandise to the stores in June.

Not all companies produce lines for all six fashion seasons. The number of lines a company will produce depends on both the product category and the target market (the group of customers for whom the line is designed). For example, a company that produces men's tailored suits may create only two lines per year (Fall and Spring), whereas a men's sportswear company may create five lines per year (Fall I, Fall II, Holiday, Spring, and Summer). Some companies produce more than six lines per year. A number of apparel and accessory companies produce smaller lines that are shipped to retailers more frequently; the frequent infusion of new merchandise appeals to customers. **Fast fashion** companies such as Zara, H&M, and Forever 21 create lines that are delivered to stores every few weeks. Many companies that are specialty store retailers of private label apparel (SPA) or produce store brands (e.g., Victoria's Secret, Abercrombie & Fitch, Ann Taylor, Gap) or other forms of private label merchandise (e.g., Worthington for JCPenney) also ship goods to their retail stores frequently. Chapters 6 and 7 discuss in more detail the development of collections and lines.

As discussed in Chapter 1, the standardization of sizing was necessary in developing the RTW industry. Sizes in RTW are based on a combination of standardized body dimensions, company size standards, and wearing and design ease. Clothing sizes were developed by grouping computed average circumference measurements of a large group of people (of average height) into specific size categories. For example, the men's size 42 relates to a male of average height (5 feet 10 inches to 6 feet) with a chest circumference of 42 inches and waist of 36 inches. These body measurements or dimensions are referred to as the standardized size. In the U.S., standardized tables of body dimensions are available from the American Society for Testing and Materials (ASTM) for various figure types.

The fashion industry does not adhere strictly to the set standardized sizes. A company may develop its "company size" based on a target customer with a smaller waist in comparison to the hip circumference, or a larger chest in comparison to the waist circumference. The term *athletic fit* refers to a men's suit built to fit the male body with a larger chest-to-waist ratio than the standardized size (for example, a size 42 athletic fit might be based on a chest circumference of 42 inches and a waist circumference of 35 inches). Because of the wide variety of body types, companies will focus on the "company size" that is most appropriate for its target customer. This is why many consumers find that one brand of apparel fits them better than other brands.

As non-store retailing (e.g., internet) of fashion merchandise has increased, direct marketing fashion companies have worked to develop consistent body measurements and related size measurements for all styles that the company produces. A fit that can be determined accurately from a body measurement chart in a catalog or at a website can reduce returns and thus increase customer satisfaction with the product and the company.

The size chart lists the body measurements for the company's apparel. Wearing ease and design ease allowances are added to the body measurements to create the garment measurements. Each company decides how much wearing ease and design ease to add to create the look for the company. Some styles are designed to fit more loosely than other styles. The company sizing will reflect these style aspects. Each company's size range is based on its predetermined body measurements plus ease. The size measurements increase and decrease in specified increments from the base or sample size to create the size range. The size increments used to create the various sizes are discussed in more detail in later chapters.

THE DIFFERENCE BETWEEN READY-TO-WEAR AND COUTURE

Designer names, such as Chanel, Christian Dior, and Yves Saint Laurent, first became famous in the realm of French haute couture (high fashion) and later became associated with expensive RTW. Because of the continued prominence and importance of these designer labels, it is important to understand the distinction and the relationship between couture and RTW. **Couture** is a French term that literally means "sewing." In general, couture fashion merchandise is distinguished by the following characteristics:

- produced in smaller quantities
- uses considerable hand-sewing techniques
- sized to fit an individual's body measurements

Generally, more expensive materials are used in couture merchandise than in RTW. When couture techniques are applied to custom-made suits or other specialty items made to an individual's specifications, the term **bespoke** is typically used.

The term *couture* is derived from **haute couture** (pronounced *oat´ coo-tur*), which literally means "high sewing." As discussed in Chapter 1, the haute couture industry developed in Paris during the nineteenth century. At that time, apparel was produced by dressmakers and tailors who custom-fit each garment to the client. The garment's style and fabric were selected for or by each client, the client's body measurements were taken, and the garment was completed after one or more fittings during the construction process. For persons who did not have personal dressmakers or tailors, apparel was produced in the home by whoever had the necessary skills.

During the early twentieth century, the French Ministry for Industry formed the *Chambre Syndicale de la Couture* to provide an organizational structure and to offer protection for designers against their designs being copied. Currently, the *Chambre Syndicale* does the following:

- arranges the calendar for the showings of the collections twice per year
- organizes accreditation for press and buyers who want to attend the showings
- assists the couture houses so each gains the maximum press coverage possible

As of 2015, the 14 official members of the *Chambre Syndicale* are Adeline André, Alexandre Vauthier, Alexis Mabille, Atelier Gustavo Lins, Bouchra Jarrar, Chanel, Christian Dior, Frank Sorbier, Giambattista Valli, Givenchy, Jean Paul Gaultier, Maurizio Galante, Maison Martin Margiela, and Stéphane Rolland. To be a member of the *Chambre Syndicale* requires specific qualifications, including the following:

- the use of one's own house seamstresses
- the presentation of Fall/Winter and Spring/Summer collections each year with at least 35 pieces for day and evening
- adherence to the dates of showings set by the *Chambre Syndicale*
- registration of the original designs to protect against copying

Each designer's business is called a **couture house**. Thus, there is the House of Dior, the House of Givenchy, and the House of Chanel. The haute couture designer is called the **couturier** (or **couturière** if the designer is a woman), or "head of the house." Whereas some couturiers control their own businesses, many couture houses are owned by corporations that finance them. In recent years, some financial backers have been known to hire and fire head designers frequently. A Paris haute couture designer typically has a **boutique** (store) located on one of several fashion avenues in Paris. The boutique sells the designer's prêt-à-porter collections as well as licensed products such as perfume, scarves, jewelry and other accessories, and home fashions.

The **salon de couture** is the showroom of the couture designer. The salon is typically located on the second floor of the building that houses the designer's boutique. Entry to the second level, the salon, is limited to those with invitations to a collection show. The **atelier** (pronounced *ah-tal´-lee-aye*) **de couture**, or workrooms, may be on the floors above the salon or in a separate building.

The twice-per-year Paris haute couture collection openings continue to be huge events in the fashion world, and the fashion press covers them in detail (Figure 5.1). Fall/Winter fashion season haute couture collections are typically shown in July, and Spring/Summer fashion season haute couture collections are typically shown in January. The press, buyers, other designers, celebrities, and wealthy clients are in attendance. While the fashion influence of the couturiers waxes and wanes, the designs presented are considered to represent a laboratory of design creativity.

In addition to the couturiers who are members of the *Chambre Syndicale*, there are other designers who consider themselves to be couture designers. Generally, a couture designer is distinguished by the following:

- uses high-quality fabrics
- creates original designs (as opposed to copying another's designs)
- uses high-quality construction and hand-finishing details
- custom-fits the garment to a client's body measurements

Couture designers may produce all custom work (ordered by a specific client), or they may present a seasonal collection and then take custom orders selected from the collection. There are couture designers in New York, Los Angeles, Tokyo, London, and other cities around the world.

The term *couture* is sometimes used in the fashion industry to impart elite ambience to a fashion collection. Indeed, Paris haute couture houses also produce

Figure 5.1
Paris haute couture collections, such as Dior Haute Couture, attract extensive press coverage. Feugere/WWD/© Conde Nast.

RTW (prêt-à-porter) collections. These RTW collections may be sold in the house boutique, in freestanding boutiques, or in upscale department or specialty stores. However, if mass-production techniques are used in producing the fashion merchandise, and if garments are not custom-fit to the client, the line should be called RTW and *not* couture.

TYPES OF FASHION BRAND COMPANIES

From large corporations to small companies, from those that produce innovative, trendy merchandise to those that produce classics, fashion brand companies come in all types and sizes and vary tremendously in their organization. Because of the diversity found in fashion company organization, any attempt to classify types of fashion brand companies is difficult. However, according to industry analysts, the major types of fashion brand companies can be grouped into the following categories: manufacturers, licensors, and retailers that sell private label fashion including SPAs (specialty store retailers of private label apparel).

Manufacturers perform all functions of creating, marketing, and distributing an apparel line on a continual basis. Historically, manufacturers produced merchandise in their own factories, and a few fashion brand companies still have their own factories (e.g., Zara). Today, manufacturers typically use outside companies, or contractors, to perform the manufacturing function. As such, the term *manufacturer* is a misnomer in that these fashion brand companies are typically not involved in the actual manufacturing of the fashion brands they oversee. However, the historical term is still used for these fashion brand companies. (A review of the categories of fashion brands was provided in Chapter 2.) In the home fashions industry, furniture manufacturers often also serve the roles of decorative fabric converter and jobber (warehouse and distribution functions). For example, Robert Allen Design provides fabrics, furniture, trims, and design consultation for the residential and hospitality design communities. Retail distribution of fashion brands created by manufacturers will vary depending on the manufacturer. Retail distribution will be further explained in later chapters.

Licensors are companies that have developed a well-known designer name (e.g., Dior, Calvin Klein, Ralph Lauren), celebrity name (e.g., Jessica Simpson, Kathy Ireland), brand name (e.g., Tommy Hilfiger, DKNY), or character (e.g., Mickey Mouse, Harry Potter, Ironman) and sell the use of these names or characters to companies to put onto merchandise. As discussed in Chapter 2, successful licensing depends on a well-known name or image (property). However, these categories are not mutually exclusive. For example, a manufacturer may use a contractor or may license its brand name to a company that produces product categories different from its own. The details of these various types of fashion brand production will be discussed in later chapters.

Retailers that sell private label fashion brands create unique fashion brands sold only in their stores. For department stores, these fashion brands are part of the overall merchandise mix of the store that also includes international, national, and regional brands. Examples of private label fashion brands sold in department stores include Alfani, Charter Club, and INC International Concepts for Macy's and Treasure&Bond and Classiques Entier for Nordstrom.

One type of retailer that sells private label fashion brands is the **SPA**, or specialty store retailer of private label apparel. Companies of this type create and sell only private label merchandise and as such are sometimes called **store brands**, since the store and the fashion brand are the same. Examples of SPAs include fast fashion companies such as Zara, Forever 21, or H&M and specialty stores such as A&F, Victoria's Secret, Gap, and Banana Republic.

All types of fashion brand companies (manufacturers, licensors, and retailers of private label fashion brands) may hire contractors for a variety of processes in the design and production of the fashion merchandise. **Contractors** are companies that specialize in the design, sewing, and/or finishing of goods. Contractors are used by

- manufacturers that do not own any manufacturing factories and contract all sewing and finishing operations
- manufacturers that have insufficient capacity in their own plants or have specialized needs for a short time and use contractors to address these needs
- licensors that contract design, sewing, and/or finishing as part of specific licensing agreements
- retailers of private label fashion brands, including SPAs

Most contractors specialize in a product category (e.g., knit tops, denim jeans) or have specialized equipment (e.g., embroidery machines) and skilled workers. The term **item house** is used to describe contractors that specialize in making one product. For example, item houses are used in the production of baseball caps. Contractors offer their customers fast turnarounds. **Full-package contractors (FP)**, in working with retailers, also offer material procurement and design services that traditionally were part of the manufacturers' role.

Some contractors produce goods for the sole use of a particular retailer (or retail corporation) as a private label brand or retail store/direct market brand merchandise. Some contractors will produce merchandise for both international/national brands and private label fashion brands; other contractors will produce merchandise for one international/national or private label fashion brand only.

CLASSIFICATIONS AND CATEGORIES OF FASHION BRAND COMPANIES

Fashion brand companies are classified in the following ways:

- by the type of merchandise they produce
- by the wholesale prices of the products or brands (price point)
- by an industry classification system for governmental tracking

An examination of these classification systems allows for a better understanding of the diversity of fashion brand companies.

Gender/Age, Size Range, Product Category/End Use

The fashion industries are divided into the primary categories of men's, women's, and children's apparel and accessory (including footwear) and home fashion brand companies. Some companies create apparel and accessories in only one of these categories; others create apparel and accessories in more than one. In some cases, companies began with one category and then branched out into one or more other categories as the companies grew. For example, Levi Strauss & Co. began as a manufacturer of men's apparel and later expanded into women's and children's wear. Nike started as an athletic footwear company and expanded into apparel and sports equipment.

The separate gender/age categories have their roots in the early history of the U.S. fashion industries. Fashion brand producers specialized in one category due to a variety of factors. The types of machinery used for producing men's apparel were often different from the types needed for women's apparel. The sizing standards developed differently for men's, women's, and children's apparel and footwear. The number of seasonal lines produced per year differs for each category; therefore, the production cycle varies.

The organizational structure of retail stores is related to these categories of apparel, which is another reason that the fashion industries remain divided into the primary categories of men's, women's, and children's apparel, accessories and footwear, and home fashions. Retail buyers are often assigned responsibilities in one of the categories of fashion brands. For example, a menswear buyer buys apparel for the retail store from men's apparel manufacturers. This allows the manufacturers and retailer to establish and maintain profitable working relationships.

Within each of the primary categories, fashion brand companies are divided into subcategories. For example, apparel or home fashion producers generally specialize in one or several subcategories. These subcategories relate to the classification of apparel or home fashions. Fashion apparel classifications are by type of garment produced (product type). Traditional classifications by product type for women's apparel include

- outerwear (coats, jackets, and rainwear)
- dresses
- blouses
- career wear (suits, separates, and career wear dresses)
- sportswear and active sportswear (separates, such as pants, sweaters, and skirts; and active sportswear, such as swimwear and tennis wear)
- evening wear and special occasion
- bridal and bridesmaid dresses
- maternity wear
- uniforms
- furs
- accessories
- intimate apparel, which is further divided into the following categories:
    - foundations (girdles or body shapers, bras, and other shapewear)
    - lingerie (petticoats, slips, panties, camisoles, nightgowns, and pajamas)
    - loungewear (at-home wear, robes, and bed jackets,)

Foundations and lingerie worn under other clothing are sometimes referred to as *innerwear*. In addition, lingerie and loungewear are sometimes divided into daywear and nightwear.

The various subcategories are organized by size category and clothing classification (Table 5.1). For example, some apparel companies manufacture apparel

Table 5.1 Children's, Men's, and Women's Wear Categories and Size Ranges

CHILDREN'S WEAR

Subcategories (organized by gender and size)

Infants	sized by weight/height or sizes 0 to 3 months (or newborn, 3 months), 6 to 9 months (or 6 months, 9 months), 12 months, 18 months, 24 months, or S-M-L-XL
Toddler	sizes 2T, 3T, 4T, 5T
Boys	sizes 4, 5, 6, 7, and 8 to 20 (even numbers only). Also Slim sizes 4S, 5S, 6S, 7S, and 8S to 20S (even numbers only), and Husky sizes 8H to 26H (even numbers only), or S-M-L-XL-XXL
Girls	sizes 4, 5, 6, 6X, and 7, 8, 10, 12, 14, 16, 18. Also Slim sizes 4S, 5S, 6S, 7S, and 8S to 16S (even numbers only), or S-M-L-XL
Girls Plus	sizes 81/2 to 201/2 (even numbers only), or 7+, 8+, 10+, 12+, 14+, 16+, 18+, 20+, or M-L-XL
Preteen (girls)	sizes 6 to 16 or 8 PT to 16 PT (even numbers only)
Young Junior	sizes 3 to 13 (odd numbers only)

MENSWEAR

Subcategories (organized by classification of apparel)

Tailored clothing	suits, sport coats, evening wear (tuxedos), overcoats: sizes: 36, 38, 39, 40, 41, 42, 43, 44, 45, 46, 48, 50, 52, 54, 56, 58, 60 based on chest circumference lengths: Regular, Short, Long, Extra Long Regular, Athletic, and Portly fit separate trousers: sized by waist (29 to 44)/hemmed at retailer
Sportswear	sport shirts: sizes S-M-L-XL-XXL-XXXL pants: sized by waist/inseam (29 to 44 waist and 28 to 34 inseam), or sizes S-M-L-XL casual jackets: sizes 36 to 50 or S-M-L-XL. Also Tall, Extra Regular, Big & Tall sizes
Furnishings	shirts: sized by neck/sleeve length (e.g., 16/34), or S-M-L-XL-XXL sizes sweaters: sizes S-M-L-XL-XXL underwear: sized by waist size robes and pajamas: sizes S-M-L-XL-XXL neckwear: sizes regular, long, and extra long socks (based on shoe size)
Active sportswear, swimwear, athletic wear, windbreakers	sizes S-M-L-XL-XXL-XXXL may include Tall and Big & Tall sizes
Uniforms and work wear	overalls, work pants: sized by waist/inseam, or S-M-L-XL-XXL-XXXL work shirts: sizes S-M-L-XL-XXL-XXXL Regular, Tall, Big & Tall sizes

WOMEN'S WEAR

Classifications include outerwear, dresses, career wear, blouses, sportswear and active sportswear, evening, bridal, maternity, uniforms, furs, intimate apparel, accessories

Misses	sizes 0 to 18 (even numbers only: 2, 4, 6, 8, 10, 12, 14, 16, 18), or sizes XS-S-M-L-XL
Women's (large size, queen, plus, custom)	sizes 14W to 26W (even numbers only), or Plus sizes 1X, 2X, 3X
Petite (under 5'4")	sizes 0P to 16P, under 5'4" (even numbers only)
Women's Petite	14WP to 20 WP (even sizes only)
Tall (over 5'9")	sizes 10T to 18T (even numbers only)
Junior	sizes 1 to 15 (odd numbers only)
Junior Petite	sizes 1JP to 15JP (odd numbers only)

Note: Not all companies produce the entire size range in the size categories listed.

Figure 5.2
Women's apparel size categories include misses (missy), junior, petites, and women's.
TORSTEN BLACKWOOD/AFP/Getty Images.

only in the misses (also referred to as *missy*) or the junior-size category. Some companies produce apparel in misses and women's sizes, while other companies manufacture misses, women's, petite, plus, and/or tall sizes (Figure 5.2). In one size range, an apparel producer may manufacture clothing in one or more of the product classifications previously listed.

In addition to the difference between size categories of misses and junior apparel, there are styling differences (Figure 5.3). The junior size range is designed for a customer who is approximately 16 to 22 years old, whereas the misses size category is designed for a target customer who is approximately 22 years old and upward. The styling, fabrics, and trims of misses apparel have a more mature fashion look than that of junior apparel.

Traditional menswear classifications include

- tailored clothing (structured or semi-structured suits, coats, and separates, such as sport jackets and dress slacks)
- sportswear (casual pants, including jeans)
- furnishings (dress shirts and casual shirts; sweaters; neckties, handkerchiefs, and other accessory items; underwear and nightwear; hosiery; and hats and caps)
- active sportswear (athletic clothing, including golf wear, tennis wear, swimwear)
- uniforms and work wear (work shirts and pants, overalls)

Figure 5.3
Junior apparel is differentiated from misses (missy) apparel through sizing for a younger customer and trendier styling.
Michael Stewart/GC Images.

The number of seasonal lines produced per year in menswear varies with the classification of apparel. Producers of tailored clothing tend to develop a large Fall line and a somewhat smaller Spring line, while most sportswear producers develop four to six seasonal lines per year.

In children's wear, the subcategories are organized by age-related size categories and by gender (see Table 5.1). Many children's wear manufacturers produce apparel in both infant and toddler sizes. In the older-size categories, apparel companies usually specialize in either boys' wear or girls' wear. Seasonal lines produced in children's wear typically include Back-to-School (the largest line), Holiday, Spring, and Summer lines.

Companies that create **home fashions** are generally divided into the following end-use categories:

- upholstered furniture coverings and fillings
- window treatments
- wall coverings
- soft floor coverings including area rugs, scatter rugs, and runners
- room and wall-to-wall carpeting
- bed linens including sheets, pillowcases, comforters, blankets, duvet covers, pillows, and quilts
- bathroom textiles including wash clothes, towels, and shower curtains
- tabletop including table cloths, napkins, placemats, and table runners
- kitchen textiles including towels, dishcloths, hot pads, and aprons
- other home accessories including textile wall hangings, decorative pillows, and throws

Accessories manufacturers are grouped into end-use product categories, including

- footwear
- hosiery and legwear
- hats and headwear
- scarves
- belts
- handbags
- gloves
- jewelry

Footwear subcategories include

- athletic footwear
- dress shoes and boots
- casual shoes sandals
- work shoes and boots
- western/casual boots
- hiking, hunting, and fishing boots
- specialized sport shoes (e.g., ski boots, bicycling shoes)

Many accessory companies specialize in manufacturing only one type of product; that is, some companies manufacture only athletic footwear, and other companies produce only neckwear. For example, many hat and headwear producers

Figure 5.4
Felt hats are molded into shape over hat blocks such as the one seen here. Ron Mullet © 2010.

are considered item houses and may specialize in one type of product, such as baseball caps. Soft-fabric hats and caps are usually sewn using construction techniques similar to those used for apparel. Handwork might be required for the more expensive hats, while less expensive hats and headwear are machine made. Traditionally styled wool felt hats and straw hats are usually formed over a hat block, using steam to mold the hat into shape (Figure 5.4). **Millinery** is a term that refers specifically to women's hats and usually denotes that handwork is involved in the hat-making process.

Within this category, men's hats are produced in sizes, from 6½ to 7½ (in ⅛-inch intervals), that correspond to head circumference, or, for less structured hats, in sizes *small*, *medium*, *large*, and *extra large*. Caps may be produced in one size. Most women's hats are made in one size; however, some designer hats are produced in several sizes. Small children's caps and hats may be sized by age, while older children's hats may be produced in sizes *extra small*, *small*, *medium*, and *large*.

The belt industry is divided into two segments: **cut-up trade** and **rack trade**. The cut-up trade includes manufacturers that produce the belts that apparel companies add to their pants, skirts, and dresses and supply as a component of the products that apparel companies ship to retailers. The rack trade is made up of manufacturers that design, produce, and market belts to retailers.

Jewelry is divided into three categories: fine jewelry, bridge jewelry, and costume jewelry.

- **Fine jewelry** is the most expensive jewelry category. It includes pieces made from precious metals, such as silver, gold, and platinum, either alone or with precious and semiprecious gemstones. Fine jewelry companies are often vertically integrated organizations with the designer, producer, and retailer under one roof.

Figure 5.5
Coach has diversified product offerings to include footwear and licensed fashion apparel. Centeno/WWD/© Conde Nast.

- **Bridge jewelry** serves as an umbrella term for several types of jewelry, including those made of silver, gold (typically of 14, 12, or 10 karats), and less expensive stones, such as onyx, ivory, coral, or freshwater pearls. One-of-a-kind jewelry designed by artists using a variety of materials is also considered bridge jewelry. From a retail price perspective, bridge jewelry typically falls between fine and costume jewelry.
- **Costume jewelry** is the least expensive of the jewelry categories. This type of jewelry is mass-produced using plastic, wood, brass, glass, Lucite, and other less expensive materials. Although the costume jewelry industry includes large companies such as Monet and Pandora, it is dominated by small companies that produce jewelry sold through a variety of retail outlets, including non-store retailers.

Some companies prefer to diversify into more than one accessory category (Figure 5.5). Dooney & Bourke and Coach, both traditionally handbag and small leather goods manufacturers, diversified into footwear. Coach further diversified with a licensed fashion apparel line.

Price Zones

Fashion brand companies typically specialize in one or more **price zones** or **price points**. These categories are based on either the suggested retail price of the merchandise or the approximate wholesale price of the merchandise.

- *Luxury or Designer*: The luxury or designer price zone is the most expensive of the price zones. It includes collections of name designer brands such as Louis Vuitton, Calvin Klein, Vera Wang, Armani, and Chanel, as well as collections of brands such as Burberry and St. John Knits and jewelry brands such as Tiffany.

- *Bridge*: Bridge lines traditionally fall between designer and better price zones. These may include designers' less expensive lines, sometimes called **diffusion lines** (e.g., Armani Collezioni), or those brands that are situated between designer and better price zones (e.g., Eileen Fisher, Adrienne Vittadini).

- *Better*: Lines in the better price zone are generally nationally known brand names, such as Emporio Armani, DKNY in women's wear, Nautica in menswear, or Nike athletic footwear. Many SPA/store brands (e.g., Banana Republic) and private label merchandise (goods that carry the retailer's name) are also in this price zone (e.g., Nordstrom's Classiques Entier private label brand).

- *Moderate*: Lines in the moderate price zone include nationally known sportswear brand names (e.g., Dockers, Guess?, Jones New York Sport) or store brands (e.g., Gap, A/X Armani Exchange) and other reasonably priced lines (e.g., Kasper suits). Moderate lines also include less expensive lines of companies that also produce better merchandise (e.g., Calvin Klein sport). Private label and store brand merchandise may also be in this price zone (e.g., JCPenney's Arizona brand and Macy's INC International Concepts brand). Fashion merchandise of exclusive licensing agreements such as Target's Mossimo brand may be at either the better or moderate price zone.

- *Budget or mass*: Found primarily at mass merchandisers and discount stores, budget lines are the least expensive price zones. These may include SPA/store brands of retailers with low prices as a competitive strategy (e.g., Old Navy—Figure 5.6). Private label merchandise for discount stores is also considered to be in the budget price zone (e.g., Kmart's Jaclyn Smith brand).

It is important to note that for classification purposes, the price zones can be considered a continuum. For example, some lines may be considered as falling between budget and moderate, while others may be considered as between

Figure 5.6
Old Navy offers merchandise at the budget price zone. Ericksen /WWD/© Conde Nast.

moderate and better. Some companies produce labels in several price zones, or brand tiers. Giorgio Armani includes the Giorgio Armani label, the Emporio label, and the A/X Armani Exchange label, each targeted for a different price zone.

North American Industry Classification System

The U.S. Department of Commerce categorizes companies based on their chief industrial activity. Industry data are compiled and reported according to these categories. In the past, Standard Industrial Classification (SIC) numbers were used. With the phasing out of the SIC system, the **North American Industry Classification System (NAICS)** was created. In this classification system, industry sectors in the United States, Mexico, and Canada can be compared. Here are the primary NAICS groups for textiles and apparel:

- NAICS 313: Textile Mills
- NAICS 314: Textile Product Mills (produce non-apparel textile products)
- NAICS 315: Apparel Manufacturing
- NAICS 316: Leather and Allied Product Manufacturing

In these major groups, additional numbers are used to designate more specific products (e.g., group 31521 refers to cut-and-sew apparel contractors). Table 5.2 lists the NAICS categories for textiles and apparel.

ORGANIZATIONAL STRUCTURE OF FASHION BRAND COMPANIES

Figure 5.7 depicts the organizational structure of a typical fashion brand company. Although the organization of companies may vary, they often include the following activities:

- research and merchandising
- design and product development
- marketing and sales
- operations
- advertising and sales promotion
- finance and information technology

Large companies may have separate departments or divisions with dozens of employees who handle each of these activities. In small companies, a few employees may handle several of these activities.

In reviewing Figure 5.7, it is important to note the connections among all of the areas or divisions. Communication among the various activities is imperative for the success of the company. Merchandisers must communicate with designers; designers must communicate with production management and marketers; those in information technology must understand the computer needs of all areas. Effective communication among the various areas can be a challenge for large companies.

Table 5.2 North American Industry Classification System (NAICS)

Primary NAICS Group	Chief Industrial Activity
313 Textile Mills	Industries in the Textile Mills subsector are establishments that transform a basic fiber (natural or synthetic) into a product, such as yarn or fabric, that is further manufactured into usable items, such as apparel, sheets, towels, and textile bags for individual or industrial consumption. The further manufacturing may be performed in the same establishment and classified in this subsector, or it may be performed at a separate establishment and be classified elsewhere in manufacturing. The main processes in this subsector include preparation and spinning of fiber, knitting or weaving of fabric, and finishing of the textile. The NAICS structure follows and captures this process flow. Major industries in this flow, such as preparation of fibers, weaving of fabric, knitting of fabric, and fiber and fabric finishing, are uniquely identified. Texturizing, throwing, twisting, and winding of yarn contain aspects of both fiber preparation and fiber finishing and are classified with preparation of fibers rather than with finishing of fiber.
314 Textile Product Mills	Industries in the Textile Product Mills subsector are establishments that make textile products (except apparel). With a few exceptions, processes used in these industries are generally cut and sew (i.e., purchasing fabric and cutting and sewing to make non-apparel textile products, such as sheets and towels).
315 Apparel Manufacturing	Industries in the Apparel Manufacturing subsector are establishments with two distinct manufacturing processes: (1) cut and sew (i.e., purchasing fabric and cutting and sewing to make a garment); and (2) the manufacture of garments in establishments that first knit fabric and then cut and sew the fabric into a garment. The Apparel Manufacturing subsector includes a diverse range of establishments manufacturing full lines of ready-to-wear apparel and custom apparel: apparel contractors, performing cutting or sewing operations on materials owned by others; jobbers, performing entrepreneurial functions involved in apparel manufacture; and tailors, manufacturing custom garments for individual clients are all included. Knitting, when done alone, is classified in the Textile Mills subsector, but when knitting is combined with the production of complete garments, the activity is classified in Apparel Manufacturing.
316 Leather and Allied Product Manufacturing	Establishments in the Leather and Allied Product Manufacturing subsector transform hides into leather by tanning or curing and fabricating the leather into products for final consumption. The subsector also includes the manufacture of similar products from other materials, including products (except apparel) made from "leather substitutes," such as rubber, plastics, or textiles. Rubber footwear, textile luggage, and plastic purses or wallets are examples of "leather substitute" products included in this group. Products made from leather substitutes are included in this subsector because they are made in ways similar to those used in making leather products (e.g., luggage). They are made in the same establishments, so it is not practical to separate them. This subsector includes leather making partly because leather tanning is a relatively small industry that has few close neighbors as a production process, partly because leather is an input to some of the other products classified in this subsector, and partly for historical reasons.

Source: U.S. Census Bureau (http://www.census.gov/eos/www/naics/).

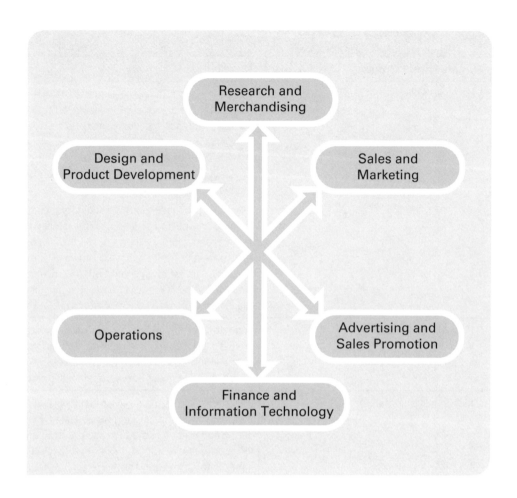

Figure 5.7
Organizational structure of a typical fashion brand company

Research and Merchandising

The term **merchandising** generally refers to the process of synthesizing information to make decisions about the characteristics of merchandise manufactured and/or sold by a company (e.g., product category, price, promotion, retail venue, etc.) This process includes conducting necessary trend and market research and developing strategies to get the right merchandise, at the right price, at the right time, in the right amount, to the right locations to meet the target consumers' wants and needs.

The merchandising area of fashion brand companies may include merchandise managers, merchandise coordinators, and fashion directors. These individuals research and forecast fashion trends and trends in consumer purchasing behavior in order to develop color, fabric, and garment silhouette directions for the company's merchandise. When making these forecasts, merchandisers interpret these trends for the company's target market, which includes characteristics of their customer's age, gender, income, and lifestyle. The role of merchandisers in fashion companies can vary. In some companies, they facilitate the creation of lines; in other companies, they oversee the fashion direction of the company. The merchandising function of the fashion brand companies is discussed in greater detail in later chapters.

Design and Product Development

The merchandisers work closely with those in the design and product development area, who interpret the trend forecasts and create designs to be manufactured by the company. Generally, merchandisers and designers work together on the seasonal and line planning. Those in the design and product development area include designers, assistant designers, product developers, stylists, pattern makers, and sample sewers. For companies that have their own factories, the design and product development area may also involve managing and operating the factories, including the employment and training of sewing operators.

The term **cross-merchandising** refers to the strategy used by fashion brand companies to combine apparel and accessories in their product offerings. Some apparel manufacturers create their own accessories to coordinate with their apparel lines. For example, Nike designs, markets, and sells "get fit kits" of merchandise for particular sports. The Nike running kit for women includes footwear, socks, running top and tights, sports bra, and running armband that holds a smartphone. Other companies form agreements to produce coordinating fashion merchandise. In skiwear, for example, one company may produce the outerwear apparel products, while another company produces the coordinating knit sweaters, headwear, and hand wear. Thus, the responsibility for manufacturing each type of product rests in the hands of the company with the required expertise and the best qualifications to produce it. Chapters 6 through 8 focus on the design and product development activities of fashion brand companies.

Figure 5.8
Sales and marketing: Designer Antonio Marras assists a model at a Kenzo showroom. Maitre /WWD/© Conde Nast.

Marketing and Sales

The marketing and sales area of the fashion brand company works to conduct marketing research and apply the results to better, design, merchandise, and sell the company's merchandise to the retail buyers and/or the ultimate consumer. The marketing and sales division includes those who conduct marketing research for the company as well as regional sales managers and sales representatives. The marketing and sales staff also show the company's merchandise to merchandisers and/or retail buyers in the company's showrooms during market weeks and at trade shows (Figure 5.8). Some companies employ their own sales staff; others contract with independent sales representatives to handle their merchandise. Chapter 9 discusses the marketing and sales activities of fashion brand companies.

Operations

The operations area includes the preproduction, material management, quality assurance, sourcing, production, distribution, and logistics functions. The preproduction, production, material management, and quality assurance areas of fashion brand companies include those people

Figure 5.9
The operations area of fashion brand companies includes sourcing, production, and quality assurance. Ye Aung Thu/AFP /Getty Images.

Figure 5.10
Sales promotions areas of fashion brand companies include sales events such as fashion shows and print advertisements in fashion magazines. Skip Bolen/WireImage/Getty Images.

involved with the material inspection and buying, production (Figure 5.9), and quality assurance. (Some companies refer to these activities as product engineering.) This area also includes those who identify and monitor domestic and foreign contractors to sew the garments, if the company contracts out these services. Once produced, merchandise is shipped and distributed to retailers. Production, planning, control, and distribution strategies of fashion brand companies will be discussed in later chapters.

Advertising and Sales Promotion

Working with the design and product development staff and the sales and marketing staff, those in the advertising and sales promotion area focus on creating promotional, advertising, and social media strategies and tools to sell the merchandise to the retail buyers and/or to the ultimate consumer (Figure 5.10). Often these services are contracted to an outside advertising agency that specializes in these activities.

Finance and Information Technology

Because all companies are in business to make a profit, effective financial management of companies is imperative to their success. More than simply "churning out numbers," those in the finance area of an apparel company are responsible for the overall financial health of companies and work closely with all other areas.

Because of the importance of computer systems in the design, production, distribution, and retailing of products and in the product data management of companies, information technology (IT) areas of companies play important roles in overseeing companies' computer operations. Those who work within IT must have technical expertise, and they must understand the operation of the fashion industries. Some companies have chosen to outsource their information technology area.

MERCHANDISING PHILOSOPHIES OF FASHION COMPANIES

The goal of the merchandising area is to make a profit by offering merchandise that meets the wants and needs of consumers. Thus, merchandisers set the overall direction for the merchandise assortment and work closely with the other areas of the apparel/accessory company that carry out the design, production, marketing, and distribution of the goods. Effective merchandising and product development depend on these factors:

- the company's product category (e.g., men's sportswear, women's dresses, children's outerwear, home fashions)
- the price zone(s) of its merchandise
- its marketing, advertising, and promotional strategies

Companies can be classified according to their merchandising philosophy, based on where in the product life cycle their merchandise belongs:

- *Design and/or technology innovators*: Design innovators depend on their innovative designs to attract their target market, which is generally composed of fashion innovators (Figure 5.11). Because their target market represents such a small number of customers, competition among design innovators is intense. The odds of a company succeeding are probably less than 1 percent. Designers for such fashion-forward companies often rely on their skill, reputation, and advertising to attract customers. Examples of brands representing design innovator companies include Alexander Wang, Betsey Johnson, Vivienne Westwood, and Anna Sui. Design innovators may also be small companies started by young designers who offer merchandise through boutiques and small specialty stores and that cater to customers who are fashion innovators. Some fashion brand companies are innovators in the incorporation of technology and performance characteristics. For example, Nike is typically an innovator in performance sportswear technologies.
- *Design or fashion interpreters*: Rather than creating their own design innovations, some fashion brand companies interpret successful innovative trends of other companies for their own target market.

Figure 5.11
A design innovator company, such as Alexander Wang, depends on innovative designs to attract its target market. Antonio de Moraes Barros Filho/Film Magic/Getty Images.

Although design skills and reputation are often key factors in the success of these interpreters, the risk of creating unsuccessful innovations is reduced.

- *Design or fashion imitators*: Imitators are those who produce affordable knockoffs or similar copies of fashions that have received media attention. Timing is crucial for the imitators, who must react immediately to new trends in the market. Companies that quickly reproduce gowns worn by celebrities at award shows (e.g., Academy Awards) are considered imitators.

Regardless of how innovative a company's merchandise is, all successful companies conduct some type of market research and typically obtain direct feedback from consumers on the product line through processes such as style testing. To be successful in today's global economy, companies must accurately assess consumer preferences, based on observational research, style testing, and analyses of trends in retail sales. Companies get sales information through their own retail venues or through partnerships with other retailers, and they can produce and ship merchandise quickly, often within weeks. As previously discussed, fashion companies such as Zara and H&M offer trendy merchandise very quickly by using a variety of methods to predict and accurately address consumers' preferences.

TRADE ASSOCIATIONS AND TRADE PUBLICATIONS IN THE FASHION INDUSTRIES

A number of trade associations in the fashion industries promote their industry segments, conduct market research, sponsor trade shows, and develop and distribute educational materials related to various segments of the fashion industries. For apparel and footwear, the largest of these associations is the American Apparel & Footwear Association (AAFA). Representatives of member companies and other professionals in the industry are active in many committees. Activities of the AAFA include

- compiling statistical information related to apparel manufacturing, industry forecasts, and trend forecasts
- publishing educational materials and information for use by industry analysts and company executives

Other trade associations focus their efforts on specific divisions of the RTW industry, such as intimate apparel, men's sportswear, or knitwear, to name just a few (Table 5.3).

Table 5.4 lists selected trade associations for accessories.

As with other fashion industries, the home fashions industry is supported by a number of industry-specific trade associations. Some overlap with the textile industry; for example, Cotton Incorporated serves all industries that use cotton. Some trade associations promote home furnishings or home fashions in general. Other trade associations, such as the Carpet and Rug Institute (CRI), focus on specific aspects of the industry. Table 5.5 lists selected trade associations in the home fashions industry.

Table 5.3 Selected Trade Associations in the Textile, Apparel, and Accessory Industries

Accessories Council	www.accessoriescouncil.org
American Apparel and Footwear Association (AAFA)	www.wewear.org
Americas Apparel Producers' Network (AAPN)	www.aapnetwork.net/
American Association of Textile Chemists and Colorists (AATCC)	www.aatcc.org/
American Textile Machinery Association	www.atmanet.org/home.aspx
Canadian Apparel Federation (CAF)	www.apparel.ca
Council of Fashion Designers of America	www.cfda.com
Fashion Footwear Association of New York	www.ffany.org/
Fashion Group International, Inc.	newyork.fgi.org
The Hosiery Association	hosieryassociation.com/
International Apparel Federation	www.iafnet.eu
International Association of Clothing Designers and Executives	www.iacde.net
International Fashion Jewelry and Accessory Group	www.ifjag.com
International Formalwear Association	www.formalwear.org/
International Glove Association	www.iga-online.com
International Swimwear/Activewear Market	www.isamla.com/
MAGIC International	www.magiconline.com/
National Shoe Retailers Association	www.nsra.org
Organic Trade Association	www.ota.com
Sewn Products Equipment Suppliers of the Americas	www.spesa.org/default.html
Sports and Fitness Industry Association	www.sfia.org
Underfashion Club	www.underfashionclub.org

Table 5.4 Selected Trade Associations for the Home Fashions Industry

Association	Website
American Home Furnishings Alliance (AFHA)	www.ahfa.us
Carpet and Rug Institute (CRI)	www.carpet-rug.org
International Furnishings and Design Association (IFDA)	www.ifda.com
International Home Furnishings Representatives Association (IHFRA)	www.ihfra.org
International Sleep Products Association (ISPA)	www.sleepproducts.org
North American Home Furnishings Association (NHFA)	www.nahfa.org
Upholstered Furniture Action Council (UFAC)	www.ufac.org
Window Coverings Association of America (WCAA)	www.wcaa.org

Table 5.5 Selected Trade Publications for the Fashion Apparel and Accessory Industries

Publication	Description	Web Address
Apparel Magazine	Targeted to apparel and soft goods businesses. Focus on business and technology.	apparel.edgl.com/home
California Apparel News	Covers fashion industry news with an emphasis on regional companies and markets on the West Coast.	www.apparelnews.net/
Earnshaw's Magazine	Targeted to retailers of fashion and accessories for newborns and young children.	www.earnshaws.com/
FN	Footwear news, fashion trends, and business strategies for footwear manufacturers and retailers.	footwearnews.com/
Just-style.com	General news for the international textile and apparel industries; market research reports and analyses.	just-style.com
Stores	Provides information of general interest, as well as reports on electronic commerce, loss prevention, and computer software and hardware.	nrf.com/connect-us/stores-magazine
WWD	Covers international news in the men's, women's, and children's fashion industry for retailers and manufacturers. Also covers textiles, accessories, and fragrances, in addition to apparel.	wwd.com

A number of trade publications focus on the fashion industries and are of use to professionals in these industries (Table 5.6 lists various trade publications in the fashion industries.) Many of these publications started as daily newspapers or weekly or monthly magazines (Figure 5.12). Most now are available in digital form, including those that are available only in electronic formats.

Table 5.6 Selected Trade Publications for the Home Fashions Industry

Publication	Description	Web Address
Bed Times	Business journal of the sleep products industry.	www.bedtimesmagazine.com
Floor Covering Weekly	Focuses on topics of interest to the flooring and interior sur-facing product industry; reports news to floor covering retailers, contract dealers, distributors, and manufacturers.	www.floorcoveringweekly.com
Furniture Today	News, trends, research and operations information for furniture store retailers.	www.fur024todaytoday.com/
HFN	Features in-depth news and analysis of products and retail trends in the home furnishings industry.	www.hfnmag.com
Home Accents Today	Focuses on merchandising and fashion news for the home accent industry; aimed at decorative accessory, specialty home accent, and gift buyers.	www.homeaccentstoday.com/
Home and Textiles Today	Focuses on marketing, merchandising, and retailing of home and textile products.	www.homeandtextilestoday.com/
Interior Design	For professional interior designers of office, commercial, and residential interiors.	www.interiordesign.net/

Figure 5.12
Digital formats of fashion media provide immediate access to marketing tools such as runway shows. Monica Schipper/Getty Images.

SUMMARY

Most of the fashion merchandise designed, produced, and sold today is considered ready-to-wear (RTW) or home fashions, ready to be used by the ultimate consumer. That is, the merchandise is completely made and ready to be worn or used at the time of purchase. RTW apparel and accessories are possible thanks to standardized sizing and mass-production techniques used in the apparel and accessory industries. Fashion brand companies typically produce four to six lines or collections corresponding to the fashion seasons: Spring, Summer, Fall I (Pre-Fall), Fall II, Holiday, and Resort or Cruise. Fast fashion companies can produce more than 12 lines per year.

Distinctions can be made between RTW and couture. In couture, garments are made to an individual's specific body measurements rather than to standardized sizes found in RTW. In addition, couture garments are generally made with some hand-sewing techniques and from more expensive materials than RTW. Haute couture collections are shown twice per year (in July and January) to the media, others in the fashion industry, and wealthy clients.

Based on their organization and operations, RTW fashion brand companies fall into the following categories: manufacturers, licensors, and retailers that sell private label fashion, including SPAs (specialty store retailer of private label apparel). Fashion brand companies are also classified according to the type of merchandise they produce, the price zones of their products or brands, and by the North American Industry Classification System (NAICS) established by the government.

A typical fashion brand company includes areas or divisions that focus on the following activities: research and merchandising; design and product development; marketing and sales; operations including production, planning, control, and distribution; advertising and sales promotion; and finance and information technology. Merchandisers set the overall direction for the merchandise assortment and work closely with other divisions of the company that carry out the design, production, marketing, and distribution of goods. Companies vary in their merchandising philosophies and may be innovators, interpreters, or imitators. All successful companies rely on consumer and market research, as well as sales data, for setting their fashion direction.

A number of trade associations in the fashion industries promote, conduct market research, sponsor trade shows, and develop and distribute educational materials related to various segments of the industries. Examples include the American Apparel and Footwear Association (AAFA) and the Carpet and Rug Institute (CRI). A number of trade publications focus on the apparel industry and are used by professionals in the fashion industries. Examples include *WWD*, *just-syle .com*, and *Apparel*.

KEY TERMS

atelier de couture
bespoke
boutique
bridge jewelry
collection
contractor
costume jewelry
couture
couture house
couturier, couturière
cross-merchandising
cut-up trade

diffusion line
fashion season
fast fashion
fine jewelry
full-package contractor (FP)
haute couture
home fashions
item house
licensor
line
manufacturer
merchandising

millinery
North American Industry
    Classification System (NAICS)
prêt-à-porter
price point
price zone
rack trade
ready-to-wear (RTW)
salon de couture
SPA
store brand

DISCUSSION QUESTIONS AND ACTIVITIES

1. Name your three favorite fashion brands. What companies manufacture these brands? How would you classify these brands in terms of product category and price zone?

2. Examine copies and/or online versions of trade publications in the fashion industry. To whom does each of the trade publications cater (i.e., what are the publications' target markets)? What types of information are included in the trade publications? How might this information be used by professionals in the industry?

3. Discuss the advantages and disadvantages of producing 4 seasonal lines per year versus 6 seasonal lines per year versus 12 lines per year. What are some examples of merchandise that is well suited to 4, 6, and 12 lines per year? Why?

4. In a fashion brand company, what role is played by each of the following divisions? Research and merchandising; design and product development; sales and marketing; operations including production, planning, control, and distribution; advertising and sales promotion; and finance and information technology. In which area would you like to have a career? Why?

Ralph Lauren:
Adding Another Diffusion Brand

According to investor relations of Ralph Lauren Corporation (2015),

Ralph Lauren Corporation is a leader in the design, marketing and distribution of premium lifestyle products in four categories: apparel, home, accessories and fragrances. For more than 47 years, Ralph Lauren's reputation and distinctive image have been consistently developed across an expanding number of products, brands and international markets. Luxury brand company, Ralph Lauren Corporation, has examined the pros and cons of adding diffusion brands over the course of its 40+ year history. The company has seen successes with diffusion brands at the bridge and better price zones including Polo Ralph Lauren, RRL & Co., and RLX. However, in 2013 they axed the diffusion line, Rugby. The time is right for the company to examine the opportunities and challenges with adding another diffusion line to their family of brands.

1. What are Ralph Lauren Corporation's current brands? For each brand, give a brief overview of the brand, price zone, and target customer. The following Ralph Lauren websites will be useful: Investor Relations website (http://investor.ralph lauren.com/phoenix.zhtml?c=65933&p=irol -irhome) and Ralph Lauren merchandise (http:// www.ralphlauren.com).

2. What are the current gaps in the company's family of brands? That is, given its orientation as a lifestyle brand, what lifestyles would add to the family of brands?

3. What are the advantages and disadvantages for Ralph Lauren Corporation to add another diffusion brand?

4. If you were a merchandiser for Ralph Lauren Corporation, would you recommend that Ralph Lauren Corporation add another diffusion brand? Why or why not?

Careers with the global fashion industry include positions in merchandising, product design and development, sales and marketing, preproduction, production, operations, information technology, and advertising/promotion. Career opportunities are identified in Chapters 6–13. Here are a few examples:

- Merchandise manager
- Accessories designer
- Product engineer
- Retail buyer

- Journalist for a fashion trade publication
- Marketing or communications professional for a fashion trade association

American Society for Testing and Materials (ASTM). http://www.astm.org/ (accessed March 4, 2016).

Fédération Française de la Couture du Prêt-à-Porter des Couturiers et des Créatures de Mode. http://www.modeaparis.com/ (accessed March 4, 2016).

North American Industry Classification System (NAICS). http://www.census.gov/eos/www/naics (accessed March 24, 2016).

PART II
Creating and Marketing a Fashion Brand

CHAPTER 6

Creating a Fashion Brand: Research

IN THIS CHAPTER, YOU WILL LEARN
THE FOLLOWING:

- the importance of research in establishing a fashion brand

- the various types of market research used to understand the target consumer

- conducting and interpreting market research for the fashion brand

- resources for fashion trends, color trend, and fabric/material trend forecasting

Step 1: Research and Merchandising

Step 1 Research and Merchandising

Market Research:	Fashion Research:
Consumer Research	Fashion Trend Research
Product Research	Color Research
Market Analysis	Material and Trim Research
Target Customer Profile	

Seasonal and Line Planning

Step 2 Design Brief

Step 3 Design Development and Style Selection

Step 4 Marketing the Fashion Brand

Step 5 Preproduction

Step 6 Sourcing

Step 7 Production Processes, Material Management, and Quality Assurance

Step 8 Distribution and Retailing

CREATING A FASHION BRAND

Developing a fashion brand involves a series of steps. Each step is closely related to and influenced by all the other steps in the process. The next several chapters will discuss these steps sequentially. The Eight Steps in the Design Process flowchart at the beginning of Part 2 will help acquaint you with the big picture. Each stage in the design process will be explored in greater detail in Parts 2 and 3. Step 1, Research, is discussed here in Chapter 6. The Step 1 flowchart at the beginning of this chapter shows the research step in detail. It is important to keep in mind that this is a generic flowchart. Some companies deviate from this sequence, for a variety of reasons. The industry is constantly changing in areas such as computer integration, speed of production, geographic location for production, regulations on goods manufactured in a country outside the domestic market, number of new products introduced each year, and distribution channels. These changes affect the sequence of steps in the design process. In addition, several activities may occur simultaneously during the progress of a brand's development.

The discussion of the creation, marketing, production, and distribution of a fashion brand in the following chapters is an overview of the processes that occur from the inception of a product until it reaches the ultimate customer. There are many variations of the specific sequence of processes used by companies. For the most part, a traditional design and manufacturing sequence of processes will be used to avoid confusion. Alternative possible sequences will be discussed where appropriate.

Just as fashion generally follows an evolutionary pattern, designers who work for companies generally create new seasonal lines and products in an ongoing, evolutionary manner. New products tend to develop from previous ones and may involve some repetition or modification of successful styles. In planning and development of a fashion brand, companies thoroughly consider the target customer, general market trends, fashion trends, color trends, fabric trends, and retailers' needs. Every successful company conducts research to determine what, why, and to whom its product should be marketed. This chapter explains how a company might conduct that research.

MARKET RESEARCH: UNDERSTANDING CONSUMER MARKET TRENDS

The most important concept for success in the fashion industry is that the company needs to know its target market and provide the merchandise assortment desired by its customers—when they want it and where they will purchase it. In other words, consumer demand is the driving force in the fashion industry. The industry expression, "You can make it only if it sells," emphasizes the concept of the consumer-driven market. Thus, the success of any fashion company depends on determining the needs and wants of the consumer. To determine what customers will need and want, and when and where they will want it, several types of research must be conducted. This process is called **market research**.

Market research can be defined as "the systematic and objective approach to the development and provision of information for the marketing management decision-making process" (Kinnear and Taylor 1983, p. 16). Market research is divided into two general categories (Kinnear and Taylor, p. 17):

1. basic research that deals with extending knowledge about the marketing system
2. applied research that helps managers make better decisions

Company executives, merchandisers, and designers conduct applied market research as a part of the planning process.

Applied market research includes three types of research:

- **consumer research**, which provides information about consumer characteristics and consumer behavior
- **product research**, which provides information about preferred product design and characteristics
- **market analysis**, which provides information about general market trends

All three types of market research are discussed in this chapter.

Each form of applied market research yields valuable information for company executives, merchandisers, and designers about the wants and needs of their target market customers. Some forms of market research take considerable time to conduct, analyze, and interpret. Thanks to the fast-paced nature of the fashion business, fashion products require a short research and development stage. Timing is crucial to the successful sale of a fashion item in the marketplace. Therefore, companies generally conduct market research continuously.

Trade associations, such as the American Apparel and Footwear Association and Cotton Incorporated, also conduct market research, providing information that can be helpful to apparel manufacturers and retailers. Examples of other sources of information to assist with conducting research are discussed in this chapter.

Consumer Research

Consumer research provides information about consumer characteristics and consumer behavior. Some forms of consumer research study broad trends in the marketplace. Research on **demographics** focuses on understanding the following characteristics of consumer groups:

- age
- gender
- marital status
- income
- occupation
- ethnicity
- geographic location

Consumer research may also focus on psychographics. Psychographic characteristics of consumer groups include

- buying habits
- attitudes
- values

- motives
- preferences
- personality
- leisure activities

Demographic information helps describe who the customer is, while psychographic information helps explain why customers make the choices they makes. Some of these demographic and psychographic characteristics are discussed further in the "Market Analysis" subsection of this chapter.

Numerous companies conduct consumer and market research. The ACNielsen Company was founded in 1928 and is considered the pioneer company in this field. Some market research companies include a fashion division. For example, NPD Fashionworld is the apparel division of NPD Group, a market research firm based in Cambridge, Massachusetts.

Fashion brand companies may conduct and interpret their own consumer research. For example, Macy's worked with the consulting firm dunnhumby to gather data through surveys, focus groups, store intercepts, and diaries of customer purchases to determine their customers' needs and wants. Peter Sachse, chief marketing director for Macy's, stated the one reassuring outcome of this research: "We don't need new customers. All we need to do is take care of the ones who already love us" ("NRF Retail Innovation" 2010, p. 22).

Consumer research is also conducted by companies expanding their markets to better understand the preferences of these new consumer groups. For example, some activewear companies in the United States have expanded into the Asian market. To successfully market a U.S. company's activewear apparel in Asia, it is important to research the Asian activewear consumer. It is essential to learn, among other things, that Asian women prefer activewear styles unlike those currently most popular in the United States.

Color preferences vary among countries and cultures. These preferences might be related to the country's climate, personal skin tones of the residents, or cultural heritage. When a company is expanding into a new market, consumer research focusing on color preferences of the intended new market is important for the success of the line.

Conducting consumer research related to fashion items can be a challenge. Purchase decisions are based on a number of factors—including psychological, social, and financial considerations—that consumers are often not conscious of. Therefore, results of market research indicate that consumers frequently do not purchase what they had indicated they would purchase when queried in advance.

Product Research

Product research provides information about preferred product design and product characteristics. When new products are developed, or existing products are modified, it is helpful to assess how well a new or revised product will fare in the marketplace. To determine customer preferences, companies could conduct product research such as the following:

- survey potential consumers orally
- send a questionnaire or post inquiries online

Sometimes a fashion brand company will conduct substantial market research before introducing a new line, especially if the company is interested in developing a new product type. Some large fashion brand companies , such as JCPenney (for its private label merchandise) and VF Corporation, have been testing style preferences for years.

Is it possible to predict how consumers will react to a style? Style testing techniques, refined by some of the most respected fashion brand companies, show that predicting what consumers will want to buy can be used. Some companies use outlet store sales to gather data on how consumers react to various styles and prices. Listening to comments from sales representatives, retailers, and customers about the success of a line provides part of the feedback necessary for continued success. Others use in-house video testing to guide the decisions of its buyers. One of the newest ways that companies are collecting data about their customers is through social media, such as Facebook and Twitter. Companies are not only setting up websites to advertise their products, but using social networking to ask customers what they want. Shannon Walton, a spokesperson for Schoeller, states, "The everyday user is available 24/7. We are taking a more social approach to the end user" (Walzer 2010, p. 18).

Market Analysis

Market analysis provides information about general market trends. Planning ahead to meet consumers' future needs is a critical part of continued success in the apparel industry. Market analysis in the apparel, accessories, and home fashions industries can be subdivided into long-range forecasting (or research) and short-range forecasting. **Long-range forecasting** projects market trends from one to five years in advance, while **short-range forecasting** focuses on market trends one year or less in advance. Both of these forecasting strategies are used in market analysis. Long-range forecasting includes researching economic trends related to consumer spending patterns and the business climate. Sample research questions include the following:

- Will interest rates be increasing on money borrowed by an apparel manufacturer to purchase fabric?
- Will corporate taxes for a company be increasing?
- Will cost-of-living expenses rise because of inflation, resulting in fewer apparel purchases by consumers?
- Will rising labor costs result in noticeable increases in the purchase price for the merchandise?

All of these trends can influence the company's plans and the consumer's future purchases.

Long-range forecasting also includes sociological, psychological, political, and global trends. For example, changes in international trade policies will affect long-range forecasting. Political fluctuations among countries can affect sourcing options when planning offshore production. Currency devaluation, economic downturn, and financial turmoil around the world affect the fashion industry.

Other aspects of long-range forecasting deal with ongoing changes in the fashion industry. Sources of information on these changes include the following:

- The *Apparel Strategist* (www.apparelstrategist.com) and *Just-Style* (just-style .com) conduct and publish market analyses in the fashion industry.
- NPD Group (www.npd.com) publishes online market research for the apparel and footwear industries.
- Kurt Salmon Associates (KSA) specializes in conducting and publishing soft goods business expertise and market analysis.

Numerous companies use these long-range market forecasts to influence their short-range fashion forecasts.

Many trend forecasting firms provide short-term and long-range trend forecasts. For example, Fiona Jenvey, CEO of Mudpie Ltd., states, "Currently there is a trend for longevity and classic as a reaction to both considered consumption and sustainability (buy better less often); this translates in fashion to vintage, design re-issues, or 'vintage inspired'. Retailers and designers should use trend information as a tool for creating an original desirable product, which represents the values of the brand" (Fibre2Fashion 2010).

Also, companies are becoming more socially responsible. As consumers' awareness about global social issues continues to grow, so does the importance these customers place on CSR (corporate social responsibility) when choosing where to shop (Taylor 2015).

"Technology has brought global connectivity and enabled advocacy and awareness for social situations that were once obscure," said Alexis Magnan-Callaway, whose fashion company Pax Cult donates 10 percent of its profits to an organization of the customer's choice. "Millennials are redefining what it means to connect and give back through this technology. It's not just about having a recycling program or sustainable products. People want to feel good about what their dollar is doing" (quoted in Taylor 2015).

Short-range forecasting is critical to a fashion brand's success. Planning meetings are held with designers, merchandisers, planners, and sales personnel to discuss the company's short-range forecasts and strategic planning. This planning includes such components as determining the desired percentage of increased sales growth for a company. For example, perhaps the company managers have determined that a 5 percent growth in sales should be planned. The designer for each apparel line the company produces may be asked to increase the line with a 5 percent sales growth factor in mind. Using sales figures from the current selling season, the designer (and merchandiser) may select one or several styles that are selling particularly well and add one or several similar styles to the upcoming line. Short-range forecasting also includes careful study of what the competition is doing. If a competitor seems to be expanding one of its lines—for example, the water sports category of apparel—then perhaps your company would be wise to study whether this growth area would be feasible to pursue. Fashion companies constantly observe the marketplace competition.

Brand Positioning

Each fashion brand company's goal is to position its lines to be different from the competition and enticing to potential customers. The merchandising and design staff's objective is to develop the right product for the company's target customer

(a)

(b)

at the right time in the marketplace. The result is called its **brand positioning**. Eddie Bauer, headquartered in Seattle, describes its brand position as follows:

> Innovation, quality and an appreciation of the outdoors: The passions of our founder, Eddie Bauer, remain the cornerstone of the Eddie Bauer business today. In conjunction with innovative design and exceptional customer service, Eddie Bauer offers premium-quality clothing, accessories, and gear for men and women that complement today's modern lifestyle. (Eddie Bauer 2016)

A company has a brand position in the marketplace, and each line produced by the brand company requires a clearly defined **target customer** (Figure 6.1).

FASHION RESEARCH

In addition to market research, fashion research is conducted. Fashion research focuses on trends in styles, colors, fabrics, materials, and trims. Similar to market research, fashion research may be conducted and interpreted by fashion research or forecasting firms.

Figure 6.1
The target customer for Marc lines (a) is similar to the target customer for the more expensive Marc Jacobs designer lines for women (b). The main difference between the two markets is the price zone. (6.1a) Chinsee/WWD /© Conde Nast. (6.1b) Aquino /WWD/© Conde Nast.

Fashion forecasting relies on understanding the current style and the evolutionary process that occurred to make a style popular. Forecasters are constantly following fashion history to determine the next trend. Events and the general spirit of popular culture might be reflected in new fashions. This social "spirt of the times" is known as the **zeitgeist**.

Fashion Trend Research

Trend research activities include reading or scanning appropriate **trade publications**. Each segment of the fashion industry has specific trade media directed toward fashion trends in that industry segment. Examples include the following:

- *WWD.com* offers comprehensive coverage of fashion, beauty, and retail news.
- *Earnshaw's (earnshaws.com)* focuses on children's wear and juvenile product industry.
- *FN (footwearnews.com)* focuses on the footwear industry.
- *Sportswear International (http://www.sportswear-international.com/)* focuses on denim and other sportswear for men, women, and children.

Online versions of these trade publications provide general information; fashion professionals will subscribe to those most relevant to their industry.

Popular fashion magazines, read by the target customer, are sources for fashion trend information and provide an insight into the preferences of the customer. Designers and merchandisers peruse the appropriate publications, depending on their target market. Examples of popular fashion magazines include *Vogue, Elle, Harper's Bazaar, W, Glamour, Allure, Vanity Fair, Essence, In Style, Seventeen, Maxim,* and *GQ* (Figure 6.2). These magazines are readily available to the public online and in print formats at news and magazine stands and bookstores. European **fashion magazines**—such as *French Vogue, Italian Vogue, Elegance,* and *Book Moda Alta Moda* (women's wear); *Book Moda Uomo* and *Vogue Homme* (menswear); and *Vogue Bambini* (children's wear)—are important sources for fashion trends.

Figure 6.2
Popular fashion magazines are a source of fashion trend information. JOEL SAGET/AFP /Getty Images.

Fashion brand companies and retailers often subscribe to **fashion forecasting services**. Some of these forecasting services cover a broad range of fashion trends. Some specialize in color trends while others provide both fashion trend and color trend analysis. Here are some examples of fashion trend forecasting services based in the United States:

- The Doneger Group, based in New York, provides merchandising consulting and fashion trend and color forecasts for the apparel and accessories markets. The Doneger Group publishes the *Tobe Report*, a fashion consulting publication for retailers.
- Margit Publications, a division of the Doneger Group, publishes a variety of trend and color forecasts.
- Here & There provides trend and color forecasts as well as collections reports, retail reports, and textile reports.
- Trend Union is a fashion trend, fabric, and color trend forecasting service based in Paris that conducts fashion and fabric trend seminars in locations such as New York, Seattle, San Francisco, and Los Angeles several times a year in addition to its forecasting publications.
- Promostyl provides trend books focusing on menswear, women's wear, sportswear, streetwear, youth, and accessories. The company produces style trends, color trends, and fabric trend books. Based in Paris, Promostyl continuously sponsors conferences in many major cities throughout the world.
- Worth Global Style Network (WGSN) is an example of an online subscription fashion resource. WGSN provides research, trend analysis, and news service daily to its online subscribers.

Recent runway shows are another source of fashion trend information. Several resources, including many websites, provide runway images of recent designs shown in Milan, Paris, London, and New York. These sources show examples of current fashions, rather than forecasting future trends. However, many of the new styles shown are those that set new trends and offer a sense of fashion direction for many moderate- and mass-priced manufacturers. Some sources are accessible without a fee, whereas other sources require an online subscription. Often a free introductory preview is available to assess the usefulness of a source before subscribing. A big advantage of these online sources, like online magazines, is their ease of accessibility.

The design team often attends fashion trade shows geared to a specific segment of the market. Trade shows are held in various locations around the world, from Las Vegas to Beijing. Attendance at trade shows might be for a variety of purposes. Often the attendee's company is represented at the trade show. Some designers and merchandisers attend trade shows specifically to view the latest trends. An added benefit for those going to trade shows is the opportunity to attend fashion trend and color forecasting seminars geared to a specific product market, such as that presented by Outdoor Retailer.

Computer software programs have been developed to assist with consumer-driven fashion forecasting. Some software programs provide more than total sales figures. The software enables an apparel company to determine specifically who is buying what, and where, taking into account factors such as weather, special events in the area, and store promotions.

Fashion trend research also involves **shopping the market**. Although this sounds like fun, it actually requires considerable focus and constant vigilance. Merchandisers and designers look for new trends that may influence the direction of an upcoming line. Design details in the bodices of evening wear may inspire a design detail in a swimsuit, for example. One aspect of shopping the market involves visiting retail stores that carry the company's line. Talking with retailers about how the line is selling can yield helpful information for predicting fashion trends. Watching retail store customers' reactions to the line provides helpful feedback. Studying the competitors' lines in retail stores is also important for predicting trends.

The fantasy aspect of trend research involves viewing the high-fashion couture and ready-to-wear collections in Paris, Milan, London, Tokyo, and New York. Designers and merchandisers for some apparel companies are assigned to view these twice-yearly collections. The high-fashion collections are often filled with avant-garde styles that target customers probably would not wear. However, important fashion trends can be extracted and then modified for a line in the moderate price zone.

Some designers and merchandisers also study customers on the street; or, if the line is an active sportswear line, they go to the ski slopes or the beach and watch potential customers participating in the specific sport. Fashion reflects the time and the lifestyle of the society from which—and for which—it is created. Therefore, trend research continuously involves collecting information from multiple sources. The design team does not create in a vacuum; instead, it is influenced by everything, on a daily basis. It is important for design teams to visit art museums, concerts, and movies, and to participate in other activities that expose them to fashion-related trends.

Color Research and Resources

When color trends in apparel, accessories, or home fashions are reviewed over time, it becomes clear that certain staple colors appear frequently in the fashion cycle. In apparel, black, navy, white, and beige are considered staple colors and are seen almost continuously season after season. Each line includes one or more **staple colors**. Pendleton Woolen Mills is known for maintaining several staple colors in its classic apparel lines. Pendleton's tartan navy and tartan green are examples of colors that are color matched season after season. If a customer has purchased a navy Pendleton jacket from its classic line, a pair of navy slacks purchased several years later will match the color of the jacket (unless the jacket has faded due to improper care or excessive wear). Pendleton tracks the sales, ranked by dollar volume and color, to ensure that long-term, high-selling colors are represented in each line. Talbots is another company that provides color-matched apparel season after season. The Talbots true red, #25, and cherry red, #26, are examples of colors that are continued season after season.

Some companies vary a staple color slightly from season to season to reflect fashion influences. In one season, a navy may be a violet-navy; in another season, the navy may be a black-navy. This variation lends an updated fashion look to staple colors. If a print fabric in the line contains navy, then the navy in the print fabric needs to match the solid navy.

Other colors, called **fashion colors**, appear less frequently over time than staple colors. Fashion colors often follow cycles, reappearing in a different shade, value, or intensity from one fashion season to the next. For example, an orange-red may evolve into a blue-red, which may evolve into a blue-magenta. It is interesting to follow the trend of a fashion color over a period of years. A color such as aubergine (eggplant) will recur every few years. It may be slightly redder one season, slightly bluer another. For those who have tried to match the color of an item purchased in a previous season or year, it becomes painfully obvious that the life cycle of some fashion colors is very short. Some customers have learned to purchase all color-matched pieces of a line at one time to avoid disappointment later, when they might be unable to match the color of a shirt they would like to purchase for wearing with the pants they bought a year earlier.

Some fashion colors sell more readily, and, therefore, tend to reappear more frequently than others. Designers and merchandisers keep in mind color preferences of their target customers as they look at color trends. For example, in the United States, dark reds and wine tones tend to recur often. Blue is a color that typically flatters people's personal coloring and therefore occurs frequently in the color cycle.

The color forecasting services used by textile producers are also used by fashion brand companies. These services study color trends in textiles, apparel, home fashions, and related fields. Some color forecasting services predict color trends 18 months in advance of when the product is available to consumers, while others, for a higher subscription fee, predict farther ahead. An apparel company subscribes to the color forecasting service based on the product category, such as men's suits or outer wear, as well as how far in advance the forecasts are provided. Most services publish color forecasts twice a year for fashion merchandise (Figure 6.3).

Resources for color forecasting services based in the United States include the following:

Figure 6.3
Color trend reports are issued by color forecasting services. Image Source/Getty Images.

- Color Association of the United States (CAUS) produces seasonal predictions with fabric swatches twice a year. Annual memberships range from $650 to $1,350 and include two seasonal forecasts for one category (women's, men's, youth, interiors/environmental).
- Pantone, based in Carlstadt, New Jersey, publishes the Pantone View Color Planner twice a year, providing seasonal color direction 24 months in advance, and offers color consulting services. Pantone View Home is targeted to the home fashions industry.
- Here & There, mentioned earlier in this chapter, provides both fashion trend and color forecasting services.
- Huepoint Color is an American color company dedicated to forecasting the best seasonal colors and color standards on different formats such as cotton yarn, cotton fabric, or color standards for printing, such as CMYK (cyan, magenta, yellow, and key (black)) and RGB (red, green, blue).

These are just a few of the many color resources available. Most fashion companies subscribe to several color forecasting services to achieve a broader view of color trends.

Many people wonder how color trends are determined. Does someone predict that ruby red will be the color of the fall season, and that all designers will then include ruby red in their lines? Although this is not the case, color forecasting services do conduct color research to assist the fashion industry in assessing the color trends. Some U.S. forecasters rely on the color directions of fabric producers in Europe. They might watch to see whether these colors are adopted by fashion-forward designers and consumer fashion innovators in the United States. Other color forecasting services will focus on analyzing trends in consumer color preferences through sales data.

From the wide variety of possible colors, the color forecasting service identifies a palette of certain hues, values, and intensities that reflect upcoming color trends. Many apparel companies subscribe to several color forecasting services. It is interesting and informative to compare the similarities and differences of several color forecasting services' predictions for the same season.

The color trends presented by the color forecasting services are represented by a grouping of paint chips, fabric swatches, or yarn pompons, arranged attractively in a spiral-bound notebook or magazine format. These color palette charts may include up to several dozen colors. The colors selected tend to span a range of darks and lights, neutrals, and fashion colors. Thus, one color service will not predict all dark colors while another service shows all light colors. Designers and merchandisers will be able to identify certain overall trends recurring among the various color forecasting services.

After studying the color trends, designers and merchandisers will select a **color palette**, or color story, for the upcoming season, taking into consideration the many factors important to the success of their line. A designer may note that varying shades of purple have appeared in many of the color forecasts, indicating a purple trend. Some services provide fashion names for the color chips. The various shades of purple might be named violet, plum, dahlia, wisteria, African violet, and lavender. The specific name may be transferred to the color name used by the fashion brand company for that color, or the fashion brand company may create a new name to identify its company's seasonal color. The theme of a line might be linked to the color names used. For example, color names such as adobe, cactus, sage, and sandstone might be selected to correlate with a Southwestern theme for a line.

Fabric and Trim Research and Resources

The designer and merchandiser research the fabric and trim market in addition to studying fashion and color trends. The designer does fabric research, beginning with such broad fabric trends as the use of spandex blended with wool for career apparel or the use of microfibers for men's suits and raincoats. This research might include such trends as using metallic fibers in fabrics or chenille yarns in suiting. Resources for this type of fabric research include the same trade publications that designers and merchandisers use for fashion trends, as well as textile trade publications.

For more specific fabric trends, textile mills, textile trade associations, and textile manufacturers are eager to acquaint designers with the latest fibers, fabrics, and textures. Fabric manufacturers employ sales representatives who supply designers with fabric swatch cards, usually in response to a phone call by the design team member to the textile sales representative. Sample yardage can also be ordered from the sales representative. Many fabric manufacturers have showrooms in New York and other cities that display the latest fabrics. The textile trade associations' headquarters are excellent resources as well. For example, a designer might visit the New York office of Cotton Incorporated to research a wide range of woven and knit cotton fabrications.

An effective way to research fabric resources is to visit one of the textile trade shows. The shows are usually held twice a year, in the fall and spring. American fabric manufacturers hold their textile trade shows in New York and Los Angeles. Here, many fabric manufacturers have booths displaying the latest and most enticing fabrics. Smaller shows also are held in cities such as Chicago and Seattle.

Some of the international fabric manufacturers bring their fabric lines to New York and Los Angeles to show to the American designers who are not able to travel to Europe. For example, Première Vision Preview New York features Italian, French, Spanish, Austrian, and Portuguese fabrics. The Los Angeles International Textile Show features both imported and domestic fabrics, trims, and findings.

Some designers travel to the European textile trade shows held twice a year to see the latest goods produced by fabric manufacturers in Europe. Most notable of the foreign textile trade shows include the following:

- Première Vision, showcasing Europe's fabric manufacturers, is held in Paris (Figure 6.4).
- Texworld is also held in Paris twice a year, showcasing fabrics from 42 countries.

Figure 6.4
Designers attend textile trade shows for fabric research and inspiration. Stan Honda/AFP /Getty Images.

- Italian fabrics are featured along with those of many other countries at Ideacomo and Ideabiella near Milan.
- Prato Expo in Florence, Italy, hosts textile companies from Europe, North America, and Asia.
- Interstoff Asia, held in Hong Kong, provides an opportunity to feature Asian-produced textiles.

Designers can place orders for **sample cuts** from the textile producers. Each cut is usually three to five yards long, enough yardage to produce a prototype garment that enables designers to evaluate possible uses of the fabric. At a trade show, an apparel company can place an order for delivery of sample cuts. Sample cuts can also be ordered directly from the sales representative after the trade show. For many designers, though, these textile shows serve a purpose similar to that of couture design shows—as an inspiration and a means to sift through the multitude of ideas for trends appropriate to their company's target customers.

Some types of apparel are especially suited to the use of specialty trims and fasteners. Outdoor activewear is one example. A new design idea might be sparked by a novelty trim or fastener. Research of new products is an important aspect for designers and merchandisers. Product trade shows, trade publications, and specialty trim sales representatives are sources of information about new products.

Armed with information from market research—fashion and color trend research, and fashion forecasts—a company's design team or creative director is ready to bring everything together and create a new line.

SUMMARY

Creating a fashion product or brand begins with research. Sales figures from the current selling season are taken into consideration as the company plans the upcoming season. However, a fashion brand company that only repeats what has sold well in the past cannot survive for long. Market research is often conducted to help predict what specific items or general trends will appeal to customers in the upcoming season. A fashion company must consider both long- and short-term forecasts. Long-range forecasting includes major social, economic, retail, apparel manufacturing, and customer trends. Short-range forecasting is also tied to the economy, political climate, availability of resources, and customer needs. The target customer profile, describing such aspects as the target customer's age, lifestyle, and intended price zone, requires constant updating and careful consideration when creating fashion brand.

brand positioning
color palette
consumer research
demographics
fashion color
fashion forecasting service
fashion magazine

long-range forecasting
market analysis
market research
popular fashion magazine
product research
psychographics
sample cut

shopping the market
short-range forecasting
staple color
target customer
trade publication
trend research
zeitgeist

DISCUSSION QUESTIONS AND ACTIVITIES

1. What are some examples of trends that can be predicted by long-range forecasting (perhaps five years from now)? How might these trends affect a company's product?

2. What are some examples of short-range trend forecasting (perhaps six months from now) in men's apparel, women's apparel, and children's apparel? How might these trends be reflected?

3. Describe what you perceive as the target customer profile for the following national brands: lululemon, Polo Ralph Lauren, and Tommy Hilfiger.

4. What are some current color trends in women's wear? In menswear? What color or colors do you predict will be popular next season in women's wear? In menswear? Why do you think these colors will be popular?

5. What are some fabric trends that are on the upswing in the fashion cycle?

6. What are some examples of specific sources of research information for designers and merchandisers? How would you locate examples of these sources?

CASE STUDY

Carter's, Inc. and Organic Cotton

Carter's, Inc. is a publicly traded corporation headquartered in Atlanta, Georgia, USA. It is "is the largest branded marketer in the United States and Canada of apparel and related products exclusively for babies and young children." The company's family of brands includes Carter's and OshKosh B'gosh national brands, which are sold worldwide through department stores, specialty stores, company-owned stores in the United States and Canada, and online. In addition, Carter's Inc. has exclusive licensing agreements with Target (Just One You, Genuine Kids, and Precious Firsts brands) and with Walmart (Child of Mine) for private label merchandise.

Cotton plays an important role in all of Carter's, Inc. brands, and sourcing ethically grown and harvested cotton materials is integral to Carter's, Inc. corporate social responsibility program. For example, because of government-sanctioned use of forced child labor in the harvesting of cotton in Uzbekistan, Carter's, Inc. prohibits the use of any cotton from Uzbekistan in its products. In addition, in an effort to end this practice, Carter's, Inc. has partnered with other companies in signing the Responsible Sourcing Network's Uzbekistan Cotton Pledge.

Should Carter's Add an Organic Cotton Line?

As Carter's, Inc. moves forward with its corporate social responsibility strategies, the company is investigating the use of organic cotton in some of its products. A number of competitors of the Carter's and Oshkosh B'gosh brands have added organic cotton options to their baby wear and accessories (e.g., blankets). The time is right for Carter's to weigh the advantages and disadvantages of adding an organic cotton line of baby clothes and accessories.

1. Select either the Carter's or Oshkosh B'gosh brand of baby wear; then answer these questions:
   a. Who is the target customer for this brand?
   b. Describe the primary merchandise offerings of this brand and where the brand is sold.
   c. What are three competitors of this brand? Describe target customer and merchandise.

2. What forecasting services might Carter's use to assist in its analysis of using organic cotton for baby wear and accessories?

3. What are the advantages and disadvantages of using organic cotton for baby wear and accessories? List and describe at least three advantages and disadvantages of using organic cotton in baby wear and accessories.

4. In your opinion, should Carter's, Inc. add a line of organic baby wear and accessories to either of its Carter's or Oshkosh B'gosh brands of baby wear and accessories? Why or why not? Justify your recommendation and cite relevant references.

Source: Carter's, Inc. (2016). Carter's, Inc. http://corporate.carters.com/corporateHome.html (accessed March 6, 2016).

CAREER OPPORTUNITIES

Possible positions in fashion research include

- Fashion forecaster
- Trend analyst
- Lifestyle analyst
- Consumer researcher
- Shopper
- Research assistant

REFERENCES

Eddie Bauer. (2016). "About Eddie Bauer." http://www.eddiebauer.com/company-info/company-info-about-us.jsp (accessed March 22, 2016).

Fibre2Fashion. (2010). "Face2Face: Ms. Fiona Jenvey, CEO and Founder, Mudpie Ltd." http://www.fibre2fashion.com/face2face/mudpie-ltd/ms-fiona-jenvey.asp (accessed March 6, 2016).

Kinnear, Thomas C., and James R. Taylor. (1983). Marketing Research: An Applied Approach. New York: McGraw-Hill Book Company, 16–17.

"NRF Retail Innovation and Marketing Conference Highlights." (2010) Stores, April 4, pp. 22–23.

Taylor, Nicole F. (2015, June 19). "What Is Corporate Social Responsibility?" http://www.businessnewsdaily.com/4679-corporate-social-responsibility.html (accessed March 6, 2016).

Walzer, Emily (Ed.). (2010a). "Consumer Connections." Textile Insight, January/February, p. 18.

Creating a Fashion Brand: Design Brief

IN THIS CHAPTER, YOU WILL LEARN THE FOLLOWING:

- development and use of a design brief

- use of a design brief in developing a line of fashion merchandise

- job responsibilities of the design and merchandising team in designing a line

- the ways computer-aided design and graphic design software systems are used in the design process

- the use of product life cycle management systems to track each style as it progresses through the design, style selection, marketing, preproduction, production, and distribution processes

Step 2: Design

Step 1 Research and Merchandising

Step 2 Design Brief

Design Inspiration

Plan the Line

Sketch Design and Obtain Vendor Samples

Select or Develop Materials and Trims

Review and Select Styles to Develop for Line

Write Garment Specifications Sheet and Quick Cost

Step 3 Design Development and Style Selection

Step 4 Marketing the Fashion Brand

Step 5 Preproduction

Step 6 Sourcing

Step 7 Production Processes,
Material Management, and Quality Assurance

Step 8 Distribution and Retailing

DESIGN BRIEF

The second step in creating a line is the development of the design brief and actual creation of the products. As shown in Figure 7.1, designing the products is the responsibility of both designers and merchandisers. This chapter explains how the design brief is used and developed to create a fashion brand.

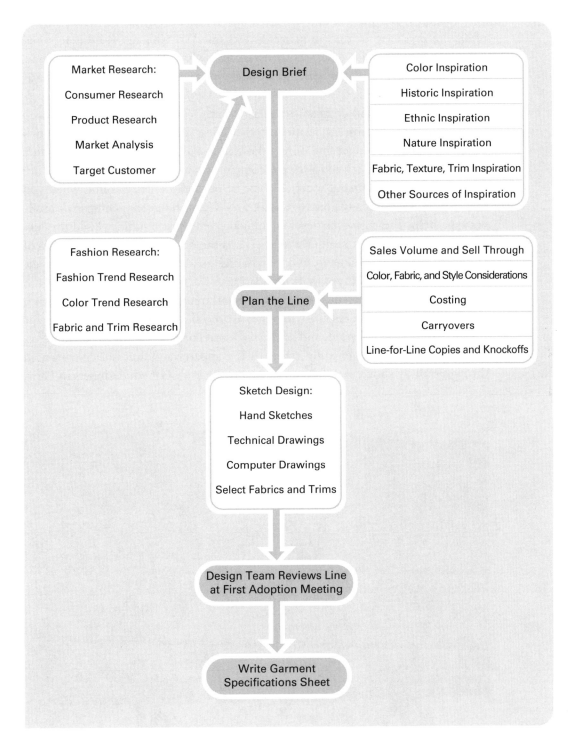

Figure 7.1
Step 2 Design expanded to show how a new line is created. Meißner /ullstein bild via Getty Images.

Most fashion brand companies collect the different parts of their research to develop what is known as a design brief. The design brief allows all aspects of the company to have a common focus in its design strategy.

The **design brief** is a document that is developed by both designers and merchandisers, often under the approval of a creative director. This document is a guide for designers and includes the business aspects of the company to help develop a unified brand identity and strategy. A brief often includes information related to target customers, target theme or inspiration, deliverables, timeline, and budget. Development of a design brief creates an outline for development of all the lines within the company. As explained in Chapter 6, designers and merchandisers conduct research to determine what the brief should include. Research and forecasting are often done at a corporate level and become the basis for the design brief.

Many fashion brand companies specialize in a certain type of product, such as casual clothes, swimwear, footwear, or evening wear. The apparel company's **product type**, or product line, forms the basis for developing its fashion brand. For example, Lacoste is known for the company's polo-style knit shirts. If you are familiar with this company, a certain type of product comes to mind when you think about the company's name (Figure 7.2). Consistency in a company's product type helps the customer develop company brand recognition, build product loyalty, and encourage repeat customers. Thus the design team, which consists of designers, product developers, and merchandisers, develops the line for the new season with the product type as its foundation.

The deliverables of a design brief for a fashion brand company are often a combination of items presented together to the buying public for a particular season. The terms *line*, *group*, and *collection* are used to describe the group of items. The term **collection** generally refers to the apparel and accessories presented through runway shows each fall and spring by the high-fashion designers in Paris,

Figure 7.2
Consumers associate the name of a company, such as Lacoste, with a specific fashion image.

Milan, New York, London, Tokyo, and other locations. The runway shows of designer collections for women's wear often include a wide range of fashion items, including swimwear, dresses, suits, sportswear, evening wear, and, of course, bridal wear as the finale. The designer collections may include from 100 to 150 items. Collections reflect the design philosophy of the head designer. The high-fashion name designers typically develop a theme for a collection and invest heavily in marketing that theme to retailers and the public. Often the designer's theme is based on historical or ethnic inspiration. Fashion silhouettes or garment details popular during historical periods are a source of design inspiration.

A **line** consists of one large group or several small groups of apparel and/or accessory items, or styles, developed around the design brief. A theme may be used to direct color, fabric, design details, or a purpose (such as golf or tennis) that links the items together (Figure 7.3). A line is composed of a variety of items or styles within a category, such as shirts, pants, jackets, vests, and sweaters. Each line is developed for a specific target customer and might include as many as 50 or 60 items. A designer, often with a team of several others, such as a design assistant and a product developer, is assigned responsibilities for creating the line. Some designers have responsibility for several lines. Sometimes, several small **groups** are developed within a line, each with its own theme. For example, a group might use three to five fabrics in varying combinations and include approximately a dozen apparel items, all carefully coordinated.

Whereas many fashion brand companies focus on developing seasonal lines (typically four to six seasons per year), some fashion brand companies develop new groups to ship every four to six weeks throughout the year. This merchandising strategy places new merchandise in retail stores at frequent intervals, so it entices many customers to shop often. Another merchandising strategy focuses on continually providing new. For example, the fast fashion company Zara uses a quick-cycle approach to design-produce-distribute. Zara designs the product as well as

Figure 7.3
A line is a group of products developed around a common theme. WWD/© Conde Nast.

owns its retail stores; therefore, it can quickly design, produce, and distribute new merchandise. New styles arrive in Zara's retail stores weekly.

Just as fashion, in general, follows an evolutionary pattern, designers who work for fashion brand companies generally create new seasonal lines in an ongoing, evolutionary manner. New lines tend to develop from previous lines, along with some repetition or modification of successful styles. Styles repeated from one seasonal line to the next are called **carryovers**. The target customer, general market trends, fashion trends, color trends, fabric trends, and retailers' needs are all carefully considered when planning and developing a line that represents the fashion brand and are outlined in the design brief.

CREATING A DESIGN BRIEF

The design team uses the design brief to communicate the common goal of a line. Balancing the relationships among the current fashion brand's look, making the changes that need to occur in the product to maintain interest and offer fashion change, and keeping the target customer happy are all responsibilities of the design team. The brief explains the target customer, but it also describes characteristics of the designs, such as the theme or inspiration, colors, and fabrics.

Target Customer

In creating a line, the design team must keep the target customer profile in mind throughout the design process. The type of product included in the line is strongly connected to the company's target customer. The blend of product type with target customer is referred to as the **market niche**. Developing and maintaining a line based on the market niche is important to the success of the line. The line for the new season will include some variation of styles to appeal to different customers' needs and tastes within the market niche. Based on the changing needs and preferences of the target customer, a company's product line may change over time. A design brief communicates these changes and is why the changes are so important. If the product line does not change at all, customers might become bored with the same look and decide they do not need to purchase another item so similar to those they already own. Here are some examples of product line changes:

- A company might decide to change the direction of its product from a focus on career suits to a focus on coordinated separates after sensing that women are no longer interested in the look of a matched suit.
- A sportswear company may decide to add a golf apparel group to its product line because golf is becoming popular among its target customers.

A design brief includes a detailed target customer profile. A photograph of typical customers might be included with the target customer profile statement to help merchandisers, designers, product developers, and sales representatives visualize them. The models used for product advertisements are also selected to portray the image of the target customer. The design team relies on the target customer profile

- to identify market trends, especially those related to its target customer
- to develop the initial direction for the line
- to develop style sketches (concept sketches) and color concepts

A study of the target customer's lifestyle might include information such as the following:

- type of career
- stage in career
- geographic location and its population size
- social or political direction
- education
- attitudes
- values
- interest in fashion (e.g., prefers classic looks or is a fashion trendsetter)
- price consciousness

Lifestyle preference descriptions could suggest that the target customer is focused on entertainment or is comfortable with technology. Obtaining such results through lifestyle research can help define the various target groups.

The term **lifestyle merchandising** was coined to recognize the importance of appealing to the target customer's lifestyle choices. The proliferation of popular lifestyle magazines, direct mail catalogs, and websites indicates the importance of appealing to customers' lifestyles. For example, the fitness market has a myriad of lifestyle magazines. Not surprisingly, some fashion brand companies design merchandise to appeal to a specific lifestyle preference.

Theme

Based on market research, design inspirations, and discussions among the designers and merchandisers who are coordinating the various lines for a company, a theme might be developed to be included in the design brief. Not every group or line will have a theme, but a theme can help sell a group or a line to retailers and consumers. In some cases, an advertising campaign may be developed around a chosen theme. For example, a company producing an outdoor fishing group might use the theme of a popular sport fish. The theme might be carried through in the graphic art used on items in the group.

Color, Fabric, and Style Considerations

The design team studies color trend reports gathered during the research phase. Members discuss possible groups of colors, also referred to as **color stories**, for the new line while thinking about a color theme. The theme might be reflected in the colors chosen for some of the new styles. For example, the colorations seen on a golden trout might inspire the color story for a group of fishing apparel. Colors for fabrics used in the group might include various hues, tones, and values of the golden trout's colorations. A graphic design of a golden trout leaping up to catch a fishing fly could be created for a T-shirt in the line. A small version of the leaping trout could be used as an embroidered or printed motif on other pieces in the group. As another example, an Americana theme might be chosen for a group of misses pieces in a Spring collection with a "country flavor" that features fabrics in ruby red, navy blue, and bisque colors in solids, small prints, and plaids.

Based on the color research conducted, the design team develops a color story. Lines need a balance between some staple colors and some fashion colors. The line needs to have a cohesive look, so the team spends a great deal of time deciding on the correct balance of colors. The group of colors selected for the line may need to include a color that the design team does not expect to sell well because they know that buyers expect to see a balance of colors in the color group (e.g., a light color may be needed to balance the color story of a group of medium and dark colors).

Most styles will be produced in more than one color. A specific style may be available in three or four different solid colors, or in three or four color variations of the same print. The varieties of colors available for a style are called **colorways**. Producing the same style in several colorways reduces development cost since fewer patterns, spec sheets, prototypes, and cost estimates need to be prepared than if each style were produced in only one colorway. This variety also offers more options to retailers that might want to buy part of a line but not duplicate the same colorways that competing local retailers will offer in their stores. It also allows retailers to select the colorway choices that they think are best suited for their customers.

Designers typically attend textile trade shows and are aware of the new colors and fabrics available. Fabric and materials vendors will provide samples of fabrics and other materials that the design team is considering for use in the upcoming line. Therefore, decisions about the colors and fabrics are frequently made before determining the garment styles. The new line needs to strike a balance among the colors, styles, and prices offered.

Design Brief Uses

Although the research and design inspiration stages of the design process—consisting of market research as well as trend, color, and fabric/trim research—continues throughout the year, at a specified time in the year, the design team must begin to develop concrete ideas from the design brief. Based on the number of lines a company produces each year, each fashion brand company maintains a master calendar with target due dates for completing the stages of creating and producing each line (see the Eight Steps in the Design Process flowchart on page 146). The design team looks at the due date for completing a line and then works backward to determine when to move from the research stage to the design stage.

The Design Team's Role

The creation of each line relies on a team of people. In creating each new style in the line, designers typically work with merchandisers and product developers (Figure 7.4 is an example of an apparel company's design team organizational chart). Many larger fashion brand companies employ a creative director or general merchandiser who is responsible for overseeing and guiding the

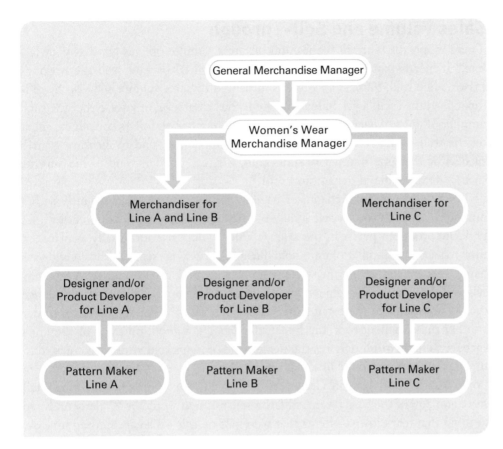

Figure 7.4
Apparel company organization
chart. Chinsee/WWD
/© Conde Nast.

development of the design brief. The design brief determines what, when, at what price, and how much product to have manufactured.

In some companies, especially smaller ones, the designer also acts as the merchandiser. Some companies employ both designers and product developers. A product developer takes the designer's idea and is responsible for developing the product. The product developer does the following:

- researches possible fabrics and trims
- works with vendors in securing all components for the style
- coordinates all aspects of style creation

At some smaller companies, the designer also handles the product development responsibilities.

The designer(s) and merchandiser(s) attend planning meetings to develop the design brief. At planning meetings, they review the sales figures (including sales volume and sell-through) for the previous season, consider the sales projections for the new season, and discuss the overall plan and schedule for the upcoming season's line. This discussion of the overall plan might include the following:

- decisions about the target number of styles to include in the line
- ratio of jackets compared to vests or the ratio of skirts compared to pants
- styles that will be repeated from the previous season (carryovers)
- types of silhouettes for various styles
- decision to add something new to the line
- colors and fabrics that will be used
- costs of all components for the line

Sales Volume and Sell-Through

There is an expression in the fashion business: "You're only as good as your last line." It means that a company's success is measured by how well the previous season's line sold. Success of a line is measured by sales volume and also by sell-through at the retail level. **Sales volume** is the actual level of sales, either the total number of units of each style sold or the total number of dollars consumers spent on the style (dollar volume). Fashion brand companies tend to measure a line's success by the total number of units sold, whereas retailers tend to measure its success by the value of the amount sold.

The designer and merchandiser have to hit the targeted sales volume with a mix of repeated styles, revised styles, and new styles. Due to the number of lines typically produced per year, the sales volume figures are not usually available in time to learn the number of units sold during the previous season. Thus it is always hard to accurately predict the strategy for the line under development. A line may sell well at market to the retailer, but a delay in delivery to the retailer could reduce the dollar volume at the retail store. This is one reason that companies consider another measurement tool, the line's sell-through, a good indicator of the line's success. **Sell-through** denotes the percentage of items sold at retail compared to the number of items in the line that the retailer purchased from the manufacturer. For example, if 300 items in a line were delivered by the fashion brand to the retail store and 250 of the items were sold, the sell-through would be 83 percent. Keep in mind that markdowns—items that were put on sale—also are figured into the line's overall success. A strong sell-through is the goal for both the manufacturer and the retailer. The sales figures from the current and previous selling seasons are important guidelines in planning how many and what types of apparel items to include in the new line.

Costing

Throughout the design stage, the production cost of each style in a line is an important factor for designers to consider. Thus, many companies include cost personnel as a part of the team during the planning meetings for a design brief. Their role is to provide cost estimates on the new styles in the line as the styles develop. Many factors must be kept in mind related to costing. Even before providing an initial cost estimate, each company has pricing strategies that guide costing. Here are examples of pricing strategies:

- It is important that two garments in the same line do not compete against each other for sales. Some manufacturers follow a pricing strategy that specifies that the prices of two different shirt styles should not be the same—and style differences in the two styles need to support the price difference. A shirt made from a more expensive fabric might have fewer garment details, while a shirt made from a less expensive fabric could have more details so it can be sold at similar (but not identical) prices.
- Pricing strategies need to make sense to the customer. When comparing two differently priced shirts in the same line, the customer needs to recognize that the higher-priced shirt is made from the more expensive fabric or that the higher-priced shirt has more complex style details to justify the price.

- With the pricing strategy called **price averaging**, a shirt manufactured from a more expensive fabric is priced to equalize a shirt manufactured from a less expensive fabric. The manufacturer averages the costs of the two shirts to keep the price of both styles similar. Thus, the shirt made from the more expensive fabric is priced slightly low, while the shirt made from the less expensive fabric is priced slightly high. If both styles sell equally, the company breaks even. If more shirts are sold that are made from the less expensive fabric, the company comes out ahead; if more shirts are sold that are made from the more expensive fabric, the company loses some profit.

- **Target costing** is a pricing strategy that developed as a result of a significant change made by the apparel industry in the design-produce-sell cycle. The process had been to create a new style and then calculate its cost based on materials and labor. Now, price tends to drive the style decisions, especially in the moderate and budget/mass price zones, as well as in private label and store brand merchandise. The style and fabric components are manipulated by setting a cost first, and then determining how many yards of fabric and at what price, estimating the cost of other components such as a zipper or buttons, and estimating how many minutes of labor are needed to produce the design, based on an hourly labor price. For example, the design team might determine that it wants to produce a jacket to sell at $75 retail ($37.50 wholesale). The team knows from previous seasons' costs that it takes 30 minutes to sew a basic jacket, and that one and one-half yards of fabric are required for a typical style. After estimating a cost per yard of a typical fabric and other components, the design team can calculate the cost. If the estimated total is less than the target cost, more design details (adding labor and materials cost) or more expensive fabrics or trims can be added to enhance the style and still meet the target cost.

The target costing process has been used for some time for certain types of goods, such as styles produced for a specific retail chain (these styles are sometimes called special makeups) and private label goods. One of the driving forces behind target costing is that in today's market (except for the couture and some designer price zones), the upper limit of price is based on what the target customer is willing to pay.

Carryovers

A line of fashion merchandise typically does not consist of only new styles. In a new line, some styles will be carryovers, some styles will be modifications of good sellers, and some styles will be new designs. A carryover will repeat the same garment style as a successful garment style from a previous season, but often in a new fabric, material, and/or color. Thus, carryovers provide a less expensive route to add a fresh look to a line. If the new fabric has identical textile characteristics as the previous fabric, the development cost will be minimal because the production patterns made for this style can be reused. However, if the new fabric is different—for example, it has a different shrinkage factor—a new pattern and prototype will need to be made.

Companies vary regarding the number of new items compared with the number of carryovers for each line. For an idea of the approximate ratio for a company that produces apparel in the moderate price zone, some companies target about one-third of the line to be carryovers, one-third as revisions of previous styles, and one-third as new designs. The percentage of new styles could be as low as 10 percent at some companies selling in the mass to moderate price zone, whereas a bridge or designer label might produce mostly new styles. Some styles in a new line might be revisions of a style from a previous season. One or more design details, such as a collar or pocket, might be changed for the new season to revise a style. This process cuts development time, saves some cost, and provides some degree of confidence that the revised style will sell well in the marketplace.

Line-for-Line Copies and Knockoffs

Rather than starting with a designer's sketch for a new design, a new style might be added to a line in another way. Sometimes while shopping the market or looking through fashion magazines, a designer or merchandiser will find a garment that seems ideal and conveys the essence of the design brief. Thus, the design team may decide to create a copy of an existing garment. Copying a garment may be done in several ways. For example, a unique design, such as a shirt with innovative design details, may seem perfect for the upcoming line. The designer might ask the pattern development department to make a **line-for-line copy** of the shirt and produce it in a similar fabric. The new shirt will be an exact replica of the original; thus, it is called the line-for-line copy.

Another example is taking a garment that exists in a higher price zone and copying it to be sold at a lower price. This can be done by selecting a less expensive fabric, or by eliminating or modifying some of the design details. These methods are used to create **knockoffs**, designs that are similar to the original but not exact replicas. Moderate price lines often knockoff successful designer looks once the style has become poplar.

Is it legal to copy an existing fashion design? The United States has laws to protect against copyright and trademark infringement A specific "invention" in a garment (e.g., a unique molding process to create a seamless panty) can be patented in the United States. However, in some countries (including the United States), the actual garment design is considered to be in the public domain. Therefore, it is quite common to see line-for-line copies and knockoffs in the U.S. apparel business. Design laws are stricter in some European countries, as evidenced by the 1994 case in which French designer Yves Saint Laurent took Ralph Lauren to court in France in a dispute over the design copy of a tuxedo dress (Figure 7.5) ("Tuxedo Junction" 1994).

Many factors need to be considered when planning a line. Among them is the overall number of styles the line will include. Some of these styles will be carryovers from the previous line, some styles will be revisions of previous styles, and some styles will be new designs. Decisions are also made about the following:

- the number of top styles in relation to the number of bottom styles
- styling variety (such as single-breasted and double-breasted jackets)
- color and fabric offerings for each style
- cost to produce each style
- overall pricing balance of the line

(a)

(b)

SELECTION OF MATERIALS, FABRICS, AND TRIMS

Sourcing for the right materials, fabrics, and trims must often be accomplished at the planning stage of the design process. The materials, fabrics, and trims are usually selected before a design is approved for inclusion in a line. Each design sketch or tech drawing includes a small sample of the intended material or fabric, called a **swatch**, which is attached to the sketch or drawing. It is essential to choose the fabric before the merchandiser, designer, and cost personnel review a design for possible inclusion in the final line. The design sketch or tech drawing will also include any trim swatches that will be used and may indicate specific findings, such as buttons and zippers. Sometimes the actual material or fabric intended for the design is not yet available from the manufacturer. In these cases, a facsimile material or fabric will be used temporarily for the design development stage.

Textile mills produce a large quantity of printed textiles each season. Many fashion brand companies purchase printed fabrics directly from textile mills for their lines. However, sometimes a fashion brand company prefers to work with a textile converter to develop a printed textile. A new textile design can be created from the following:

- an existing print that is revised into a new colorway
- a new textile print developed by the designers, assistant designers, or product developers (e.g., if they cannot find the right print on the market)
- a textile design that is purchased from a company or a freelance textile designer who creates and sells original artwork for the printed textile industry

When a fashion brand company purchases a piece of textile design artwork, it owns the rights to copy or change the print as it wishes. Thus, the fashion brand company's staff can reconfigure a textile design's scale, motif, colors, or repeat to suit their needs.

THE DESIGN SKETCH

At some point in the design stage (usually determined by the master calendar due date), the designer will begin to transform interpretations of the design brief information into sketches. By constantly seeking inspiration from a variety of sources and from the design brief information, most designers have plenty of new ideas.

Technical Drawing

Design sketches that do not include the body silhouette are referred to as a *technical drawing*, or **tech drawing**. The design is drawn as it would appear lying flat, as on a table, so sometimes the term **flat**, or **flat sketch**, is used to indicate this type of drawing. Most companies use tech drawings in place of design sketches, especially in the active-sportswear industry. Activewear garments might have many details. Tech drawings might include a close-up sketch of a detail, such as a pocket, cuff, or collar, as well as the back view. Tech drawings are especially useful and often necessary for pattern making and production needs. Sometimes the tech drawing indicates specific dimensions, such as the size and/or placement of a patch pocket.

Computer-Aided Design and Graphics Software

Computer-aided design (CAD) software was in use by the 1970s. CAD software developed specifically for the fashion industry was introduced in the early 1980s. Since then, software upgrades have dramatically improved apparel CAD software. Current CAD software used for pattern making (and also for preproduction and production) is much easier to learn than the software used in the 1980s. Adobe Creative Suite™ has become a popular graphics software and is especially useful for drawing and textile design. Software upgrades have also improved the ease of using these programs. In the past, the cost of CAD and graphics systems was a hurdle for some companies. The price for computer systems has dropped substantially, making CAD and graphics systems affordable for even small fashion brand companies.

Apparel Design

Some designers prefer to draw flats or tech drawings by hand. However, many, if not most, fashion brand companies expect their designers to create tech drawings using CAD or graphics software programs (Figure 7.6). CAD systems used for pattern making, pattern grading (sizing), and marker making (developing the master cutting plan) will be discussed later in the book.

Two major advantages of using a CAD or graphics system to create design sketches are the time-saving potential and the capability to try out numerous design ideas quickly. The designer may select a garment sketch from the previous season's line as a starting point and simply modify design details for the new design for the upcoming line. This procedure greatly speeds up this phase of the design process.

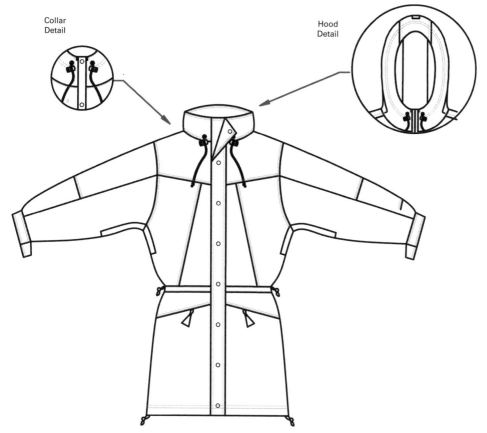

Collar
Detail

Hood
Detail

Figure 7.6
Tech drawings can be used
to show design details.
WWD/© Conde Nast.

Some designers may think it stifles their creativity to sketch on a computer. They prefer to "think" with pencil in hand. To assist the artist, some graphics computer programs allow the designer to use a pencil-like stylus to simulate the act of drawing. After becoming familiar with the process of sketching by CAD or graphics software, most designers find that the ability to speedily modify a design is a great advantage. Designs can be created using the following approaches:

- The computer can store a croqui (Figure 7.7), or a series of croquis, in various poses. The designer selects a desired pose, which then appears on the computer screen. The desired garment sketch can be drawn onto the croquis.
- Some software programs provide a style library of basic garment silhouettes, such as shirts and pants, as well as garment components, such as collar and pocket styles. The designer creates the new style by bringing the desired components together (Figure 7.8).
- New garment designs are drawn by using true proportions from a croqui stored in the system.
- New garment designs are drawn by specifying exact measurements.

To visualize what the garment style might look like in a specific color or print, the computer-generated garment drawing can be colored in several possible ways. For example, designers can use computer graphics programs to simulate the color of a specific fabric swatch by blending colors on the computer monitor to create an accurate color match. They can then print the drawing of the new garment style to compare the printed color on paper to the actual color of the fabric swatch.

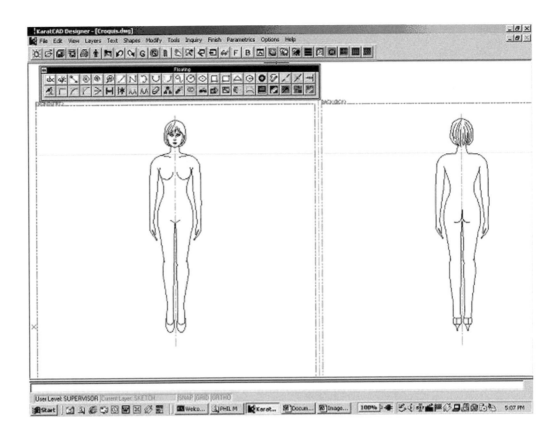

Figure 7.7
A body image, called a croquis, can be used as the lay figure for drawing the new garment style.

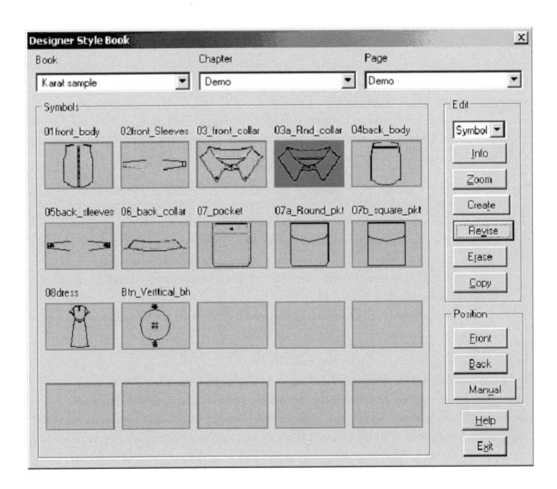

Figure 7.8
A library of garment components stored in the computer can be selected and imported into a tech drawing to develop a new style. Freeboarders.

Some of the graphics software programs are integrated with the same color system used by textile producers, so that an exact match can be produced quickly by keying in the color number. The Pantone color system is supported by a number of graphics software programs, and textile producers use it to match the printed visual version of the garment with the actual fabrics. These integrated systems can be used to produce accurate color matching of the line sheet used later to sell the line at market.

A scanner can be used to input an existing fabric print into the computer system. A facsimile of the fabric will appear on the computer screen. The scale of the print or plaid fabric motif can be adjusted to approximate the correct size of the motif for the scale of the drawing. This process is much faster than manually drawing and coloring fabric motifs.

Some of the more complex software programs can simulate the drape of the fabric on the designer's computer drawing (Figure 7.9). The computer technology of simulating the three-dimensional drape of fabric is called **virtual draping**.

Using CAD or graphics software at the design stage helps to integrate later steps in the design process. The designer's CAD drawing will be the basis for garment technical drawings used in developing and producing the design. Integration of computers in the entire design process is discussed later in this chapter and at each step in the design process.

It is becoming even more important for designers to be proficient with CAD and graphics software systems, and design students will increase their opportunities for future employment by developing the ability to use a computer system to sketch their design ideas.

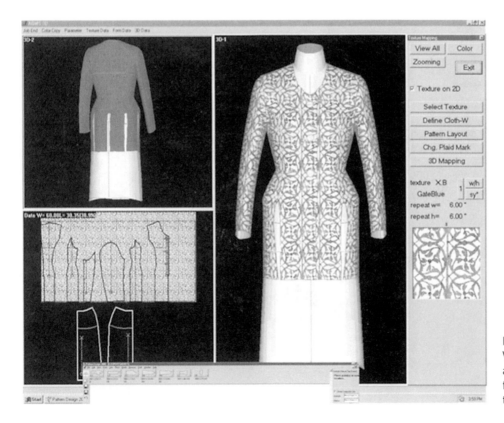

Figure 7.9
Virtual draping software creates a visual image of the scanned fabric shown on the 3-D image of the garment style.

Textile Design

Computer-aided design and graphics software programs are also important tools for textile design. Since textile design is such an integral part of the garment design, apparel designers and merchandisers need to know as much as possible about the textile design process. More frequently today than in the past, apparel designers find textile design and/or graphic design assignments a part of their responsibilities. For example, apparel designers may need to design a graphics logo for a T-shirt to coordinate with a print fabric used in a line, or perhaps they will need to redesign or recolor an existing textile print.

At some companies, textile designers work side by side with the apparel design team. For example, at Pendleton Woolen Mills in Portland, Oregon, the design of the woven plaid fabric is integrated with the garment design. The textile designers calculate the spacing of the plaid repeat to coincide with the pleat widths of the skirt pattern, or vice versa, depending on the style requirements specified. This is not an easy task, for the designer also must keep in mind the size range in which the style will be produced.

Computer software systems offer many advantages for textile design. Some of the computer textile design systems can print the newly created print design directly onto fabric. Several repeats of the print design can be joined together to simulate a large piece of the printed textile. Viewing a large section of the print design helps textile designers visualize the scale, repeat, and color combination (Figure 7.10), so they can immediately make changes. This process is much faster and less expensive than sending a printed paper sample to a textile mill to make a length of sample yardage of the print, called a **strike off**.

Figure 7.10
Textile designers experiment with various color combinations while designing prints.

PRODUCT MANAGEMENT SYSTEMS

Today's fashion brand companies face increasing demands to produce new styles quickly. Traditional methods of designing, marketing to retail buyers, producing, and distributing to retailers are no longer effective for many companies. Many forces have affected the need to accelerate the pace of these industries. Several of the most critical factors include

- the length of time a style is in process
- the international scope of sourcing and production
- the need for all partners in the pipeline to communicate accurately and quickly

Here is a typical scenario in today's fashion industry: Suppose that you are a New York–based apparel designer, carefully formulating the next season's color palette while meticulously developing the Summer line that will use the palette. Here's the catch—your design partner is based in Los Angeles, your patternmaker and sample maker are 8,000 miles away in India, and your dyeing mill is in China. How do companies handle all the necessary data, in the shortest time possible, across thousands of miles?

Computer technology provides the means to help meet these requirements. Beginning in the early 1990s, product data management systems, also known as product information management or product development management systems, were developed to track via computer the technical information package for a style. That package would then be supplied to the preproduction and production facilities. Generally, this management approach began once the new style had been adopted. Often the design team members worked through the initial stages of creating a new style by using their computer-drawn garment sketches (or tech drawings) along with computer-generated style information sheets (spec sheets). Once the style moved to the preproduction department, style information was transferred seamlessly through the computer network.

By the late 1990s, it became increasingly important to begin using electronic management of product information related to the style at its inception. This situation led to expanding the tracking process for style information to include information from the very beginning of a style's design through its delivery at the retail store. The two technologies that provide electronic management of files are

- **product data management (PDM)**, also referred to as **product development management (PDM)**
- **product life cycle management (PLM)**

These technologies differ somewhat. PDMs software takes product-centric data and allows it to be managed as information. Unlike image- or document-focused management systems, PDM centers on the product, or style at hand, grouping together everything related to that product, including specifications, sketches, and other information, which can then be reviewed and updated by other parties.

Sometimes referred to as **PDM/PLM** when combining product data (development) management and product life cycle management, this approach requires all computer systems in the pipeline to be compatible so they can share product data. The designer's sketch is created in a software program that interfaces with the garment spec sheet software, and on down the product production pipeline. All partners have online access to the style information. All users have access to the full range of data and can visualize each step in the development of a collection: design, technical specifications, bills of materials, size charts and measurements, sewing instructions, costing, planning control, pattern making, marker making, and packaging.

Because all partners have instantaneous access to any change made for a style, the person responsible for accurately entering the data carries a heavy responsibility. A product developer at Nike commented on how nervous she was the first time she logged into the PDM system. She knew that if she input data incorrectly, the error would be transmitted to everyone in the system. Despite this concern, the advantages of using a PDM/PLM system are tremendous in managing total workflow.

DESIGN TEAM REVIEW OF LINE

Typically, many more design ideas are sketched than will appear in the final line. At a line review meeting (also called a **first adoption meeting**), the designer presents the design sketches to the review team (e.g., the merchandiser, fit or production engineer, and head of sample sewing) according to the timeline on the master calendar (Figure 7.11). Some designers unveil the new line at a formal presentation. Design presentation boards or concept boards may be included as a part of the presentation, showing fabrics, various colorways, inspirational pictures, and sketches. The presentation might include information about

- the concept or inspiration for the line
- how the styles coordinate or work together
- the target customer profiles for various styles within the line

The designer might make an oral presentation to the design team, upper management, or private label managers to sell the line.

This initial adoption meeting is the first of several review processes that the line must undergo. Several line reviews will take place before the final adoption. The review team discusses and evaluates each of the designs. The team will have determined during previous planning meetings how many of each type of apparel item the line will include. Out of 60 design ideas presented for review, perhaps only 30 or 40 sketches are selected to continue into the design development stage. Some of these designs will be dropped at later stages as well. At other companies, the merchandisers may request that all or most of the designs be developed as prototypes to better visualize the product.

Guided by the total number of pieces previously determined for the line, other factors enter into the decision to accept or drop designs from the line. The balance of the line is an important factor in deciding which designs are included. For a misses career line, jacket style variations are considered so that there will be a range of styles to suit a variety of customers. For example, it is important to include a balance of the number of short versus long, boxy versus fitted, single- versus

Figure 7.11
At review meetings, the designer, merchandiser, and production engineer discuss the feasibility of each style in the line. Digital Vision/Getty Images.

double-breasted jackets, and jackets with collars versus collarless jackets. The ratio of solid to plaid or print fabrics is another consideration. Skirt style variations must be balanced—short versus long, fitted versus flared, full versus pleated. The skirts need to coordinate with as many of the jacket styles as possible. The mix of classic and fashion-forward styles needs to be considered.

Anticipated cost is an important factor in the review process. The anticipated prices need to be similar to the previous season's prices, unless a new market niche is sought. Some cost considerations are discussed in the section on planning the line earlier in this chapter. It is important for style features to match price. For example, a customer expects to pay less for a short, single-breasted style than for a longer, double-breasted jacket. The team discusses cost estimates and possible style, design details, findings, and fabric changes that might reduce cost.

Other factors to consider include ease of adjusting the style to fit varied body types. For example, elastic added at the sides of the skirt waistband can enhance the adaptability of a garment to fit more figure shapes, especially in the misses and larger-size markets. However, for the junior market, elastic in the waistband may be considered a negative feature and could adversely affect sales. Ease of alteration is another consideration. A wrap skirt with a curved, faced hemline is not easily shortened and cannot be lengthened.

A constant struggle goes on among the following personnel:

- production personnel, who want new styles to be similar to previous styles and as simple to construct as possible
- merchandisers, who want the line to sell itself in the marketplace with great prices and high quality
- designers, who want highly creative, complex styles

This atmosphere may explain why some companies call the conference room where design reviews are conducted the *war room*. During the review, designers must be prolific with design ideas and develop an impersonal attitude about the designs that need to be modified or are dropped from the line.

In short, the merits of each style as it fits in the design brief are discussed at the design review meeting. Sometimes design details will need to be modified to lower the expected cost or to coordinate better with other styles. The team is guided in the review process by the following aims:

- to create a cohesive theme
- to include an appropriate number of items and a balance of styles
- to fit the overall merchandising orientation of the company for the season (e.g., fit the price and lifestyle of the target customer)

The reviewed and selected styles are sent to the design or product development team for implementation. The next chapter will explain the process used to transform a sketch into a product that is ready for production.

SUMMARY

In creating a fashion brand, the design team uses a design brief as a guide for developing a product line. The brief documents the target market, inspiration or theme, color story, and possible materials and fabrics for the line.

The line is planned to provide the right product type for the target customer at the right time and at the right price. The sales volume and sell-through of a line at the retail level are important indicators used to plan the upcoming line. Striking the right balance between carryover styles, revisions of popular styles from the previous season, and new styles is critical to the success of the line.

Increasing demands for the fast development, production, and delivery of goods has put pressure on the fashion industries. These demands are coupled with the physical distance between various partners in the global marketplace that rely on one another for sourcing. Electronic technologies have provided the means for instant communication and accurate tracking of each style. Product data management and product life cycle management systems provide electronic connectivity for instantaneous communication among all parties in the creation, design development, style selection, preproduction, marketing, production, and distribution of goods.

KEY TERMS

carryover
collection
color story
colorway
computer-aided design (CAD)
croqui
design brief
findings
first adoption meeting
flat
flat sketch
group

knockoff
lifestyle merchandising
line
line-for-line copy
market niche
price averaging
PDM/PLM
product data management
    (PDM)
product development
    management (PDM)

product life cycle management
    (PLM)
product type
sales volume
sell-through
strike off
swatch
target costing
tech drawing
virtual draping

DISCUSSION QUESTIONS AND ACTIVITIES

1. Review current designers' collections, and try to identify their source of inspiration. Do any of the designers share a common inspiration?

2. What are some current styles in the stores that might be considered knockoffs of designers' styles?

3. What are some job responsibilities of a merchandiser and a designer in the design stage of the design process? What are some activities that might be helpful for you to complete as students to help prepare you for these job responsibilities? Examples include preparing a target customer collage for a specific company, a trend board for a jacket line for a year in advance, or an inspiration board for a children's wear beach group.

CASE STUDY

Writing a Design Brief

A design brief is a document that communicates the design objectives and describes how to solve a design problem. A design brief allows designers to succinctly describe the design process they used and explain their design. A design brief should include all of these components:

- a brief explanation of the problem being solved (this may also identify the design limitations)
- goals and objectives of the design
- the target audience of the design
- techniques and elements used in the design (shape, materials, color) and why
- a description of the overall style of the design

To practice writing a design brief, you will select a recent design innovation in apparel, footwear, or other accessories and write a design brief for that innovation.

1. Select a recent design innovation in apparel, footwear, or other accessories. Examples include performance apparel or footwear; apparel designed for infants or older adults; accessories that assist the user to perform a task more efficiently; or apparel, footwear, or accessories designed and/or manufactured in socially responsible ways. Include a photograph, drawing, or image of the design innovation in the design brief.

2. Write a design brief for this innovation:
   a. Introduce the design problem. Help the reader understand the problem the design solves.
   b. Articulate the goals of the design. What emotions was the designer trying to evoke through the design? What kind of reactions was the designer trying to create?
   c. Describe the target audience. Who was this design meant for? How did the designer reach that audience?
   d. Describe the important technical aspects of the design. What were some of the techniques, shapes, and colors used to create the design? Why were these techniques, shapes, and colors used?
   e. Characterize the design's style. What inspired the design? What types of design are similar to this? How is this design different/better than other designs?

Sources: Adapted from Cameron Chapman, "7 Basics to Create a Good Design Brief," *Webdesigner Depot RSS*, March 17, 2011 (http://www.webdesignerdepot.com/2011/03/7-basics-to-create-a-good-design-brief/); and Brian Ling, "5 Steps to a Better Design Brief," *Design Sojourn*, August 4, 2009 (http://designsojourn.com/5-steps-to-a-better-design-brief/).

CAREER OPPORTUNITIES

Working to develop and complete a design brief requires many different people. Some positions that might be available include these as well as the positions listed in upcoming chapters.

- Creative director
- Lead designer

- Merchandise manager
- Data/Costing analyst

REFERENCES

"At Ease." (2010). Women's Wear Daily, June 17, 7.

Bowles, Hammish. (2006). "Show Business." *Vogue*, May, pp. 142, 144, 146.

Knight, Molly. (1999). "Globetrotting for Inspiration." *DNR*, September 24, pp. 14–16.

Saint Laurent, Yves, Diana Vreeland, Costume Institute. (1983). *Yves Saint Laurent*. New York: Metropolitan Museum of Art.

"Tuxedo Junction: YSL, Ralph Square Off." (1994). *Women's Wear Daily*, April 28, pp. 1, 15.

Wilson, Eric. (1999). "The Culture of Copycats." *Women's Wear Daily*, November 2, pp. 8–9.

Design Development and Style Selection

IN THIS CHAPTER, YOU WILL LEARN THE FOLLOWING:

- development of garment specifications

- the steps required to develop a sketch into a prototype garment and to prepare the garment for design team review

- the use of computers for product life management

- reasons for eliminating a style from the line during the review process

- style factors that influence the estimated cost of a new garment style

- relationships among traditional design development processes and private label and store brand product development

At this point in the design process, a design brief has been developed and a group of sketches with fabric swatches have made it through the design team's preliminary selection process. This chapter discusses how the first pattern is developed from the designer's sketch, swatch, and garment specification sheet and how the prototype garment is cut and sewn from the first pattern (see Step 3: Design Development and Style Selection flowchart, at the beginning of this chapter, and Figure 8.1, an expanded view of Step 3). The prototype is then tried on a fit model whose body measurements match the company's size standard.

DESIGN DEVELOPMENT

Participating in the development of a new style from its sketch (or the first drape) to a finished prototype is an exciting part of the design process. On the other hand, it can be a difficult decision to cut some styles from the line after seeing the prototypes and liking all of them. After the final styles have been approved and final cost has been determined, sales samples are cut and sewn.

This chapter focuses on the development process typically used by fashion brand companies that design and market name brand merchandise. These fashion brand labels are well recognized by the public, including Levi Strauss & Co., Tommy Hilfiger, Calvin Klein, and Nike. Later in the chapter, private label and SPA/store brand product development processes are discussed. Although the processes are almost identical, with private label and SPA/store brand product development, retailers are an integral part of the design team. Such changing roles and relationships among design, production, and retail will continue in our complex economic market.

The design development stage of creating a line occurs within the design development department of a fashion brand company. Other names for this department include design department and product development department. Design development teams in this department include designers, assistant designers (also called design assistants), and product developers (also called technical designers). Merchandisers may also be part of the design department. At some companies, the patternmakers and production engineers (also called cost engineers or product technicians) are a part of the design development team. If the apparel company also has production patternmakers, they may be a part of the design development department. At other companies, a pattern development department may be separate from the design development department.

Writing the Garment/Product Specification Sheet

The designer often has some specific design details in mind that need to be conveyed to the patternmaker and sample sewer in order to create the sample or prototype garment at the next stage of the design process. These details, as well as other vital information, are conveyed on a **garment/product specification sheet**, also called a *garment/product spec sheet*, or shortened still more to *spec sheet*. Examples of types of design details that need to be specified include the following:

- placement and spacing of buttons
- any edge stitching or topstitching

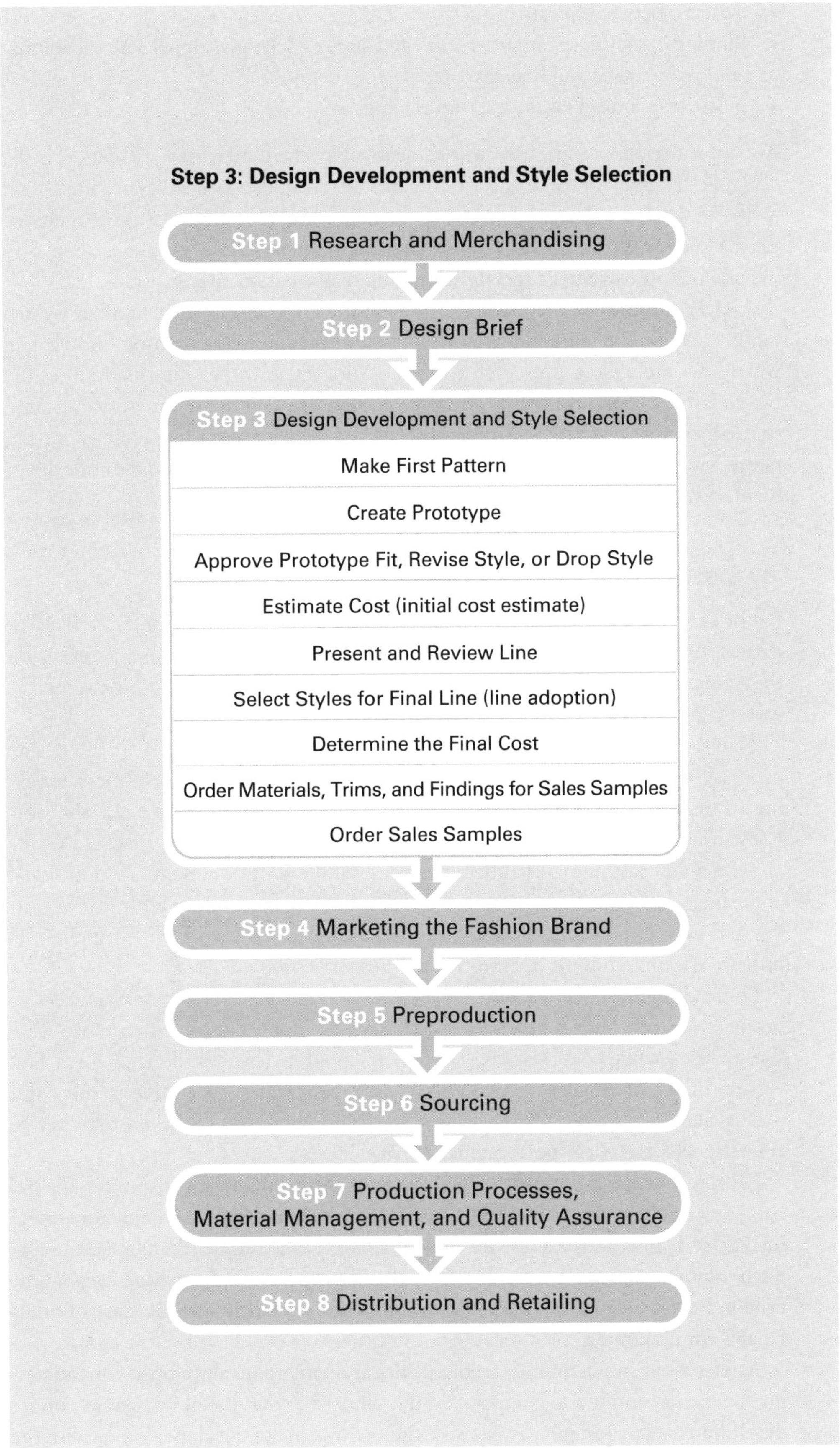

Step 3: Design Development and Style Selection

Step 1 Research and Merchandising

Step 2 Design Brief

Step 3 Design Development and Style Selection

Make First Pattern

Create Prototype

Approve Prototype Fit, Revise Style, or Drop Style

Estimate Cost (initial cost estimate)

Present and Review Line

Select Styles for Final Line (line adoption)

Determine the Final Cost

Order Materials, Trims, and Findings for Sales Samples

Order Sales Samples

Step 4 Marketing the Fashion Brand

Step 5 Preproduction

Step 6 Sourcing

Step 7 Production Processes, Material Management, and Quality Assurance

Step 8 Distribution and Retailing

Figure 8.1
Step 3 Expanded:
Design Development
and Style Selection.

- spacing between pleats or tucks
- findings, such as the number, size, and style of buttons; zipper length, color, and style; snaps and buckles
- pocketing, lining fabric, and interfacings

Any information not specified will be decided by the patternmaker. Thus, it is the designer's responsibility to specify all garment/product aspects that are important to the look of the design. A drawing of the garment/product design is included on the spec sheet along with material/fabric swatches. The spec sheet may also include the measurement specifications and construction specifications.

A **style number** is assigned to each new style in the line. This number (which might include a letter code as well) is coded to indicate the season and year in which the line will be presented to buyers, along with other information desired by the fashion brand company. The style number may include a category indicator, such as swimwear or footwear, and the size or size category (e.g., junior, misses, petite, tall). The style number is used as the style's reference throughout development, marketing, and production.

FABRIC/MATERIAL DEVELOPMENT

Fabrics and materials are a key element of a new style. At the same time that the pattern for the new style is under development, potential fabrics and materials for the new style are under consideration. A product developer might be assigned to work with textile mills to develop a new fabric or finish.

New fabrics and materials under consideration are tested early in the design process (before making the prototype) for such properties as colorfastness, crocking (transfer of color from one fabric to another fabric), pilling, and abrasion. Sometimes an independent testing laboratory is used to perform specified textile tests on a new fabric/material being considered for adoption. Some fashion brand companies maintain their own testing labs that might conduct both textile testing and garment testing. Product developers might also work with suppliers to procure specific findings or trims for the new style.

Some designers and product developers work with fabric manufacturers to produce custom fabrics to meet specific needs. For example, after Gore-Tex's success as a woven fabrication, activewear apparel designers longed for a knit version of the breathable fabric. The fabric's manufacturer was able to meet this need when W. L. Gore & Associates and Nike employees worked together to create special technical-performance fabrics.

Fabrics that have been developed by a textile producer for a specific apparel company can be restricted for use solely by that fashion brand company for a specified period. This adds exclusivity to the product, which in turn can enhance sales. Such a fabric is **proprietary**; that is, it is the property of the private owner (the fashion brand company). Dri-FIT® is a proprietary fabric for Nike, as is Omni-Heat® for Columbia.

As discussed in Chapter 7, textile prints are sometimes developed for the new line by the fashion brand company. At the same time that the new styles are under development, the designer, assistant designer, or product developer works with the textile converter to ensure that the prints will be approved and ready for production on schedule.

The designer responsible for the line will have selected a color story, or palette, for the line. The colors for the line might be represented by color chips or fabric swatches. **Color management** deals with handling the technical aspects of matching the colors of the fabrics, trims, and findings to ensure that the colors of the finished product match the designer's color swatches. Much work goes into selecting the specific hue, value, and intensity for each color in the color palette. Therefore, it is essential that the fabrics and trim colors of the finished product match the intended color swatch. Color management begins during design development, as the product developer, assistant designer, or designer work with textile mills to procure the exact color match.

For prints, the colors used need to match any solid-colored fabrics intended to coordinate with them. Color matching is challenging, especially when the various fabrics used in a line are composed of a variety of fibers. Different fibers require different types of dyes, so color matching the wide variety of fibers, fabrics, thread, buttons, zippers, and other findings requires constant attention during the design development and preproduction steps. Color management continues in production processes.

Preparation for Pattern Development

After the design team approves the style for development, the designer's sketch, fabric swatch, and garment/product specification sheet are delivered to the design development department to begin the patternmaking process. In the case of fashion brand companies that use contractors, the first pattern may be developed by the contractor, or the pattern may be developed by the design department of the fashion brand company. The responsibility for developing the first pattern is fairly common for contractors who provide full-package (FP) contractor services.

Making the First Pattern

As noted earlier, some fashion brand companies develop the line, create the design sketches with accompanying fabric/material swatches, and write the garment/product specification sheet. Then they use either domestic or offshore contractors to manufacture the garments/products. These firms are called *CMT contractors* because they cut, make, and trim the garments/products. The steps between those involving making the pattern and cutting and sewing/creating the **prototype**, or **sample**, may be performed by either the design department of the fashion brand or the contractor.

Patterns can be made using a variety of methods. Three methods that may be used are

- **drafting:** Measurements are used to develop the pattern shape.
- **flat pattern:** A base pattern is manipulated and changed to create a new pattern.
- **draping:** Fabric is draped on a body form to create the garment style. A pattern is developed for the fabric pieces.

It may be advantageous for fashion brand companies that use contractors to retain the capability to develop the pattern and prototype in-house, because schedule delays and communication and visual interpretation problems are possible when a contractor develops the pattern and prototype. Each fashion brand must consider a number of factors regarding the patternmaking, grading, and marker making responsibilities. One potential problem area when using contractors for pattern-making has to do with the base pattern used. A **base pattern** is a non-stylized, basic pattern in the sample size from which the stylized pattern is derived. Two contractors producing different styles for the same line might not use identical base patterns for patternmaking. This can cause differences in the fit of the finished stylized garments between a style produced by one contractor and another style produced by another contractor.

At some companies, the designer is also the first patternmaker. This tends to be the case in very small companies or in some specialty areas, such as children's wear. Some designers enjoy being involved in developing their design ideas from sketches into patterns and then prototypes. For designers who also are responsible for making the first pattern and prototype, their design ideas or the construction procedure might evolve during the development process. Thus, they might modify the design during the process of making the pattern and/or sewing the prototype.

From the designer's sketch, the assistant designer or patternmaker begins the patternmaking process. The patternmaker's role is critical to the accurate transla-tion of the designer's idea. It is important that the patternmaker accurately assesses from the sketch the following information:

- overall silhouette desired
- amount of ease (from very snug to very oversized)
- designer's desired proportions for the design details

Patternmaking Using a Base Pattern

An existing pattern may be used to begin the new design. This pattern could be a base pattern (also called a **block** or a **sloper**) in the company's sample size. For example, a basic shirt block might be used as the base pattern for a new shirt style. The patternmaker creates the new pattern by adding pattern design details such as a collar, pocket, button band, back yoke, and sleeve pleats to the base pattern, as indicated in the designer's sketch or tech drawing.

Another process that patternmakers frequently use is to select a similar style from a previous season. For example, a shirt style for a new season might be simi-lar to a pattern that has already been made for the previous season. Modifying an existing pattern can be the fastest way to create the pattern for the new style. Selecting the most appropriate previous style for the starting point of a new style may require some discussion between the patternmaker (or assistant designer) and the designer. Alternatively, the designer might make a note to the patternmaker on the design sketch or tech drawing suggesting a previous style to start from.

The intended fabric for the final garment is an important consideration during patternmaking. For example, the amount of gathers to incorporate into a sleeve depends on the hand, or tactile qualities, of the fabric specified by the designer. The patternmaker may experiment by gathering a section of the intended fabric or a facsimile fabric to better determine the ideal quantity of gathers. To develop patterns for garments made from stretch fabrics, it is necessary to know the exact amount of stretch of the fabric in all directions. The patternmaker selects the base pattern or previous style pattern to correspond to the specific stretch factor of the intended fabric for the new style.

Fabric shrinkage is another patternmaking consideration. After the fabric sample has been test washed to accurately determine its shrinkage in all directions, the pattern is enlarged just enough to account for the shrinkage factor. All pattern pieces are expanded, based on accurate length and width shrinkage ratios.

Patternmakers need expertise/knowledge in the following areas:

- patternmaking, so that a garment/product illustration can be translated into a pattern
- understanding of fit and the ways in which shape and fullness are incorporated into the design
- textiles, so that fiber and fabric characteristics are accounted for in the design development
- production aspects, such as the sequence of sewing/manufacturing operations used by a production facility that affect how the pattern is built, so the style can be made easily and cost effectively in the factory
- types of equipment at the production facility, in order to produce a pattern that the factory can sew/manufacture satisfactorily

The patternmaker may work with traditional paper patterns, or the pattern might be created using a computer-aided design system.

Many fashion brand companies use **pattern design systems (PDS)** for some or all of the patternmaking functions (Figure 8.2). The computer patternmaking process is similar to the flat-pattern process. The base patterns and all previous style patterns are stored in the computer's files or on a server. To begin a new style, a patternmaker selects an electronic file of either a base pattern or the pattern

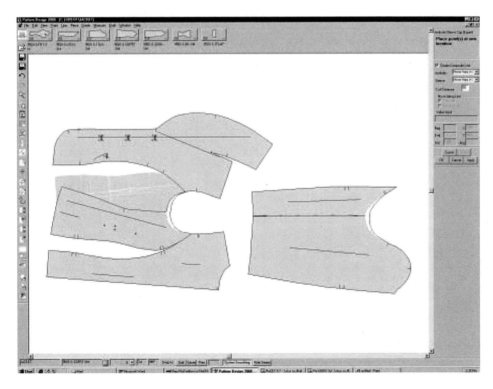

Figure 8.2
Pattern design systems provide speed and accuracy for patternmaking.

pieces for a similar style from a previous season. After opening the file so it appears on the computer screen, the patternmaker uses a mouse, or stylus (similar to a pen) to select specific areas to change on the pattern. Patternmaking commands are either selected from a menu shown on the screen or typed on a keyboard. Once the patternmaking is completed, the pattern can be plotted (drawn) in full size (Figure 8.3).

Note that using PDS does not automatically produce a pattern. Knowledge of patternmaking is essential in developing a pattern using a computer. Just as word processing software cannot write a sentence unless the user understands grammar, PDS cannot develop a pattern.

Computer technology continues to bring remarkable advances in ease of use, adaptability, and cost effectiveness of PDS. Here are some advantages of PDS:

- *Speed:* Since the base patterns and patterns from previous styles are stored in the computer system and used to begin the pattern for a new style, no time is spent tracing an existing pattern to begin patternmaking. To add seam and hem allowances, the patternmaker specifies the amount of seam and hem allowances to add to selected edges, and the cutting lines are added in an instant. The lengths of two seam lines that need to match can be compared for accuracy with a computer command. Markings and labels, such as grainlines and notches, are stored in a library and can be quickly added to the pattern pieces. If the design is modified later in the design process, changes in the pattern can be made more quickly by PDS than they usually can with a paper pattern. Another advantage of using a PDS that enhances the speed of patternmaking is its capability to adjust other pattern pieces automatically. For example, a change made by the patternmaker on the jacket front pattern

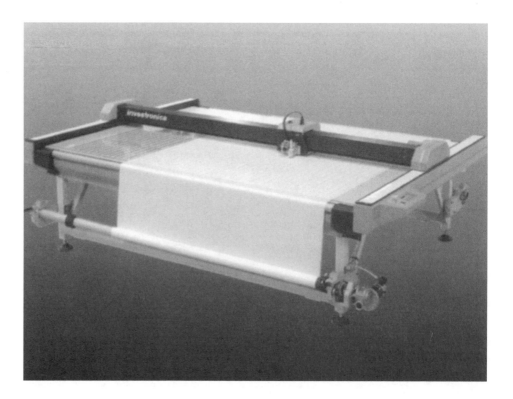

Figure 8.3
After a pattern is completed on a pattern design system, the pattern pieces are drawn full size on a plotter. Elaine Pederson.

would generate the same change to be reflected on the facing and lining pattern pieces.

- *Accuracy:* Using PDS, seam lengths and seam allowance widths are more exact than is possible by hand. By always using a stored pattern for the base pattern, consistency in pattern design across all styles is assured. When the patternmaker makes a modification in one pattern piece that affects other pattern pieces, some PDS software programs make an automatic change in the corresponding pattern piece(s). For example, if a change is made in the front side seam length, the back side seam length is automatically corrected. This feature can greatly reduce potential errors, as well as increase the speed of patternmaking.
- *Integration with spec sheets:* Some computer software programs provide an interface between the patternmaking process and the garment/product specification sheet (spec sheet). Some PDS programs allow the patternmaker to write parts of the spec sheet as the pattern is being made on PDS. A file of potential sewing steps is retrieved and edited on one screen while the pattern is being made and viewed on another screen. The measurement specifications can also be written during the patternmaking process. With some PDS software programs, the widths and lengths of the pattern being made in the sample size can be requested at any time during the patternmaking process. This information is the basis for completion of the measurement specifications. The possibility of an error in the spec sheet is reduced when the patternmaker writes the spec sheet simultaneously with making the pattern.
- *Integration with production:* Later in the product development process, production is faster if the pattern pieces have been stored in the computer than if it is necessary to input the pattern pieces for computerized grading and marker making.

Although the advantages of PDS are many, some patternmakers and company executives note that there are disadvantages.

Possible disadvantages of using PDS include the following:

- *Cost:* The initial cost of PDS is high, although some of the new technology systems cost less than earlier versions. Some apparel manufacturers, especially smaller companies, may not see a substantial return on their investment for some years. If a company produces only a limited number of new styles per season, PDS will not be used to its full extent.
- *Time:* Another aspect of cost has to do with time involved in training patternmakers. One hurdle with learning a computer software system is knowing its operating system and memorizing the commands and the various steps needed to complete a process. There is the cost of lost time while training occurs and the increased time required for making patterns while the new system is being mastered.
- *Technical support:* If the system goes down, the delay can cause great problems and affect the subsequent production steps. Any delays can be extremely costly to the fashion brand company and retailer. Fortunately, most PDS companies have excellent technical support by phone and online, easing the time loss and stress.

- *Visualization difficulties:* For patternmakers who are used to working with full-size patterns, using PDS requires an adjustment because they are looking at reduced-size pattern pieces on the computer screen. With experience, it becomes easier for patternmakers to visualize scale using PDS.

Costs of PDS programs have been reduced as more price competition among CAD companies has developed and technology costs have decreased. Many CAD systems operate with standard computer industry PCs, providing additional price competition in the huge PC market. Most large apparel manufacturers already rely completely on computer-generated patternmaking. An increasing number of small apparel companies use CAD systems in order to be fully integrated with their manufacturers.

Patternmaking by Drafting

Rather than beginning the patternmaking process with a base pattern, some companies prefer to draft the pattern by using body measurements. The pattern shapes are drawn based on the body dimensions plus ease allowances. Pattern drafting can be accomplished using paper and pencil, or using a CAD program. Pattern drafting to create stylized patterns is used more frequently in Asia than in other parts of the world.

Patternmaking from a Draped Design

Some designers, especially in the designer and bridge price zones, create the initial garment by draping the design on a mannequin. The fabric, either fashion fabric or muslin, is draped onto the sample size mannequin. The design is developed by cutting into the fabric, molding the fabric to the desired shape, and then pinning the fabric in place. After finalizing all aspects of the design, the style lines and construction details of the drape are carefully marked so they can be removed from the mannequin. The fabric pieces are removed and laid flat over pattern paper. The shapes of the pattern pieces are traced onto paper; then the pattern is perfected, and markings such as grainlines, notches, buttonholes, seam and hem allowances, and facings are added.

Figure 8.4
Patterns may be digitized into a computer.

Some companies digitize the paper pattern into a computer pattern design system (Figure 8.4). This allows the remaining stages of the design development process, preproduction, and production processes for the new style to be handled electronically.

Regardless of the process used to make the pattern—flat pattern design with paper, PDS, drafting, or a draped design—the full-scale, final pattern of the style is now ready to be cut and sewn into a prototype for style review.

MAKING THE PROTOTYPE OR SAMPLE GARMENT

The next step in the design development process is to cut and sew the prototype or sample garment/product. As mentioned in Chapter 7, some fashion brand companies use computer software systems to create three-dimensional replicas of the styles in the line; these computer images show simulated fabrics draped on the mannequin (Figure 8.5). Rather than continuing the development process by cutting and sewing the sample, some companies use these computer-generated images to sell their styles to retail buyers.

Most companies produce a sewn prototype. This provides the opportunity to

- test the design in the selected materials/fabric(s)
- evaluate the style on a live fit model
- test the construction sequence
- use a physical sample to perform a cost analysis for materials and labor costs
- see all the styles in the line as a whole

The prototype made from the first pattern for the new style may be cut and sewn by an in-house sample or sewing department, or it might be made by a contractor. If the contractor has a compatible computer system, the pattern can be sent electronically to the contractor. Many contractors realize that their business opportunities expand greatly if they invest in computer systems that are the same as the fashion brand companies they work with.

Sample Cutting and Sewing

The completed pattern is delivered to the sample sewing department, accompanied by a swatch of the intended fabric/material for the actual garment/product and the garment/product specification sheet. If the intended fabric is available

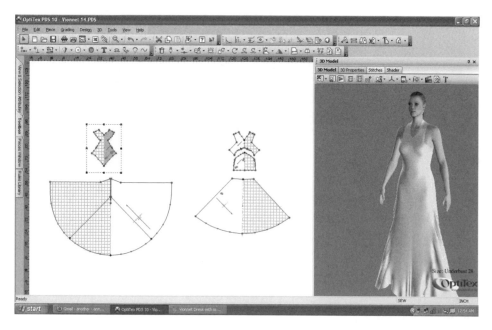

Figure 8.5
Computer-generated sample garment.

(sometimes as a sample cut ordered from the textile mill), it will be used to make the prototype garment. Sometimes the intended fabric is not yet available, so a substitute or facsimile fabric, as similar as possible to the intended fabric, is used.

The garment/product spec sheet will indicate any special cutting instructions. For example, a shirt with back yoke may require that the shirt's striped fabric be cut on the lengthwise grain for the body, sleeves, and collar, and on the crosswise grain for the yoke. Stretch fabrics for swimwear and bodywear may require some pattern pieces to be cut with the greatest stretch in the horizontal direction and other pattern pieces to be cut with the greatest stretch in the vertical direction. The sample cutter will match plaids where specified and make other decisions about how the pattern pieces are laid on the fabric (layout). The sample cutter will cut all pieces needed for the prototype. A sample room may use a cutter that cuts directly from a PDS program used to develop the pattern (Figure 8.6). The pattern is removed from the fabric after cutting; then the pattern is usually returned to the design development department rather than accompanying the fabric pieces of the prototype through the sample sewing process.

The **sample sewer** is highly skilled in using a variety of sewing machines as well as knowing the production processes used in factories. Without an instruction sheet and rarely consulting the pattern pieces, the sample sewer sews the entire prototype garment. The sample sewer moves from one piece of equipment to the next, until the garment is finished. The sample sewer may need to send a section of a prototype to another area for work. For example, it may be necessary to embroider a logo onto a shirt front after it is cut out and before the shirt is sewn. Keeping the work flowing smoothly is also part of the process. Generally, for companies that produce prototypes in-house, the prototype is completed within a few days after cutting.

If the design development department is located near the sample sewing room, sample sewers might consult with the patternmaker regarding a specific sewing process or technique, or they may discuss possible alternative solutions to a pattern

Figure 8.6
The sample cutter is used to cut the garment pieces for the sample or prototype. Inti St. Clair/Getty Images.

Figure 8.7
The patternmaker and the sample sewer discuss possible alternatives for a design detail.

or construction problem (Figure 8.7). A team approach among patternmaker, cutter, and sample sewer is an advantage. After the sample sewer finishes making the prototype, it is sent back to the design development department for evaluation. Often the patternmaker reviews the prototype first to assess whether any changes need to be made before the designer and merchandiser review the style.

Approving the Prototype

The fit of the company's products is important in achieving a competitive advantage through product differentiation. Therefore, an assessment of how each style fits can be very important to a company. A **fit model** is used to assess the fit, styling, and overall look of the new prototype. The fit model is a person selected to represent the body proportions that the fashion brand company feels are ideal for its target customer and that correspond to the base pattern size used to make the prototype. Some fit models, called in-house models, may work for the company in another capacity and are asked to try on prototypes as needed as a part of their job duties. Other companies hire a professional fit model who may work for a number of fashion brand companies. With professional fit models, specific appointments will be made for fit sessions, requiring both lead time to book the appointment and on-time delivery of prototypes for the fit session. Fit models can provide valuable information about the comfort and ease of the garment.

Menswear fit models tend to have well-proportioned bodies and usually are about 5 feet, 10 inches to 6 feet tall. In misses apparel, fit models differ from runway models and photographic models. A misses fit model has body proportions that are "average," with a height of 5 feet, 5 inches to 5 feet, 8 inches, as compared to the tall and svelte runway models. Large-size, tall, and petite fit models are used for their respective size categories.

Body forms (such as dress forms, torso forms, and pant forms) can be a valuable tool for assessing the fit and design of a prototype. Many fashion brand companies use body forms based on specified body dimensions. Customized body forms, made to a company's measurement specifications, are also available from a variety of body form companies. New developments in 3-D body scanning allow a fashion brand company to have its fit model's individual shape duplicated as a body form. Thus, assessing the fit on a true-to-life body form can offer great accuracy when the fit model is not available. Other developments in body forms include the use of more pliable materials that better replicate the malleable characteristics of flesh. Body forms made from these materials are especially valuable for swimwear, underwear, and lingerie companies.

When several prototypes are ready for assessment, a fit session is scheduled with the fit model. Whereas the garment fit is a part of the assessment, much of the discussion among designer, assistant designer, and patternmaker may focus on the prototype's overall style and garment details. Sometimes production engineers are asked to provide feedback about potential difficulties in factory production of the style. If any of these aspects need revision, either the existing prototype will be redone or the pattern will be revised and a new prototype will be cut and sewn. The final design will be approved by the designer and/or the merchandiser. The style might be eliminated from the line at this point if reworking the design does not seem feasible.

After the prototype garment has been completed, it might undergo a wash test using a home-laundry-type washer and dryer. The wash test performed on garments to be sold in other countries would use the type of laundering equipment found in those countries, to simulate the conditions under which the garment will be laundered. Occasionally, problems that were not evident when the individual fabrics or trims were tested arise after laundering a garment.

THREE-DIMENSIONAL TOOLS

Three-dimensional technology provides the ability to move from the two-dimensional pattern to a three-dimensional image of a garment draped onto a body form. When using 3-D for patternmaking, a designer can construct garments over a digital image, rotate them, zoom in, and visualize how the piece will look. Even different fabric drape can be selected to stimulate how the final garment will hang. Originally developed as a virtual dressing tool at the retail level, three-dimensional technology enables customers to envision how a garment might look on them. Software such as My Virtual Model™ allows the customer to input personal data such as coloring, body build, and favorite colors. The program shows the virtual model on the computer screen, wearing suggested styles in several colors.

In addition to allowing designers and product developers to view a design three-dimensionally before the pattern is made and the sample cut and sewn, 3-D technology has many applications in the fashion industry. The concept of designing entirely on the computer may seem far off, but the reality is that not only can designers create the three-dimensional image of the garment style with replica fabric on the computer screen, but retail buyers can write their orders from the garments viewed on the screen. No prototype samples need to be sewn. The cost savings related to design development are substantial.

Advances in computer technology will allow the three-dimensional virtual garment to be transferred into a two-dimensional pattern. Other advances include the technology to compute the cost difference (in material usage and time to sew) between slightly different versions of a design.

DETERMINING THE INITIAL COST ESTIMATE

The cost to mass-produce the style is an important consideration when selecting styles for the final line. Thus, preliminary costing needs to be done before making the decision to adopt or reject a style. An **initial cost estimate**, also called **precosting**, for the style is based primarily on material cost and labor cost. A quick cost may have been calculated during the design stage; however, until the prototype is constructed, the quick cost serves only as a preliminary estimate. To calculate the cost more accurately, an initial cost estimate is determined based on the components of materials, trims and findings, labor, and other related costs.

Material Cost

The cost of the materials is estimated based on the number of yards of fabric or other materials required for making the prototype. Included in the cost of materials are such items as interfacing, pocketing, and lining needed for the prototype. To calculate the quantity of yardage required to make a new style, a layout plan of the pattern pieces, called a **marker**, needs to be made. The term *costing marker* refers to the layout plan for the pattern pieces that are used to determine the yardage (called **usage**) to produce one garment of the new style (Figure 8.8). If the pattern for the new style was made using PDS, the pattern pieces for this style have been stored in the computer and can be brought into a computer program that is used to develop the costing marker. The pattern pieces are arranged within a rectangular space representing the width and length of the intended fabric. Various layouts can be analyzed to determine the best arrangement of pattern

Figure 8.8
A costing marker created from the pattern pieces stored in the pattern design system is used to determine the quantity of material required for one garment.

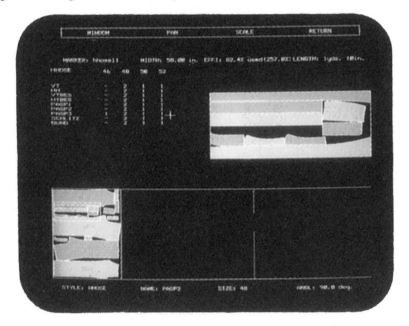

pieces using the least quantity of fabric. This process is repeated for the lining and other materials required for the new style.

In theory the quantity of the various fabrics needed to produce one medium-size garment in the new style, multiplied by the fashion brand company's cost for the fabrics, would be used to arrive at a total materials cost. If the company produces the same number of small sizes and large sizes as medium sizes, then using the size medium to average the quantity of fabrics needed should yield a good estimate of the yardage required for one garment. However, if the company in fact sells many more size small items than size large items, the average cost of materials would be higher than the actual cost. Conversely, if many more size large items were sold than size small items, then the average cost of materials would be too low. Therefore, some companies may use a size other than size medium to calculate their average usage.

Trim and Findings Cost

The quantity of all trims and findings used for the new style must be included in the initial cost estimate. Examples of trim items include braid or lace, and findings include items such as elastic, zipper, and buttons. For the initial cost estimate for the cotton pants shown in Table 8.1, one button and one zipper are needed to make this style. Note that the cost of one button is based on the cost when a gross of buttons is purchased. The cost per item is based on a large-quantity purchase for other trims and findings as well.

Labor Cost

The other major component of the initial cost estimate is the cost of labor to cut and sew/construct the new style. The labor cost is determined by estimating the number of minutes required to cut (and fuse interfacing), sew/construct, and finish the garment/product multiplied by the cost per minute of labor for a specific factory. To estimate the number of minutes required to cut, sew/construct, and finish a new style, sewing/construction time data from similar styles produced in the previous season can be useful. For an accurate labor cost estimate, it is necessary to select a possible site for production since labor costs vary considerably around the world. In some countries, the labor cost varies month by month. One approach to estimating the labor cost for a new style is to use the known cost of labor to sew a similar garment from the previous season. However, due to economic and political conditions, it may not be feasible to use the same factory that produced a similar style for the previous season. At this point in the development process, the cost is just an estimate. An exact cost will be calculated later. As production time nears, costs might be researched in several countries because production cost is used as one criterion in selecting where to source production (see Chapter 11).

Other Costs

When establishing the initial cost estimate, it is necessary to include other items that affect the cost. Table 8.1 details some of these items: packaging and/or hangers, hangtags, labels, and freight charges. If a style is produced offshore, other costs might include duty charges (tariffs) and fees to shipping agents and freight consolidators.

Table 8.1 Cost to Manufacture a Pair of Cotton Pants in the United States

Style #8074	Quantity	Price/Yard	Amount	Subtotal
1. Materials				
fabric	1.7 yd.	$2.90	$4.93	
interfacing	0.2 yd.	$0.55	$0.11	
ship fabric to company ($0.20 x 1.7)		$0.20	$0.34	
Total Materials Cost				$5.38
2. Trim/Findings				
buttons	1	$2.00/gross	$0.02	
zipper (7″)	1	$0.13	$0.13	
Total Trim/Findings Cost				$0.15
3. Labor				
marking ($45/order)		$0.23		
grading ($70/order)		$0.35		
cutting ($75/order)		$0.38		
sewing labor (0.5 hour @ $15.00)		$7.50		
Total Labor Cost				$8.46
4. Other				
packaging/hanger, hangtag, labels		$0.15		
freight		$0.35		
duty (none, U.S. production)		$0.00		
shipping agent, consolidator fees (none)		$0.00		
Total Other Costs				$0.50
5. Cost to Manufacture				$14.49
6. Wholesale Price*				$28.98

*The manufacturer determines the wholesale price to include overhead and profit. If keystone markup is used, then the wholesale price paid by the retailer to the manufacturer will be double the cost to manufacture.

Target Costing

Designing a product based on target costing (also discussed in Chapter 6) works a little differently from the product development sequence discussed previously. The designer's sketch is reviewed by the cost engineer, also called a product technician. The cost is carefully estimated from the designer's sketch. The design team works out fabric choices, garment details, and construction factors to bring the design within the required cost for each style in the line. The design sketch may need to be reworked to meet the target cost and be approved; then a prototype garment is cut, sewn, and given final approval after a careful cost estimate has been made. Each style that is approved is added to the line. The line might be composed of five groups with three to four styles in each group.

Fashion brand retailers frequently use target costing as they develop private label or store brand merchandise. The retailer's design department sets a specific cost for each item that will be produced. During the design development process, style features and fabrics are adjusted to meet the target cost.

STYLE SELECTION

Each style in the new line goes through a similar process of development and costing. When all the styles have been approved by the designer (and merchandiser), the line is ready for design review. Because of the lag time in receiving some fabrics, the review garments may have simulated textile elements in order to visualize the style in the intended fabric. For example, sometimes a print or stripe is painted onto a fabric to simulate the final textile design. Occasionally, these simulated prototypes are even used for promotional photos, since the difference between the mock-up and the actual garment will not be apparent in the photograph.

First Line Review Meeting

On the scheduled master calendar date, the new line is presented for review. The merchandiser, designer, assistant designer, production engineer, and any other review team members (such as a selected sales representative) assemble for the line review meeting. Upper management may also be included in the review session. The individual garment styles may be displayed on walls in the conference room (sometimes referred to as the war room), or fit models may try on the garments to present the styles to the review team.

Each style in the line is reviewed, and the review team asks questions to determine how well the style works in the areas of cost, production, styling, relationship to the rest of the line, and fabric and trims.

- *Cost:* Will the estimated cost result in a retail price that is within the range of the target customer's expectation? Is its cost in proportion to that of other similar styles? Are there changes in design that might reduce the cost? Could less expensive buttons be substituted? For companies that do cost averaging among several similar items, is this approach feasible?
- *Production:* Are there any potential difficulties in production? Are there changes in design that could make production easier or less expensive? Could a seam be eliminated?
- *Styling:* Does the style fit the look of the target customer? Does the styling look too fashion forward or too conservative when compared to the rest of the line? Could pockets be added if this is important to the target customer? Does the style look sufficiently different from competitors' styles?
- *Relationship to the rest of the line:* Does the style work well with other styles in the line? Is there another style so similar that the two will compete with each other? Is the style so different from others that it looks out of place in the line?
- *Fabric and trims:* Are there potential problems with the fabric? If the fabric is new to the line, will it snag, pill, or wrinkle? Has the fabric been adequately

tested? Are there potential problems with lengthy lead time required for a fabric or high minimum yardage requirements by the textile mill?

The review team discusses all of these points, as well as others, for each of the styles in the line.

Final Line Adoption Meeting

After the line review meeting, some styles will be eliminated, and some changes may be required in a few styles. For styles in which changes are required, patterns are modified and new prototypes are sewn and approved. The line is thus honed to develop a tight group, line, or collection of styles with the hope that all styles will sell well at market.

Occasionally, one or more styles are included in a line that the review team speculates may not sell well to the retail buyers. A company may want to experiment with a slightly more fashion-forward look. The line may include one or two jackets with more updated styling than has been shown in the past to see how the retail buyers react to these styles.

Thus, the styles that have been approved become part of the new line. It is reviewed and finalized at the final adoption meeting.

Determining the Cost to Manufacture

The cost to manufacture each of the styles to be shown in the new line must be determined before showing the line at market. Establishing as accurate a cost as possible is important to the successful financial outcome of the line. A design that sells well but is underpriced can be a disaster for the apparel company. The amount that the company calculates will be spent to make the garment is called the **cost to manufacture**.

Calculating the cost requires knowledge about production techniques and facilities. Production engineers, or cost engineers, use known costs as well as estimated costs for unknown factors to arrive at the cost to manufacture each of the styles. There is always the possibility that a style will actually cost more than was calculated, or perhaps less. However, it is critical that the cost to manufacture be as accurate a figure as possible. Forgetting to include the cost of a hanger or plastic bag can affect the overall profit when multiplied by thousands of items produced in that style.

If a fashion brand company uses contractors for production, they can be asked to do one of the following:

- examine a prototype garment of the style to provide a cost figure
- sew a sample garment and thus provide a cost figure
- review a complete and detailed spec sheet and provide a firm cost

The **wholesale price** is the price quoted to the buyers at market and is the amount the retail store will pay the fashion brand company for the goods. The wholesale price is the cost to manufacture the style plus the manufacturer's overhead and profit. Some fashion brand companies double the cost to manufacture (sometimes referred to as "keystone") to arrive at the wholesale price (see Table 8.1).

PRELINE

Some fashion brand companies invite their key retail accounts (those retail buyers who place large orders with them) to preview the line before its introduction at market. The preview is sometimes referred to as **preline**. The line might be composed of actual samples, or virtual samples shown on the computer. These retail buyers give the apparel company their opinions about the potential success of the styles they are shown. Retailers might place orders at this time. Advantages to the apparel company of holding a preline showing include

- knowing in advance which styles will sell well, thus allowing the fashion brand company to plan production needs accordingly so it has adequate quantities of anticipated successful products and avoids producing poor-selling styles
- maintaining a strong working relationship with key retail accounts
- receiving feedback from retailers about styles that might sell better if changes were made

A disadvantage of preline showing is that, since the styles have not yet been produced in the factory, unknown factors may still emerge that will require later changes in a style that buyers have already ordered.

Some companies forecast sales without receiving actual written orders from retailers. For example, black ski pants tend to be constant sellers at market. In advance of orders being placed, the skiwear company may begin production of a certain number of black ski pants to avoid the pressure on production during that industry's very short production season.

PREPARATION FOR MARKET

Once the new line is ready to be shown to retail buyers, additional **samples** or **duplicates** need to be made so that sales representatives throughout the country or world can sell the line by showing samples to retail store buyers.

Ordering and Making Sales Samples

Each sales representative and/or each market center showroom will require a representative group of styles from the new line to show to the retail store buyers. Because of cost limitations, not every style in every colorway will be made for sales representatives' samples, or duplicates. However, line catalogs, or line sheets, will show all colorways. As soon as the line is final, the styles that will be made as samples to sell the line at market are selected. The quantity of fabric is calculated and ordered, along with the linings, buttons, zippers, and other supplies required for the samples. If the textile producer is late in delivering the ordered fabrics, complications in producing the samples on time may occur. Late arrival of fabric could result in the samples not arriving in time for the sales representatives to show at market.

Contractors, or the fashion brand company's factories, cut and sew/construct the sample garments/products. If any production difficulties arise during this small production run, there is an opportunity to make an adjustment to ensure a smooth run later during production of the retailer's goods. Late delivery of samples from the sewing/construction facility could also cause complications at market.

Line Catalog or Line Sheet

As soon as the new line has been finalized, a **line catalog** (also called a **line sheet** or line style book) is prepared. This is a catalog, usually with color illustrations, of all the styles available in the line in the various colorways available for each style. Color photographs of featured styles may also be included. Charts show the sizes and colors available for each style and can serve as order sheets as well. Wholesale prices and sometimes suggested retail prices for each style are included. Figure 8.9 shows a typical line catalog page. Sales representatives and buyers use the line catalog to augment the sample garments shown during presentations.

Most companies use specialized CAD or graphics software to produce color illustrations of the garments for the line catalog. Typically, if the first sketch used in the design stage is produced using a computer system, this sketch is revised as needed and then used for the line catalog.

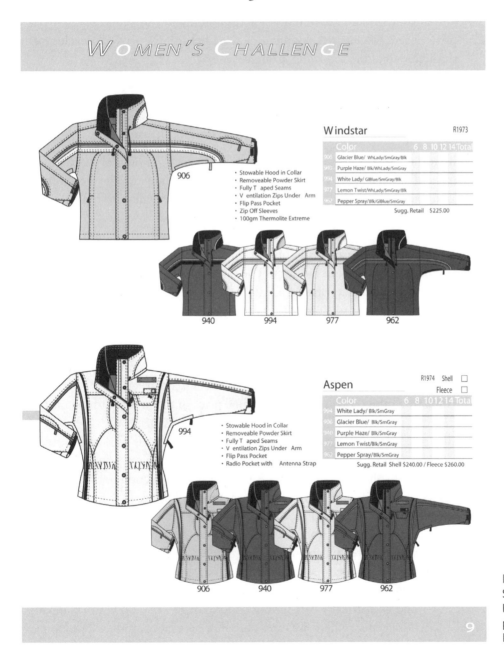

Figure 8.9
Sales representatives use line catalogs in their presentations. Dimitrios Kambouris/Getty Images.

It is important that the line catalog accurately represents the colors of the actual fabrics for each style. Retail buyers expect the finished goods to match the colors depicted in the line catalog. Some fashion brand companies show actual fabric swatches in their line catalogs, or they send a set of fabric swatches with the line catalogs. Seeing the actual fabric texture, plaid repeat, or variety of print colorways helps sell the line to the retail buyers.

PRIVATE LABEL AND STORE BRAND/SPA PRODUCT DEVELOPMENT

In today's marketplace, the creation and development of a fashion line occurs in a variety of ways. Possible design–retail relationships include the following:

1. traditional design development in which the garment/product carries the brand name or designer brand of the fashion brand company
2. private label product development or store brand/SPA product development through one of the following arrangements:
    *   The retailer provides the garment specifications and the contractor sources the goods (**specification buying**).
    *   The retailer and the contractor collaborate in creating the retailer's line.
    *   The contractor designs the entire program for the retailer.

It is important to understand the differences between traditional design development and private label or store brand/SPA development. The development approach affects the design, production, and pricing strategies for apparel, accessories, and home fashions.

We have traced the progress of a style from its creation through its development stages, using a model based on a conventional marketing channel used for **brand merchandise** in the fashion industry. The fashion brand company conceives the design, controls manufacturing (using its own factories or contractors it selects), and then markets the product to the retailer. The retail buyer evaluates the sample garment and decides whether to purchase the style in anticipation of the retailer's target customer desiring the product. A profit is expected at each step of the marketing channel. Conventional design development, marketing, and production involve several profit-making steps, including sewing/construction by a contractor and selling by a sales representative. The final price of the product to the ultimate consumer usually reflects the number of profit-making steps.

As the price of fashion merchandise at the retail level has escalated in recent years, retailers and fashion brand companies have sought ways to reduce costs and increase their share of the profit. Using offshore production in countries with lower labor costs is one solution. Another approach is to reduce the number of steps involved in the marketing channel. By reducing the number of profit-making steps, either the cost of the product can be reduced, or the profit to the remaining companies can be increased (or both). If a retailer works directly with a fashion brand company to co-create a product or a line, the sales representative's position is no longer needed. If a retailer decides to create a product to sell in its retail stores and goes directly to a sewing contractor, the fashion brand company's services are not needed. These are examples of private label product development or store brand/SPA product development.

Private Label and Store Brand/SPA Product Development Processes

Creating private label or store brand/SPA merchandise can be achieved in several ways. One method for developing private label or store brand goods is for the retailer to work directly with the contractors or their agents, providing them with garment/product specifications. Retailers such as Target, JCPenney, and Nordstrom have their own product development departments for developing their store brand merchandise. These companies work directly with contractors to source and produce the goods to their very detailed specifications. Target, JCPenney, and Walmart, among others, have sourcing offices in Asia. Thus, the retailer assumes the responsibility of designing the product as well as overseeing its production.

One advantage to the retailer in dealing directly with the contractor for production is that the retailer has no intermediaries to deal with, thus avoiding communication pitfalls and eliminating the need to share the profits. From the contractor's viewpoint, working directly with the retailer has certain risks. The contractor usually carries the financing for the materials during the production process. After delivering the goods to the retailer, the contractor is paid for both labor and materials. This is different from the conventional market channel discussed earlier, in which the fashion brand company often carries the financing of the materials. As these new marketing channels expand and are modified, the advantages, disadvantages, and risks to contractor and retailer may vary as well. Some retailers own their production facilities, carrying all the risk while reducing the number of intermediaries in the marketing channel.

Another of the private label or store brand development processes uses the fashion brand company's design and development staff to create the entire program for the retailer. Nike, an apparel company that produces lines of sports apparel under its own label, also develops special lines for other sports specialty retail stores carrying the retailer's label. This type of collaborative business is common in the fashion industry. One advantage to the retailer is that the fashion brand company handles all the production processes. Often the fashion brand company has a strong working relationship with vendors, relieving the retailer of developing systems to oversee the production.

Development of Private Label and Store Brand/SPA Products

The British retailer Marks & Spencer was a leader in private label apparel. "The company's low prices were the result of trading directly with manufacturers for cash, a principle which remains unchanged to this day. Marks & Spencer's goods are immediately recognized by their 'St. Michael' trademark, which first appeared on 'pajamas and knitted articles of clothing' back in 1928" (Bressler, Newman, and Proctor 1997, p. 68). Rather than purchasing lingerie items from apparel companies to sell in their retail stores, Marks & Spencer determined the goods it wanted to produce and then went directly to contractors who produced the goods. By eliminating the apparel company's role (and its profit) in the design and manufacturing process, Marks & Spencer could produce and sell its goods at very appealing prices.

Soon, other retailers began to realize the advantages of private label product development. In the 1950s, Hong Kong was well known for its knitwear manufacturing, especially sweaters. The quality was good, production was dependable, and prices were low. Retailers such as Frederick and Nelson (no longer in business) contracted with knitwear companies in Hong Kong to produce exclusive products, such as sweaters, for their retail stores. The sweater label read, "Made Exclusively for Frederick and Nelson in Hong Kong." This private label product development remained a small part of the specialty and department store retail picture in the United States until the 1980s.

The growth of off-price stores and factory outlet mall stores in the 1980s increased pressure on department and specialty store retailers to offer products at competitive prices. Added to retailers' pressures was the fact that apparel companies such as Tommy Hilfiger, Polo Ralph Lauren, and Nike opened retail stores of their own. One remedy for department store retailers was to increase the percentage of private label merchandise they carried. Thus, the private label business continues to expand, both within department store retailers and with specialty retailers.

Figure 8.10
Department stores offer a number of private label apparel brands, such as INC International for Macy's.

With private label goods, all the risk in selling is in the retailer's hands. The risk to retailers is lessened because basic goods (as compared to fashion goods) have long-term sales potential. Thus, as department store retailers built and expanded their private label business in the early 1990s, most of them chose to produce basic garment styles such as polo shirts, shorts, casual pants, and jeans—all well suited for private label manufacturing. Another advantage of producing these types of private label goods is that the difference between a national brand and a private label item is difficult to discern. A customer could purchase a private label polo shirt for several dollars less than the national brand shirt that looked nearly identical. The price-conscious customer would eagerly select the private label polo shirt and be well satisfied with its quality (Figure 8.10).

Some retailers link their private label lines to celebrities to enhance the stature of the label and the retail store. Kmart offers Jaclyn Smith labels. In an interesting twist, some retailers have signed licensing deals with Seventh Avenue fashion designers. Target signed an exclusive licensing deal with designers Mossimo, Issac Mizrahi, and Cynthia Rowley. For these fashion designers, the financial risk of designing under their own business has been transferred to the retailer.

As sales volume of private label merchandise increased, retailers developed more fashion-forward private label merchandise in addition to the basic items that were safe choices for beginning their private label businesses. To do so, retailers organized product design teams similar to the design teams at apparel companies. Mass retailers such as Target and JCPenney were some of the first retailers to have private label product development departments (Table 8.2).

Table 8.2 Selected Apparel Private Labels

Store	Labels
Dillard's	Allison Daley, Investments, Westbound, Copper Key, Aigle, Caribbean, Daniel Cremieux, Murano, Roundtree & Yorke, Class Club, First Wave, Starting Out
Macy's, Inc.	Charter Club, Karen Scott, INC International, Alfani, Greendog, Club Room, Style & Co.
JCPenney	Worthington, St. John's Bay, Arizona/Arizona Kids, Stafford, Okie Dokie
Kmart	Joe Boxer, Jaclyn Smith, Basic Editions, Route 66, Small Wonders
Kohl's	Apt 9, Croft & Barrow, Sonoma, Urban Pipeline
Nordstrom	Caslon, Classiques Entier, Halogen, Baby Nay, Façonnable
Sears	Canyon River Blues, Covington, Classic Elements, Personal Identity, Stacy Adams
Target	Merona, xhilaration
Walmart	Starter, No Boundaries, George, Faded Glory

Store Is Brand/SPA

During the 1980s and early 1990s, a number of specialty retailers opened businesses that sell 100 percent private label merchandise or store brands. This strategy, known as **store-is-brand**, results in the retail outlet (i.e., store, catalog, website) and the apparel brand being one and the same in the consumer's mind. These are now referred to as specialty retailers of private label apparel (SPA). Examples of companies that employ this strategy include The Limited, Victoria's Secret, Express, Gap, Banana Republic, Old Navy, Zara, H&M, Eddie Bauer, Talbots, and Benetton. As with other retailers that offer private label merchandise, companies that offer only store brands either employ their own designers and/or product developers who turn their designs over to contractors for production, or their buyers seek out full-package contractors who design, develop, and produce specified merchandise exclusively for the store. Exceptions include Benetton and Zara, both vertically integrated companies that control production from fabric to finished garment.

Advantages and Disadvantages of Private Label and Store Brand/SPA Product Development

Retailers may decide to offer private label merchandise, expand their private label business, or offer only store brands. As noted earlier, a major advantage to private label and store brand product development is the reduced number of intermediaries involved, providing an increased profit (gross margin) to the retailer and/or a reduced price for the consumer.

Another advantage of private label and store brand business is that the retailer can fill in voids in some product categories. Also, the customer is looking for value, and private label merchandise can provide that value. Quality private label products offered at a good price can build and maintain store loyalty as well as private label loyalty among customers. One goal for retailers is to make the private label into a well-defined brand in the customer's mind. Creating a brand that the customer can associate with and understand creates brand loyalty. The brand then becomes a destination brand or go-to brand. Store differentiation is another advantage. National-brand merchandise is available at many retail and specialty stores, creating sameness in these stores' merchandise. Once customers become familiar with retailers' private label brands or store brands, they may choose to shop at that retailer's location because the store merchandise has an appeal and is different from what other stores offer. Presenting exclusive merchandise to the customer who wants to associate with the retailer's image is an advantage of private labeling.

Retailers have the closest tie to the customer. They have a finger on the pulse of what the customer is really buying and what she or he wants. Retailers want increasing control over more aspects of the product than branded manufacturers are offering them.

The major drawback to private label and store brand business has been mentioned: The retailer takes all the risk. Since the retailer usually owns the merchandise, if it does not sell well, the retailer loses profit.

SUMMARY

The designer, merchandiser, patternmaker, and production engineer analyze the fit and design, and they discuss cost factors. An initial cost estimate is calculated. This is an important factor in deciding the feasibility of producing the style. Changes may be made to the prototype, or perhaps the pattern will be modified and a new prototype will be cut and sewn. This process continues with all the styles proposed for the line. The styles in the line are reviewed, and final decisions are made to determine which styles will be adopted for the final line.

The design development stage in the progress of a new line begins with delivery of the designer's approved sketch. Development of the new style includes making the first pattern. A prototype is cut from the pattern and sewn by a sample sewer, using the intended fabric (or a substitute facsimile if the actual fabric is not yet available). The new prototype is tried on a fit model for review of the design and fit by a design team and revised if necessary. Sometimes, several prototypes of a new style are sewn to perfect the design. The cost for the final design is estimated. The line is reviewed again, at which time the design team carefully scrutinizes each style. The final line consists of styles that have been approved at this stage. Additional samples of styles in the line are sewn for sales representatives, and a line catalog and other types of promotional materials are prepared for marketing purposes.

Computer applications in design development continue to expand. Each year, more fashion brand companies realize the need to use this technology to survive in today's marketplace. The computer integration of design, patternmaking, and production is another critical step for continued survival in the ever-increasing pace of the fashion industry.

The changing structure of marketing channels will continue to bring about changes in the relationship between the fashion brand company, contractor, sales representative, and retailer. Trends in the fashion industry include continued expansion of private label and store brand product development, the use of product life cycle management systems, and 3-D tool development.

KEY TERMS

base pattern
block
brand merchandise
color management
cost to manufacture
drafting
draping
duplicate
fit model
flat pattern

garment/product specification
    sheet
initial cost estimate
line catalog
line sheet
marker
pattern design system (PDS)
precosting
preline
proprietary

prototype
sample
sample sewer
sloper
specification buying
store-is-brand
style number
usage
wholesale price

DISCUSSION QUESTIONS AND ACTIVITIES

1. Discuss how an apparel company interested in converting from paper patternmaking to a pattern design system (PDS) might decide what system to purchase.
2. Discuss why a designer might use draping techniques as opposed to patternmaking when developing a garment design. What are advantages and disadvantages of each method?
3. Select a garment, such as a jacket. How might the design and materials be changed to reduce the cost?
4. For a retailer, what are some advantages and disadvantages in producing private label merchandise?
5. For an apparel company, what are some advantages and disadvantages in producing a special private label apparel line for a retailer?

CASE STUDY

Importance of Specifications in Design Development

Lauren's Fashion Boutique is a regional specialty store chain with eight locations. To provide unique merchandise to its customers, Lauren's Fashion Boutique has contracted with Lee's Manufacturing to manufacture a line of private label wool trousers for its stores. Lee's Manufacturing is a well-known full-package contractor. Merchandisers for Lauren's Fashion Boutique worked with Lee's Manufacturing in a process known as specification buying. Merchandisers for Lauren's Fashion Boutique met with Lee's Manufacturing and selected the product style, colors, and sizes needed from specifications developed by Lee's Manufacturing. Upon completion of the line, the Lee's Manufacturing production facility sent the private label trousers directly to the Lauren Fashion Boutique stores.

Lauren's Fashion Boutique stores received the trousers, but also received many complaints from customers that the trousers did not fit and the fabric was not consistent across the colors. When the merchandisers from Lauren's Fashion Boutique reviewed the specifications with Lee's Manufacturing, the specifications agreed upon in the contract were met. Unfortunately, what appeared to happen was that the merchandisers from Lauren's Fashion Boutique did not specify the length of the pant, and Lee's Manufacturing produced and delivered only petite sizes to the stores. The specifications for the waist and hips were correct for petite sizes only and therefore met the contract. Similarly, specifications approved by the merchandisers for Lauren's Fashion Boutique required a 100 percent wool fabric in three colors to be used for the private label trousers. However, the 100 percent wool fabric used by Lee's Manufacturing was a different weave structure for each color.

1. Lauren's Fashion Boutique is now requesting that Lee's Manufacturing produce and deliver trousers in misses sizes in fabrics that are consistent across colors at no cost to them. Do you believe that Lee's Manufacturing should consider this request? That is, who was responsible for the garment specifications?
2. In hindsight, what should the merchandisers at Lauren's Fashion Boutique have done to ensure that the trousers they received were to the specifications they thought they were agreeing to?
3. How might Lauren's Fashion Boutique prevent this problem in the future?

CAREER OPPORTUNITIES

Possible positions in the area of design development and style selection are

- CAD Designer/engineer
- Costing manager
- Developer
- Patternmaker
- Production engineer
- Product developer
- Sample maker
- Specification developer
- Technical production assistant

REFERENCES

Bressler, Karen, Karoline Newman, and Gillian Proctor. (1997). *A Century of Lingerie*. Edison, NJ: Chartwell Books.

Cohen, Marshal. (2009, August 1). "The Challenges of Private Label Apparel." *License Global*. Retrieved from http://www.licensemag.com (accessed March 12, 2016).

D'Innocenzio, Anne, and Miles Socha. (1998). "Punching Up Private Label." *Women's Wear Daily*, October 7, pp. 14–15.

"Private Label's New Identity." (1999). *Women's Wear Daily*, March 11, 1, 8, 20.

Ryan, Thomas J. (2003). "Private Labels: Strong, Strategic & Growing." *Apparel*, June, pp. 32–37.

Workman, Jane E. (1991). "Body Measurement Specifications for Fit Models as a Factor in Clothing Size Variation." *Clothing and Textiles Research Journal* 10 (1): 31–36.

CHAPTER 9

Marketing
Fashion Brands

IN THIS CHAPTER, YOU WILL LEARN

THE FOLLOWING:

- the marketing processes used by fashion brand companies

- the functions and activities of fashion brand market centers, marts, market weeks, and trade shows

- the nature of the selling function of fashion brand companies

- the sales promotion strategies used by fashion brand companies

Step 4: Marketing the Apparel Line

Step 1 Research and Merchandising

Step 2 Design Brief

Step 3 Design Development and Style Selection

Step 4 Marketing the Fashion Brand

Designer and National Brands
Sales Representatives Show Line at Market and
through Other Promotion Strategies

Retail Buyers Place Orders

Private-Label Brands
Design Team Shows Line to Merchandisers/Buyers

Buyers Place Orders

Step 5 Preproduction

Step 6 Sourcing

Step 7 Apparel Production Processes,
Material Management, and Quality Assurance

Step 8 Distribution and Retailing

Within the organizational structure of fashion brand companies, the area called research and merchandising typically focuses on market research and developing sales, promotion, and distribution strategies. Marketing divisions or departments in fashion brand companies are organized in a number of ways, depending on the company size and goals. Figure 9.1 shows a variety of organizational structures for marketing divisions of fashion brand companies.

The marketing area of a fashion brand company is most often associated with product promotion and sales. But without an accurate understanding of the target

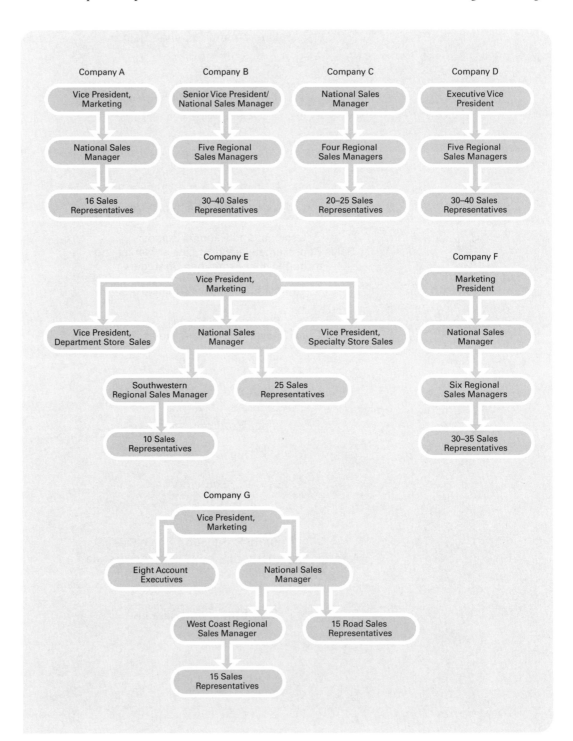

Figure 9.1
Examples of marketing division organizational structures.

customer attained through market research, and without designing and producing goods and services that meet the needs of the target customer, even the best promotion strategies will undoubtedly fail. Thus, the marketing of fashion merchandise connects the research conducted previously with the appropriate strategies for getting the product to the right consumers at the right price and in the right place.

The term **market** can be used in the following ways:

- When someone says that a particular product has a *market*, it means there is consumer demand for the product. As noted in earlier chapters, research is used to assess the consumer demand or market for a product.
- People also use *market* when referring to a location where the buying and selling of merchandise takes place. For example, retail buyers often talk about going to market to purchase merchandise for their stores.
- We also use *market* to mean promoting a product, typically through advertising in the media and public relations efforts.

This chapter examines fashion markets as locations where fashion brand companies sell their merchandise to retailers. It also explores the promotion strategies that fashion brand companies use in marketing their goods to retailers and ultimate consumers.

MARKET CENTERS AND MARTS

The term **market center** refers to those cities that are the headquarters of major fashion brand companies, house marts and/or showrooms, are home to important trade shows, and have important retailing industries. Internationally, these cities include New York City, Los Angeles, Paris, London, Milan, Tokyo, Hong Kong, Seoul, Taipei, Rio de Janeiro, and Buenos Aires.

Marts

A **mart** is a building or a group of buildings that houses showrooms in which sales representatives show apparel and home fashions lines to retail buyers. Many fashion market centers have marts; some are devoted entirely to textiles, apparel, accessories, home fashions, and related goods (e.g., Los Angeles's California Market Center, aka the CMC); some also house showrooms for a variety of products. For example, the Merchandise Mart in Chicago includes showrooms for apparel, home furnishings, kitchen and bath, commercial furnishings, outdoor furnishings, and gift and home accessories. Some marts are also part of larger market center complexes (e.g., Dallas Market Center) that include multiple mart buildings for an array of merchandise.

All marts also include exhibition halls that are filled with temporary showrooms or booths. These are used during **market weeks**, the primary times during the year when retail buyers are shown seasonal lines by apparel, accessories, or home fashions companies or sales representatives without permanent showrooms at that mart. Exhibition halls are also used for trade shows. To facilitate the buyers' trips to market, merchandise marts publish and/or post on their websites directories for market weeks that list the fashion brands being offered, sales representatives, and services available at the mart.

Retail Relations Programs

Marts compete for retailer buyers' attention through a variety of programs and services designed to enhance the buyer's experience and help them to be more efficient and effective in their jobs. These programs are commonly known as **retail relations programs**. For example, in response to shorter turnaround times and faster delivery of apparel, and because buyers are purchasing less merchandise more often, the larger marts are open year-round, typically 5 days a week, 52 weeks a year. This schedule allows buyers to come at any time during the year, not just during market weeks. Most marts currently have ongoing retail relations programs, including a number of services designed to assist retail buyers during market weeks and trade shows. These services include

- educational seminars (e.g., trend reports, visual merchandising, new merchandising strategies)
- seminars for first-time or new buyers
- fashion shows
- programs to connect buyers with representatives and vendors
- opportunities for buyers to join together for purchasing, marketing, and advertising purposes
- credit and financing assistance
- discounts on travel expenses
- entertainment (e.g., concerts, food fairs)

A number of marts offer seminars focusing on international markets and sourcing (purchasing goods and services) in other countries. Topics include how to do business in Mexico or China, labeling requirements for exporting goods, and other issues surrounding exporting. Many marts attract international buyers with services including travel assistance and translation services.

Marts are sometimes viewed as self-contained in that they generally house consultants' offices, restaurants, banks, hotels, auditoriums, health clubs, dry cleaners, business centers, and other services for retail buyers. Marts may also be involved in many aspects of fashion industries. For example, the California Market Center includes offices of fixture and display companies, employment agencies, buying offices, trade associations, and private label manufacturers. Thus, when buyers come to market, the mart serves as a one-stop location for all their needs.

MARKET WEEKS AND TRADE SHOWS

Market weeks and trade shows are the primary opportunities for designers, manufacturers, and retailers to connect and conduct business.

Market Weeks

Market weeks are the times of the year when retail buyers come to showrooms or exhibit halls to see the seasonal fashion lines. During market weeks, retail buyers attend to the following activities:

- set appointments with manufacturers' sales representatives of name brands
- set appointments with contractors for private label and store brand merchandise

- discover new brands
- attend fashion shows
- attend trend seminars and other educational sessions
- review manufacturers' lines
- place orders for name brand merchandise for their stores
- place orders for private label and store brand merchandise

The buyers typically come to market weeks with a specific amount that they can spend (referred to as their **open-to-buy**) for specific categories of merchandise. Marts generally sponsor a variety of market weeks throughout the year, each focusing on a particular product category (e.g., women's, juniors', men's, children's, bridal, swimwear, maternity) and fashion season (e.g., Pre-Fall, Fall, Holiday, Resort, Spring, Summer). Market week dates are typically set years in advance. In general, market weeks for Fall fashion season are held in March and April, and market weeks for Spring fashion season are held in October and November. Market weeks may also be sponsored in conjunction with an industry trade association. Through these joint efforts, buyers are exposed to a greater variety of apparel manufacturers at a single location than they would be otherwise. Table 9.1 outlines the typical months in which U.S. women's and children's ready-to-wear market weeks are held for each fashion season.

Market weeks provide advantages for the fashion brand and the retailer. Following are some advantages of market weeks for fashion brands:

- Sales representatives can show the new lines to a large number of retail buyers in a very short time. Retailers may also place orders during market week shows.
- Sales representatives can talk with the buyers and acquire information regarding consumer and retail trends.
- Based on buyer interest, sales representatives also can determine which pieces in the line will most likely be put into production.
- Through such market week activities as fashion shows and displays, apparel and home fashions companies can receive publicity for their lines and increase the potential for securing new retail accounts.
- Lines of competing companies may be viewed (although many exclusive lines are available for viewing to retail buyers only).

Table 9.1 Women's and Children's Ready-to-Wear (RTW) Market Weeks	
Fashion Season	**Market Weeks**
Summer	NYC market: October All other markets: January
Fall I (Pre-Fall)	NYC market: January All other markets: March–April
Fall II	NYC market: February All other markets: June
Holiday and Resort	NYC market: June All other markets: August
Spring	NYC market: September All other markets: October–November

Figure 9.2
Retail buyers attend trade shows such as WWDMAGIC to view seasonal lines of fashion brands. Churchill/WWD/© Conde Nast.

Figure 9.3
Trade shows provide opportunities for retail buyers to see and review new fashion brands. Bryan Steffy/WireImage /Getty Images.

For retail buyers, market weeks offer the following advantages:

- Market weeks allow them to review many lines of merchandise in a very short time.
- By attending seminars held during market weeks, they are also able to acquire information about fashion trends, promotional strategies, visual merchandising, and a number of other topics.
- Buyers can also become aware of new lines that they may want to purchase for their stores.

Individuals involved with product development often attend market weeks to identify contractors that may be able to produce private label or store brand merchandise. Thus, market weeks are important times for the fashion brand companies in determining the success of their lines.

Trade Shows

Trade associations and specialized trade show producers sponsor their own shows for the purpose of promoting lines of apparel, accessories, and home fashions (Figures 9.2 and 9.3). These **trade shows**, lasting anywhere from three to eight days, are typically located in the exhibition halls of marts, at large hotels, or at convention centers. For example, the Javits Center in New York City is the home to many fashion industry trade shows each year including MODA, Accessories The Show (ATS), Coterie, Project New York, Sole Commerce, and FAME trade shows. Las Vegas has become a U.S. hub for trade shows including ATS and MAGIC, one of the largest fashion brand trade shows covering men's, women's, and children's apparel, footwear, accessories, and resources. Tables 9.2 through 9.5 present selected examples of trade shows for several categories of merchandise.

Table 9.2 Examples of Footwear and Accessories Trade Shows

Trade Show	Location
Accessories The Show	New York City and Las Vegas, NV
WSA@ MAGIC (World. Shoes. Accessories) Show	Las Vegas, NV
FN Platform	Las Vegas, NV
Fashion Footwear Association of New York (FFANY)	New York City
Toronto Shoe Show	Toronto, Canada
GDS	Dusseldorf, Germany
The MICAM	Milan, Italy
China International Footwear Fair	Shanghai, China

Table 9.3 Examples of Apparel Fashions and Accessories Trade Shows

Trade Show	Location
MAGIC • The Collective—branded and licensed apparel for men and young men • WWDMAGIC—young contemporary and juniors', women's sportswear and accessories • Project—contemporary apparel and accessories for men and women • WSA@ MAGIC—fast fashion footwear for men, women, juniors, and children • FN Platform—luxury to lifestyle branded footwear for men, women, juniors, and children • CURVENV @ MAGIC—lingerie, swimwear, loungewear, activewear, and men's underwear • POOL TRADESHOW—boutique-ready fashion and accessories • THE TENTS—luxury and designer men's brands • Playground—contemporary fashion for children • Sourcing at MAGIC—manufacturing, component, technology, and services providers from around the world	Las Vegas, NV
ENK International Trade Events • Accessorie Circuit • Fashion Coterie • Children's Club • Intermezzo Collections • Sole Commerce	New York City, Las Vegas, Beijing, Shanghai
TMRW Fashion Avenue Market Expo (FAME)	New York City and Las Vegas
MODA: juried modern contemporary ready-to-wear collections	New York City
STYLEMAX: women's apparel and accessories	Chicago
International Fashion Jewelry and Accessory Show	multiple cities

Table 9.4 Examples of Active Sportswear and Sporting Goods Trade Shows	
Trade Show	**Location**
Outdoor Retailer (Outdoor Industry Association)	Salt Lake City, UT
Action Expo	Atlantic City, NJ

Table 9.5 Examples of Interior Design and Home Fashions Trade Shows	
Trade Show	**Location**
NeoCon World's Trade Fair: Design exhibition and conference for commercial interior designers	Chicago, IL
NY NOW: Home, lifestyle, handmade, and gift items including a wide range of home fashions and accessories	New York City
Home Textiles Sourcing Expo: Fabrics and finished soft goods for home applications	New York City
High Point Market: Largest home furnishings industry trade show in the world	High Point, NC

Some companies rely heavily on trade shows for presenting their lines; others present their lines primarily during market weeks in New York City and/or at apparel and merchandise marts and may exhibit at only one or two of the primary trade shows. Retail buyers, product developers, and sourcing agents may attend both market weeks and trade shows to review lines and services for their stores.

In addition, websites for trade shows include exhibitor information, buyer information, product search services, show information and registration, and show evaluations. Because of the expense of attending trade shows in person, online exhibits of lines and expanding buyers' opportunities to purchase goods online have grown in popularity. Virtual trade shows for textiles, home fashions, graphics (e.g., T-shirt graphic designs), and specialized apparel (e.g., protective clothing, uniforms) are quite common.

FASHION BRAND MARKET CENTERS

Fashion brand market centers include New York, Los Angeles, Paris, London, Milan, Rome, Tokyo, Hong Kong, Seoul, Taipei, Rio de Janeiro, Buenos Aires, and Sydney. These cities play important roles within the global fashion industries in marketing fashion brands. They are home to thriving fashion industries including design, marketing, and distribution/retail. New York and Los Angeles are the preeminent fashion market centers in the United States. Paris, London, and Milan have long histories as fashion capitals in Europe. Hong Kong and Tokyo reign as the fashion capitals of Asia, and Rio de Janeiro and Buenos Aires are important fashion market centers in South America.

All fashion brand market centers focus on design and marketing, and their respective fashion weeks are covered by all major media outlets. Trade shows in Europe (e.g., Premiere Vision) and Asia (e.g., Hong Kong Fashion Week, TITAS) attract attendees from around the world. Although all of these cities—and their respective countries—also have production industries (production centers are discussed later in the book), the following subsections focus on their roles in marketing fashion brands.

U.S. Fashion Brand Market Centers

New York City was the first fashion market center in the United States. Buyers from large, upscale stores traveled to New York City once or twice a year to view the new lines and purchase merchandise for their stores. In addition, manufacturers' salespeople traveled from town to town within a specific region, inviting buyers from local stores to see the lines in a hotel room or in the retailers' stores. With the growth of manufacturing and retailing of fashion merchandise in the 1950s, regional market centers began to be established. In the early 1960s, the first regional apparel and merchandise marts were built. After experiencing growth throughout the 1980s, some regional fashion and merchandise marts saw a decline in the 1990s. This drop was because of consolidation of companies within the industries, increased competition among marts, the growth of private label merchandising and store brands, the growth of trade shows as an important means for retailer buyers to connect with manufacturers, and the growth of electronic and web-based communications between manufacturers and retailers. With the decline in the importance of regional marts, there was growth in the importance of market centers for the industries—including New York City, Los Angeles, Dallas, and Atlanta.

New York City

New York City (NYC) is considered the preeminent U.S. fashion brand market center. NYC does not have a designated apparel or merchandise mart. Instead, showrooms are located throughout a portion of Manhattan known as the *garment district*, the *garment center*, the *fashion center*, or the *fashion district*. NYC's fashion center is an area in midtown Manhattan located between Fifth Avenue and Ninth Avenue and between 35th Street and 42nd Street (Figure 9.4). The central area is between Seventh Avenue (designated *Fashion Avenue* in 1972) and Broadway.

Currently, the NYC garment district or fashion center includes design and marketing headquarters for thousands of textile, trims, apparel, accessory, and home fashion companies. Virtually all name designers (e.g., Vera Wang, Calvin Klein, Donna Karan, Ralph Lauren, Jill Stuart, and Michael Kors) have offices in NYC. NYC is also home to New York Fashion Week, where nearly 100 U.S. and international designers hold their runway shows twice a year (Fall/Winter is held in February and Spring/Summer is held in September; see Figure 9.5). Some designers also present their lines/collections for other fashion seasons through runway shows.

Figure 9.4
New York City's fashion center, located in midtown Manhattan, is home to the studios and design and marketing headquarters of hundreds of companies. Eichner/WWD/© Conde Nast.

Figure 9.5
Designers present new collections twice per year at New York City's fashion week. Antonio de Moraes Barros Filho/FilmMagic/Getty Images.

Given that the city is expensive, crowded, and inconvenient, why does NYC continue to serve as an important market center? In addition to its historic foundation as a fashion center, NYC offers companies access to buying offices, textile wholesalers, findings and trim wholesalers, consultants, advertising agencies, offices of major trade associations, and publishing companies located in the city. Similar to other international fashion market centers, NYC is a cultural center where designers can draw inspiration from the continuous influx of art, theater, dance, opera, and other cultural events.

Los Angeles

Whereas NYC is considered the primary market center on the East Coast of the United States, Los Angeles is considered the primary market center on the West Coast. Located in Los Angeles' downtown Fashion District, the California Market Center (CMC), which opened in 1964, houses hundreds of showrooms for women's wear, menswear, children's wear, accessories, textiles, and gifts and home decor (Figure 9.6). In addition to the major markets, the CMC offers a number of category-specific specialty markets.

Similar to New York City, Los Angeles was once one of the nation's largest garment manufacturing centers, but it too has shifted its emphasis to design and

Figure 9.6
(a) The California Market Center in Los Angeles is the largest fashion brand market center on the West Coast of the United States. Boye/WWD/© Conde Nast. (b) Boye/WWD/© Conde Nast.

(a)

(b)

marketing. When we think of California, casual apparel and sportswear come to mind; Los Angeles is best known for sportswear, swimwear, and the "L.A. Style" of casual chic. Companies with headquarters in the Los Angeles area include BCBG Max Azria Group, Inc. (Vernon, CA), Guess? Inc., Joe's Jeans, Inc., Lucky Brand Jeans (Vernon, CA), Quiksilver, Rock & Republic, Sketchers USA, Inc., St. John Knits International, Inc., Tarrant Apparel Group (maker of JCPenney's Arizona jeans and other private labels), and Pacific Sunwear of California (PacSun in Anaheim, CA), to name a few. California is also home to the headquarters of a number of other large apparel/retailing companies including Ashworth, Inc. (Carlsbad, CA), Bebe Stores, Inc. (Brisbane, CA), Levi Strauss & Co. (San Francisco), Patagonia (Ventura, CA), and Wet Seal (Foothill Ranch, CA).

Chicago

The Chicago Merchandise Mart and the Chicago Apparel Center cater to industry customers from around the world. For apparel and accessories, their clientele come primarily from the northern and Midwestern regions of the United States. Since its opening in 1930, the Chicago Merchandise Mart (Figure 9.7) has remained one of the largest trade centers in the world. As a design center, the Merchandise Mart is the venue for the gift and home markets, as well as for NeoCon. Stylemax trade show offers over 4,000 brands of women's apparel and accessory lines. The Chicago area is also home to the headquarters of Sears Holdings Corporation (owner of Sears and Kmart).

Figure 9.7
The Chicago Merchandise Market is the venue for numerous gift and home markets. Raymond Boyd/Michael Ochs Archives/Getty Images.

Dallas

In the south, Dallas has become the key apparel market center. The Dallas Market Center (DMC) includes four buildings:

- World Trade Center—gifts, decorative accessories, furniture, rugs, fabric, and toys (FashionCenterDallas® showcases fashion apparel and accessories.)
- Trade Mart—gifts, decorative accessories, housewares, tabletop, and stationery
- International Floral and Gift Center®—floral and holiday trim industries
- Market Hall—temporary exhibit space for a variety of trade and consumer shows

DMC offers more than 50 markets a year for merchandise including textiles; women's, men's, and children's apparel and accessories; and home furnishings and gifts.

VF, the world's largest manufacturer of jeans, has operations in Texas. Dallas is also home to the corporate headquarters of Haggar Clothing Co., a menswear manufacturer, and Williamson-Dickie Mfg. JCPenney Corporation is headquartered in Plano, Texas, near Dallas.

Atlanta

AmericasMart in Atlanta hosts more than 55 markets per year, including apparel (men's, women's, children's, bridal), accessories, gifts, furniture, home fashions, jewelry, and toys. Corporate headquarters of Carter's, Inc., Oxford Industries, Ballard Designs, and Rich's department stores are also located in Atlanta.

Other U.S. Fashion Brand Market Centers

Figure 9.8
San Francisco is home to international fashion brands including Levi Strauss & Co and Gap, Inc. Claire R Greenway /Moment Mobil ED/Getty Images.

San Francisco, CA

Apparel, home fashions, and retailing companies with headquarters in San Francisco include Levi Strauss & Co., Gap, Inc. (Figure 9.8), Jessica McClintock, Gymboree, and Williams-Sonoma, Inc. In addition, a number of apparel companies have headquarters near San Francisco including Bebe (Brisbane, CA), The North Face (San Leandro, CA), JanSport (San Leandro, CA), Restoration Hardware (Corte Madera, CA), Ross Stores (Pleasanton, CA), and Marmot (Santa Rosa, CA).

Seattle, WA

Proximity to Asian contractors is an advantage for Seattle companies that source in that region of the world. Thanks to established sport and outdoor wear companies/retailers, such as Cutter and Buck, Tommy Bahama, Zumiez, Eddie Bauer (Bellevue, WA), and Recreational Equipment Incorporated (R.E.I.) in Kent, Washington, as well as successful bricks-and-mortar retailers such as Nordstrom, and e-retailers such as Amazon.com, Seattle has gained prominence in the fashion industry.

Portland, OR

Over the past 20 years, Portland, Oregon, has grown as a market center for active-wear and outdoor gear. With the headquarters for Nike, Columbia Sportswear, and Adidas North America, Inc., Portland has attracted a variety of smaller sportswear and footwear companies including KEEN Footwear and LaCrosse Footwear, Inc. In addition, Portland is home to the headquarters of other apparel companies including Pendleton Woolen Mills and Hanna Andersson.

South American Fashion Brand Market Centers

Argentina and Brazil are South America's largest consumer markets and also the countries that have the strongest design, marketing, research, and retailing capabilities. Sao Paulo, Brazil's fashion week is considered the fifth largest in the world. International brands with headquarters in Brazil include Havaianas, Grendene, Mormaii, Osklen, Carlos Meile, Gloria Coelho, and TNG. International brands with headquarters in Argentina include Cardon and AY Not Dead.

European Fashion Brand Market Centers

Western European countries including France, Germany, Italy, Great Britain (UK), and Spain are known for their fashion market centers (i.e., Paris, Milan, London), luxury brands, and influential fashion weeks. The Paris, London, and Milan fashion weeks are some of the most influential worldwide.

Figure 9.9
Paris fashion week is widely covered by the media in promoting luxury fashion brands. Antonio de Moraes Barros Filho /WireImage/Getty Images.

- France, the birthplace of haute couture, is best known for luxury fashion brands including Chanel, Dior, Givenchy, Louis Vuitton, Nina Ricci, and Yves Saint Laurent. Paris fashion week (Fall/Winter is held in February, and Spring/Summer is held in September) highlights these and other luxury brands and is widely viewed as one of the most important media events for fashion (Figure 9.9).
- Germany is best known for textile and production machinery design and production, important trade shows (e.g., Igedo), and brands including Adidas, PUMA, Escada, Buffalo, Hugo Boss, and Etienne Aigner.
- Italy, as with the other countries in Western Europe, has a long history of supporting the fashion industry, and the "made in Italy" label is often described as a brand in its own right. Milan fashion week is held twice per year (Fall/Winter is held in February/March, and Spring/Summer is held in September/October). Italian luxury brands include Giorgio Armani, Roberto Cavalli, Dolce and Gabbana, Etro, Fendi, Gucci, Prada, and Versace.
- Great Britain (UK) influence on fashion has traditionally included quality woolens, custom-tailored suits (Saville Row), and trendy London nightclubs. London fashion week is held twice per year (Fall/Winter is held in February, and Spring/Summer is held in September). UK fashion brands include Alexander McQueen, ASOS, Burberry, Dr. Martens (Doc Martens), Duchamp, Stella McCartney, Vivienne Westwood, and Topshop.
- Spain is best known for its fast fashion companies (e.g., Zara, Mango) and brands including Desigual, Massimo Dutti, and Bershka.

Asian Fashion Brand Market Centers

After the Second World War, Japan's textile and apparel industries were important to the growth of Japan's economy. Now, as a developed country, Japan is best known for specialty textiles (e.g., recycled polyester, performance materials), designer fashion (e.g., Issey Miyake, Hanae Mori, Rei Kawakubo, Yohji Yamamoto), international fashion brands (e.g., Cheat Sheet, Onitsuka Tiger), fast fashion retail (e.g., Uniqlo), and department store retailing (e.g., Sogo, Takashimaya). Tokyo Fashion Week is highly regarded in promoting Japanese luxury fashion brands.

Hong Kong has a long history of serving as an important port for East Asia, as well as a key port for the British Empire. After the 1949 communist revolution in China, refugees who fled to Hong Kong developed a strong fashion industry, manufacturing inexpensive apparel and footwear. As wages went up, Hong Kong's fashion industry moved from manufacturing to serving as design and merchandising operation hubs for international fashion brands. In 1997, Hong Kong left British rule to be a Special Administration Region of China. Since 1997, Hong Kong continues its importance as an Asian hub for supply chain management, marketing, licensing, and trade. One of the best known Hong Kong–based supply chain management companies is Li and Fung, Ltd., a world leader in design, development, sourcing, and distribution of fashion brands (Figure 9.10).

As with Japan and Hong Kong, South Korea's textile and apparel industries contributed to its economic development. Centered in Seoul, the South Korean fashion industry is now focused on (1) market center of budget and moderate priced merchandise for the Asian and Russian markets, (2) luxury fashion designers, and (3) companies that serve as merchandisers and supply chain managers for fashion brands producing merchandise in China. South Korean department stores, including Hyundai and Lotte, are often anchors for large shopping centers throughout South Korea.

Taiwan (Chinese Taipei) has had a rich history of textile and apparel production and is now considered a world leader in manufactured fibers, high-tech and performance materials, and materials used in footwear production. Through a combination of investments from government, industry, and higher education, researchers in Taiwan have furthered the development of footwear materials, design, marketing, and production. The Taipei Innovative Textile Application Show (TITAS) is one of the largest trade shows of functional, performance, and sustainable materials.

Figure 9.10
Li and Fung, Ltd., headquartered in Hong Kong, is a world leader in supply chain management of fashion brands. Li & Fung.

THE SELLING FUNCTION

The selling function of fashion brand companies is handled in one of the following ways:

- internal selling for private label merchandise and store brands
- corporate selling
- sales representatives and showrooms

Internal Selling

With private label merchandise (e.g., JCPenney's Arizona brand) and SPA/store brands (e.g., Gap, Victoria's Secret, Banana Republic, Niketown), the selling of merchandise to retail buyers is handled internally. This is because merchandise is designed and produced for a particular fashion brand retailer. With **internal selling**, the design team presents seasonal lines to in-house merchandisers who select specific pieces of the line for production. Merchandisers also determine which items of the line will be sold at specific stores.

Corporate Selling

Corporate selling is used by (1) companies that manufacture designer price zone merchandise and sell to a limited number of retailers; and (2) very large companies that sell moderately priced merchandise to large corporate retailers. In these cases, selling processes are often conducted through their corporate headquarters without the use of sales representatives or showrooms.

Sales Representatives and Showrooms

The **sales representative** or *sales rep* is the individual who serves as the intermediary between the fashion brand company and the retailer, selling the fashion line to retail buyers (Figure 9.11). Other names for sales representatives are *vendor representative*, *account executive*, and *manufacturer's representative*. **Showrooms** are the rooms used by sales representatives to show samples to retail buyers. Depending on the size of the company, showrooms can be decorated elaborately or very simply. They always include display racks for the samples and tables and chairs for the retail buyers.

Showrooms can be either permanent or temporary. Permanent showrooms are located in buildings in market centers, in marts, in buildings adjacent to marts, or within a company's design headquarters. During market weeks, sales representatives for companies that do not have permanent showrooms in that area use temporary showrooms or booths. Booths are set up and staffed by either the company's sales representative or a multiline representative. Some sales reps always use temporary

Figure 9.11
Seasonal fashion lines are sold to retail buyers through showrooms and at trade shows. Keenan/WWD/© Conde Nast.

showroom or booth space during market weeks. Some companies will use temporary showroom or booth space to "test the water" in a new region during a market week without having to commit to a sales rep or the mart on a permanent basis. Although using temporary space can provide companies with a feel for the mart and the sales opportunities, it also has disadvantages. Because buyers are looking for long-term customer service from sales reps, they may seek the assurance of continued service from reps who do not have a permanent showroom.

Types of Sales Reps and Showrooms

One of the most important decisions made by marketers of fashion brands is whether to open an exclusive **corporate showroom** with company sales representatives or to use established independent **multiline sales representatives**. The primary difference between the two is that company sales reps work for a particular company and are housed in corporate showrooms owned by the company; independent multiline sales reps work for themselves and typically represent lines from several different noncompeting, but related, companies. For example, a multiline sales rep may offer a variety of noncompeting children's wear lines from several companies. In addition, this sales rep may represent lines of children's toys and nursery accessories. Both company and multiline sales reps are assigned and work in a geographic territory (**regional sales territory**) that may be quite large (e.g., the West) or quite small (e.g., northern California), depending on the company and product line.

A fashion brand company considers two main criteria in deciding whether to have a corporate showroom or a multiline sales rep: the type of product line and the amount of business the company expects to do. The corporate showroom is appropriate for a company with a large sales volume in a particular region of the country. For some marts, it is recommended that the company be capable of producing at least $1 million in sales at the mart in order to support a corporate showroom.

Corporate showrooms are managed by company sales representatives who represent the lines of that company only. (Note that because company sales reps generally represent large companies, most of them are based in a showroom.) Company sales reps may work on salary plus commission or on a straight commission basis, depending on the company's sales philosophy. If the company pays the sales reps' expenses, which is often the case for company sales reps, then commission is lower than if expenses are not paid. In addition to managing the showroom, company sales reps may travel to other marts' market weeks and trade shows. Corporate showrooms have advantages and disadvantages. With a corporate showroom, the staff can devote 100 percent of their time to the company's line(s) and the company's customers. In addition, the showroom can better portray the company's image and style of merchandise to retail buyers. However, a corporate showroom is an expensive investment. Space is leased from the mart; lease contracts should be evaluated in terms of services offered (e.g., janitorial services, utilities, mart-sponsored promotion activities, directory listings), because they can vary from mart to mart.

Rather than opening a corporate showroom, many companies choose to go with an independent multiline sales representative. Multiline sales representatives typically work for small manufacturers that cannot afford or do not want to hire their own sales representatives. The multiline sales rep works on straight commission, typically 5 to 10 percent of the wholesale price of goods that are shipped by the company. This means that if the company ships $100,000 (wholesale) in goods that are, in turn, sold by the sales rep, the sales rep would receive 5 to 10 percent of this amount ($5,000 to $10,000) as payment.

Independent multiline sales reps must pay all their own expenses, including

- the cost of leasing and furnishing showrooms (if they have them)
- travel expenses to market weeks or to visit retailers
- in some cases, the purchase of manufacturers' sample lines

For smaller companies, using an independent multiline sales representative can have several advantages. The main advantage is that no initial capital investment in the showroom is needed. In addition, established sales reps are familiar with local accounts and can promote the line with buyers. Although the initial costs of using an independent rep are lower than with opening a corporate showroom, the following additional expenses are to be expected:

- fees for market week activities
- cooperative advertising expenses
- costs for hospitality service
- fashion shows or other promotional activities

Some companies begin with an independent multiline rep and then, as they grow, they will move into their own corporate showroom.

Finding the right fit between the product line and the sales representative is important to both the fashion brand company and the sales rep. Companies want to find a rep who has access to the types of retailers appropriate for the product line. Independent multiline sales reps should not represent competing lines. The company must be assured that the sales rep will spend the appropriate amount of time in promoting its line(s). Another consideration is whether the sales rep needs to travel to different retail accounts before market weeks. Table 9.6 compares the advantages and disadvantages of corporate showrooms and multiline sales representatives.

Table 9.6 Comparisons between Corporate Showrooms and Multiline Sales Representatives

Type of Selling	Advantages for the Manufacturer	Disadvantages for the Manufacturer
Corporate showroom	Control over image of showroom possible	Capital investment is necessary
	Staff can devote 100 percent of time to line	Lease agreements may vary from mart to mart
		In addition to commission, there may be other promotion expenses
Multiline sales representative	No initial capital investments needed	Determining right fit between sales rep and line may be difficult
	Established reps know local accounts	Rep may not devote adequate time to the line
	Buyers are exposed to related but noncompeting lines in the same showroom	Lack of control over image of the showroom

Home Fashions Brands—Decorative Fabric Converters and Jobbers

In addition to manufacturers' showrooms, decorative fabric converters and jobbers also play an important role in the marketing of home fashions. Textile converters in the home fashions industry design and sell finished textiles to jobbers, designers, and manufacturers, who use the textiles in home fashions end-use products. Some converters also produce end-use products such as bed linens and window treatments. Similar to manufacturers, converters also create and distribute sample books. They also have showrooms in New York City or elsewhere where they display and sell their goods to jobbers as well as to interior design, manufacturing, and retailing customers.

Decorative fabric jobbers are also involved in the marketing and distribution of home textile piece goods, particularly upholstery and drapery fabrics. Traditionally, jobbers have served a warehousing and distribution function in the industry. More recently, the jobber market has changed as jobbers have started providing a number of services, such as importing fabrics, creating exclusive in-house fabric designs, converting fabrics, and marketing fabrics through showrooms. Similar to manufacturers and converters, jobbers also put together sample books for their customers. Thus, the differences between the functions of textile mills, converters, and jobbers are less distinct than in the past. In fact, as some jobbers have turned to converting, some top converters have begun to perform jobbing/distribution functions.

Sample Lines

The manufacturer provides the sales representatives with a set of samples for the line(s) being presented to retail buyers. The samples include an example of each style included in the line in one colorway. The line catalog or brochure is used in conjunction with the samples to provide information about the line to the retail buyer. Some companies require the sales rep (usually independent multiline sales reps) to purchase the samples. In these cases, the sales reps are generally allowed to sell the samples at the end of the selling season. Other companies provide the samples to the sales rep (usually company sales reps). In these cases, the sales rep generally returns the samples at the end of the season. Computer technology has made it possible for sales reps to use alternatives such as virtual samples and computer-generated buying instead of actually showing sample lines.

Product Life Cycle Management Applications

Product life cycle management (PLM) applications have altered the way many fashion brand companies work with their retail clients. Three-dimensional computer technology is now in place to show a line with **virtual samples**, which are viewed on a computer screen. The intended fabric color and print of the style is also shown. Retail buyers and sales representatives can view the line and place orders without having the manufacturer produce actual prototypes or samples. Pieces of the line can be combined in a video presentation to show a variety of coordinating combinations.

An advantage of PLM applications to the buying/selling function is that key buyers can "forecast" the hot-selling styles. As design, development, and production software programs become more fully integrated, the time savings increase exponentially. A designer can create the new style on a three-dimensional CAD system, the design team can revise it, it can be shown to buyers (even in remote locations), and orders can be placed without the cost of developing a prototype or sample.

Computer-generated buying systems that are part of an integrated computer-generated garment design, pattern, and material utilization system enhance the entire process of creating and marketing a new line. Linking the computer-aided design system to the computer-integrated manufacturing system provides the maximum cost efficiency, speed, accuracy, and quality. For example, it is possible to predict the efficiency of the fabric usage for a style and to revise the garment design to use the fabric more efficiently without going through the patternmaking process.

Job Functions of the Sales Representative

The sales representative (whether a company sales rep or an independent multi-line sales rep) performs a number of job functions, including selling activities, selling support activities, and non-selling activities (Figure 9.12). The most obvious of the functions that sales representatives perform are the selling functions. These include

- showing lines to retail buyers and demonstrating product features
- negotiating terms of sale
- writing orders for merchandise

Figure 9.12
Sales representatives show home textiles to designers, manufacturers, and retailers. Alamy Robert Daly/Alamy.

In negotiating the terms of sale, the sales representative and retail buyer focuses on several areas, including delivery date, cooperative advertising, and discounts (see the "Terms of Sale" subsection later in this chapter). Using integrated order-writing, sales representatives access up-to-date inventory information, enter orders for next-day shipment, and analyze information from the order database. Sales representatives also perform a number of activities that support and expand the selling function:

- advising retail buyers regarding trends related to the target customer
- providing retailers with product and merchandising information
- training buyers and/or salespeople to promote and advertise the merchandise
- ordering and reordering merchandise for retailers to guarantee sufficient inventory
- dealing with complaints from retail customers regarding merchandise orders
- promoting customer relations

In addition, sales representatives perform many non-selling activities:

- making travel arrangements
- writing reports for the company
- keeping books of account
- attending sales meetings
- participating in market week activities, such as fashion shows
- managing and maintaining the showroom or trade booth

Although their career paths vary greatly, many sales representatives have retail buying experience before they become sales representatives. With this background, they understand the retail buying process and can address the needs of retail buyers.

Orders and Canceled Orders

The sales reps work with the retail buyers in placing orders for merchandise to be produced and delivered to the retailer. It is important to keep in mind that not every style in the line that is presented to buyers will be produced. Usually, only those styles that have a sufficient number of orders from retail buyers will be produced. Therefore, at the time the buyer places the order for a specific style, in specified colors and sizes, the order is tentative. Whether a specific style in a specific color will be produced is based on the cumulative orders from other retail buyers. The style will be produced only if the style reaches the minimum number of orders from retail buyers. The minimum number of orders required to put a style into production is based on any of numerous factors. Sometimes a minimum order is based on the fabric manufacturer's minimum yardage requirement. Or the minimum order might be determined by the contractor who will sew the style. In some cases, a minimum of 300 units might be required, whereas with another company, the minimum order might be 3,000 units.

Thus, retail buyers place orders without knowing for certain whether every style they order in the preferred color will be produced. Orders can be canceled for the following reasons:

- There are insufficient orders for a particular style or color.
- The fabric is not available from the textile manufacturer. The textile company will produce the fabric only if a sufficient number of yards have been ordered by various apparel companies to meet the textile manufacturer's minimum order. This creates a domino effect in these interrelated industries.
- A variety of production problems can occur, both with the textile manufacturer and with the production facilities.
- Natural disasters and political crises in countries where the merchandise is being produced can make it impossible to meet retailers' orders.

When a retailer's order for a style cannot be filled by the manufacturer, the retailer may be willing to accept a substitute style or color. Or, the retailer may cancel the order, filling in any gaps in style choices on the retail floor with merchandise from other companies.

Terms of Sale

The sales representative and retail buyer will negotiate various **terms of sale**, including

- a specific time when the goods are to be delivered
- guarantees related to whether styles ordered will, in fact, be produced
- reorder capabilities and timing of the reorders (especially important for basic merchandise, such as jeans or hosiery, for which continuous inventory is essential to optimum sales)
- promotional discounts paid by the manufacturer to assist the retailer with advertising or other promotions
- payment terms and any discounts if invoices are paid within a certain period
- transportation costs of the merchandise ordered
- introductory allowances including incentives for a retailer to purchase the brand for the first time
- discounts if a certain quantity is purchased
- discounts if merchandise is bought either early or late in the season
- markdown allowances (Is any credit given on merchandise that had to be marked down?)
- return privileges (Can any unsold merchandise be returned at the end of the season?)
- creation of floor-ready merchandise by the manufacturer
- availability of promotion tools such as gift-with-purchase promotions or displays
- possibility of creating merchandise unique to the retailer

As the retailer places orders for styles in the new line, delivery dates and payment terms are arranged between the manufacturer and the retailer. If the manufacturer does not meet the delivery date, that manufacturer may be required to take a reduced payment for the shipment, or the retailer may be allowed to cancel the order. Late delivery may be the result of late arrival of materials to the production facility, production delays with the contractor, or delays in transportation.

MARKETING STRATEGIES

Distribution Policies

The primary goal of a fashion brand company's distribution policies is to make sure the merchandise is sold to stores that cater to the customers for whom the merchandise was designed and manufactured (the target customers). Thus, fashion marketers must be able to identify store characteristics and geographic areas that will optimize the availability of the merchandise to the target customers. For example, a manufacturer of men's suits in the designer price zone may identify specialty stores in areas where residents have above-average incomes as its primary retail customers. A manufacturer of moderate-priced women's sportswear, on the other hand, may identify department stores as its primary retail customer. Once these basic criteria are established, fashion brand marketers must next decide on the company's policy regarding merchandise distribution. In general, there are two basic distribution policies: open-distribution policy and selected-distribution policy.

Open-Distribution Policy

With **open-distribution policy**, the manufacturer will sell to any retailer with whom they have satisfactory business experience and with whom they negotiate appropriate terms of sale.

Selected-Distribution Policy

With **selected-distribution policy**, fashion brand manufacturers establish detailed criteria that stores must meet in order for them to carry the manufacturer's merchandise. Typically, the criteria focus on

- expected sales volume
- geographic area
- retail image

For example, some fashion brand companies sell their merchandise to only one or two retailers within a certain geographic region; others sell only to retailers that portray an image that is consistent with the merchandise; others sell only to retail accounts that can purchase a specified amount of merchandise.

Based on these decisions, fashion brand marketers focus on retail accounts that are consistent with their distribution policy. Distribution strategies are discussed further in Chapter 13.

International Marketing

As fashion brand companies expand their businesses to include foreign markets, a review of the ways in which fashion merchandise is marketed internationally is in order. There are four basic ways fashion merchandise is marketed internationally:

1. *Selling through direct sales*: In some cases, fashion brand companies will sell merchandise directly to foreign retailers through independent or company sales representatives.

2. *Selling through agents*: In some cases, fashion brand companies prefer to use international agents to handle the selling function in other countries. These agents have expertise in market demand, import/export issues, and international currency issues. Therefore, they can facilitate the establishment and processing of international accounts.

3. *Selling through exclusive distribution agreements*: In some cases, fashion brand companies have established agreements with specific international retailers for the exclusive distribution of their merchandise.

4. *Marketing through foreign licensees in a specific country or region*: In some cases, fashion brand companies license their lines to foreign companies. These licensing arrangements with foreign companies facilitate the marketing of the goods internationally.

Sales Promotion Strategies

Fashion brand companies have essentially two groups of customers that need to know about their lines: retailers and consumers. Thus, sales promotion strategies developed by fashion brand companies will focus on both of these groups. Fashion brand companies use a number of promotion strategies to let retailers and consumers know about their merchandise. Decisions regarding promotion strategies are based on these factors:

- company's advertising budget
- characteristics of its target customer
- characteristics of the product line
- area of distribution

Promotion strategies include advertising, publicity, and other promotion tools made available to retailers. Use of social media in promoting fashion brands can be considered either advertising or publicity, depending on who pays for and/or controls the content.

Advertising

Through paid **advertising**, fashion brand companies buy space or time in the print, broadcast, and/or digital media to promote their lines to retailers and consumers. Although some large companies may have in-house advertising departments, most companies hire advertising agencies to develop print, broadcast, and/or digital campaigns for them. Large fashion brand companies (e.g., Nike, Ralph Lauren, Burberry) can spend millions of U.S. dollars per year on advertising. Companies can also share the cost of the advertisement with a retailer, trade association, or another manufacturer through **cooperative advertising**, or **co-op advertising**. For example, a company and a retailer may share the cost of an advertisement that features both the merchandise and the retailer (see Figure 9.13).

Figure 9.13
Cooperative advertisements are often used to connect a brand name with a retailer in the consumer's mind. Scott Olson /Getty Images.

The specific print, broadcast, and/or digital media used in advertising campaigns depends on the following:

- advertising budget
- target audience
- product line
- company image

For example, a company may rely on advertisements in print and online trade publications when targeting retailers. When targeting consumers, designer/luxury brands may focus on advertisements in print and/or online fashion magazines; national/international fashion brands (e.g., Levi's, Fruit of the Loom, Nike) or SPA/store brands (e.g., Gap, Victoria's Secret) may use broadcast and digital media to reach a wide audience.

Publicity

Although positive publicity has the same effect as advertising (promoting merchandise to retailers and consumers), the two strategies differ. Unlike advertising, **publicity** is not controlled by the marketer or company. With publicity, the company or the company's fashion brand merchandise is viewed as newsworthy and thus receives coverage in print, broadcast, and/or digital media (including social media). For example, media coverage of designers' runway shows often results in news stories, photographs, and/or videos of the designers' collections in multiple media formats. Sometimes the company creates news by sending out or posting news releases about its company or merchandise. For fashion brand companies, the primary advantage of publicity is that they do not have to pay the media source for communicating information about the company. In addition, consumers may respond positively to publicity that includes a third-party endorsement, since the endorsement may be perceived as more credible than a marketer-controlled advertisement. The primary disadvantage of publicity is that the company has little control over how the company or its merchandise are portrayed.

Social Media

Social media include all of the internet-based applications that allow communication among users. Fashion brand companies use a variety of social media (e.g., Facebook, Twitter, Pinterest, YouTube, Instagram, Tumblr, LinkedIn) to create **brand communities** through advertising, sharing product information, providing promotional incentives and discounts to consumers, and providing opportunities for consumers to interact with each other and with company representatives. The impact of social media for the fashion industries has been impressive. For example, in 2012 the UK SPA, TopShop, partnered with Facebook to allow website users watching the live-streamed fashion show to click on favorite items to share online. In addition, over 2 million people from 100 countries watched the online video in the first three hours after it was live-streamed. The first dress seen in the fashion show sold out before the fashion show ended. In 2014 Kohl's, a U.S. department store, launched Life's S.o. R.a.d., a YouTube series that combined entertainment with information about its S.o. R.a.d. junior fashion brand. Viewers were encouraged to use the hashtag #SoRad on social networks such as Twitter and Instagram.

Because of the immediacy and influence of social media, fashion brands must monitor both positive and negative communications. Responding to customers' posts, resolving problems or issues, and creating engaged brand communities is imperative for effective use of social media. Companies' applications or apps for smartphone technologies have furthered their connections to customers in building brand loyalty.

Other Promotion Tools for Business Partners

To promote their lines to business partners, including retailers, fashion brand companies provide a number of other tools:

- media kits
- line catalogs or brochures
- B2B electronic communications
- visual merchandising tools

The following subsections describe these promotion tools.

Media Kits

Media kits are promotional tools that fashion brand companies use when launching a new company, brand, or service; enhancing or changing a company or brand identity; and/or promoting the company or brand to the media. The companies provide background information, photographs, videos, media releases, displays, giveaways, and other information and promotional items for publicity purposes for print, broadcast, and digital media sources and for retailers to use in promoting the brand.

Line Catalogs or Line Brochures

Line catalogs or line brochures (print and/or digital) provide important information about the line to retail buyers (Figure 9.14). They include photographs or drawings of the items in the line, along with style numbers, sizing information, colors (some even include fabric swatches), and information about ordering procedures and guidelines.

B2B Electronic Communications

Fashion brand companies use several types of electronic business-to-business (B2B) communications to promote their brands and merchandise to retailers and ultimate consumers. Some companies use websites with virtual showrooms where retail buyers can "walk" through the showroom and view new seasonal lines. Other companies use private networks called *extranets* or communications software to communicate with their business partners. Benefits include the ease of communication and simplification of order tracking. A number of companies use web-based and/or cloud

Figure 9.14
Line brochures show all of the styles, colors, and sizes available and the area used by sales representatives in selling lines to retail buyers.

technology systems that allow retail buyers to place orders for merchandise online. Manufacturers and retailers enjoy the following advantages of B2B technologies:

- No appointments are necessary.
- Paperwork is reduced.
- Because buyers need an ID and password to log on, security issues are resolved.

Visual Merchandising Tools

A variety of visual merchandising tools may be provided by apparel companies. These can range from providing posters and signs to setting up actual in-store shops and supplying all the necessary fixtures (e.g., Ralph Lauren's in-store shops).

Other Promotion Tools for Consumers

Fashion brand companies use a number of additional promotional tools for consumers. These tools, described in the following subsections, include

- B2C electronic communications
- direct mail
- trunk shows
- merchandise representatives
- style testing and participation promotions

Figure 9.15
Fashion brands use social media to create brand loyalty with their customers. Jason Kempin /WireImage for Victoria's Secret/Getty Images.

B2C Electronic Communications

Fashion brand companies use a variety of business-to-consumer (B2C) electronic communications to promote their brand and/or merchandise. Examples include

- email communications
- websites with blogs, videos, consumer reviews, and brand community engagement
- social media pages (Facebook), boards (Pinterest), and/or other postings that are initiated and controlled by the fashion brand company (As noted earlier, these platforms encourage two-way interactions with the customer; see Figure 9.15.)

Direct Mail

Although email and other electronic communications have grown in popularity, direct mail opportunities still exist. As a form of cooperative advertising, some manufacturers provide promotion inserts to be included with retail store mailings (e.g., credit card bills). Some companies also send out postcards or other mailings directly to consumers.

Trunk Shows

Typically, a retail buyer does not purchase a company's entire line for the store. Through the use of **trunk shows**, a representative from the company (or the designer of the line) will bring the entire line (or part of a line) to a store. Customers invited to attend the showing can purchase or order any piece in the line, whether or not it will be carried by the store. Designers often make appearances at their trunk shows to promote their collections. Trunk shows can benefit manufacturers, retailers, and consumers in the following ways:

- Manufacturers use trunk shows not only to promote their lines but also to get consumers' reactions to their merchandise.
- For retailers, trunk shows provide an opportunity to offer an exclusive service to their customers. They also provide feedback from their customers about their tastes and preferences.
- Customers benefit because they have access to the full line of merchandise.

Merchandise Representatives

Some companies use *specialists, merchandisers,* or *sales executives.* These individuals are paid either partly by the fashion brand company and partly by the retailer or entirely by the fashion brand company, but they work with the retail store(s). They may be based in one store or may travel to various stores within a region. Their role is to do the following:

- educate the retail sales staff and consumers about the merchandise
- demonstrate display procedures
- assist retailers in maintaining appropriate stock
- get feedback from the retailers and consumers for the apparel company

Style Testing and Participation Promotions

Active sportswear companies often ask retail executives and athletes to test styles in a line or participate in sports activities as a way of promoting the line to retailers and ultimate consumers. For example, Columbia Sportswear invited selected retailers, sales reps, and skiers to test a new performance-oriented outerwear line on the slopes of Oregon's Mount Hood. The retailers could learn about the product, and Columbia Sportswear could hear suggestions from both retailers and ultimate consumers. Nike has invited retailers to go golfing, and Patagonia has sponsored kayaking trips for retailers. REI Adventures offers hiking, bicycling, backpacking, rafting, and climbing trips to give current and potential customers the opportunity to experience those activities.

SUMMARY

The marketing of fashion brands connects market research with the appropriate strategies for getting the right product to the target consumers at the right time, at the right price, and in the right place. Markets for fashion brands can be any city where marts and/or showrooms are located. During specific times of the year, known as *market weeks*, buyers visit fashions markets to purchase merchandise for their stores. They may also attend trade shows sponsored by marts and/or trade associations. Fashion brand marketing centers such as New York, Los Angeles, Paris, London, Milan, Rome, Tokyo, Hong Kong, Seoul, Taipei, Rio de Janeiro, Buenos Aires, and Sydney play important roles within the global fashion industries in marketing fashion brands. These large cities are home to thriving fashion industries including design, marketing, and distribution/retail.

The selling function of fashion brand companies is handled either through corporate selling or through sales representatives who work out of permanent or temporary showrooms. Sales representatives serve as liaisons between manufacturers and retailers. Some sales representatives work from a corporate showroom and focus on the line(s) of one company; others are multiline sales reps, representing a number of related but noncompeting lines. The job of sales representatives includes both selling and non-selling functions.

Fashion brand marketers develop distribution and promotion strategies for their company. In general, there are two basic distribution policies: open distribution and selected distribution. These policies help determine which retail customers will be the focus of selling efforts. Sales promotion strategies of fashion brand companies are directed to both retail customers and consumers. Strategies may include advertising, publicity, social media, and other promotion tools to business partners and to the ultimate consumer.

KEY TERMS

advertising
brand community
co-op advertising
cooperative advertising
corporate selling
corporate showroom
decorative fabric converter
decorative fabric jobber
internal selling

market
market center
market week
mart
multiline sales representative
open-distribution policy
open-to-buy
publicity
regional sales territory

retail relations program
sales representative
selected-distribution policy
showroom
social media
terms of sale
trade show
trunk show
virtual sample

DISCUSSION QUESTIONS AND ACTIVITIES

1. Interview a retail buyer in your community. Document the type of retailer (e.g., specialty store, department store) and the type of merchandise offered (e.g., children's wear, menswear). Ask which markets or trade shows the buyer attends and why. Compare your findings with those of your classmates. Are there any patterns in market attendance related to geographic area, type of retailer, or type of merchandise?

2. Find two examples of co-op print advertisements in either a trade publication, consumer publication, or online. What companies and/or associations joined forces for each advertisement? What are the advantages and disadvantages for the companies in using co-op ads as part of their promotion strategy?

3. Locate the website of a fashion brand company. What type of information is provided on the site? Would this information be useful to retailers, to the target customer, or to both? Evaluate the site's effectiveness. What social media platforms are used by the fashion brand company? How effective is the social media? Why?

CASE STUDY

Future of *Black Friday* Promotions

Since the early 1960s, the term *Black Friday* has referred to the post–Thanksgiving Day shopping frenzy of retail sales and promotions. Because most government and non-retail business employees have the day after Thanksgiving off, retailers viewed the Friday after Thanksgiving as the opportune time to start promotions for the holiday shopping season. Some people say the term originated with the police in Philadelphia, who used it to describe the traffic challenges they faced on the day after Thanksgiving. Others claim it was first used to label the day when retailers went from losing money ("in the red") to making a profit ("in the black").

Through the early 2000s, Black Friday became associated with deep discount price promotions, shopping chaos, huge crowds, and longer shopping hours—including Thanksgiving day itself. And with the advent of online shopping, the Monday after the Thanksgiving holiday weekend came to be called Cyber Monday, a reference to consumers using that day to continue their purchasing.

Although originally associated with a U.S. holiday, with the growth of international retailing, Black Friday promotions are now seen worldwide. In recent years, however, Black Friday has been losing its appeal for consumers. Reports of violence, injuries caused by stampeding consumers, and general unruliness are keeping many consumers from participating in the tradition. In addition, in an effort to extend the promotional period beyond just one day, retailers now offer Black Friday sales throughout November. Retailers also offer discounts to consumers shopping online, and this strategy is appealing to many consumers who no longer want to fight the crowds at the bricks-and-mortar stores. Analysts agree that consumers are changing the way they shop.

You will take the role of the VP of merchandising for Bed Bath & Beyond to lead the discussion and ultimate decisions being made about your company's future retail calendar, specifically around Black Friday and Cyber Monday promotions.

1. Summarize the facts surrounding the analysis of Black Friday and Cyber Monday promotions. Use sources at the end of this case study and other references for this background.

2. Describe the organization of Bed Bath & Beyond Inc.

3. List and evaluate three alternative solutions to address changes in consumer shopping habits during Black Friday, Cyber Monday, and other holiday promotions. What are the advantages and disadvantages of each alternative?

4. What is your recommendation for Bed Bath & Beyond's future retail calendar, specifically for Black Friday and Cyber Monday promotions? Why?

5. What data should you keep track of to evaluate the effectiveness of your recommendation? Why?

Sources:
Barrie, Leonie. (2014, December 1). "Viewpoint: Is Black Friday Losing Its Luster?" http://www.just-style.com.
Bed Bath & Beyond Inc. (2014). *Corporate Responsibility*, http://www.bedbathandbeyond.com/store/static/CorporateResponsibility Report.
Brustein, Joshua. (December 1, 2014). "Shopping Relics: Why Black Friday and Cyber Monday Don't Really Matter." *BloombergBusiness*, http://www.bloomberg.com/bw/articles/2014-12-01 /why-black-friday-and-cyber-monday-dont-really-matter-any-more.

CAREER OPPORTUNITIES

The marketing of fashion brands offers career opportunities including

- Mart and showroom manager
- Market week and trade show organizer
- Sales representative
- Advertising professional who focuses on fashion brands
- Public relations and social media professional who focuses on fashion brands

REFERENCES

Aderibigbe, Niyi. (2015, February 21). "Social Media Is Revolutionizing Apparel Industry." *Fibre2fashion.com*, http://www.fibre2fashion.com/industry-article/54/5347/social-media-is-revolutionising-apparel-industry1.asp (accessed March 13, 2016).

AmericasMart. (2015). "AmericasMart Atlanta. The Nation's #1 Product Destination." http://www.americasmart.com (accessed March 13, 2016).

California Market Center (CMC). (2015). http://www.californiamarketcenter.com (accessed March 13, 2016).

Chicago Merchandise Mart. (2015). *The Merchandise Mart*, http://www.mmart.com/ (accessed March 13, 2016).

Dallas Market Center. (2015). http://www.dallasmarketcenter.com (accessed March 13, 2016).

New York City Garment District. (2015). *The Garment District NYC*, http://garmentdistrictnyc.com/ (accessed March 13, 2016).

New York City Javits Center (2015). http://www.javitscenter.com/ (accessed March 13, 2016).

Preproduction Processes

IN THIS CHAPTER, YOU WILL LEARN
THE FOLLOWING:

- the role of financial agencies, called factors, in the fashion industry

* the process and timing used by fashion brand companies to order production fabrics and trims

* scheduling and management considerations in ordering production fabrics and trims

* the processes used to finalize a production pattern, grade the pattern, create a production marker, and then cut, spread, and bundle the fabric pieces

* ways in which grade rules, size range, styling, cost considerations, and grading processes influence pattern grading

Step 5: Preproduction

Step 1 Research and Merchandising

Step 2 Design Brief

Step 3 Design Development and Style Selection

Step 4 Marketing the Design Brand

Step 5 Preproduction

Order Production Materials, Trims, and Findings

Finalize Production Pattern and Written Documents

Grade Production Pattern into Size Range

Make Production Marker

Inspect Fabric/Materials

Spread, Cut, Bundle, and Manage Dye Lots for Production

Step 6 Sourcing

Step 7 Production Processes, Material Management, and Quality Assurance

Step 8 Distribution and Retailing

PRODUCTION ORDERS

The sales force has shown the new line to retailers during market week, and the retail buyers have placed their orders with the fashion company. As discussed in previous chapters, those styles in specific colors and sizes that meet the company's required minimum order will continue in the development process. Usually, styles that do not attain the minimum number of orders are dropped from the line. Sometimes after a week or two of selling the line, a fashion brand company will decide to drop a style that is not selling well. Suppose that, for the style we are following through the development process, enough orders have been placed to warrant a production run (see Step 5 of the flowchart on the previous page).

FACTORING

A company's financial credit line is an important consideration before it can approves any business transactions or work orders. Therefore, fashion brand companies, contractors, and retailers need to establish a credit line or cash advance so they can buy materials in advance of the season when they will receive payment.

Due to the nature of retailing fashion products, the fashion industries face a high level of financial risk. Some fashion companies use commercial banks for their financial backing. However, their interest rates may be high, and some commercial banks are not willing to accept the degree of risk involved with fashion-related companies. Therefore, another type of financial agency, called a **factor**, is often used. **Factoring** is a short-term plan that allows business owners to receive a cash advance based on the value of their current invoices, so that they do not have to wait several weeks or months to receive their payments. Factoring is not a loan. Rather, the factoring company is actually purchasing the outstanding invoices and then sending the fashion brand company an advance on the invoice value (Factor Funding Co. 2015). As an example, the factoring agency advances money to the fashion brand company so that the company can pay the textile mill for the fabric that has been delivered. The advance allows the fashion brand company to pay for fabrics well before the date when it receives its payment for the new styles that the retailer has purchased from the fashion brand company.

Factoring agencies are the companies that provide protection against bad debt losses, manage accounts receivable, and provide credit analysis in the apparel industry. The factor's procedures include the following:

- running a credit check on the company
- approving a credit line to the company
- approving the orders for shipping to the company
- receiving the invoices from the company's suppliers
- advancing the cash needed to pay the invoices to the company

The company pays interest on the money advanced until the company can repay the factor. Usually, a 60-day or 90-day payment period has been arranged between the factor and the fashion company. The length of the payment period is determined by the length of time the company usually waits to be paid by its customers. For example, based on the terms of agreement, the textile producer might need to wait 90 days after shipping the fabric to the fashion brand or contractor to receive payment for the fabric. The factor's fees are similar to the interest paid on credit card debt. For example, a large fashion brand company might be charged the prime rate plus 1 percent of the value of each invoice.

Small fashion brand companies often do not qualify for financial backing by a factor, because their sales volume is lower than the factor's minimum. Therefore, such companies go to refactor agencies. Refactors are factors that give their credit, collection, and check-processing functions to larger, full-service factors and concentrate on acquiring new clients and businesses.

Factoring has advantages and disadvantages. Possible advantages are as follows:

- A company would be able to increase its working capital almost instantly by getting up to 85 percent of its invoice value in advance.
- Usually as invoice amounts increase, so does the total amount a company can factor.
- Factoring companies provide professional assistance by performing accounts receivable duties such as issuing customer statements, collecting on invoices, and keeping records of payments.
- Faster access to cash enables a company to make necessary improvement or grow the business. Since the money is available right away, a company can use some capital to fund future work.

Despite the ease and convenience of factoring, it also has some disadvantages:

- The factoring company may enforce credit limits for customers to keep them from owing too much at once and then possibly defaulting later. These credit limits can potentially affect business.
- If a company needs to leave the factoring agreement early, it may be difficult to do so.
- If a customer disputes the charges on an invoice, settlement is needed immediately to avoid the factoring company collecting on the debt obligation (recoursing). Since accounts receivable are the responsibilities of the factoring company, a fashion brand company depends entirely on the factor to collect on the invoices and uphold its part of the agreement.

Keep in mind that many months before the retailer pays the fashion brand company for the goods, the fashion brand company has paid the textile producer for the fabric and the contractor for the labor. Some type of lending institution is used by all of these participants. After credit is approved for these parties, production can proceed. Some fashion brand companies will decide to take an account on their own without the factor's approval. For example, a fashion brand company may decide to sell to a new retail account, such as a specialty store that has just opened and has not yet established credit. In this situation, the fashion brand company carries the financial risk that the specialty store will pay the fashion brand for the merchandise delivered to the store.

Now that sufficient orders have been placed and the retailers' credit standings have been approved, the style is ready for the next step in development: preproduction.

PRODUCT LIFE CYCLE MANAGEMENT

Enterprise Resource Planning

As fashion companies expand and integrate operations, a need to coordinate all aspects of the business is necessary. Enterprise resource planning (ERP) is a category of business management software that facilities the flow of information using common databases. An Apparel ERP system gives a real-time view of business processes every step of the way from design to delivery. All parts of the process are coordinated because the system consolidates applications into a single platform from design, through sales, purchasing, and warehouse management ("ERP Suits Fashion Industry" 2015). ERP software can integrate with PDM/PLM software. These software programs are essential to tracking a product from design through production and will be discussed in more detail.

Product Data (or Development) Management

Software provides seamless integration among all of these segments of a new style's development process (Figure 10.1). A drawing created by the designer on a graphics program can be integrated into the garment specification sheet (spec sheet) used by design development, preproduction, and production personnel. Data from the garment specification sheet can be integrated with the bill of materials and other forms needed for production.

Figure 10.1
A PLM system, such as GalleryWeb software, enables a system server to provide authorized access to style information anywhere in the world by means of electronic communication.

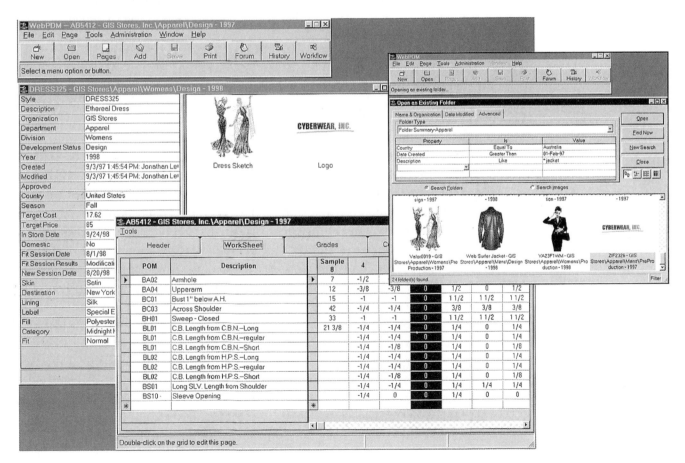

The first pattern is created by the patternmaker using a pattern design system (PDS) and is used for the production pattern. The PDS base pattern used for the new style can include the measurement dimensions and sizing standards (grade rules) coded into the base pattern, providing integration between design development and preproduction. In addition, some software programs are integrated so that a change on one form triggers that change to be made on all other forms in the database system. For example, changing the zipper length on a garment spec sheet will trigger a change on the bill of materials, the form used to order the zippers. While this system has many advantages, it can also mean that a mistake will be transmitted throughout the system.

Companies rely more and more on computer system integration, both within the company and outside the company. Maintaining accurate and up-to-the-minute information about each style and every change in each style during design development in the line will increase the speed of workflow and increase accuracy of the system for all company personnel who need access to the data.

In his article "The Three Stages of Retail PLM Adoption," Jeremy Rubman (2010) states that retailers who connect their internal product development with sourcing functions and also include their external suppliers in their PLM systems will realize greater reductions in costs and time and increase product quality and innovation. Providing external contacts, such as vendors and contractors, with electronic access to style information speeds information exchange and increases accuracy as well. Garment specifications can be shared instantly with contractors that intend to bid on production jobs. Web technology provides global exchange of product specifications and other pertinent information within companies and throughout contractor networks.

ORDERING PRODUCTION MATERIALS, FABRICS, TRIMS, AND FINDINGS

In an ideal situation, the fashion brand company would be able to wait until most of its retail buyers have placed their orders before ordering the needed quantity of fabrics from the textile/material producers (a production run of one style might require 6,000 yards of fabric), as well as ordering the trims and findings for each style in the new line. Such a situation would eliminate any financial risk that would result from ordering fabrics/materials that might turn out to be unneeded. But if fashion brand companies were to wait to order fabrics/materials until they knew exactly how much of each fabric/material in their lines would be needed, they would have to wait weeks for the fabrics/materials to arrive from the material producers.

If textile/material producers, not wanting to risk manufacturing excess fabric /material, also were to wait until the fashion brand companies had ordered fabric before beginning to produce the yardage to fill the manufacturers' orders, the fashion brand company would have to wait even longer, perhaps months, for the production yardage to be manufactured and delivered to the sewing facility. Producing the merchandise would probably take several more weeks. As you can imagine, these cumulative delays would be so lengthy that the retailers would not receive the goods at the peak selling time. Thus, the fashion brand company is positioned between the textile/material producer and the retailer and pressured from both sides.

CUT ORDERS

A production **cut order** is issued in either of these two situations:

- when a targeted number of orders for a style has been placed by retailers and received by the fashion brand company
- when the fashion brand company decides to produce a style before receiving orders

The cut order specifies the number of items in each color and each size that will be included in the production run. A cut order for a specific style might include cutting fewer small sizes and more large sizes and may contain a mix of colors for each size. For example, a cut order for Style XXYY might include 80 items of size 6, divided into 24 of color A, 24 of color B, 16 of color C, and 16 of color D; 160 items of size 8 of the same style, divided into 40 of color A, 60 of color B, 40 of color C, and 20 of color D; and so forth. The cut order includes the date when the goods must be delivered to each retailer. Thus, the production schedule is calculated from end to beginning—that is, backward from the retailer's delivery date, to the date when production of the goods must be finished, to the date production must begin, to the date when the materials, fabrics, trims, and findings must be ordered.

Timing of Cut Orders

In reality, few fashion brand companies can afford to wait until all, or nearly all, of the buyers' orders are placed before ordering production fabric for the line. Therefore, fashion brand companies use a variety of means to determine how much yardage to order and when to order the yardage from the textile/material producers. Furthermore, some companies begin production on some styles before the buyers' orders have been received. This helps maintain an even workflow during production. These methods of timing production include the following:

- starting early production of proven sellers in basic colors
- initiating preline selling
- using early-season lines to predict sales
- using past sales figures

Some companies will make production estimates of some of the more staple styles and colors, especially if these items are carryovers from a previous season. Some colors are known to sell especially well. For example, baseball cap companies know that the colors of Major League Baseball teams sell well every year. Therefore, they may decide to begin early production on several styles of proven sellers in these colors. Early production also allows the company to maintain a constant production flow and thus avoid times when the factories are overcommitted.

Preline selling is discussed in Chapter 8. Some fashion brand companies invite key retail accounts to place orders before market weeks. Early production of these styles can be advantageous to both retailers and apparel companies. Swimwear companies might use an early-season line to help predict which styles will sell well. An early January line of swimsuits sold at resorts in Florida could be used to help forecast production of the Spring line to be introduced to northern climates in April. Some of the hot-selling styles from Florida retail sales could be put into production for the main selling season before the line is sold at market to retailers in the rest of the country.

Past sales figures and the opinions of leading sales representatives and leading retail buyers can be used to determine which styles and colors might go into early production. For styles that are carryovers, production might be started before receiving buyers' orders since management is fairly certain these styles will sell well.

Selection of Vendors

Using as much information as possible and as early as possible, fashion brand companies order production yardage, trims, and findings from the various **vendors** (or **sources** or **suppliers**) of materials, textiles, trims, and findings. Many variables influence the selection of vendors, including the following:

- lead time needed to secure the goods
- past history of on-time delivery
- the quality of goods
- whether the vendor uses supply chain management strategies
- the minimum yardage (or quantity) requirement for an order
- the financial stability of the vendor
- the geographic location of the vendor in relation to where the merchandise will be manufactured

Some fashion brand companies will ask for bids from several vendors as part of the decision-making process. Software programs are available to perform cost comparisons based on inputting variables such as material costs from different vendors. Clearly, the selection of material, fabric, and trim vendors is based on many important considerations.

Production Fabric/Material Considerations

During the process of planning production fabric/material orders, constant communication occurs between the fashion brand company and the fabric/material vendors. Vigilance is required to ensure that the production fabric/material matches the fabric/material used for the samples. Some of the fabric/material considerations include color control, lab dips, and strike offs (Figure 10.2). Various requirements are also important considerations when ordering finished materials, printed fabrics, staple fabrics, and trims and findings.

Preproduction Color Management

During preproduction processes, the fashion brand company needs to finalize several aspects of the fabrics/materials that will be ordered for the new line. Color management is very important. It is essential that all components of the prototype accurately match the intended color for the new style.

The design development department might be responsible for working with the materials, textile, trims, and findings vendors to develop and maintain exact color matching of all components of each style and to ensure that all products in the entire production run maintain the specified color match. Color management may begin at the prototype stage if a textile/material is to be dyed to match a color

STRIKE OFF/LAB DIP APPROVAL FORM

TO: KATHY SIMSES

CC: J. LEIBY, D. RAINEY, G. HUNTER, PRODUCT TECHS, PATTERNMAKERS, A. BEYMER

PATTERN NAME: URBAN LUAU   COLOR CODE: S31 OLIVE

PATTERN NUMBER: 35323-C   STYLES: Y2109, Y2020

VENDOR: A.G.X   SEASON: CRUISE 2011

PRINTED ON: COTTON SHEETING   SECTION: MAY COMPANY

APPROVAL   A. BEYMER 8/17/10

COMMENTS: APPROVED PENDING PSO. SAND NEEDS TO BE A LITTLE DARKER AND LESS RED—MATCH SWATCH TO ATTACHED.

Figure 10.2
Fabric color and design must be approved before producing the textile print in large quantities.

chip or swatch provided by the fashion brand company. If available, the specially dyed sample goods are used to make the prototype. Trim, findings, sample yardage, and production yardage will be ordered to match the prototype color.

It is important to the consumer, and thus to the retailer and the fashion brand company, that colors remain consistent throughout all the components that are used to make a garment style. First, the color of the garment/product style needs to match the color intended by the design team. This could require that the fabric/material vendor submit test samples until the perfect color is achieved. The trims and findings, such as buttons, zippers, and thread, must also match the garment/product color. For example, if the color of the rib knit used for the sleeve band of a rugby shirt is not the same shade as the body of the shirt, the consumer will quite likely decide not to purchase the garment. Thus, when contractors supply the trims and findings for the products they make, it is important that they receive approval of the color match from the fashion brand company. An acceptable color match for contractor-provided matched goods is referred to as a **commercial match**.

When producing coordinated items in a line, color management can be a challenge. A fabric composed of one fiber might be selected for pants, and a fabric composed of another fiber or blend of fibers might be selected for the top. For example, rayon crepe pants might be planned to match a silk jersey tank. However, the color of the pants may not look like an exact color match to the tank because the fibers and fabrics have different reflective qualities. As another example of color management concerns, adjacent colors in plaid and print fabrics tend to affect their neighboring colors' hue, value, and intensity. Because of this optical effect, a color in a print or plaid may not look like it matches its solid-colored coordinate, even though when viewed by itself the color in the plaid or print does match the color standard. Thus, much time can be spent on perfecting the colors in a line.

Lab Dip

To ensure that color matching will be as perfect as possible, the vendor will supply a sample of the product (such as fabric, rib knit trim, or buttons) in the color requested (the fashion brand company might supply the vendor with a fabric swatch or paint chip that needs to be color matched). The sample the vendor supplies to the fashion brand company is called a **lab dip** because, in most cases, the fabric swatch (or trim or finding) was dipped in a specifically prepared dye bath in the lab to dye the sample. Vendors submit lab dips (called *submits*) for all the individual components required in a line. Since various blends of fabrics and other materials absorb dyestuffs differently, accurate color matching of all components may require multiple attempts by vendors.

Fashion brand companies usually have equipment to view colors to assess their match accuracy under controlled lighting conditions. Various lighting conditions can be simulated, such as daylight, fluorescent lighting, and incandescent lighting. The fabrics/materials under consideration are placed into a cabinet and observed under controlled lighting conditions to assess the color accuracy.

The fashion brand company may require that the fabric/material vendor submit results of textile tests, such as colorfastness and lightfastness, performed by approved textile testing laboratories for each sample. These testing procedures are especially important for certain fabrics/materials, such as nylon fabrics in neon bright colors. Each fabric, trim, and finding that is to match the line's color choice will require approval on a form supplied by the fashion brand company.

Printed Fabric Considerations

Not all printed fabrics are printed by the textile mills that produce the fabrics. Sometimes the fabric is printed by a textile converter to the specific textile design requested by the fashion brand company. Thus, many fashion brand companies work with textile converters as well as textile mills. The fabric might be purchased from the textile mill and then sent to a textile converter to print before it arrives at the cutting facility. For fashion brand companies that use textile converters, careful scheduling is required to ensure that the printed fabric is ready on time. Custom print fabrics require substantial lead time for orders; therefore, decisions about custom prints occur early in the design/production process. As mentioned in Chapter 7, some fashion brand companies create some or all of their textile designs in-house. This process also requires careful planning for lead time, as well as the considerations discussed earlier.

New developments in digital printing have helped advance this technology, which is now a viable production option. Improvements in dyes and printing have overcome some of the earlier challenges of this technology. Digital printing provides for one-of-a-kind, exclusive items and is increasingly being evaluated to support customization scenarios and niche market opportunities.

Strike Off

A strike off is a fabric sample that is printed by the textile converter—the company printing the fabric (Figure 10.3). Usually, a strike off consists of no more than a few yards of fabric. It shows the rendition of the textile print made from the artwork submitted to the textile converter by the apparel company (or textile company that develops the print). The fashion brand company carefully examines the strike off before giving approval to print production yardage. For screen prints composed of more than one color, each color requires a separate screen. Each of these screens must be positioned exactly, or the print will appear blurred. The accuracy of placement, or **registration**, of each of the color screens is checked (Figure 10.4). The color match of each screened color is compared to color chips or fabric swatches submitted to the textile converter. The accuracy of the pattern repeat match is checked. Sometimes the textile converter must make several strike offs before receiving approval to print the production yardage.

Figure 10.3
A strike off is a sample of the fabric provided by the textile vendor and sent to the apparel company for approval before the textile print is produced in large quantity. Courtesy of Nancy Bryant. In Figure 10.3, the strike off has poor registration—the screen printing of the two colors was not properly aligned. In Figure 10.4, the approved strike off has perfect registration.

Figure 10.4
The strike off is sent from the textile mill or converter to the apparel manufacturer for approval. Sometimes it takes several attempts to gain approval. Courtesy of Nancy Bryant.

Trims and Findings

It may be necessary to order special trims very early in the planning process. For example, elastic for a waistband might be ordered in a three-color stripe to match the print colors used for pants. On the other hand, elastic in a standard width and color might be ordered just in time for production. Findings such as snaps, hooks, zippers, and thread tend to be kept in stock in large quantities at the production facility. Sometimes a new fashion color requires ordering thread or other findings that are not in stock. Thus, careful planning needs to take place to ensure that all the needed trims and findings are available for production at the appropriate time.

Decisions about findings, such as specifying the type of thread, may be more complex than most people might imagine. Some of the issues to consider for thread selection include the following:

- capability of thread type to match fabric characteristics
- type of stitch or machine used for the operation
- wash procedures to be used
- degradation that will occur during washing

Thus, the selection process for findings may involve research and testing of some products in order to ensure a quality finished garment/product.

PATTERN FINALIZATION AND WRITTEN DOCUMENTS

The pattern for the style that has been approved for production needs to be finalized. Every detail needs to be perfect for production to run smoothly. Sometimes, minor pattern adjustments need to be made to improve ease of production. The production pattern, which has been made in the company's sample size, is then ready for **grading**; that is, each piece of the pattern in the sample size is remade in each of the sizes specified. Next, all the pattern pieces in all the sizes are arranged into a master cutting plan, called a **production marker**. The style is ready to move to the next stage, the production cutting and sewing operations. In the following subsections, each of these steps is discussed in more detail.

Finalizing the Production Pattern

A specialist called a **production engineer** or pattern engineer may be part of the team that is responsible for getting the pattern ready for production. Production engineers are familiar with factory production processes and types of equipment. The pattern may need some minor changes to facilitate production. Production engineers are responsible for suggesting such changes in the pattern. They might also be responsible for suggesting the specific factory where production can best be accomplished.

Finalizing the Garment Specifications

When the designer's sketch or drape of the style is delivered to design development, a specification sheet accompanies the design. The spec sheet lists all materials, fabrics, trims, findings, and important construction details, such as logo placement, label type and placement, and color and weight of topstitching thread

(Figure 10.5). Any changes that may have occurred while developing the style must be transferred to the spec sheet. Any requested change not transferred to the spec sheet can cause difficulties in production. If a PDM/PLM software system is used to create and maintain the spec sheet, all changes can be made easily as soon as they have been approved, and they will automatically be changed on any other necessary documents.

nbintl. COLOR MATRIX PAGE — NB01

INSTALL DATE: 3–28–00   REV DATE:
DESCRIPTION: SOLID WOVEN SHORT   FINAL NAME: NANCY'S WALKING SHORT
SEASON: Y00/S02   BLOCK: WALKING SHORT

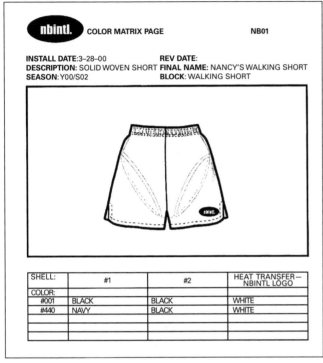

SHELL:	#1	#2	HEAT TRANSFER— NBINTL LOGO
COLOR:			
#001	BLACK	BLACK	WHITE
#440	NAVY	BLACK	WHITE

(a)

nbintl. COMPONENT PAGE — NB01

INITIAL DATE: 3–28–00   REV DATE: 3–28–0
DESCRIPTION: SOLID WOVEN SHORT   FINAL NAME: NANCY'S WALKING SHORT
SIZE: S–M–L–XL   SM NAME: NBWKSH
SEASON: Y00/S02   BLOCK: WALKING SHORT

SHELL #1	SHELL #2
VENDOR: FABRICS GALORE	VENDOR: KNITS & MORE
FAB#: OF1234	FAB#: LF5678
PHYS. WIDTH: 58"	PHYS. WIDTH: 60"
CONTENT: 100% NYLON	CONTENT: 100% POLYESTER
PIECES:	PIECES:
1 RIGHT FRONT	1 FRONT LINER
1 LEFT FRONT	1 BACK LINER
2 BACK	1 KEY POCKET

TRIMS:

VENDOR	ITEM	ITEM#	PLACEMENT	YIELD/QTY
STRETCH INC.	1" ELASTIC	5564	WAISTBAND	.800
STRETCH INC.	1/4" RUBBER	EL26-BLACK	LEG OPENINGS OF LINER	1.400
BOND RITE	HEAT TRANSFER	NBINTL LOGO	LOWER LEFT LEG	1 EA.
NB INTL.	CARE CONTENT LABEL W/SIZE	CL00001	CENTER BACK WAIST	1 EA.
THE PRINTHOUSE	I.D. TAG: WOMEN'S	WID	SWIFT-TACHED DIRECTLY INTO LEFT WAISTBAND	1 EA.
WEST COAST PAPER CO.	8x10 POLYBAG–SEALED WITH TAPE			1 EA.

(b)

nbintl. CONSTRUCTION PAGE — NB01

INITIAL DATE: 3–28–00   REV DATE:
DESCRIPTION: SOLID WOVEN SHORT   FINAL NAME: NANCY'S WALKING SHORT
SIZE: S–M–L–XL   SM NAME: NBWKSH
SEASON: Y00/S02   BLOCK: WALKING SHORT

CUTTING:
SEAM ALLOWANCE: 3/8" ON ALL SEAMS. 1/4" SERGE ON KEY POCKET.
TOPSTITCHING: TRIPLE NEEDLE WAISTBAND. SERGE AND TOPSTITCH VENTS.
COVERSTITCH:
HEM ALLOWANCE: 1/2" DOUBLE ROLL HEM. LINER: SERGE RUBBER ON LEG OPENINGS, AND TOP STITCH
ELASTIC: 1" ELASTIC FOR WAIST. RUBBER: 1/4" RUBBER FOR LEG OPENING OF LINER
BUTTONS OR SNAPS:
ZIPPERS:
PULLS:
BAR TACKS: 1 AT EACH END OF VENT (2).
WELTS:
MISCELLANEOUS: CLEAN FINISH KEY POCKET: FOLD, SERGE AND TURN. SEWN AT WAIST/LINER SEAM TO WEARER'S LEFT FRONT SIDE. SET TO NOTCHES.
DRAWCORD:
LABEL: CARE CONTENT LABEL SEWN AT CENTER BACK WAIST.
LOGO: NBINTL LOGO HEAT TRANSFER – 2 1/2" IN FROM SIDE RAW EDGE, 2 1/2" UP FROM BOTTOM RAW EDGE. (MEASUREMENT IS TO CENTER OF LOGO). PARALLEL TO WAISTBAND.
PACKAGING: FOLD IN HALF, TURN CROTCH IN, THEN FOLD IN HALF, I.D. TAG WITH STYLE NUMBER MUST BE VISIBLE THROUGH POLYBAG.

(c)

nbintl. MEASUREMENT PAGE — NB01

INITIAL DATE: 2–28–00   REV DATE:
DESCRIPTION: SOLID WOVEN SHORT   FINAL NAME: NANCY'S WALKING SHOES
SIZE: S–M–L–XL   SM NAME: NBWKSH
SEASON: Y00/S02   BLOCK: WALKING SHORT

SIZE	TOT. + OR.	S	M	L	XL
WAIST ON THE HALF RELAXED	1/4"	11"	12"	13"	14"
WAIST ON THE HALF STRETCHED	1/2"	18 1/2"	19 1/2"	21"	22 1/2"
HIP ON HALF: 6" DOWN FROM TOP OF WAISTBAND	1/2"	22"	23"	24"	25"
RISE: FOLD GARMET IN HALF TOP OF WAISTBAND TO CROTCH	1/4"	14"	14 1/2"	15"	15 1/2"
INSEAM	1/4"	4"	4"	4"	4"
LINEAR RISE ON THE HALF	1/4"	13"	13 1/2"	14"	14 1/2"
LINER LEG OPENING ON THE HALF: RELAXED	3/8"	11 1/4"	11 3/4"	12 1/4"	12 3/4"
LINER LEG OPENING ON THE HALF: STRETCHED	3/8"	12 1/4"	12 3/4"	13 1/4"	13 3/4"

(d)

Figure 10.5
(a) The garment specification or spec sheet includes important information for producing the style, including the color matrix. (b) Fabric, trim, and findings are specified on the component page of the garment spec sheet. (c) This page of the garment spec sheet details construction-related instructions. (d) The measurement page details finished garment dimensions and allowable tolerances. Photos courtesy of Kristen Sandberg.

A GUIDE TO SEWING BLUE JEANS — Union Special

Sequence Of Operations For Traditional Blue Jeans

	OPERATION NUMBER	OPERATION	RECOMMENDED MACHINE STYLE	STITCH & SEAM TYPE
PRELIMINARY				
✓	1	Hem top of hip and watch pockets	56500R18 or FS311L51-2H72	401 EFb-2(inv.)
✓	2	Decorative stitch hip pockets	56500R18 or FS311L51-2H72	401 OSa-2
	3	Precrease hip and watch pockets	Pocket Creaser	
✓	4	Make belt loops	FS321J01-2A60Z	406 EFh-1
✓	5	Attach facings to front pockets	FS311L41-2H64CC1Z3	602 LSbj-1(mod.)
	6	Set watch pocket to right front facing	Juki LH2178	301 LSd-2
	7	Bag pockets	Juki MO3716	516 SSa-2
✓	8	Serge left and right fly pieces	39500CRU	504 EFd-1
✓	9	Attach zipper tape (continuous) to left fly piece	56400PZ16	401 SSa-2
✓	10	Attach zipper tape to right fly piece	56300G or FS311S01-1M	401 SSa-1
FRONTS & BACKS				
	11	Set left fly piece and edgestitch	Juki DLN5410	301 SSe-2
	12	Topstitch left fly	Juki LH2178	301 EFa-2 (inv.)
	13	Set right fly piece and cord fly	Juki DLN5410	301 LSq-2b
	14	Hang front pockets	Juki LH2178	301 LSd-2
✓	15	Attach risers to backs	FS315L63-3H36CC2PA1	401 LSc-3
	16	Set hip pockets to backs	Juki LH2178	301 LSd-2
✓	17	Join backs (seat seam)	FS315L63-3H36CC2PA1	401 LSc-3

✓ (Union Special machine available)

Figure 10.6
Union Special, an industrial sewing machine producer, distributes this guide, which illustrates a typical production sequence to manufacture jeans. Courtesy of Union Special Technical Training Centre.

Another component of the spec sheet is the bill of materials. It lists the materials, fabrics, trims, and findings requirements for each color of a style in the line.

Construction Specifications

The spec sheets that accompanies the style will include additional construction specifications related to the production sequence (Figure 10.6). The production engineer or product technician often determines the sequence of steps (what will be sewn first, second, third, etc.) required for factory production of the style. When the style is made in a factory owned by the fashion brand company, the production engineer is an employee of the company. When the style is made by a contractor, the contractor's production engineer determines the production sequence. The sequence of production is related to the cost to manufacture the goods. Thus, the production sequence may have been determined at the time the final cost was calculated.

Experienced production engineers can examine a finished sample garment/product and quickly provide a reliable estimate of the number of minutes—and thus, the actual labor cost—required to sew a specific style. One of the reasons production engineers are often included in the development design team is that their engineering and costing experience is highly valuable as a factor in style decisions. Computer software programs can be used to help analyze cost in comparing various production sequence options.

Point of Measurement Specifications (POM)

The actual measurements at specific locations on the finished goods for each size specified for the style will be listed on the **measurement specification** chart. Measurement specs are part of the garment specifications (Figure 10.7).

Since garments are measured flat, sometimes the circumferences are measured across just the front width or just the back width. These half-circumference measurements are listed as the *sweep*. This dimensional information is important to maintain accurate sizes, especially if several factories will be used to produce the same style for a large production order. Two jackets in the same style and size may fit differently if one factory is less accurate in sewing than another.

The measurement specifications also include a **tolerance**, usually listed as "+/−", a certain fraction of an inch that indicates a narrow range of acceptable dimension variations. This means that a stated dimension on the measurement specifications may vary by the stated tolerance amount. The tolerance amount might be one-half inch (1.3 cm) for larger circumferences (such as the chest) or lengths (such as back length), and one-quarter inch (6 mm) for smaller circumferences (such as the neck). The stated dimensions, with allowable tolerance, serve as a contract between the fashion brand company and the sewing facility. If dimensional accuracy is not maintained within the tolerance range, the fashion brand company can reject the goods.

The fashion brand company's quality assurance department is usually responsible for checking the finished dimensions of the delivered goods. Since it would be too time consuming to measure the specified dimensions of every garment in a production order, quality assurance departments use a sampling technique to measure a specified number of garments/products in specific sizes. If goods sewn by a contractor must be rejected due to size inaccuracy, the fashion brand company may miss the deadline for delivery of goods to the retailer. Therefore, it is important for fashion brand companies to carefully select the contractors they do business with, and it is critical for contractors to carefully adhere to the garment specifications.

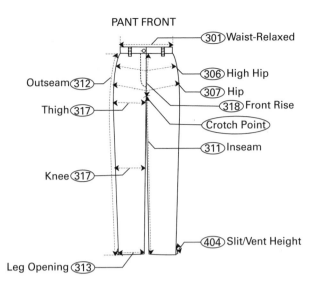

PANT FRONT

- 301 Waist-Relaxed
- 306 High Hip
- 307 Hip
- 318 Front Rise
- Crotch Point
- 311 Inseam
- Outseam 312
- Thigh 317
- Knee 317
- 404 Slit/Vent Height
- Leg Opening 313

Figure 10.7
The measurement specifications include the location of the points of measure.

GRADING THE PRODUCTION PATTERN

Pattern grading involves taking the production pattern pieces that have been made in the sample size for the new style and creating a set of pattern pieces for each of the sizes listed on the garment spec sheet. Grading a garment pattern is much cheaper than developing a sample garment of each size. Therefore, grading is a cost factor and does not ensure the fit of the other sizes.

The written documents and production pattern are delivered to the pattern-grading and marker-making department if the fashion brand company is responsible for the grading and marker-making operations. When contractors are used for production, they will be responsible for one of the following activities:

- making the first pattern and production pattern, grading and making the marker, cutting and sewing (full-package contractor)
- making the production pattern (based on a first pattern developed by the apparel company), grading and making the marker, cutting and sewing
- grading and making the marker (based on a production pattern developed by the apparel company), cutting and sewing
- cutting and sewing (termed CMT, for "cut, make, and trim") only (based on a marker delivered by the fashion brand company). The fabric may be supplied by the fashion brand company, or it may be supplied by the contractor.

Some fashion brand companies that use contractors prefer to take responsibility for grading and marker making. However, if anything is incorrect on the pattern or marker that the fashion brand company has provided, the contractor can blame the fashion brand company for a late delivery or other related problems. For the fashion brand company that provides the marker, maintaining an even workflow in the grading and marker-making department is difficult, especially when the time frame for producing a season's line—determining that a style will be produced and having the marker ready for cutting—is very tight. Most contractors communicate data such as patterns, markers, and garment specifications electronically.

Grade Rules

Grading requires different amounts of growth (for a larger size) or reduction (for a smaller size) at various points on each pattern piece. Thus, it is not possible to place a pattern piece into a photocopy machine and enlarge or reduce the pattern piece uniformly. The amounts and locations of growth/reduction are called the **grade rules**. There is no industry standard for these grade rules, and some fashion brand companies guard their grade rule standards carefully. The grade rule itself is the combination of a specific length and width that the pattern pieces need to increase or decrease at a specified point on the pattern. For example, the shoulder–neck point may need to increase for each subsequent larger size or decrease for each subsequent smaller size by one-eighth inch in height and one-sixteenth inch in width for each pattern size.

Pattern grading is more complex than it may appear. There are different grade rules for garments with set-in sleeves, raglan sleeves, kimono sleeves, and shirt sleeves. Style variations magnify the complexity of the different grade rules. For example, a shirt with raglan sleeves could also include a front panel, so the grade rules would need to be modified for the extra style line added to the shirt front. Also, some companies use different grade rules for various sizes: for sizes 4, 6, and 8, a 1-inch width change increment per size may be used for the waist and hip dimensions; for sizes 10, 12, and 14, a 1½-inch width change increment per size may be used for the waist and hip dimensions; and for sizes 16, 18, and 20, a 2-inch width change increment per size may be used for the waist and hip dimensions.

Size Range and Style Cost Considerations

Depending on the style and the fashion brand company's policy, the size range might include a large number of sizes—for example, from size 4 to size 18 for a misses dress. Another fashion brand company might produce garments in a size range of small, medium, large, and extra large (designated S-M-L-XL). The cost to grade a pattern with many pattern pieces into a wide range of sizes may be more than the cost to grade a pattern with only a few pattern pieces in just four sizes. These cost differences are considered from the design stage onward. Another cost variation related to styling concerns designs that are asymmetrical—that is, different pattern pieces are required for the left and right halves of the body. An asymmetrical design might also require different left and right facings and interfacing patterns. Each separate pattern piece needs to be graded and multiplied by the number of sizes in the size range. Thus, asymmetrical designs can be more costly to grade. With computerized grading, the same grade rules can be quickly applied to a back facing pattern as was used for the front pattern.

The fabric/material selected may influence the size range in which the style will be produced. Some fabrics/materials will look best in a narrow size range. Based on the scale of a plaid size and repeat, a plaid pleated skirt in misses sizes may look attractive only in certain mid-sizes—for example, sizes 8 through 16. It would be ideal to select a fabric that looks good in a wide size range, but this is not always possible. Some styles look best in certain sizes. Thus, the style may be offered in a limited size range.

Grading Processes

The pattern-grading process can be accomplished by a variety of methods. Computer grading, combined with computer marker making, has gained widespread acceptance. It is the method of choice for fashion brand companies and contractors that can invest in a computer grading and marker-making system.

Computer programs for pattern grading and marker making have been in use since the 1970s. The combined process is called **computer grading and marker making (CGMM)**. Companies that use computer systems to grade and make markers may refer to the department as the computer grading and marker-making department. Many large fashion brand companies began their shift to computerization and formed CGMM departments early on.

Some PDS programs include the option to select a grading function as the pattern is being made. These systems are integrated so that the pattern blocks used to begin making the style have specific grade rules embedded in them. Once the pattern has been completed, the grading is completed automatically (Figure 10.8). With PDS, the operator can distribute the new measurements to all affected pieces automatically without having to manually choose each pattern piece to be graded. For example, when a measurement change is made on the front shirt piece, the program automatically modifies the measurements of the opposite front, side, and back pieces, thus saving patternmakers substantial time and effort.

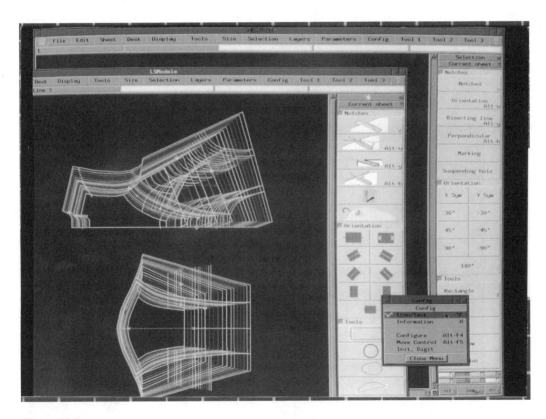

Figure 10.8
The computer screen shows a nested grade of the entire size range for this dress pattern piece.

MAKING THE PRODUCTION MARKER

A costing marker is used to calculate the usage (yardage) required for one garment. At the preproduction stage, another type of marker is required. The **production marker** is the full-size cutting layout of all the pattern pieces for all the sizes specified for the style. The marker is drawn on paper, showing the outline of all the pattern pieces. Arranging all the pattern pieces into an efficient layout can be a challenge. The goal for the marker is a tightly arranged layout so that very little fabric is wasted. The waste, called **fallout**, represents fabric that cannot be used, and it is thus money lost to the apparel company. The efficiency of a marker's layout plan (marker efficiency) is measured in the percentage of fabric used. Thus, a high-utilization percentage represents a cost-effective marker. Highly efficient markers attain utilization with percentile figures in the high 80s and into the 90s (90 percent utilization means that there is about 10 percent fallout).

If a pattern for a style requires 10 pattern pieces, and 7 sizes are produced, the marker will include 70 pattern pieces. Sometimes, a marker is planned so that the layout will have two sets of pattern pieces in the most frequently purchased sizes—often those in the mid-size range. Therefore, the marker for a misses style could have two sets of sizes 10 and 12, for a total of 90 pattern pieces for the marker with 10 pattern pieces. For styles offered in the S-M-L-XL size range, it is fairly common to cut one set each of size S and size XL pattern pieces, and two sets each of size M and size L pattern pieces (or, one set of size S and two sets each of size M, L, and XL, especially in men's athletic wear). The cut order specifies the sizes and number of size sets in each of these sizes needed for the marker (as well as the colorway by size if various colors of fabrics will be stacked up for the cut order).

Before computerized marker making was developed, markers were typically made by hand. The layout is planned on a long sheet of paper (e.g., 30 feet long)

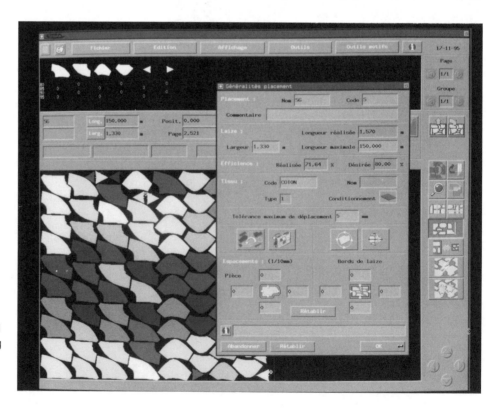

Figure 10.9
A production marker is displayed on the computer screen, showing the tight layout on the left and the utilization percentage on the right.

that is the width of the fabric/material to be cut. Pattern pieces were traced onto the paper. The marker was laid onto the stacked layers of fabric. The cutter, using an industrial cutting knife, followed the drawn outlines of the pattern piece on the marker.

Although various marker-making methods are used in today's industry, computer marker making is the most efficient and effective method. With CGMM, the marker-making function is tied to the pattern-grading function. Thus, a company that grades by computer also makes markers by computer. Once the pattern pieces have been graded by computer and stored in the computer's memory, the marker maker can retrieve all the pattern pieces needed in the size range (Figure 10.9). The marker-making software calculates the usage, or fabric utilization, so the marker maker can continue to arrange pattern pieces until the utilization goal has been reached. After the marker is completed, the system generates a letter-size printout of the layout. The small-scale marker can be analyzed for utilization and accuracy. It can also be used for reference during preproduction and production.

PRODUCTION SPREADING, CUTTING, BUNDLING, AND DYE LOT CONTROL

Several steps are involved in preparing the fabric for garment production. They include

- spreading the fabric/material onto cutting tables
- cutting the fabric/material
- preparing the cut fabric/material pieces for production

These steps might be done at the production facility, such as at the contractor's facility. If the fashion brand company owns its production factories, then these steps might take place at one or more of the fashion brand company's facilities. Sometimes the fashion brand company is responsible for cutting and bundling. Then it ships the bundled pieces to a production facility. This might happen if the fashion brand company wants to control the cutting of the goods, or if the selected contractor only makes and trims garments.

Spreading

Spreading (or laying up) is the process of unwinding the large rolls of fabric onto long, wide cutting tables. The fabric is stacked, layer upon layer, depending on the size of the cut order. For **production cutting**, the fabric is laid flat across its entire width from selvage to selvage (nothing is cut on a fold, as is frequently done in the home sewing industry). The length of each layer of fabric is determined by the specific style's marker length. For large cuts, thin sheets of paper may be laid between every 12 layers of fabric, in order to count the stacked layers of pieces quickly by dozens. This saves a great deal of time after cutting, when the stacks of cut pieces need to be assembled into different groups (bundles) for sewing. When a style will be produced in several colors, the fabric layers will reflect the correct number of layers for each color needed.

Extra costs may be involved when spreading fabric. Fabrics that have a directional print or napped fabrics, such as corduroy and velvet, need to be laid so that

Figure 10.10
Fabric is spread carefully and stacked layer upon layer in preparation for production cutting. A spreading machine is used to roll the fabric onto the cutting table. Photos credit of Gerber Technology.

all layers face the same direction (called *face-up*). This is a more time-consuming process than face-to-face spreading (two-directional), and the effort it requires is reflected in the labor cost for cutting. Fabrics such as stripes and plaids require matching, so they also take more time to lay up; therefore, these fabrics cost more to cut. Stretch fabrics, such as fabrics used for swimwear or intimate apparel, require great care during lay-up to avoid distorting the fabric. Stretch fabrics also require time to relax on the table after laying up and before cutting.

A variety of equipment speeds the fabric laying process. **Spreading machines** guided on tracks along the side edges of the cutting table carry the large rolls of fabric, spreading the fabric smoothly (Figure 10.10). For face-up cutting, a cutting knife is sent across the fabric at the desired length corresponding to the length of the marker, the spreading machine is returned to its origin, and another layer is spread on top of the previous layer. This process allows each layer to be laid face up. This process is also used if a print fabric is one directional—that is, the motifs on the print all need to face in the same direction. For plaids and stripes, each layer is stacked so that the plaids or stripes match the layer beneath.

Cutting

Either the fashion brand company or the contractor is responsible for making the production marker. The marker, whether drawn by hand or plotted by computer, is sent to the cutting facility or contractor for the cutting process. The marker made during preproduction is laid onto the top layer of fabric, serving as a cutting guide if the fabric will be cut by one of several hand processes. Several types of specialized hand-guided electric knives and rotary cutters are used for cutting the multiple thicknesses of fabric. Most electric knives look similar to a band saw and have a reciprocating blade that oscillates vertically to saw through the fabric layers.

Die cutting is another type of cutting process used for specific purposes. For very small pieces that will be cut repeatedly, season after season, a die is more precise and more economical in the long run. The die is similar to a cookie cutter—a piece of metal with a sharp edge, tooled to the exact dimensions of the pattern piece. The die is positioned over several layers of fabric. Then, a pressurized plate is applied to the die to cut through the thicknesses of fabric/material. Leather and plastic materials are often die-cut. The die is expensive, but its continued use defrays the initial cost and increases the cutting accuracy compared to hand-cutting the same piece.

Facilities that have computerized cutting require special tables to accommodate the cutting equipment (Figure 10.11). The table surface is covered with bristles that allow the cutting blade to slide between them. The fabric layers are compressed with air to reduce the cutting height, thus increasing the accuracy of the cut. The table surface is designed to accommodate the required suction. The computer-generated marker is laid onto the top layer of fabric. The cutting equipment is guided by computer coordinates, not by "seeing" the pattern piece outlines on the marker. The plotted marker is used for two purposes: (1) to ensure that the marker is laid properly onto the fabric, especially when plaids or stripe notations must be aligned; and (2) to indicate the sizes of the pattern pieces and styles for the workers who will bundle the pieces after cutting. Computerized cutting is much faster and generally more accurate than hand cutting or even die cutting. This cutting process uses either a reciprocating knife blade or a rotary cutting blade. The rotary cutting blade is effective for cutting very stretchy fabrics, such as swimwear fabrics. The rolling action of the blade minimizes fabric stretching and thus reduces distortion of the fabric during cutting.

Laser cutting is also driven by computer. It offers many of the same advantages as knife-blade computer cutting, including high speed and accuracy. Laser cutting can be done economically with one or several layers of fabric (called *single-ply* cutting and *low-ply* cutting), compared to the many stacked layers used with computer cutting. Several low-ply cutters will cost about the same as one high-ply computerized cutting system. Since low-ply cutters offer the flexibility to produce small runs very quickly, they offer additional benefits to consider. Several low-ply

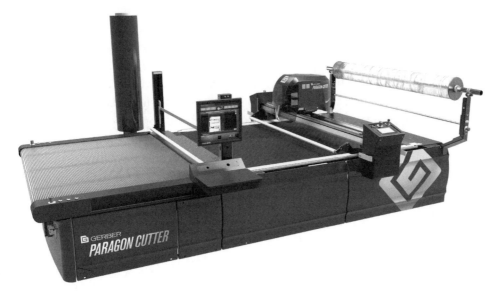

Figure 10.11
A computerized cutter requires a special table surface to accommodate the knife blade requirements. This Gerber cutter automatically conveys material from a spreading table to the cutting area and then directly on to the bundling area. Photos credit of Gerber Technology.

cutters can be working on different orders at the same time. They lend themselves well to the short-cycle manufacturing environment. Single-ply cutting systems are needed for individually customized cuts for the mass-customization manufacturing environment. On the other hand, if a production facility handles primarily large orders for mass production, a large-scale computerized cutter that cuts up to 300 dozen pieces per hour may be more efficient.

Computerized cutting and sewing facilities may be linked electronically to the apparel company's computer so that the marker file can be downloaded electronically. This increases the speed of delivering the marker to the cutting facility or contractor.

Bundling

After cutting, the component pieces for each size and in each color must be grouped together in some way. **Bundling** is the process of disassembling the stacked and cut pieces and reassembling them in groups according to garment size, color dye lot, and number of units in which they will proceed through production. Bundling is done by one or more workers who hand-pick the required garment/product parts from the stacks and group them in bundles that are ready for production. The type of production process determines the number of garments to be included in each bundle. This amount varies from bundles containing the cut fabric/material pieces for an individual unit (one garment) to bundles of a dozen units (or sometimes specified parts of a dozen garments), usually in the same size and color (including same color dye lot) for all twelve garments. For some types of production, up to three dozen units might be bundled together.

Dye Lot Color Management

All coordinating pieces of an outfit, and those styles that are to coordinate in a line, need to be color-matched exactly. Mismatching can occur if strict color management is not maintained. Even with adherence to color management, slight variations in shading can occur in the same dye lot of a production order. Therefore, it is important to code all fabric bolts with the dye lot number and to maintain accuracy in matching dye lots throughout spreading, bundling, production, and distribution processes.

Often a fashion brand company uses one sewing contractor for producing the suit pants and another contractor for the suit jacket. Each contractor receives a shipment of matching fabric from the textile producer. If dye lots are not matched, the suit pants might be a slightly different shade from the suit jacket. This discrepancy may not be noticed until the goods arrive at the apparel company's distribution center, the retailer's distribution center, or the retail selling floor, where the sale may be lost when the customer is trying on the jacket and pants and notices that the colors do not match exactly. The importance of maintaining dye lot consistency for pieces that are intended to match in color is critical to the success of the line.

SUMMARY

Retail buyers' written orders, in sufficient quantity to warrant production, trigger the chain of events involved in producing a new style. The preproduction steps include ordering production materials, fabrics, trims, and findings; maintaining color management, including the use of lab dips and strike offs; and finalizing the production pattern and written documents. To ensure quality production, the documents that accompany the pattern are as important as the pattern itself. These documents comprise the garment specification package. They include a tech drawing of the garment style; a list of all fabrics (with fabric swatches), trims, and findings in all colorways; construction specifications (construction details and sewing steps in sequence); and measurement specifications with stated tolerances. Accurate documentation is essential.

In company-owned production facilities, the production pattern is graded into the specified size range, and a production marker is made by the fashion brand company. For contracted production, either the fashion brand company or the contractor is responsible for the grading and marking procedures. Computer grading and marker making (CGMM) systems have gained widespread use in the fashion industry. The advantages of CGMM include increased speed and improved accuracy. Integrated computer systems provide product information management, including instantaneous electronic linkage between the pattern design system (PDS) and CGMM, whether the two systems are separated by miles within a city (e.g., the design development department is located at company offices, and the grading and marking department is located at the company's factory) or by an ocean (e.g., the design development department is located in the United States, and the contractor's grading and marking department is located at the factory in Hong Kong).

Pre-production processes require many different identities, and communication between them all is important. The future promises continued advances in a seamless integration of all aspects of design, development, marketing, production, and distribution of fashion brands.

KEY TERMS

bundling
commercial match
computer grading and marker
   making (CGMM)
cut order
die cutting
factor
factoring
fallout

grade rules
grading
lab dip
measurement specification
pattern grading
point of measurement (POM)
product life cycle management
   (PDM)
production cutting

production engineer
production marker
registration
source
spreading
spreading machine
supplier
tolerance
vendor

DISCUSSION QUESTIONS AND ACTIVITIES

1. Describe or bring to class a product that exemplifies lack of color management and has one or more components not matching. Explain how you think this mistake could have been avoided.

2. Give several examples of problems that may occur with fabric quality. Discuss options available to the fashion brand company to correct the problem, and explain how such problems—and their corrections—affect production and delivery to the retailer.

3. Select a garment and determine how many pattern pieces were cut to assemble the garment. What findings or trims were used?

4. Discuss why garment specifications are important for the manufacturer. What areas of a garment might be essential information for a specification sheet?

CASE STUDY

Chico's Sizing

Part of the preproduction process is to develop the sizes in which the product will be offered. As noted earlier, understanding the target customers and providing products that meet their specific needs is imperative for the success of fashion brand companies. One company that prides itself in addressing consumer wants and needs is Chico's. Founded in 1983, Chico's is a SPA that has been successful in offering products that are a "combination of great style, one-of-a-kind details, and warm, personal service that has captured the hearts of women nationwide" (Chico's 2016). With over 700 retail stores as well as its catalogs and website, Chico's creates new designs weekly and uses a specialized sizing system to address its customers' fit requirements.

Chico's has developed a unique sizing system. The company states that its "unique sizing chart runs from 000–4.5. Because size is just a number—the simpler, the better (and the more consistent, so you always know your size at Chico's)."

Review Chico's sizing charts on the website: Chicos.com.

1. Who is the target customer for Chico's?

2. Why would Chico's develop its own sizing system? What are the advantages and disadvantages of this unique sizing system?

3. Compare Chico's sizing system with the sizing systems used by at least two other companies that cater to a similar target customer (e.g., Talbots, Ann Taylor). How are the sizing systems used by these companies the same? How are they different?

4. From a production perspective, what costs might be associated with having a unique sizing system of one that is different from other companies' systems?

Source: Chico's, http://chicos.com (accessed March 15, 2016).

CAREER OPPORTUNITIES

Career opportunities in preproduction processes include

- Trim buyer
- Materials librarian
- Marker maker
- Pattern grader

- Production engineer
- Product life cycle manager
- Global production manager
- Factor

REFERENCES

"Apparel Software Trends 2015: Future Investment Focus." *just-style*, http://www.just-style.com/management
-briefing/future-investment-focus_id124809.aspx (accessed March 14, 2016).

Cole, Michael D. (2005). "Technology's Next Frontier on Display at Tech Conference." *Apparel*, November,
pp. 20–22.

DesMarteau, Kathleen. (2003). "The Potential for 3-D & e-Collaboration." *Apparel*, April, pp. 33–36.

Dundish, Harold. (2009). "The Factoring Business: How Times Have Changed." *Apparel Magazine*, April 18.
http://www.apparelmag.com (accessed March 14, 2016).

"ERP That Suits the Fashion Industry." (2015). Blog post, October 26, 2015. http://info.fdm4.com/blog/erp-that
-suits-the-fashion-industry (accessed March 18, 2016).

Factor Funding Co. (2015). "What Is Apparel Industry Factoring?" http://www.factorfunding.com/blog/what-is
-apparel-industry-factoring/#sthash.LXP4rmzo.dpuf (accessed March 14, 2016).

Gaffney, Gary. (1999). "SCM: In Reach for $5M to $25M Firms?" *Bobbin*, May, pp. 74–78.

Hill, Thomas. (1994). "CAR Study: UPS, CAD Provide 300%+ Return on Investment." *Apparel Industry
Magazine*, March, pp. 34–40.

King, Kerry Maguire, Genevieve Garland, Lujuanna Pagan, and Jack Nienke (2009). "Moving Digital Printing
Forward for the Production of Sewn Products." *AATCC Review*, February, pp. 33–36.

Rubman, Jeremy. (2010). "The Three Stages of Retail PLM Adoption (Including Five Myth Busters for Better
Product Development)." *Apparel Magazine*, April 24. http://www.apparelmag.com (accessed March 14, 2016).

"Saber Introduces First Truly Robotic Spreader." (1995). *Apparel Industry Magazine*, August, pp. 46–48.

Speer, Jordan K. (2004). "Color Profile: Examining Processes." *Apparel*, June, pp. 22–26.

Young, Kristin. (1996). "The F Word." *California Apparel News*, February 2–8, pp. 1, 8–9.

CHAPTER 11

Sourcing Decisions and Production Centers

IN THIS CHAPTER, YOU WILL LEARN THE FOLLOWING:

- the criteria used by fashion brand companies in their sourcing decisions

- various sourcing options available to fashion brand companies

- advantages and disadvantages of these sourcing options

- current issues related to sourcing decisions

- locations and characteristics of the primary global production centers

- sourcing philosophies and strategies used by fashion brand companies

- steps used by fashion brand companies in sourcing materials and production

Step 6: Sourcing

Step 1 Research and Merchandising

Step 2 Design Brief

Step 3 Design Development and Style Selection

Step 4 Marketing the Fashion Brand

Step 5 Preproduction

Step 6 Sourcing
Select Production Facility Domestic or Foreign
Company-Owned or Contract

Step 7 Production Processes,
Material Management, and Quality Assurance

Step 8 Distribution and Retailing

SOURCING DECISIONS

Some of the most important decisions a fashion brand company makes are (1) who will design your products; (2) how, when, and where materials will be purchased; and (3) how, when, and where the merchandise will be produced and distributed. This decision-making process is called **sourcing**. Sourcing decisions around design, materials, and production are important to all fashion companies because these decisions play an important role in achieving a competitive advantage. The first section of this chapter outlines decision criteria, production options for companies, and issues surrounding **domestic production** (producing in the same country as where the merchandise with be sold at retail) and **offshore production** (producing outside the country where the merchandise will be sold at retail). At the beginning of this chapter is the Step 6 flowchart, which summarizes the sourcing process. Figure 11.1 diagrams the sourcing options available to fashion brand companies.

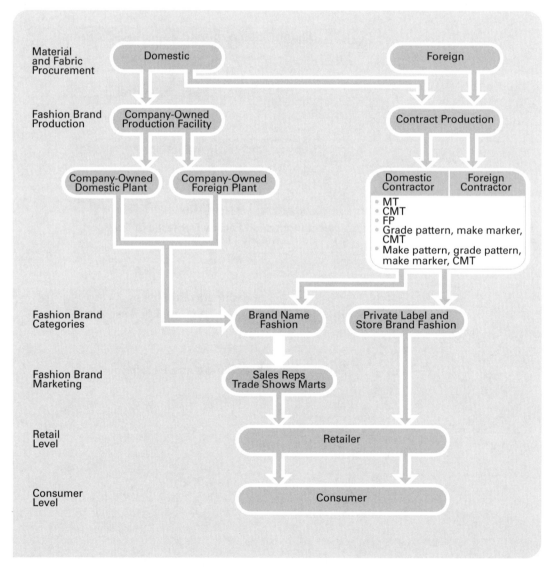

Figure 11.1
Sourcing options for fashion brand companies.

Criteria Used in Sourcing Decisions

Before comparing the options available to companies for **sourcing** materials and production, this section outlines the criteria they will use in making sourcing decisions. Companies consider a number of criteria when deciding what design processes they will used and how, when, and where they will purchase materials and manufacture products. The answers to some questions related to each criterion will help determine the best sourcing option for a company. These criteria include the following:

- company and design criteria (internal to the company)
  - the company's sourcing philosophy around design and production
  - labor requirements, costs, and productivity
  - fabric/materials quality and availability
  - quality assurance/control standards
  - equipment and skills requirements
  - required plant/factory capacities and capabilities
  - social responsibility and environmental impact
- political and geographical criteria (external to the company)
  - trade and other government rules and regulations
  - geographic location, shipping distance, and expected turnaround time
  - infrastructure of the country to support production
  - availability of materials and supplies
  - political and economic conditions of the country
  - natural disasters

Criteria used in sourcing decisions are extremely complex. Thanks to the competitiveness of the textile, apparel, accessory, and home fashions industries as well as the labor-intensive nature of the industries, labor costs have traditionally been a primary criterion for companies in their sourcing decisions about production. Subsequently, where production happens is generally an important criterion for design and material sourcing decisions. However, other factors such as geographical location, infrastructure needs, and trade regulations must be considered when companies make sourcing decisions. These criteria are continually assessed to meet the sourcing philosophy, standards, and production needs of a company.

In small companies, sourcing decisions are generally the responsibility of merchandisers. In larger companies, merchandisers may work with sourcing agents, sourcing analysts, or sourcing managers in making these decisions. Some very large companies have a staff of individuals who make the sourcing decisions for a specific product category such as men's cotton trousers or women's wool sweaters. Those who work in design and product development, fabric procurement, and production sourcing must coordinate their efforts so that the product line will be successfully designed, produced, and distributed to the retailers at the agreed-upon time.

Company and Design Criteria

Some of the criteria that must be considered when making sourcing decisions are controlled by the company through its overall sourcing philosophy and design decisions, which directly affect its material and production needs.

Figure 11.2
For some U.S. fashion brands, sourcing production in the United States is an important aspect of their overall sourcing philosophy. David Engelhardt/Getty Images.

The Company's Sourcing Philosophy

Often companies have a general philosophy toward sourcing that serves as a guideline or framework for sourcing decisions. For example, some companies that retail their merchandise in the United States are committed to **domestic production** and want to be able to add "Made in the U.S.A." labels to their products (Figure 11.2). Other companies that retail their merchandise in the United States have strong ties and positive working relations with contractors in other countries and, therefore, generally prefer **offshore production**. In some cases, companies will take advantage of trade agreements by working with contractors in these countries. This strategy is referred to as **partner shoring** or, if sourcing is close to the ultimate consumer, **nearshoring**.

Many companies also adopt a sourcing philosophy that incorporates **social responsibility** or **corporate social responsibility (CSR)**. For these companies, in addition to costs and profits associated with sourcing decisions, the decisions must also take human rights, labor conditions, and environmental implications of the decisions into account. This position is often referred to as a **triple bottom line** for sourcing decisions; that is, people, planet, and profit factors are all considered. These philosophies are implemented in the selection of countries and factories and in the monitoring of factory conditions. Questions companies might ask include the following:

- How do we design, produce, and distribute the highest-quality fashion merchandise under the best factory and business conditions?
- How do we design, produce, and distribute fashion merchandise and services that are both sustainable and provide consumers with what they want and need?

These topics are discussed in greater detail later in the chapter.

Labor Requirements and Costs

Apparel, footwear, and other accessory production is very labor intensive, even though technological advances are increasingly automating the processes. Therefore, labor costs are an important consideration in sourcing decisions. Questions companies might ask include the following:

- How many workers will be required to produce the goods efficiently and to the quality standards specified?
- What is the cost of labor in a particular country, including benefits? What are the labor and employment laws in a particular country (e.g., wages, unions, minimum age)? How are the workers treated?
- Based on religious, cultural, and communication orientation of the workers in a particular country, what are the best practices for building business relationships?
- What investments in technology and personnel training will need to be made?

As discussed in Chapter 1, workers in the textile, apparel, and footwear industries have historically been some of the lowest compensated. These industries have always sought out cheaper labor—first in England; then in the United States; then in Japan, South Korea, and Hong Kong in the 1950s; in the Caribbean Basin from the 1960s to the 1980s; in Mexico, Canada, the Caribbean Basin, and eastern Europe and Turkey in the 1990s; in China, South Asia, and Southeast Asia after quotas were phased out for most World Trade Organization members in the early twenty-first century.

Over the past 50 years, U.S. and western European fashion brand companies have moved a great deal of production offshore, where labor costs are considerably lower than in the United States or Western Europe. For example, in 2014, the average hourly compensation cost (in U.S. dollars, including social charges) for apparel production workers in developed markets included the United States at $17.71, Italy at $22.67, Japan at $25.10, Germany at $30.03, and France at $31.61. Average hourly compensation of emerging markets included India at $1.12, China at $2.65, Mexico at $3.06, and Turkey at $5.48. Average hourly compensation of developing markets included $0.62 in Bangladesh, $0.74 in Vietnam, and $0.62 in Pakistan. Obviously, the labor costs in emerging and developing markets is much lower than those in developed markets (Table 11.1).

When comparing labor costs, companies must also take worker productivity into account. For example, since 2008, labor costs in China have steadily increased. However, when companies explore less costly alternatives, they must account for the productivity of Chinese workers. Although many companies have left China for production facilities in South Asian countries such as Bangladesh or Southeast Asian countries such as Vietnam or Cambodia, many have stayed with Chinese sourcing because of the Chinese workers' relatively high productivity.

However, even though the labor costs are lower in a particular country, the overall production costs are not necessarily lower in that country. Other costs must be taken into consideration:

- costs of fabrics, materials, and trims
- costs associated with support services and infrastructure
- cost of transportation and shipping
- costs associated with **duties** or tariffs (taxes on imports)

Companies must examine both fixed and variable costs associated with manufacturing in the various countries in order to accurately assess the financial benefits of manufacturing in any one country (Table 11.2).

Fabric/Materials Quality and Availability

Tied closely with sourcing decisions about production are sourcing decisions about fabric and materials procurement. Typically, companies want to procure needed fabrics, materials, and trims as close as possible to where the finished product will be manufactured. This option reduces shipping costs and lead time, and because less energy is used in shipping materials and merchandise, it contributes to a more environmentally sustainable product. For example, if a company is manufacturing premium denim jeans in the United States, it will most likely also be procuring the denim fabric in the United States. If it is manufacturing denim jeans in China, then the fabrics will also most likely be procured in China.

Table 11.1 Minimum Wages in Apparel Manufacturing Countries (monthly wages in US$, 2015)

Country	Monthly Minimum Wage $US
Bangladesh	68
Sri Lanka	79
Vietnam	107–156
Pakistan	116–125
Lesotho	125
Mexico	130–175
India	137–179
Cambodia	140
Haiti	153
China	155–321
Mauritius	283
Peru	284
Honduras	319–457
Guatemala	384
Turkey	454

Source: EmergingTextiles.com (2015).

Table 11.2 Comparison of Costs of Producing a 96% Cotton/4% Spandex Knit Skirt and Top in US$

	Garment Made In		
	Mexico	**Peru**	**China**
Fabric cost per garment	10.70	10.30	9.35
Trim cost per garment	1.80	1.80	1.60
Cut/Make/Finish cost per garment	3.66	3.19	2.90
Average profit per garment	1.62	1.53	1.38
Average shipping cost per garment	0.09	0.11	0.12
Duty cost into United States (2005 level)	0.00	0.00	1.44
Total landed U.S. cost	**17.86**	**16.93**	**16.78**
Importers/brand owner price to retailer	21.97	20.82	20.64
Suggested retail price	59.00	59.00	59.00

Source: EmergingTextiles.com (May 23, 2008).

Figure 11.3
One aspect of quality assurance is the ability to maintain specialized equipment. WWD/© Conde Nast.

Another important consideration when comparing options for sourcing fabric is trade agreements that have a **yarn forward rule of origin**. This stipulation to a trade agreement means that apparel products could be traded duty-free (i.e., without duties or tariffs on the product) if the yarn and all manufacturing operations "forward" (e.g., textile production, apparel production) occur among the countries involved in the trade agreement. For example, The U.S.–Peru Trade Promotion Agreement, enacted in 2009, requires that for imported apparel from Peru to come into the United States duty-free, the yarn forward standard must be met, although the agreement outlines certain exceptions.

Quality Assurance/Control Standards

The importance of maintaining specific quality assurance/control standards is one criterion in a company's sourcing decision. Maintaining a consistently high quality of product is often a reason for the few companies that own their production facilities to continue doing so. When using either domestic or offshore contractors, companies will specify quality standards that the contractors must meet and will also expect to see in sample merchandise. Companies will maintain quality assurance programs with their contract facilities to ensure that quality standards are constantly met (Figure 11.3).

Equipment and Skill Requirements

Depending on the product category, equipment and skills needed to produce the product line will vary. Some products require specific types of equipment or sewing skills. For example, the manufacturing of brassieres requires specialized materials, equipment, and skills; and because of the importance of fit, it is typical for brassiere manufacturers to require that finished products be within 0.125 inches (0.3175 cm) of the specifications or standard pattern. Therefore, to ensure quality standards, companies will ask the following questions:

- What equipment is needed to produce the goods efficiently?
- How specialized are these equipment needs?
- What specific skills are required to produce the product line?
- Will different equipment be needed next season or next year to produce goods for the company?

Companies will analyze the factory's equipment and the skills of sewing operators when determining their production needs and making their sourcing decisions (Figure 11.4).

Figure 11.4
When specialized production equipment is required, companies will select contractors that have the required equipment. Leslie Burns.

Required Plant/Factory Capacities and Capabilities

Certainly factories must have the needed equipment to produce the product lines, but they also must have the capacity relative to expected production needs and timing of production. To determine whether these resources are sufficient, companies will first estimate production needs and then assess the production capabilities and capacities of all the factories they work with. If they are found to be insufficient, the company may decide to hire (additional) contractors. Financial capacities to invest in any new or upgraded equipment will also need to be analyzed. If factory capacities are found to be greater than needed, then downsizing strategies are in order. If a contractor is relying on subcontractors to meet the capacity needs, the company must be assured that the subcontractor meets the same standards regarding quality of merchandise and social responsibility. Facility costs will vary across countries, as will the terms of contracts. Some factories also require minimum orders. Companies must read the fine print of lease contracts to determine what is included.

Corporate Social Responsibility and Environmental Impact

Companies are increasingly using corporate social responsibility and environmental impact factors in their sourcing decisions. Because of limited natural resources and the importance of human rights, many fashion brand companies have included corporate social responsibility and environmental impact in their design, production, and distributions sourcing decisions. Corporate social responsibility in sourcing decisions can happen throughout the supply chain.

- *Socially responsible design*: As discussed in earlier chapters, designers can influence environmental and social systems through their design decisions and contributions. These decisions can include using environmentally responsible materials, zero waste design, inclusive/universal design, and design decisions that do not have a negative impact on factory workers.

- *Socially responsible production*: Also as discussed in earlier chapters, socially responsible companies use factories that provide safe and healthy working conditions, offer fair wages including appropriate overtime wages, and are environmentally responsible. They may also focus on **fair trade** production. For example, Patagonia recently launched a line of sportswear certified by Fair Trade USA. Table 11.3 presents widely used fair trade criteria.
- *Socially responsible marketing*: As also discussed in earlier chapters, consumers like to be associated with fashion companies that are contributing members to the community and encourage employee service, advocacy of social causes, and responsible business practices. A fashion brand can positively affect its image with consumers by communicating these contributions.
- *Supply chain transparency*: **Supply chain transparency** is the effective communication of where, how, and by whom all aspects of a fashion product are made and distributed. Examples of effective supply chain transparency (Figure 11.5) include Patagonia's Footprint Chronicles (www.patagonia.com/us/footprint).

Political and Geographical Criteria

In addition to those factors that are internal to and/or controlled by the company, various other considerations external to the company must be monitored and taken into account when making sourcing decisions.

Trade Agreements and Other Governmental Rules and Regulations

Companies must continually monitor changes in trade agreements as they compare the advantages and disadvantages of sourcing in any particular country. Under many international trade policies, imported textile and apparel goods imported into the country are often subject to tariffs and, in limited cases, quotas. **Tariffs** or **duties** are taxes assessed by governments on imports; **quotas** are limits on the number of units, kilograms, or square meters equivalent (SME) in specific categories that can be imported from specific countries (the metric system for measurement is generally used for these numerical limits). When producing offshore, the company must decide if and how these tariffs may affect the expense of exporting its goods into other countries. Because tariffs add to the overall cost of production, companies reflect on the relative advantage of any free-trade agreements that the country has negotiated.

Documentation providing evidence of country of origin or rules of origin has become important when implementing trade agreements. **Country of origin** of a product is defined as the country where the last step that added value (i.e., substantial change) to the product took place. Because trade agreements are country specific, country of origin documentation (along with product category and fiber content/material) determines tariff rates.

Table 11.3 Fair Trade Criteria

- Paying a fair wage
- Opportunities for advancement
- Engaging in environmentally sustainable practices
- Being open to public accountability
- Building long-term trade relationships
- Providing healthy and safe working conditions within the local context
- Providing financial and technical assistance to producers whenever possible

Figure 11.5
Patagonia's Footprint Chronicles provide effective supply chain transparency. Patagonia.

Other government regulations that companies consider when making sourcing decisions include country-specific laws associated with government intervention regarding

- industrial pollution
- the monitoring of air and water quality
- minimum wage requirements
- child labor laws
- other labor laws (e.g., terms of employment, unions)
- tax laws

When laws in other countries with contract facilities are less strict than companies believe is appropriate, or when enforcement of the laws is problematic, companies may establish their own codes of conduct—guidelines that address human resources, health and safety, and labor and environmental laws—and require their contractors to follow them. Codes of conduct are discussed later in the chapter.

Shipping Distance and Expected Turnaround Time

In an era when getting products to the consumer as quickly as possible is important to company success, production, shipping, and distribution times need to be determined and compared. Here are some questions asked by companies:

- How fast can goods be produced, shipped, and distributed to retailers?
- Would turnaround time be faster if production location changed?
- Would shipping costs be reduced if production location changed?
- What are the energy costs associated with shipping and distribution options?

Companies should consider the distance and shipping time between the production factory/contractor and the company's distribution center. For example, a company with a distribution center in New York may choose a contractor in Mexico over a contractor in Thailand because of shipping time, costs, and environmental impact. In addition, with improved supply chain management strategies such as enhanced communication and transaction technologies (e.g., business-to-business web technologies), information, business forms, and money can be transferred electronically and thus reduce the time involved.

Infrastructure of the Country to Support Production; Availability of Materials and Supplies

When making sourcing decisions, companies must also analyze the availability and reliability of each country's infrastructure and support areas. Questions asked by companies include the following:

- Are quality trims and threads readily available?
- Are sewing machine technicians and parts available?
- Are power sources, transportation methods, and shipping options reliable?

These questions are particularly important when exploring production in developing countries such as Bangladesh, Cambodia, or Pakistan.

Political and Economic Conditions

Companies continually monitor the political and economic conditions of countries where production is taking place. Political instability or economic problems can dramatically affect the availability of materials and the reliability of transportation and shipping alternatives. Safety of employees must also be considered when violence or terrorism could pose threats to employees. Exchange rates of monetary currency are also monitored, particularly by large multinational corporations that are sourcing production around the world.

Natural Disasters

Companies must also monitor the impact of natural disasters such as hurricanes or earthquakes on production capabilities, in addition to possible disruptions to the supply chain. For example, the devastating floods that hit Pakistan and the earthquake that hit Haiti in 2010 had damaging effects on each country's infrastructure and apparel production industry. Rebuilding after these disasters can be slow and can consequently affect companies' decisions whether to remain or return to the country as a sourcing option or to move production to another location.

SOURCING OPTIONS

Based on these company and design criteria and political and geographical criteria, a number of options for sourcing design, materials, and production are available to companies. In general, major sourcing decisions focus on interrelated decisions including whether fabric and materials will be procured and production will be domestic, offshore, or a combination of both; and whether production will be in a company-owned facility, contracted to other companies, or a combination of both.

When using contractors, the company must also decide which of the following types of **contractor** to employ based on the services they offer:

- *Cut, make, and trim services*: With the **cut, make, and trim (CMT)** option, the company provides the tech package, production patterns, fabrics, and trims, and the contractor provides labor and supplies. The contractor cuts, makes, and trims. In some cases, the contractor receives precut fabrics and performs only make and trim (MT) services.
- *Full-package services*: With the **full-package (FP)** option, the contractor provides design and preproduction services, fabrics, trims, supplies, and labor.
- *Other options*: For example, the apparel company provides the fabric, and cuts and bundles the fabric; the contractor sews and trims.

Companies must weigh the advantages and disadvantages of each option in light of their product line, operation strategies, and sourcing philosophy. For some companies, the flexibility afforded by using contractors is necessary; other companies believe they have greater quality control by producing products in their own factories. Some companies produce offshore to take advantage of lower labor costs elsewhere. However, just because labor costs are lower in another country does not necessarily mean that overall production costs are lower, or that producing

Table 11.4 Advantages and Disadvantages of Domestic and Offshore Production

	Advantages	Disadvantages
Domestic production	Trade barriers not a concern Shipping time and costs may be lower Known infrastructure Known culture Supported by consumers who prefer products "made locally"	Labor costs may be higher than in other countries Some types of fabrics may not be readily available
Offshore production	Labor costs may be lower than domestic production Can take advantage of trade agreement incentives Some types of fabrics are more readily available	Differences in cultural norms Monetary/currency differences Language barriers Possible trade barriers

offshore is the right decision for a company. What follows are the basic sourcing alternatives available to companies. Table 11.4 outlines the primary advantages and disadvantages of these options for sourcing production.

Domestic Production

With **domestic production**, the fashion goods are manufactured in the same country where they are sold at retail. In these cases companies may be vertically integrated, controlling most stages of the supply chain, or they may choose to use contractors in the same country where the merchandise is sold.

Vertical Integration

Vertically integrated companies often produce the materials, have their own production facilities and retail the merchandise in the same country. This option allows for the greatest control over quality and timing of production. To be competitive, companies that own their own facilities need to (and have the control to) invest in technology to increase productivity and reduce sewing costs. Companies that choose this option typically produce similar types of goods each year, so their equipment requirements do not change drastically. Companies must also invest in training personnel and plan to maintain consistent and continuous production so that personnel are not continually laid off during slow periods and then rehired during busy periods. Labor costs are generally higher for companies that own their own factories, but many companies are dedicated to making domestic production competitive through increased productivity. For example, Pendleton Woolen Mills, headquartered in Portland, Oregon USA, is involved with multiple steps in creating home and men's and women's fashions: processing wool, weaving fabric, designing and constructing products, and distributing merchandise. Such involvement allows Pendleton to directly monitor these stages.

Figure 11.6
Headquartered in Portland, Oregon, Pendleton Woolen Mills creates and sells wool blankets using vertically integrated operations. Photo courtesy of Pendleton Woolen Mills.

Domestic Contract Production

With this option, fabric is procured either domestically or from a foreign vendor, and production is contracted to a domestic company (contractor) that specializes in the type of production and services (CMT or FP) required. However, with contractor production, the company does not have to invest in factories, equipment, or training personnel. By using contractors, companies have increased flexibility in production methods. This is important for companies with product lines—and, therefore, equipment needs—that vary from year to year. Sometimes companies that typically produce in their own factories choose this option when orders outpace their production capacity. If the fabric is procured from another country, certain trade barriers (e.g., tariffs) need to be handled. Otherwise, trade barriers are not a concern, and shipping costs and production time may be advantageous.

An example of a successful U.S. contractor is Koos Manufacturing, Inc., a Los Angeles–area high-end jeans manufacturer. Koos has produced denim jeans for store brands such as J.Crew, Gap, The Buckle, and Abercrombie & Fitch. Its competitive advantages include its responsiveness to customers' needs, the specialty sewing and quality production expected in the designer price zone, and its proximity to denim laundry facilities where denim fabric takes on its faded or distressed appearance (Figure 11.7).

Figure 11.7
Among U.S. fashion brands, Koos Manufacturing is a successful domestic contractor for denim merchandise. Anne Cusack/Los Angeles Times via Getty Images.

Advantages of Domestic Production

Advantages of domestic production include

- ease of doing business in terms of language, processes, and regulations
- no tariffs or customs issues
- no monetary currency exchange issues
- transportation and shipping time and costs may be less than other options
- consumers may prefer to have merchandise produced in their home country

Disadvantages of Domestic Production

Disadvantages of domestic production include

- possibly fewer options for suppliers and capabilities of contractors
- labor costs may be higher than other options

Offshore Production

Foreign contractors engaged in **offshore production** can provide both CMT and FP services to companies (see Figure 11.8).

Advantages of Offshore Production

When weighing sourcing options, offshore production may provide advantages to the fashion company. Advantages of this option can include the following:

- Lower labor costs may be found in other countries.
- Availability of materials may be closer to production facilities in other countries.
- Factories in other countries have the needed capacities and/or capabilities.
- The finished merchandise may be closer to the ultimate consumer when produced in other countries.

Figure 11.8
Contract factories such as this lingerie factory in Nicaragua provide CMT services for specific product categories. WWD/© Conde Nast.

Disadvantages of Offshore Production

Disadvantages of offshore production include

- possible trade restrictions and/or tariffs on imported merchandise, which may require the hiring of a customs broker
- language and cultural differences that might affect working conditions or communications
- understanding and abiding by laws that may be different from those in the company's own country
- costs and environmental impact associated with shipping merchandise
- monitoring exchange rates of monetary currency

Combination of Domestic and Offshore Production

Many companies diversify their sourcing; that is, they use a combination of options depending on their production requirements at any point in time. Using various sourcing options gives companies the flexibility needed to change production in response to consumer demand, production requirements, and international relations. Diversification of sourcing options also safeguards companies against natural disasters and political or economic crises that may occur within a country or region of the world.

Companies often combine domestic and offshore production. For example, Patagonia, headquartered in Ventura Beach, California USA, sources from fiber suppliers in the United States and Peru, textile mills in the United States, Europe, China, South Korea, Taiwan, and Japan and produces its lines in factories in the United States, China, Thailand, Vietnam, Philippines, India, Sri Lanka, Jordan, Mexico, Nicaragua, El Salvador, and Colombia. To ensure product quality and that the contractors abide by environmental requirements, minimum wage, and minimum age standards set by Patagonia, Patagonia has a published code of conduct, and company representatives visit each contractor.

One of the most diverse contracting systems is that of Nike, Inc.—the world's largest footwear company, headquartered near Beaverton, Oregon. In 2015, Nike contracted with 692 factories in 42 countries, including 180 factories in China, 29 in Thailand, 67 in the United States, 68 in Vietnam, 44 in Indonesia, and 19 in Mexico. The company also requires contractors to comply with a code of conduct and conducts internal and external third-party factory audits.

GLOBAL SOURCING ALTERNATIVES

Sourcing decisions are complex, and companies continually assess sourcing options to best meet their needs. To be competitive, production facilities—both domestic and offshore—must be responsive, flexible, efficient, and cost effective.

Global Patterns of Production

Worldwide production of textiles and apparel has focused on providing the world's largest consumer markets (i.e., North America and Western Europe) with a steady supply of fashionable apparel, accessories, and home fashions.

Currently, apparel production facilities can be found in developed countries (highly industrialized countries) such as the United States, Canada, Australia,

Figure 11.9
Developing countries such as Bangladesh rely on apparel manufacturing for their economic development. WWD/© Conde Nast.

Brazil, and countries in western Europe with large domestic consumer markets; developed Asian countries with historically strong textile and apparel industries including Japan, Hong Kong (administrative region of China), South Korea, and Taiwan (Chinese Taipei); and emerging and developing countries such as China, India, Bangladesh, Costa Rica, and Guatemala (Figure 11.9).

Reasons for the increase in contract production include the number of contractors that have design and/or production capabilities (full-package services) and the progress that has been made in computer compatibility. Technology advances have led to increased transmission of electronic information, such as tech packages, garment specification sheets, and/or patterns. Movement of production to China and other countries was spurred by the following developments:

- phaseout or elimination of quotas for members of the World Trade Organization in 2005
- relatively low labor costs
- specialization in certain types of fabrics and/or production processes that cannot be found elsewhere
- relatively fast production and worker productivity

Apparel industries in countries and world regions with large consumer markets—such as in North America, the European Union, Brazil, Australia, and Japan—have typically focused on both domestic and export opportunities. Industries in countries and world regions without large consumer markets generally have focused on exporting merchandise. However, as consumer markets have grown in highly populated countries such as China and India, greater attention is being paid to both domestic and export production.

Worldwide, according to the World Trade Organization, the two largest textile exporters in 2014 were China (35.6 percent share of world exports of textiles, not including its domestic market) and the European Union (23.8 percent share of world exports of textiles, not including its domestic market). India, the United States, Turkey, the Republic of Korea, and Taiwan (Chinese Taipei), accounted for a combined additional 21.5 percent share of world exports, not including their domestic markets.

Also worldwide in 2014, according to the World Trade Organization, the two largest apparel exporters were China (38.6 percent share of world exports of apparel, not including its domestic market) followed by the European Union (26.2 percent share of world exports of apparel, not including its domestic market). Bangladesh, Vietnam, India, and Turkey combined accounted for another 16.3 percent share of world exports of apparel (Table 11.5). As the world's largest consumer markets for apparel, the European Union in 2014 had a 37.7 percent share of world imports of apparel; the United States had an additional 19.7 percent share of world imports, and Japan an additional 5.9 percent share.

Table 11.5 Leading Exporters and Importers of Clothing, 2014	
Exporters	**Share of World Exports**
China	38.6
European Union	26.2
Bangladesh	5.1
Vietnam	4.0
India	3.7
Turkey	3.5
Indonesia	1.6
United States	1.3
Cambodia	1.2
Pakistan	1.0
Sri Lanka	1.0
Mexico	1.0
Thailand	0.9
Importers	**Share of World Imports**
European Union	37.7
United States	17.7
Japan	5.9
Canada	1.9
Russian Federation	1.6
Switzerland	1.2
Australia	1.2
China	1.2

Source: World Trade Organization.

Table 11.6 Textile and Clothing Exports' Percent Share in Country Economies' Total Merchandise Exports, 2014	
Country	**Textile Exports' Percent Share in Economy's Total Merchandise Exports**
Pakistan	36.7
Nepal	29.5
Turkey	7.9
Bangladesh	7.8
El Salvador	6.0
Egypt	5.7
India	5.7
Syrian Arab Republic	5.2
Country	**Clothing Exports' Percent Share in Economy's Total Merchandise Exports**
Haiti	91.1
Bangladesh	80.9
Cambodia	54.3
Sri Lanka	43.5
El Salvador	39.4
Honduras	39.4
Lesotho	38.8
Mauritius	26.1
Madagascar	20.7
Tunisia	16.2
Turkey	10.6

Many developing countries rely on textile and apparel manufacturing for their economic development and compete worldwide as low-wage production centers (Table 11.6). Indeed, a significant proportion of these countries' exports are in textiles and apparel, as can be seen by the following statistics (2014):

- 91.1 percent of Haiti's total merchandise exports are apparel
- 80.9 percent of Bangladesh's total merchandise exports are apparel
- 54.3 percent of Cambodia's total merchandise exports are apparel
- 43.5 percent of Sri Lanka's total merchandise exports are apparel
- 39.4 percent of both Honduras' and El Salvador's total merchandise exports are apparel
- 38.3 percent of Lesotho's total merchandise exports are apparel

Several characteristics of textile and apparel manufacturing account for the importance of apparel exports in the economies of many developing countries. Because textile and apparel production is highly labor intensive, the industry provides work for many people. Compared with other manufacturing industries, apparel production is fairly inexpensive to establish. Essentially, all that a manufacturer needs are industrial sewing machines, pressing equipment, and a building. In addition, because of continuously changing fashion trends, there is a constant demand for textile and apparel products. Therefore, developing countries in Southeast Asia, Africa, the Caribbean Basin, and South America greatly contribute to the global production of textiles and apparel.

North America

North America (United States, Mexico, and Canada) represents one of the largest trading partnerships, in which with each country brings strengths and challenges as a sourcing option. Passage of the North American Free Trade Agreement (NAFTA) in 1994 further solidified reciprocal reductions in tariffs among the United States and countries within North America.

United States

As the world's largest consumer market, the United States is best known as an international hub for design, research, marketing, retailing, and niche production capabilities. Many national and international designer brands (e.g., Calvin Klein, Ralph Lauren, Michael Kors, Tori Burch), lifestyle brands (e.g., Tommy Bahama, Timberland), sportswear (e.g., Nike, Under Armor, Columbia Sportswear), and fast fashion brands (e.g., Forever 21) are headquartered in the United States with a focus on design, research, marketing, and retailing operations. Most of these brands contract production both domestically and offshore.

Once one of the largest manufacturing industries in the United States, the apparel manufacturing industry has experienced continued decreasing employment over the past 25 or more years. According to the United States Bureau of Labor Statistics, in 2014, employment in apparel manufacturing nationwide was estimated at 142,860—down from 929,000 in 1990. Small pockets of employment in apparel production can be found in almost every state, although the states with the largest employment are California, New York, North Carolina, Texas, and Florida. This distribution reflects the historical concentration of apparel manufacturing in the New York City and Los Angeles areas and the lower wages found in the southern states in comparison to other states. Southern California has a pool of skilled labor, primarily from the Latino and Asian populations in the area.

Southern states have benefited from trade agreements (NAFTA, CAFTA-DR) that have enhanced production activities such as garment cutting in these states, as well as from vertically integrated manufacturing facilities. For example, Miami has grown as a hub for numerous cutting operations for companies taking advantage of lower labor costs outside the United States and these various trade incentives. U.S. production facilities pride themselves in offering flexibility, innovation, speedy turnaround time, and efficient delivery to retailers.

Canada

Similar to the United States, Canada is known for its design, research, marketing, retailing, and niche production capabilities. Its companies primarily use a combination of domestic and offshore contractors. International brands with headquarters in Canada include Roots, Arc'Teryx, and lululemon athletica.

Mexico

Mexico's importance as a sourcing option for apparel production grew as a result of the passage of NAFTA, and Mexico is currently the fifth-largest supplier (value based on US$) of apparel to the United States. Its proximity to the United States and foreign investments in technology contributed to the growth of CMT, MT, and full-package contractors. Employment in apparel production is currently at approximately 320,000 workers. Examples of brands that currently contract production in Mexico include Levi's, Zara, Nike, Patagonia, and Pendleton Woolen Mills. Mexico is also the headquarters for large domestic brands including Milano (Mexico City) and Andrea footwear (Guanajuato).

Caribbean Basin and Central America

With its relatively close proximity to both the United States and South American consumer markets and relatively lower wages than other countries, countries in the Caribbean Basin and Central America have historically been viable sourcing options for U.S. and South American companies. Starting with the Caribbean Basin Initiative and solidified with the passage of the Dominican Republic–Central American–United States Free Trade Agreement (CAFTA-DR) in 2005, trade privileges and reciprocal reductions in tariffs continue to exist, particularly for companies that use U.S. fabric with production in these countries. Lower shipping and transportation costs (compared to Asia) and the convenience of doing business in the same or nearby time zones also contribute to making countries in the Caribbean Basin and Central American advantageous sourcing options for North and South American companies.

South America

Similar to North American countries, South American countries have formed trade alliances to enhance economic development. Mercosur is considered a common market of South America. With Argentina, Brazil, Paraguay, Uruguay, and Venezuela as members and Chile, Bolivia, Peru, Columbia, and Ecuador as associate members, Mercosur's goal is to advance free trade among these countries (Figure 11.10). In addition to fostering trade among these countries, the trade policies are considered highly protectionistic in terms of trade with other countries: policies include high tariffs and (in Buenos Aires) bans on used clothing imports. The United States has free trade agreements with Chile, Colombia, and Peru. In addition, Chile and Peru are part of the Trans-Pacific Partnership negotiations.

Figure 11.10
Winter Sun produces hand-painted fair trade apparel in Ecuador. Winter Sun.

Europe and the European Union

Made up of twenty-eight member countries (plus six candidate countries), the European Union (EU) is the second-largest consumer market in the world. The EU is considered a common single market with free trade of goods and services among member countries. The euro (€) is the common currency in seventeen of the member countries, and environmental, agricultural, and fisheries policies are coordinated among member countries. From a fashion industries sourcing perspective, Europe consists of two sets of countries:

1. Western European countries including Germany, Italy, Great Britain (UK), Spain, and France. These countries focus on niche textiles, design, marketing, niche production, and retailing.
2. Central and eastern European countries including Poland, Hungary, Czech Republic, Romania, and Bulgaria. These countries often serve as lower-wage production centers for western European brands.

Australia and New Zealand

As the world's largest producer of wool, particularly Merino wool, Australia exports to textile mills around the world. In addition, Australia is the home to numerous brands sold in both Australia and exported to other countries. These brands include Redback footwear, Billabong, Driza-Bone, Akubra, CUE, and Bonds. New Zealand is also known for its high-quality wool production. Icebreaker is a global brand of merino wool clothing headquartered in New Zealand.

South Asia

South Asia is comprised of India, Pakistan, Bangladesh, Sri Lanka, Nepal, and Bhutan. Textile and apparel exports account for a significant proportion of total exports from these countries and contribute greatly to the economies of these countries. Regarding textile production, India and Pakistan are well known for cotton production for domestic textile mills and for export to mills elsewhere. All of the countries are considered lower-wage production centers for efficient manufacturing of moderate and budget-priced apparel (Figure 11.11).

Bangladesh and Pakistan, in particular, have made headlines about the unsafe working conditions in apparel factories. In Bangladesh, the collapse of the Rana Plaza commercial building in 2013—resulting in the death of over 1,100 people (mostly garment workers) and injuring over 2,400 others—brought media attention to the plight of workers in that country. As a result of this tragedy, companies throughout the world have come together to work on improving conditions. Two organizations, The Bangladesh Safety Accord and the Alliance for Bangladesh Worker Safety, have emerged. The Bangladesh Safety Accord was signed in 15 countries by over 70 companies including H&M, Inditex (Zara), PVH, Carrefour, and Tesco. The Accord is governed by companies and worker representatives with a focus on independent inspections and remediation plans. The Alliance for Bangladesh Worker Safety was signed by over 25 North American apparel companies and retailers, including Children's Place, Costco, Gap, JCPenney, Kohl's, Macy's, Nordstrom, Target, VF, and Walmart. The Alliance conducts safety

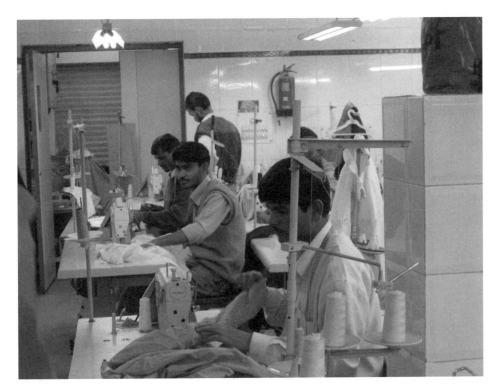

Figure 11.11
Contract factories in India produce merchandise for both domestic and export markets. Photo by Elaine L. Pedersen.

assessments of apparel factories as a means of improving conditions. Whereas strides have been made in worker safety and Bangladesh remains a popular location for apparel production, much still needs to be accomplished to bring conditions in all factories to acceptable levels.

Southeast Asia

The Association of Southeast Asian Nations (ASEAN) is comprised of Singapore, Indonesia, Malaysia, Philippines, Thailand, Brunei, Vietnam, Myanmar, Lao PDR (Laos), and Cambodia. Even with differing economic and political systems, these countries all play an important role in global production of fashion merchandise. They have each developed unique niches for the design, manufacturing, and distribution of fashion. For example, Singapore is an important design, merchandising, and port for fashion trade; Vietnam and Thailand's industries have grown as niche suppliers for apparel with complex construction; and Lao PDR is considered a low-wage production center. Political and social unrest in Indonesia and Philippines have negatively affected these countries' attraction as sourcing options in their part of the world. However, many of these countries, including Vietnam and Cambodia, have been attractive destinations for foreign investments to build and support strong apparel, footwear, and accessories industries (Figure 11.12).

East Asia

Once known as the "Big 4" of textile and apparel production, Japan, Hong Kong, South Korea, and Taiwan continue to have strong industries in high-end and high-performance textiles, niche production, design, marketing, sourcing services, and retailing. Investors from these countries have also provided financial and management resources to countries such as Vietnam, Cambodia, and Thailand in developing their fashion manufacturing industries.

Figure 11.12
Vietnam has become an important country for contracting apparel and footwear production, drawing investments to build and support the industry. Leslie Burns.

China

China is the world's largest apparel-producing country and the largest exporter of apparel. As previously noted, China accounts for a 34.8 percent share of world exports of textiles (not including their domestic market) and a 38.6 percent share of world exports of apparel (not including their domestic market). China also dominates in the production of many sectors of the apparel industry. For example, according to the U.S. Office of Textiles and Apparel, China supplies 88 percent of the cotton sweaters, 84 percent of men's wool sweaters, and 91 percent of women's wool sweaters imported by the United States. Apparel manufacturing companies in China range from small contractors to megafactories, some of which have hundreds of designers and design staff and tens of thousands of sewing operators producing millions of garments per year.

Why is China so dominant? There are a number of reasons:

- large capacity for fiber and fabric production, including fabrics made from cotton, silk, and synthetics
- large textile machinery industry that supports production needs
- diversified apparel industry; production ranges from lingerie to sportswear to luxury fashion brands
- large population of skilled workers with a very high level of productivity
- government and private investments in the manufacturing industries and infrastructure needed to support them
- large trade shows or sourcing fairs that connect fashion brands with contractors (Figure 11.13)

Figure 11.13
Large trade shows and sourcing fairs in China connect fashion brands with Chinese contractors. Leslie Burns.

SOURCING STRATEGIES: STEPS IN GLOBAL SOURCING

Faced with the complexities of making sourcing decisions and the range of options worldwide, how do fashion brand companies find the right factory/contractor to produce their merchandise? They follow this process:

1. Determine the company or corporate philosophy regarding sourcing. For example, when asked the question, "How do you select your factories?" Patagonia (2016) answered:

    > Quality, business factors (technologies, skill, location, price, customer service, ability to deliver on time); and environmental and social performance are the four factors. Quality continues to be our principal criterion for sourcing. Reduced environmental harm is a strong second criterion.

2. Design the product line and determine its fabric and production needs.

3. Identify sourcing options for materials and production. Material suppliers and production contractors can be located in various ways:

    *   Some very large companies may have their own design and material libraries, which provide services to designers and sourcing analysts for the company. For example, Nike has an extensive materials library where Nike designers, product engineers, and sourcing analysts can explore the newest materials available. However, most companies are not large enough to have an in-house materials library.

    *   Online resources are helpful in exploring options for materials and findings, and for finding suitable production contractors. Material ConneXion (materialconnexion.com) and Le Souk (www.lesouk.co) offer fashion brand companies searchable databases of materials. Designers and sourcing analysts can purchase samples for possible use in current and future lines.

    *   **Sourcing fairs** are trade shows that bring contractors and companies together. At these fairs, contractors have booths with samples of their merchandise and information about their expertise and capacities. Sourcing fairs are also held in conjunction with other trade shows, such as MAGIC. Contractors use sourcing fairs to connect with companies, and companies use them to find appropriate domestic and foreign contractors. Sourcing fairs can be face-to-face or online.

    *   Contractors and companies also use classified advertisements in trade publications, such as *WWD Classifieds*, to advertise their needs or availability.

    *   Headquartered in Atlanta, Georgia, the *American Apparel Producers' Network* is the primary trade association for contractors and other companies across the global supply chain that produce apparel for the U.S. consumer market. The association provides educational forums, research and data on sourcing effectiveness and on supply chain management technologies, and opportunities to build relationships among companies through networking events and travel.

4. Evaluate sourcing options. This step is carried out either by the company or by independent sourcing agents/analysts. Criteria for evaluation include trade and investment incentives and/or barriers, human relations and cultural challenges/benefits, product development capability and capacity, and labor compliance.

5. Inspect and evaluate factories according to the company's or auditing firm's codes of conduct.

6. Conduct negotiations between the fashion brand and the suppliers.

SOURCING STRATEGIES: IMPLEMENTING CODES OF CONDUCT

Before signing contracts, and periodically afterward, fashion brands perform inspections of the factories they use. This strategy has become an important component of compliance processes for fashion brands. The following subsections consider two aspects of codes of conduct: the sweatshop issue and the role of factory auditing in implementing codes of conduct.

What Is a Sweatshop?

From the time of the Triangle Shirtwaist Co Factory fire in 1911 to the Rana Plaza disaster in 2013, the apparel industry has been associated with sweatshops. But what is a sweatshop? The meaning of this term varies depending on the source of the definition. According to the U.S. General Accounting Office, a **sweatshop** is an employer that violates two or more federal or state labor, occupational safety and health, workers' compensation, or other laws regulating an industry. The International Labor Organization defines a sweatshop as an establishment where fundamental rights are denied, and the International Labor Rights Forum defines sweatshops as "workplaces where basic worker rights are not respected." Global Exchange's definition includes employees' inability to form independent unions and the absence of a wage that can support the basic needs of a small family (i.e., living wage).

A review of the various definitions reveals some common characteristics. In general, a sweatshop is a workplace where workers are exploited, including being denied a living wage or benefits; working excessively long hours, often without overtime pay; suffering poor working conditions; undergoing arbitrary discipline, including verbal and/or physical abuse; and/or having no ability to organize to negotiate better terms of work.

Codes of Conduct and Factory Auditing

As a result of media attention, stakeholder and consumer demands, consumer interest, and company philosophy, fashion brands have taken greater responsibility for auditing the working conditions of their contractors and subcontractors. Many fashion brands have adopted sourcing guidelines and regularly inspect contractors' facilities to ensure that workers are not being exploited. One of the first companies to implement such guidelines was Levi Strauss & Co. In 1991, it established guidelines for its hired contractors, covering issues such as the treatment of workers and the environmental impact of production (Tables 11.7 and 11.8). Levi Strauss & Co., which works with contractors throughout the world, regularly inspects its contract factories. It has published terms of engagement along with corrective actions for noncompliance, timelines, and verification methods.

Most large companies have established their own guidelines and codes of conduct. Table 11.9 outlines the JCPenney guidelines.

Table 11.7 Levi Strauss & Co. Terms of Engagement, 2013

1. *Labor:* Use of child labor is not permissible. Workers can be no less than 15 years of age and not younger than the compulsory age to be in school. We will not utilize partners who use child labor in any of their facilities. We support the development of legitimate workplace apprenticeship programs for the educational benefit of younger people.

2. *Prison/Forced Labor:* We will not utilize prison or forced labor in contracting relationships in the manufacture and finishing of our products. We will not utilize or purchase materials from a business partner utilizing prison or forced labor.

3. *Disciplinary Practices:* We will not utilize business partners who use corporal punishment or other forms of mental or physical coercion.

4. *Legal Requirements:* We expect our business partners to be law abiding as individuals and to comply with legal requirements relevant to the conduct of all their businesses.

5. *Ethical Standards:* We will seek to identify and utilize business partners who aspire as individuals and in the conduct of all their businesses to a set of ethical standards not incompatible with our own.

6. *Working Hours:* While permitting flexibility in scheduling, we will identify local legal limits on work hours and seek business partners who do not exceed them except for appropriately compensated overtime. While we favor partners who utilize less than sixty-hour work weeks, we will not use contractors who, on a regular basis, require in excess of a sixty-hour week. Employees should be allowed at least one day off in seven.

7. *Wages and Benefits:* We will only do business with partners who provide wages and benefits that comply with any applicable law and match the prevailing local manufacturing or finishing industry practices.

8. *General Labor Practices and Freedom of Association:* We respect workers' rights to form and join organizations of their choice and to bargain collectively. We expect our suppliers to respect the right to free association and the right to organize and bargain collectively without unlawful interference. Business partners should ensure that workers who make such decisions or participate in such organizations are not the object of discrimination or punitive disciplinary actions and that the representatives of such organizations have access to their members under conditions established either by local laws or mutual agreement between the employer and the worker organizations.

9. *Discrimination:* While we recognize and respect cultural differences, we believe that workers should be employed on the basis of their ability to do the job, rather than on the basis of personal characteristics or beliefs. We will favor business partners who share this value.

10. *Community Involvement:* We will favor business partners who share our commitment to improving community conditions.

11. *Foreign Migrant Workers:* All requirements defined in the Sustainability Guidebook i.e., child labor, freedom of association, forced labor, disciplinary practices, health and safety, and so on shall equally be followed for foreign migrant workers.

12. *Dormitories:* Business partners who provide residential facilities for their workers must provide safe and healthy facilities.

13. *Permits:* Factories must have all current permits as required by law (including business and operating permits, fire-safety and electrical certificates, permits for equipment such as boilers, generators, elevators, fuel and chemical storage tanks, etc. and building, emissions and waste-disposal permits).

Source: Levi Strauss & Co.

Table 11.8 Levi Strauss & Co. Environment, Health, and Safety, 2013

Levi Strauss & Co. has prepared this Environment, Health and Safety (EHS) chapter to help our business partners meet our Social and Environmental Sustainability requirements. EHS requirements are no less important than meeting our quality standards or delivery time.

Safety Guidelines: Including requirements around safety committees, risk assessment, emergency preparedness, building integrity, aisles and exits, lighting, housekeeping, electrical safety, control of hazardous energy (lock-out/tag-out), machine guarding, powered industrial trucks, noise management, personal protective equipment, ventilation, chemical management, extreme temperatures, asbestos management, occupational exposure, signs and labels, and maintenance.

Finishing Guidelines: Applies to all factories that finish/launder garments for Levis Strauss & Co. and ensure that factories have hazard controls in place to protect workers from exposure to chemicals, high noise levels, airborne silica, high temperatures, and machine hazards associated with finishing processes.

Health Guidelines: Including requirements around first aid and prevention of the spread of communicable diseases among factory workers

Environmental Guidelines: Including requirements around industrial wastewater discharges, domestic wastewater management, bio-solids management, prevention of storm water pollution, hazardous materials storage, and waste management.

Source: Levi Strauss & Co.

Table 11.9 JCPenney Supplier Principles, 2015

ETHICAL BUSINESS PRACTICES   At JCPenney, we commit ourselves to the values expressed in our Statement of Business Ethics, which is derived from the belief of our founder, James Cash Penney, in doing business according to the Golden Rule: "Do unto others as you would have them do unto you." The JCPenney Statement of Business Ethics sets out the standards by which all JCPenney associates promote a culture of integrity and legal compliance, including guidance on relations and interactions with suppliers. Suppliers who do business with JCPenney must share our values and ethical commitments.

WORKING CONDITIONS   JCPenney is committed to having a diverse and inclusive workforce where everyone is respected, valued and has a voice in contributing to our business success. We also recognize our responsibility to follow the employment and human rights laws of every country in which we operate. We ask our suppliers to adopt similar practices in their business operations and in their relations with component, raw material and service providers.

SAFE QUALITY PRODUCTS   At JCPenney, we take special care to ensure that JCPenney merchandise meets the highest quality and safety standards. We have long been a leader in consumer product safety measures to make sure all products we sell meet or exceed product safety requirements. However, JCPenney cannot meet its product safety and quality goals alone; we rely on suppliers to implement procedures to fulfill our high standards.

SOCIALLY RESPONSIBLE SUPPLY CHAIN   JCPenney is dedicated to preventing the sale of products produced at the expense of communities, workers or the environment. We work with suppliers who share our commitment to a socially responsible supply chain.

ENVIRONMENTAL IMPACT   JCPenney continually seeks to use good judgment with respect to the environmental impact of our business operations, and to develop and implement plans, programs and policies for eliminating or minimizing significant threats to the environment. We work with our suppliers to develop products, packaging and procedures that are environmentally responsible. We set ambitious goals to improve our Company's performance in this area and expect our suppliers to set similar commitments.

COMMUNICATION, COOPERATION AND COMPLIANCE   These Principles are an integral part of our supplier selection process. JCPenney works with suppliers, industry groups and experts to identify best practices and to develop tools for assessing, monitoring and improving suppliers' performance and compliance. We require our suppliers to cooperate with all audit assessment, investigation, and monitoring processes requested by JCPenney. We require suppliers to work with JCPenney to remediate issues that may be discovered during monitoring. If a supplier fails to meet our requirements, we will take decisive corrective action, up to and including cancellation of contracts and termination of our relationship. Suppliers are encouraged to contact JCPenney with any questions or concerns about our expectations and are expected to report a potential ethical or legal violation involving JCPenney business which may be reported confidentially in local languages. To that end, we provide a hotline, which can be accessed via a toll-free telephone number 1-800-527-0063 or website found at www.jcpjline.com. We will never retaliate against someone for raising good faith concerns about potential violations of law, ethics, or JCPenney policy.

Source: JCPenney.

Organizational and company **codes of conduct** are guidelines that address human resources, health and safety, and labor and environmental laws. Codes of conduct typically address the following areas:

- *Corporate principles* or general statements that describe the company's values, objectives, and commitments to the rights of workers.
- *Management philosophy statements* that describe upper management's personal philosophy and its commitment to enforcing the code.
- *Compliance codes* that offer guidance about appropriate or prohibitive conduct. For example, a code of conduct may indicate that the contractor will use no child labor.

To be effective, codes of conduct must be credible—that is, taken seriously by governments, consumers, and all companies involved. Credibility, in turn, depends on the level of auditing, enforcement, and transparency associated with the codes. *Transparency* is the extent to which the contractors, workers, organizations, governments, and consumers are aware of the codes and how they are enforced.

Thus, the need for effective enforcement of company codes of conduct resulted in the development of **factory auditing programs** by companies and organizations. The overall goal of these factory auditing programs and organizations is to improve the working conditions in factories that produce fashion merchandise around the world. These audits will occur before a factory is contracted with or assigned to produce the fashion merchandise and periodically after that. The timing will depend on the fashion company. Some factories are audited on a daily basis, and others are audited annually or every few years.

Fashion brand companies either conduct their own factory audits or contract with an independent factory auditing organization to conduct periodic reviews of factories. The different types of auditing processes are referred to as first-party, second-party, and third-party audits.

- First-party auditing, or internal auditing, occurs when the employees of the company that also owns the factory conduct the audit. For example, a factory that produces fashion brands may have its own set of auditors who ensure compliance with a set of standards.
- Second-party auditing occurs when the fashion brand does not own the factory but has or intends to have a contract with the factory. Employees of the fashion brand company will audit the factory to ensure compliance with the fashion brand company's supplier code of conduct.
- Third-party auditing occurs when employees of an organization independent of either the fashion brand company or the factory conducts the audit to ensure compliance with their own set of standards or the supplier code of conduct provided by the fashion brand company. Third-party organizations that conduct audits include Worldwide Responsible Accredited Production (WRAP) and Verité.

Some organizations also provide auditing services to fashion brand companies. The Fair Labor Association conducts audits for member companies; the Worker Rights Consortium may conduct audits based on worker complaints filed. The Fair Factories Clearinghouse provides its members with auditing tools and factory profiles. Although not involved with audits per se, the Clean Clothes Campaign directly supports workers in factories that may have been audited or will undergo audits.

Factory audits typically include the following areas of evaluation:

- efficiency and capacity of the factory
- working conditions—safety, health, and hygiene
- worker compensation, including overtime and any hiring broker arrangements
- opportunities for freedom of association and collective bargaining
- labor laws
- environmental law compliance
- quality assurance
- security of brand name and merchandise
- subcontractor arrangements

Factory audits are conducted through visual observation of the factory, financial audits, management interviews, worker interviews, and review of government regulations/laws and reports.

Challenges with Factory Auditing

Challenges for the Fashion Brand

Even as fashion brands adopted guidelines, improvement of working conditions in factories was difficult, particularly if local agencies did not enforce country or state regulations. In some cases, factories resisted adopting certain guidelines, which they viewed as Western standards of business. Large fashion brands that may contract in more than fifty countries and work with hundreds of different contractors also found it difficult to inspect and regulate working conditions in every factory. They also found that some factory managers created false documents, coached or threatened workers to lie, or even created small false factories to comply with standards outlined in the codes.

Challenges for the Factory

Factories and workers also faced challenges with codes and auditing procedures. In particular, workers developed false hope if fashion brands had codes but did not inspect factories and enforce their codes. According to critics, some companies were interested only in the public relations appeal of sourcing guidelines but did very little to enforce the rules. For fashion brands and factories that were diligent about audits and follow-ups, it was observed that factories holding contracts with multiple fashion brands often experienced **audit fatigue**—the challenge of being audited multiple times with only slight differences in the standards being addressed.

Given the amount of resources needed to conduct audits, one question is constantly asked: How effective are these auditing programs? In fact, reputable companies that effectively live up to their corporate responsibility philosophies have used factory audits as a fundamental strategy for improving the lives and working conditions of individuals worldwide.

In short, the effectiveness of audits depends on their authenticity, credibility transparency, and enforcement.

TRENDS IN SOURCING

As companies continually reevaluate their sourcing options, a number of factors are currently affecting those decisions:

- *Sustainability*: Fashion brand companies have a number of options when shipping merchandise. The cost of the shipping options is definitely a factor in the decision. Sourcing agents are also considering the impact on the environment. More sustainable decisions include
  - using recycled cardboard for shipping
  - using less packaging, where possible
  - using biodegradable vegetable-based garment bags
  - sourcing materials as close to production as possible
  - if shipping long distances, shipping by sea for transporting components and/or finished goods
- *Stakeholder concerns for corporate social responsibility*: Consumers, shareholders, and other company stakeholders are demanding that companies be more aggressive in their corporate responsibility efforts. Companies have responded through a variety of initiatives and programs.
- *Brand management*: The availability of counterfeit products has caused sourcing agents for name brands to focus on security services offered by production facilities and to make sourcing decisions based on the security of their brand.
- *Supply chain management orientation to sourcing decisions*: Companies are focusing on all aspects of materials procurement, production, and distribution in their sourcing decisions. This requires greater communication among decision makers throughout the supply chain. For example, designers must be aware of their decisions on materials procurement as well as production.
- *Local sourcing, Nearshoring, Onshoring, Reshoring*: Producing merchandise as close as possible to the ultimate consumer has resulted in a number of strategies. Local sourcing is a business strategy whereby companies procure materials within a specified radius of the site where their products are produced and/or distributed. Whereas this strategy has achieved attention in food, restaurant, and building industries, it has not been as popular in the textile, apparel, and home fashions industries. This is because raw materials (e.g., cotton, wool, polyester, silk, etc.) are produced in limited areas of the world. However, some small companies that have a discerning target customer are identifying strategies to locate their materials and production as close as possible to each other and to the ultimate customer, or nearshoring. For example, Imperial Stock Ranch's production of wool and finished wool products are all carried out in central Oregon. Other companies are contracting with manufacturers in the same country where the merchandise will be sold (**onshoring**; Figure 11.14) or moving production back to the domestic market (**reshoring**). For all these strategies, a desire to better meet consumers' needs is essential to their success.

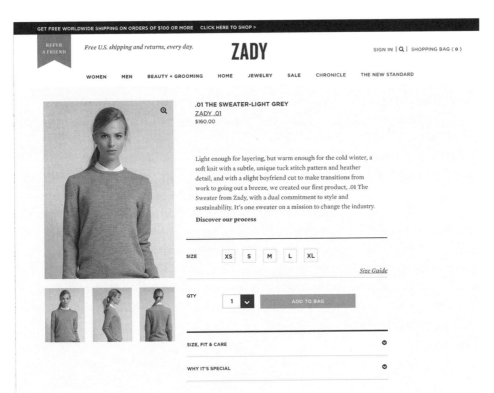

Figure 11.14
Fashion brand company Zady works with U.S. partners, including Imperial Stock Ranch in Oregon for wool, to create sustainable merchandise. Zady.

SUMMARY

The term *sourcing* refers to the decision-making process companies use to determine how and where the textile and apparel products or their components will be procured and produced. In making sourcing decisions, companies must consider factors that are internal to the company: sourcing philosophy; labor requirements, costs, and productivity; fabric/materials quality and availability; quality assurance/control standards; equipment and skills requirements; required plant/factory capacities and capabilities; and corporate social responsibility and environmental impact. Factors external to the company are also monitored and considered: trade agreements and other government regulations; geographic location, shipping distance and expected turnaround time; infrastructure of the country; availability of materials and supplies; political and economic conditions of the country; and natural disasters. Based on these criteria, various sourcing options are available to apparel companies and retailers. Major sourcing decisions focus on whether procurement and production will be domestic, offshore, or both; and whether production will take place in a company-owned facility, be contracted to others, or be a combination of both. When contracting, companies also must decide whether cut, make, and trim (CMT), full-package (FP) services, or other options will be used. Fashion brand companies evaluate the advantages and disadvantages of options when making sourcing decisions.

Worldwide production of textiles and apparel has focused on providing the world's largest consumer markets—North America and Western Europe—with a steady supply of fashionable apparel, accessories, and home fashions. Thus, apparel production occurs in both developed and developing countries. Because of the labor-intensive nature of the apparel industry, China, India, Bangladesh, Vietnam, and other Asian countries have emerged as large producers of both textiles and apparel. However, textile, apparel, accessory, and footwear production occurs throughout the world, and each region has its advantages and disadvantages depending on the criteria used by the fashion brand company.

When making sourcing decisions, fashion brand companies first decide on their overall sourcing philosophy. Then, in coordination with their line development, they determine their sourcing needs and identify options to be evaluated. Potential factories are then inspected/audited for compliance to the fashion brand's or other organization's standards or codes of conduct. If the factory meets these standards, negotiations are conducted.

Companies have attempted to improve working conditions by adopting and implementing codes of conduct and factory auditing. First-, second-, and third-party auditing systems are currently used by fashion brand companies. To be effective, codes of conduct must be credible, enforced, and transparent. Only then will factory audits result in needed improvements for workers worldwide. Trends in sourcing include sustainability issues, corporate social responsibility, brand management, supply chain management, and strategies for producing merchandise as close to the final customer as possible.

KEY TERMS

audit fatigue
code of conduct
contractor
corporate social responsibility (CSR)
country of origin
cut, make, and trim (CMT) contractor
domestic production

duty
factory auditing program
fair trade
full-package (FP) contractor
nearshoring
offshore production
onshoring
partner shoring
quota

reshoring
social responsibility
sourcing
sourcing fair
supply chain transparency
sweatshop
tariff
triple bottom line
yarn forward rule of origin

DISCUSSION QUESTIONS AND ACTIVITIES

1. What does a sourcing philosophy of corporate social responsibility mean for a company? How might a company implement this sourcing philosophy?

2. Explore the website of a large apparel and/or footwear manufacturer. What guidelines are included in the company's code of conduct? How are these codes of conduct implemented? How are these codes of conduct beneficial to consumers?

3. Examine the labels on at least three garments or accessories in your closet. What country of origin is on the label of each item? Why do you believe the item was manufactured in that country? What are the advantages and disadvantages of producing fashion merchandise in that country?

Analyzing Sourcing Options:
Sourcing in China

The misses' sportswear buyer/sourcing analyst for a major specialty store chain, Lucinda Maze, is preparing to leave her office for two weeks on an overseas trip to China. The goal of her trip is to evaluate the potential of foreign sourcing for the production of basic synthetic knit merchandise for her department. Lucinda's company is interested in importing exclusive private label merchandise. However, the production of this private label merchandise must be consistent with the company's strong human rights and environmental ethic. Currently, they are using a U.S.-based contractor that is unionized. Through the specialty store's resident buying office, her attendance at a Chinese sourcing fair, and a trade organization operated through the Chinese government, Lucinda was able to communicate with several contract apparel factories in China. She has made appointments to personally meet with the factory managers and to review her merchandise needs as they relate to the manufacturing capabilities and cost of the Chinese factories.

After two days of long and exhausting travel, Lucinda arrives at her first appointment. Through an interpreter the factory has provided, Lucinda learns that the factory can produce the goods she needs for her chain of over 100 stores. The basic shirts, turtlenecks, and cardigan sweaters can be produced in the exact color assortment she has previously determined at wholesale prices that are approximately 35 percent below the wholesale prices offered by the U.S. contractor/factory she is currently using. The Chinese factory is prepared to use any sizing specifications that the store prefers. Ad valorem tariffs (import taxes based on the value of the merchandise) on the merchandise to import them back to the United States are 30 percent of the export value of the merchandise.

Lucinda continues her investigation of Chinese factories over the next few days. She finds the other factories to be fairly competitive in their merchandise offerings, delivery schedule, and pricing. She then works with her store office (via email and company internet sites) and with various representatives of the Chinese factories to calculate the landed costs on the goods. Landed costs include the original price plus additional fees associated with foreign and domestic inland freight, ocean transport, wharfage and handling, insurance costs, both import and export tariffs on the merchandise, and any currency conversion. After they have computed the costs associated with importing the goods, Lucinda develops quotations for the overseas purchases with each of the Chinese factories.

Lucinda is aware that if she decides to use the foreign sourcing, it would be best to work with a single factory to ensure color and sizing consistency in the merchandise assortment. She concludes that if she decides to import merchandise, she would select the first factory she investigated based on the company's pricing structure, its production quality, and its experience in manufacturing for other major retailers in the United States. The single purchase with this manufacturer will represent 40 percent of her total department inventory for the start of the fall season. This is a critical decision for Lucinda as a professional buyer/sourcing analyst and for the profitability of the company as a whole.

Next, Lucinda evaluates the pros and cons of manufacturing and importing merchandise from China. She determines that the primary advantages include merchandise exclusivity, an opportunity for private label goods, lower labor costs, higher markup potential, and opportunity to have merchandise made to the store's specifications. She then carefully examines the disadvantages of importing the goods and decides that they include the requirement for a large quantity purchase, lack of control during the merchandise production process, possible difficulties and delays in communicating with the resource, the potential for delayed shipments, tariffs, possible strikes, governmental constraints, and shipping difficulties.

Lucinda is faced with a dilemma. She must immediately decide whether she will purchase nearly half of her inventory from a Chinese factory or stay with the domestic producers. The pros and cons need to be weighed; the advantages and disadvantages must be evaluated.

1. Lucinda's company has a strong human rights and environmental ethic. It believes in a three-prong bottom line: people, planet, and profits. What questions should Lucinda ask the Chinese factory manager and workers that would assist her in understanding the factory's approach to labor and environmental issues?

2. What might Lucinda do to ensure that the Chinese factory follows her company's human rights and environmental ethic?

3. If you were the manager of the Chinese factory, what would you do to secure Lucinda's order of your merchandise?

4. If you were the manager of the U.S. contractor, what would you do to convince Lucinda to keep your firm as a primary contractor of her company's merchandise?

5. If you were the chief executive officer of Lucinda's specialty store chain, how would you advise Lucinda in this situation?

6. If you were in Lucinda's position, what would you decide to do in this situation? Why?

CAREER OPPORTUNITIES

Career opportunities associated with sourcing decisions include

- Materials buyer
- Sourcing analyst for materials and/or production
- Purchase planning analyst
- Production facility auditor
- Corporate social responsibility professional for a fashion brand or supply chain management firm

REFERENCES

Clean Clothes Campaign. (2015). http://www.cleanclothes.org/ (accessed March 15, 2016).

Fair Factories Clearinghouse (FFC). (2015). http://www.fairfactories.org/ (accessed March 15, 2016).

Fair Labor Association (FLA). (2015). http://fairlabor.org (accessed March 15, 2016).

International Labour Organization (ILO). (2015). http://www.ilo.org/global/lang—en/index.htm (accessed March 15, 2016).

Patagonia (2016). Patagonia Corporate Responsibility FAQs. http://www.patagonia.com/us/patagonia .go?assetid=67517 (accessed March 28, 2016).

U.S. Department of Commerce. (2015). International Trade Administration. Office of Textiles and Apparel. Trade Data. http://otexa.trade.gov/ (accessed March 28, 2016).

U.S. Department of Labor. (2015). Bureau of Labor Statistics. "Apparel Manufacturing: NAICS 315." http://www.bls.gov/iag/tgs/iag315.htm (accessed March 15, 2016).

Worker Rights Consortium (WRC). (2015). http://www.workersrights.org (accessed March 15, 2016).

World Trade Organization (WTO). (2015). "Statistics: Merchandise Trade." https://www.wto.org/english/res_e /statis_e/merch_trade_stat_e.htm (accessed March 15, 2016).

Worldwide Responsible Accredited Production (WRAP). (2015). http://www.wrapcompliance.org/ (accessed March 15, 2016).

Production Processes

IN THIS CHAPTER, YOU WILL LEARN
THE FOLLOWING:

- goals and benefits of lean manufacturing

- the production processes used in manufacturing fashion merchandise

- the components of quality assurance and the importance of quality assurance in delivering on-time, acceptable merchandise to the retailer

- the role of agents who assist manufacturers in bringing products produced offshore into the United States

**Step 7: Production Processes,
Material Management, and Quality Assurance**

Step 1 Research and Merchandising

Step 2 Design Brief

Step 3 Design Development and Style Selection

Step 4 Marketing the Fashion Brand

Step 5 Preproduction

Step 6 Sourcing

Step 7 Production Processes,
Material Management, and Quality Assurance

Production Order (may include approval
of rst size run by contractor)

Finish, Inspect, Press, Tag, and Bag Order

Step 8 Distribution and Retailing

PRODUCTION CONSIDERATIONS

The previous chapters discuss the development of a product line from market research, creation, design development, pattern development, and preproduction through sourcing options. The product line is now ready for production. Production is the construction process by which the cut material, fabric pieces, findings, and trims are incorporated into a finished apparel, accessory, or home fashions product (see Step 7 of the flowchart on the previous page). The cost to produce the product is affected by the product design and pattern, as well as by the production process used. Therefore, it is essential to the company's success that the designer, product developer, and patternmaker be well versed in the production processes used to manufacture the product. Some of the decisions regarding the relationship among the design, pattern, and production processes occur during the planning and review meetings. Other production decisions take place as the new style proceeds through preproduction. However, if difficulties arise during the production of a new style, the designer, product developer, and patternmaker are typically consulted, along with the production engineer.

Production sequences and **manufacturing environments** (the production facility, location of production, choice of production process, and cycle time) vary greatly, depending on factors such as the following:

- available technology
- price zone
- geographic location of production

Continual new developments in supply chain management and product life cycle management (PLM) create great flexibility in production processes and manufacturing environments. This chapter is an overview of the production processes, methods assuring product quality, and auxiliary agents needed for distributing finished goods to market.

LEAN MANUFACTURING

Lean manufacturing is an approach for achieving the shortest possible cycle time by eliminating process waste. This strategy makes the operation very efficient and consisting only of value-adding steps from start to finish. Simply put, lean manufacturing takes place without wasted time or materials. Its main benefits are lower production costs, increased output, and shorter production lead times. Lean manufacturing involves some specific goals:

- Reduce manufacturing lead times and production cycle times by reducing waiting times between processing stages.
- Minimize inventory levels at all stages of production, particularly works in progress between production stages.
- Maintain lower inventories, which also leads to lower working capital requirements.
- Increase labor productivity by reducing the idle time of workers and ensuring that when workers are working, they are using their effort as productively as possible (not doing unnecessary tasks or unnecessary motions)

- Possess the ability to produce a more flexible range of products with minimum changeover costs and changeover time.
- Use equipment and manufacturing space more efficiently by eliminating bottlenecks and maximizing the rate of production though existing equipment, while minimizing machine downtime.
- Reduce defects and unnecessary physical wastage, including excess use of raw material inputs and the costs associated with reprocessing defective items.
- Omit unnecessary product characteristics that are not required by customers.

Another way of looking at lean manufacturing is that it aims to achieve the same output with fewer inputs—less time, less space, less human effort, less machinery, less materials, less cost.

How a manufacturer approaches production varies based on the product and quality needed. Different production sewing systems and processes can be used in lean manufacturing.

PRODUCTION SEQUENCE AND COSTING

Different categories of products may require very different processes and types of equipment. For example, men's tailored suits require many more steps in production than men's casual sportswear. In addition, the types of sewing and pressing equipment are quite different for tailored apparel as compared to sportswear. Boys' and girls' clothing requires similar sewing processes and equipment and could be manufactured at the same facility, whereas men's tailored clothing needs to be handled by different production facilities.

An important aspect of preproduction and production is planning the sequence of operations required to produce the garment style. Production includes the sewing sequence, as well as other tasks performed at the sewing facility that relate to completing the product, such as pressing and labeling.

These production steps, and the time required for each step, need to be determined for each garment style to determine the final cost. This information is referred to as the *construction specifications* (see Chapter 8) and is part of the tech pac.

As discussed in Chapter 8, the sequence of sewing operations may have been determined when calculating the style's cost. The production sequence used to construct the sales representatives' samples, made to market the style to retail buyers, is frequently the same as the sequence used to sew the production orders. Any problems in production might be corrected while making the sales samples.

Determining the most efficient production sequence and cost depends on many factors, such as the following:

- the equipment capabilities of the specific production facility (e.g., the availability of a pocket-setting machine can greatly speed production of a style with a welt pocket)
- the labor cost of the operators (in some factories where labor is very inexpensive, more work may be done by hand than with expensive equipment)
- whether certain steps should be subcontracted (e.g., a shirt with a pleated front inset might be less expensive to produce if the fabric for the front inset were sent to a pleating contractor and then returned to the production facility for cutting and sewing into the shirt)

Some operations may be performed before the sewing process, such as the following:

- Interfacing may be fused to garment sections before sewing. The pieces to be fused are laid on conveyor belts and moved through large fusing ovens to adhere the interfacing.
- Patch pockets, such as those sewn to the back of jeans, are prepared for sewing by prepressing the raw edges to the inside. Hundreds of pockets are prepared and then delivered to the site where they will be attached to the pants. Many processes are streamlined to provide the most labor-effective production.

Sometimes several different factories are used to produce a large order. In such cases, the different factories may not use exactly the same production sequences to produce the same style. Each contractor submits a sample sewn at its factory to the fashion brand company for approval. For the samples sewn for sales representatives by contractors, the same process of submitting a sewn sample is used. The contractor's sample is called a **sew by** or a **counter sample**. After approval, this sample is used as the benchmark for comparison of the sewn production goods.

Although great effort is expended to plan a smooth production run, many problems can stall production. Some problems involving the procurement of materials have already been discussed. Production problems include complications due to delays in receiving a shipment of zippers, or late arrival of subcontracted work. Troubleshooting is an integral part of production. When sourcing offshore, unexpected problems can be difficult to solve. A flood in Bangladesh, a hurricane in the Dominican Republic, or a rail workers' strike in France may cause production or delivery delays that cannot be planned for or avoided. Management personnel of fashion brand companies often travel to production facilities (whether company-owned or contractor-owned) to check on production or help solve production problems.

MANUFACTURING ENVIRONMENTS

The three manufacturing environments, or strategies, include mass production, fast fashion production, and mass customization. The product type as well as the strategy used for replenishing the product will determine which of these three environments is used for production. This section discusses each of the three manufacturing environments.

Mass Production

The mass-production manufacturing environment is suitable for cutting and sewing/constructing very large quantities of each product, using one of several possible mass-production processes (discussed later in this chapter). Mass production capitalizes on economies of scale. Basic staple products such as T-shirts, jeans, underwear, hosiery, pillowcases, and slippers fit this manufacturing environment. These products have a low fashion risk, in part because they can remain on the retail floor longer than many fashion goods. The focus of mass production is on in-store replenishment of products (see Chapter 13). Seasonal goods include some staple products, such as turtlenecks, produced in seasonal colors. The selling time for seasonal goods falls between the selling time for staple goods and for fashion goods. Thus, some seasonal goods are manufactured in the mass-production environment while other seasonal goods are manufactured in the short-cycle manufacturing environment, which is discussed in the next subsection.

The demand for staple goods and some seasonal goods tends to be easier to forecast than the demand for fashion goods. This situation gives the mass-production manufacturing environment the opportunity for a slightly longer lead time than that of the other manufacturing environments. Longer lead time means that production can be sourced globally. Because of the longer production time and retail selling time for these goods, the cost of carrying them (both to the fashion brand company and to the retailer) is greater than for goods that are manufactured closer to the time of their market demand.

Fast Fashion Production

To respond to the demands of fast fashion, retailers employ a variety of techniques, including strategic sourcing, production, and stocking. These practices accelerate the design-to-delivery cycle of their clothing by as much as 90 percent compared to the rest of the garment industry. They also cut costs throughout the design, delivery, and sales cycle. As the name implies, this manufacturing environment is well suited to goods that are produced closer to the time of their market demand than mass-produced products. Fast fashion or **short-cycle production** is well suited for trendy products, which are placed into the market for short selling seasons (six to eight weeks) with no intention of in-store replenishment.

Successful fast fashion retailers source labor and materials close to home and produce many small manufacturing runs to reduce cycle time. To accelerate the design process, these companies employ many in-house designers who can create thousands of designs based on upcoming trends. Due to the ever-increasing speed of production—thanks to the application of computer technology to supply chain management, PDM/PLM, and the monitoring of consumer sales—**fast fashion production** (where products go from concept to retail stores in less than three weeks) is greatly reduced. The Spanish retailer Zara is particularly successful in reducing cycle time; the company claims that some of its items go from concept to delivery in as little as two weeks (Barry 2004).

Mass Customization

A short-cycle manufacturing environment that is applied to an individual customer is called the mass-customization manufacturing environment. **Mass customization** involves the ultimate consumer in the customization of fit, design, or personalization of the product. Because the ultimate consumer is involved with design and/or fit choices, it may appear that mass customization can best be categorized as a design variation. However, mass customization deals with products that are already designed; the customer is simply customizing the product.

The emergence of new technology has provided a means to link the customer at the retail store with the apparel factory, resulting in mass customization. The cost efficiency of mass production is maintained. One key point in mass customization is that the customer selects and pays for the product before it is produced. Thus, the phrase "sell one, make one" is appropriate.

For the manufacturer and retailer, mass customization has the following advantages:

- reducing large inventories
- minimizing returns
- reducing distribution costs
- building strong customer relationships
- solidifying brand loyalty
- identifying customer preferences and buying habits

To operate, mass customization requires electronically linked, seamless integration of components throughout the entire supply chain. It requires a manufacturing environment suited to individualization, yet with a fast turnaround time and at a low cost. Custom tailors and dressmakers are not producing these goods; within the mass-customization manufacturing environment, agile manufacturing is required. This production process is discussed along with other production processes later in this chapter.

The mass-customization manufacturing environment uses all the newest computer technologies, supply chain management, PDM/PLM, and some level of customization of the product for the individual customer (Figure 12.1).

A Sales clerk measures the customer using instructions from a computer as an aid.

The clerk enters the measurements, and adjusts the data based on the customer's reaction to samples.

The final measurements are relayed to a computerized fabric-cutting machine at the factory.

Bar codes are attached to the clothing to track it as it is assembled, washed and prepared for shipment.

Figure 12.1
Mass customization is made possible by computer technology. Illustration by Mike Miranda.

Figure 12.2
Body scanners capture
precise body measurement
data into a computer
system.

Pattern alteration software allows customers to customize a garment for their specific size. (More traditional approaches to developing a design for a target market were discussed in previous chapters.) The pattern is developed based on a company's target customer size standard. The standard-size apparel fits some bodies better than others. With the development of new computer technology, PDM/PLM, and supply chain management, a type of custom apparel different from the custom-made apparel produced by personal tailors or dressmakers of the past is possible. Mass customization is a consumer-driven strategy that allows limited customization of a standard style, such as size, color, or trim choices. On the other hand, **made-to-measure** apparel is a fully customized process in which a garment is made specifically for one individual based on his or her measurements and preferences. The difference between made-to-measure and mass customization is the degree of customization offered. However, the difference is blurring as technology provides tools to blend made-to-measure with mass customization (Figure 12.2).

Brooks Brothers, a retailer and manufacturer of men's and women's classic professional clothing, provides an example of mass customization that customers can use to build their own dress shirt. Ordering shirts from the catalog is a simple process that gives customers basic choices, such as neck size, sleeve length, choice of three body styles, choice of three cuff styles, and 17 top-end fabric selections. Patternmaking software provides the capability to adapt the standard pattern to specific design and sizes. Delivery takes two to three weeks.

Early ventures in made-to-measure using mass production at the factory included men's tailored suits. The customer was measured at the tailor's retail store. In some systems, front, back, and side-view photographs of the customer standing in front of a measurement grid were also sent to the factory. The customer's measurements were input into the computer system that was linked electronically to the apparel factory's computer. The body dimensions were translated into specific differences between the standard pattern and the customer's needed adjustments. The pattern changes were made by computer calculations, and a customized pattern was plotted. Laser cutters allowed fast, single-ply computerized cutting of the garment pieces. With careful tracking through production, the cut pieces for each customized suit were sent through the mass-manufacturing process. Before receiving the finished goods, the customer returned to the retail store for a final fitting for pant hemming and other minor adjustments (handled by the retailer).

One of the challenges of made-to-measure apparel is assessing customer fit preferences. Some customers prefer a looser fit while others prefer a snug fit to their suits. The system "suggests a try-on size from the store's inventory, which is an integral part of the process" (Rabon 2000, p. 40). Mass-customization options that include customizing the fit have expanded greatly with the continued development of electronically linked body measuring, patternmaking, cutting, and production technology (Figure 12.3).

Figure 12.3
Mass customization links the customer's style preferences, selected at the retail store or through the internet, to the production site. Courtesy of Astor & Black.

Another product well suited to mass customization is footwear. Most people's left foot is somewhat different in size from the right foot. By scanning each foot, the shoes can be customized to fit each foot precisely. The huge inventories of shoes stocked in varying lengths and widths, styles, and colors can be greatly reduced by mass customization while the customer's shoe fit can be enhanced by scanning technology.

FINISHING

At the end of the production line, the goods await various finishing steps. Pressing may occur only at this stage of production. Edge stitching or topstitching may be used to reduce the need to press during production, thereby cutting labor costs. Specialized pressing equipment quickly produces excellent results on finished goods. For tailored jackets, a steam mannequin might be used to press the entire jacket while on a three-dimensional form. Other types of specialized equipment perform other functions, such as turning pant legs right side out (pants come off the production line inside out). Finishing operations include trimming thread,

Figure 12.4
Finishing processes include the application of tagless labels.

attaching buttons and snaps, tacking shoulder pads and linings, pressing, and buttoning the garment.

Some labels are sewn in during production. These might include care labels, brand labels, and size labels. Printed care, fiber content, and size information can also be heat-sealed directly onto the product. This method, called **tagless labels**, eliminates the potential for skin irritation from a woven label, as well as the bulk created by applying one or more sew-in labels to a product. Tagless labels debuted first on T-shirts, then underwear, performance wear, and children's wear—products where labels can be particularly annoying. The market trend is toward increased use of tagless labels (Figure 12.4).

Other labels, as well as hangtags, might be attached during finishing operations. Hangtags can be used to provide additional product marketing information. For example, the water resistance or UV protective properties of a jacket's fabric might be explained on the hangtag. Providing goods with floor-ready labels and hang-tags takes place at this stage in production. Garments might be laundered before shipping. Laundering might be performed to enhance the hand or visual appeal of the fabric. For example, stone washing is used to soften denim fabric. Other treatments are used to age or distress denim. Another reason for laundering is to shrink a product before shipping. While we are familiar with purchasing some products large enough to "shrink to fit," many consumers find it advantageous to know that the garment has been preshrunk. They know that the way the garment fits when they try it on at the retail store is how it will fit after washing at home. For garments that will be laundered after production and before shipping, each pattern piece for the garment has to be very carefully created and incorporate the exact shrinkage factor.

Many fashion brand companies produce dyed products in color allotments based on the quantity of orders for each color. Other manufacturers produce colorless garments and then dye the garments during finishing. Such goods are referred to as **garment dyed**. Dyeing finished goods has several advantages. It can provide quick delivery of the goods to the retailer because production can begin on the colorless garments while the sales force is accumulating the sales totals by color.

Goods are prepared for shipping by being folded or hung. At some facilities, folding might be done by hand using cardboard, tissue, straight pins, and plastic bags. At other facilities, machines are used to fold the goods. For garments placed on hangers, overhead conveyors bring the garments to equipment that covers each item with a plastic bag. Some hanger and bagged garments are moved from a conveyor belt at the factory directly onto an overhead track on the truck that delivers the bagged garments to the manufacturer's distribution center, to the retailer's distribution center, or directly to the retail store (see Chapter 13).

PRODUCTION SEWING/ CONSTRUCTION SYSTEMS

It is important to understand the variety of production systems in order to make informed decisions about the production system most suitable for the garment style, price range, and sourcing option. This section describes several of these systems and ends by discussing a combination of systems.

Single-Hand System

As discussed in Chapter 8, the prototype product is produced by a single individual. The sample maker (also called a *sample hand*) completes all the steps required in production, moving from one type of specialized equipment to another as needed, based on the garment or product style's requirements. Some apparel and accessory goods are produced in limited quantities using a system similar to that used to sew the prototype. In a single-hand system, one individual is responsible for sewing an entire garment. The bundle for this production system would include all the garment or product parts for one style in one size. In today's market, the **single-hand system** is used for couture and for some very high-priced fashion merchandise produced in a limited quantity. This system is slower than mass-production systems, and it may include considerable detail or handwork during production.

While some fashion merchandise is still sewn one at a time in a single-hand system, most merchandise is manufactured using one of several production systems of large-quantity or *mass manufacturing*. The most common categories of these production systems are progressive bundle systems and flexible manufacturing systems.

Progressive Bundle System

Worldwide, the progressive bundle system is the most common production system used by factories making fashion merchandise. With the **progressive bundle system**, garment/product parts for a specified number of garments (e.g., a dozen garments) are bundled together and put in carts that are rolled from one sewing machine operator to another. Each machine operator is responsible for the following activities:

- opening the bundle of the garment parts
- performing one or two construction steps on each garment in the bundle
- rebundling the garment parts for transport to the next operator

Figure 12.5
With the bundle system, a sewing operator performs one or several sewing steps on each garment in the bundle.

The progressive bundle system of production frequently uses a piece-rate wage system. Each operator's pay is based on individual productivity. The number of units the operator has completed at the end of each workday or week is the basis for the operator's pay for that period. New developments in software enable companies to set accurate piece rates in a manufacturing environment (Figure 12.5).

The progressive bundle system is especially well suited to large bundles of work, usually from one dozen to three dozen units per bundle. At each operator's workstation, one bundle is in process while one or several more bundles are waiting. Sometimes referred to as a *batch* or *push* system, the progressive bundle system tends to generate high levels of **work-in-process (WIP)**. Also, a considerable investment of inventory is tied up with the WIP.

With the progressive bundle system, equipment is selected and sometimes customized to perform one or several functions needed to produce a specific style. Each piece of equipment is positioned on the floor in relation to the equipment and sewing sequence required before and after each step in the production sequence. The machine operator is highly trained to perform one or several steps on specific equipment. Each sewing facility tends to specialize in certain types of products, such as athletic footwear, backpacks, or swimwear. This specialization occurs partly because different types of equipment are needed for producing different categories of products.

Sometimes the facility is arranged so that the body of the jacket is assembled in one part of the facility, and the lining is assembled in another. The two parts of each garment are united at the final assembly stage. This requires careful tagging to ensure that sizes and dye lots are matched correctly at the final assembly stage. The nature of the progressive bundle system can make it difficult to pinpoint where a quality problem originates.

A new style ready for production may differ from previous styles in its production sequence or equipment needs. Machine operators might need additional training, so it can take time to develop the expertise to run at full capacity. Equipment may have to be moved within the facility to prepare for a different production sequence.

Flexible Manufacturing Systems

For mass-manufactured products, the bottom line is cost containment. This is affected by:

- how much time is required to prepare the product for production
- how much time the product is in process (WIP)

Reduction in one or both of these measures will result in a lower production cost. Some companies focus on developing more **flexible manufacturing systems** involving one or all of the following activities:

- reorganizing existing equipment on the floor into a new systems approach
- developing new equipment
- reorganizing the way garments are routed through production
- reorganizing workers into teams that are cross-trained to handle a variety of operations using an assortment of equipment

Flexible manufacturing (FM) is defined as "any departure from traditional mass-production systems of apparel toward faster, smaller, more flexible production units that depend upon the coordinated efforts of minimally supervised teams of workers" (AAMA, Technical Advisory Committee 1988; quoted in Hill 1992). FM systems are known by many names, including

- modular manufacturing
- self-directed work teams
- compact production teams
- flexible work groups

The strategy emphasizes group effort, employee involvement, and employee empowerment.

In FM systems, manufacturing management makes a shift away from high individual productivity and low cost to short manufacturing cycles, small quantity of WIP, and quick delivery of the finished product. Flexible manufacturing is well suited to smaller production runs as compared to the large production runs of the progressive bundle system. The term **modular manufacturing** is most often used in the U.S. fashion industry to describe flexible manufacturing.

With modular manufacturing, which is often referred to as a *pull system*, the sewing facility is organized into teams of seven to ten operators each. Operators are cross-trained in all areas of garment construction. Each operator might work on two or three machines. Operators might perform several tasks at each machine, or one machine could be used for a series of assembly operations. Every team is responsible for producing entire garments, instead of one operator being assigned a single operation, such as setting in a sleeve or a zipper (as in the progressive bundle system). Equipment is arranged in modules so that work can be passed from one team member to another, who may work either while standing or sitting. The number of units in each operation may vary from only one to as many as ten.

Within a module, operators work as a team and solve problems, thus creating a more productive environment. Flaws in production are handled as a team; if a mistake is found, the entire garment is returned to the team, where the operators decide how best to fix it. Therefore, the traditional piece-rate wage is not applicable. The team is paid not only according to the quantity it produces but also by the quality of its work. Pay is based on a collective effort. In theory, if an apparel factory were completely modular, it would be redesigned into modular units, each one capable of producing complete garments in a few hours.

Before deciding to change to a modular manufacturing system, a company must consider these factors:

- Downtime is particularly critical with modular manufacturing methods. Each minute a machine is down costs money, for it can slow down the entire team's work progress. A worker's absence can also slow down production.

- Converting to a modular manufacturing system requires the involvement of all employees, an investment in education and training, a shift of management responsibilities from a few people to the team as a whole, and support from management.
- The shift to modular manufacturing requires a cultural change within a company. Success in creating effective teams depends on knowing how employees think and perform.

Some manufacturing facilities shifted to modular manufacturing in hopes of reducing manufacturing costs. For some companies, however, costs rose at first. New equipment might need to be purchased, cross-training employees costs money, and reduced productivity during training is an additional start-up cost. It may take months before the facility realizes a cost savings (Abend 1999).

For companies that commit to modular manufacturing, its cost benefits have been realized by containing costs through inventory reduction, a reduction in WIP, and for some facilities, an improvement in product quality (Figure 12.6).

Another advantage of modular manufacturing is that production facilities can shift quickly from manufacturing one type of product category to another. For example, a manufacturer can change its production facilities to accommodate producing intimate apparel, backpacks, and swimwear. At one facility, "Engineers swap out the equipment as the last items in one product go through the line. Overnight the facility is ready for the new line, and then it's a matter of training operators, which can take one to three weeks to reach full capacity" (Hill 1998, p. AS-8).

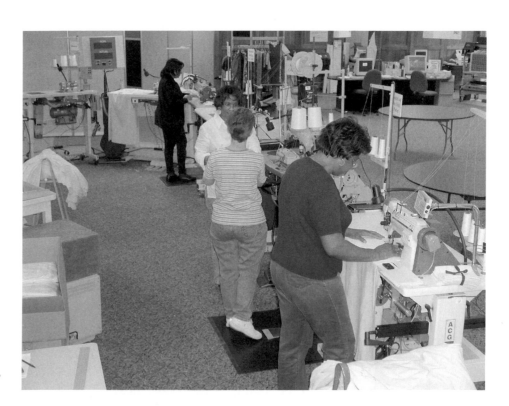

Figure 12.6
In modular manufacturing, operators work as a team. [TC]², Gary, NC, USA (www.tc2.com).

Figure 12.7
A unit production system delivers the pieces of each garment to the sewing operator. The operator may not need to remove the garment from the conveyor while performing the sewing operation. Guang Niu /Getty Images.

Unit Production Systems

To achieve efficient manufacturing, some companies have invested in a computerized overhead transport system such as the **unit production system (UPS)**. With UPS, garment parts are fed on overhead conveyors, usually one garment at a time, to sewing machine operators. Garment parts are delivered directly to the operators' ergonomically designed workstations. This dramatically reduces operator handling time during production. Workstations can be moved easily to accommodate different equipment needs for various garments. Operators are cross-trained in a number of procedures in the manufacturing cycle, similar to the way they are for modular manufacturing. The transport system is designed to include bar codes to track WIP (see Figure 12.7).

A study by Clemson Apparel Research (Hill 1994) determined that UPS would provide the hypothetical apparel manufacturing plant a 329 percent return on its investment and would pay for itself in 11 months. Primary savings to the company would be in the areas of reduced direct labor costs (shorter waiting periods, less overtime, improved ergonomics) and reduced WIP inventory levels. Many production facilities have shown substantial increases in production with UPS. Other companies have found UPS to be less successful. As with modular manufacturing, many variables enter into the success of UPS.

Agile Manufacturing

Agile manufacturing combines a variety of technologies that together form a totally integrated, seamless exchange of information linking retailers and suppliers to the manufacturing facility. An example is mass customization. This manufacturing environment allows for individual changes in style, color, and fit, using a customer's body measurements and modifications of a pattern based on a style developed by the fashion brand company. The manufacturing facility cuts an individual customized style from a pattern design system (PDS) and marker-making system linked electronically to a single-ply cutter. White fabric prepared for digital printing might be printed before or after cutting (see Chapter 6) to the customer's color and print specifications. After printing and cutting, the garment is manufactured using a production system that is designed to accommodate units of one).

Combination of Systems

Some production facilities use more than one type of production system. For example, a contractor may use UPS for certain garment styles that suit this production system, while using a progressive bundle system for other styles. As discussed earlier, the number of units to be made influences the production system. For example, in small production runs the modular manufacturing may be more economical than the progressive bundle system.

QUALITY ASSURANCE

Quality assurance involves making sure the product meets the standards of acceptance set forth by the contracting party. The contracting party might be the apparel manufacturer for goods produced by a contractor. The contracting party might be a retailer for private label or store brand goods. Many of the fabrics and trims and sewing operations are specified in detail on the garment specification sheet and are an important part of quality assurance. Visual inspection after production is complete—for loose threads, for example—forms another important part of quality assurance.

In developing quality assurance programs, companies are relying less on after-the-fact inspection and more on building quality into the products during production. Through modular manufacturing methods, operators are responsible for product quality throughout production.

Current emphasis in quality assurance focuses on actively monitoring the manufacturing methods, materials, work environment, and equipment to continually achieve the expected specifications.

The fabric inspection component of quality assurance was discussed in Chapter 4. The spreading and cutting operations include considerations such as on-grain garment parts and color-matching the dye lots. Quality assurance also takes place during the sewing and finishing operations. Garments are inspected during production to assure the specified quality standard. Inspectors can include machine operators, team quality auditors, plant supervisors, or quality auditors sent by the contracting party (apparel manufacturer or retailer).

Quality assurance includes the use of quality thread, buttons, zippers, snaps, elastic, hem tape, and other products; and the quality and accuracy of sewing operations such as stitch type and length, stitch tension, seam type, edge finish, topstitching, turned edges, buttonhole stitching, hem stitching, and plaid matching. Quality assurance personnel are well versed in evaluating all aspects of production quality and accuracy.

Another component of quality assurance is the consistency of the size specifications for all products produced in each size. All the finished products must conform to the specified tolerances (the amount the product can deviate, plus or minus, from the garment dimension) stated on the measurement spec sheet (see Chapter 10). Many fashion brand companies check a specified number of garments in each shipment received from the contractor to determine whether the measurement specs have been met.

AUXILIARY PRODUCTION AGENTS

A substantial portion of the fashion industries relies on offshore factory production. Thus, it is important to discuss some of the aspects related to shipping goods out of the country where they were produced and into the country where the merchandise will be sold. Many foreign countries have export regulations for shipping goods out of the country. It can be helpful for a U.S. fashion brand company that contracted the goods (the *importer*) to appoint an **export agent** in the producing country to assist with exporting the products.

A **freight forwarding company** arranges to move a shipment of goods from the country where the goods were produced to the country where they will be sold. Tariffs and quotas (regulations affecting companies that import and export products) are discussed in Chapter 11.

The U.S. Customs and Border Protection (CBP), a part of the federal government, is the regulatory agency in the United States. A **customs broker** (licensed by the CBP) in the United States is an agent hired by the U.S. fashion brand company to assist the company in importing the goods produced in another country. The customs broker is familiar with the complex U.S. customs regulations for importing textiles, apparel, and accessories and will assist the fashion brand company to gain customs clearance. The broker charges the fashion brand company on a transaction basis, not by the number of items in a transaction.

Although using a customs broker is optional, it can be very helpful to the fashion brand company. Sometimes, a shipment of goods is stalled by customs or sent back to the country of origin to correct the documentation. In that case, the fashion brand company faces losing the retailer's business and it may also be fined by the shipping company that cannot unload the shipment. Of course, additional transportation costs would be involved. The fashion brand company might also need to hire a consolidator to serve as an intermediary for the freight forwarder and the customs broker.

SUMMARY

This chapter examines some of the important aspects of production. Building on previous chapters, it describes the interrelationship among research, design, pattern development, marketing, preproduction, sourcing, and production. All systems must work together for production to flow smoothly. Any problem along the way may slow production of a style. Delays to the contracted delivery date may cost the manufacturer not only profits from the style, but future business from retailers.

The labor required to cut and sew the goods makes up a significant portion of the cost to produce fashion merchandise. Reducing labor costs can help retain reasonable prices for finished goods. New technology in equipment and manufacturing systems has dramatically changed apparel production and achieved more efficient use of the labor team. Workers are more actively involved in providing an efficient production system and a team responsible for the quality of the goods produced. The number of different garment styles produced per season has increased for many production facilities. This makes it more difficult for production to flow smoothly. Flexibility in production systems will continue to be a cornerstone of increased efficiency and decreased labor costs.

With the growth in offshore production, it is increasingly important for fashion brand companies to understand the various processes, agencies, and personnel involved in these complex business transactions. Changes in regulations, as well as in political and economic conditions and environmental considerations, can affect the production of goods.

KEY TERMS

agile manufacturing
counter sample
customs broker
export agent
fast fashion production
flexible manufacturing (FM)
flexible manufacturing system
freight forwarding company

garment dyed
lean manufacturing
made-to-measure
manufacturing environment
mass customization
modular manufacturing
piece-rate wage
production

progressive bundle system
quality assurance
sew by
short-cycle production
single-hand system
tagless label
unit production system (UPS)
work-in-process (WIP)

DISCUSSION QUESTIONS AND ACTIVITIES

1. Select a garment such as a blouse or T-shirt. How many seams are used to construct the garment? Are all the stitches the same? Discuss what aspects of the garment are the most difficult to construct, and suggest changes that could be made to reduce the amount of time of production.

2. Compare and contrast the advantages and disadvantages of these two systems of apparel production: progressive bundle and flexible manufacturing.

3. Describe a quality defect that you have encountered with an apparel/home fashions product or accessory. How might quality assurance have prevented this problem?

lululemon athletica:
Production and Quality Assurance

The fashion brand lululemon athletica Inc. was founded in Vancouver, BC, Canada in 1998. "The first lululemon shared its retail space with a yoga studio" (Lululemon 2016) and it continues to design, market, and distribute athletic apparel for yoga, running, dancing, and other active sports. The company prides itself on high-quality merchandise for the active woman. Lululemon also is known for its strong commitment to women's empowerment and fitness, and for hosting events including self-defense and goal-setting workshops.

This reputation began to fall apart in 2013, when 17 percent of Lululemon yoga pants were recalled because the poor quality and too-sheer fabric pilled and fell apart. In defense of the merchandise, founder Dennis "Chip" Wilson then gave an interview that questioned the characteristics of the women wearing the yoga pants, implying that the problems were because the women wearing the yoga pants were too large to be wearing them. A public relations nightmare ensued, and Mr. Wilson left the company. Since that time, Lululemon has regrouped and is attempting to rebuild its reputation for quality merchandise.

1. Who is the target customer for lululemon, and why is it important for lululemon to rebuild its reputation for quality merchandise?
2. What are five possible strategies that lululemon can use to assure quality merchandise in its fabric selection and production processes? Describe and evaluate the advantages and disadvantages of each strategy.
3. If you were advising lululemon on the best two strategies for assuring quality merchandise, what would those strategies be, and why?

Sources:
Kell, John. (2015, September 10). "High Costs at Lululemon Mean Bad Karma for Profits." *Fortune*, http://fortune.com/2015/09/10/lululemon-profits-margins/ (accessed March 17, 2016).
Lululemon athletica. (2016). "Who Is lululemon athletica?" http://www.lululemon.com/about (accessed March 17, 2016). (accessed March 17, 2016).
Warnica, Richard. (2014, March 7). "Can Lululemon's New CEO Save the Company?" *Canadian Business*, http://www.canadian business.com/companies-and-industries/can-lululemons-new-ceo-save-the-company/ (accessed March 17, 2016).
Wilkinson, Kate. (2013, November 19). "After Its See-through Pants Debacle, Lululemon Is at a Crossroads." *Canadian Business*, http://www.canadianbusiness.com/companies-and-industries/after-see-through-pants-debacle-and-still-without-a-ceo-lululemon-is-at-the-crossroads/ (accessed March 17, 2016).

CAREER OPPORTUNITIES

Careers in production and quality assurance include the following positions:

- Production cutters
- Sewing operators
- Production supervisors

- Plant managers
- Quality assurance coordinators

REFERENCES

Abend, Jules. (1999). "Modular Manufacturing: The Line between Success and Failure." *Bobbin*, January, pp. 48–52.

Barry, Neil. (2004). "Fast Fashion." *European Retail Digest*, Spring, pp. 75–82.

Hill, Ed. (1992). "Flexible Manufacturing Systems, Part 1." *Bobbin*, February, pp. 34–38.

Hill, Suzette. (1998). "VF's Consumerization: A 'right stuff' strategy." *Apparel Industry Magazine*, December, pp. AS-4–AS-12.

Hill, Thomas. (1994). "CAR Study: UPS, CAD Provide 300 Percent Return on Investment." *Apparel Industry Magazine*, March, pp. 34–40.

Rabon, Lisa. (2000). "Mixing the Elements of Mass Customization." *Bobbin*, January, pp. 38–41.

Rabon, Lisa, and Claudia Deaton. (1999). "Pre-production: Laying the Cornerstones of Mass Customization." *Bobbin*, December, pp. 35–37.

Reda, Susan. (2004). "Retail's Great Race." *Stores*, March, p. 38.

Swank, Gary. (1995). "QR Requires Floor Ready Goods." *Apparel Industry Magazine*, January, p. 106.

Speer, Jordan K. (2004). "A Label-Conscious World." *Apparel*, April, pp. 24–29.

Winger, Rocio Maria. (1998). "The Nygård Vanguard: The Way to Chargebacks." *Apparel Industry Magazine*, December, pp. AS-14–AS-18.

Distribution
and Retailing

IN THIS CHAPTER, YOU WILL LEARN
THE FOLLOWING:

- the strategies and processes for distributing fashion products to the ultimate consumer, including omnichannel strategies

- the nature of communications among companies in carrying out supply chain management and product life cycle management activities related to distribution

- the definitions and characteristics of the various categories of retailers

- the primary trade publications and trade associations involved in the distribution of fashion products

Step 8: Distribution and Retailing

Step 1 Research and Merchandising

Step 2 Design Brief

Step 3 Design Development and Style Selection

Step 4 Marketing the Fashion Brand

Step 5 Preproduction

Step 6 Sourcing

Step 7 Production Processes,
Material Management, and Quality Assurance

Step 8 Distribution and Retailing

Send Retailer's Order to Manufacturer's Distribution Center

Pick Orders (may include quality assurance check)

Send to Retail Store Distribution Center or Directly to Retailer

Review Season's Sales Figures

DISTRIBUTION STRATEGIES

We have followed apparel, accessory, and home fashions products from their design through their production. The next stage is distribution to retailers and, finally, to the ultimate consumer (see Step 8 of the flowchart on the previous page). Companies must decide on the strategies they will use to distribute merchandise to their customers. Decisions about distribution strategies are based on a number of factors, which are examined in detail in this chapter.

Factors Affecting Distribution Strategies

Decisions made around distribution strategies implemented by fashion companies are based on a number of factors:

- *Type of marketing channels to which the company belongs*: Companies using **direct marketing channels** will sell directly to the ultimate consumer. Companies using **limited marketing channels** will sell merchandise through store or non-store retailing venues. Companies using **extended marketing channels** will sell merchandise through a wholesaler, who then sells the merchandise to a retailer (these channels—direct, limited, and extended—were described in previous chapters). Multichannel and **omnichannel distribution** strategies include more than one of these marketing channels. Opportunities and challenges with omnichannel distribution will be discussed in greater detail later in the chapter.

- *Buying characteristics of the target customer:* Certain target market customers will prefer certain distribution strategies. Questions a company might ask include how and where does our target customer like to shop? And what are the customer's decision-making processes in purchasing our merchandise? For example, a manufacturer of women's career apparel may focus on **omnichannel retailing** strategies that include both bricks-and-mortar and online stores that are service oriented. A fashion brand company for men's golf accessories may focus on retailers including both large sports stores as well as small specialty stores such as golf club pro shops. Companies that sell merchandise targeted to a young customer may use strategies involving mobile shopping and social media.

- *Product type:* Categories of merchandise may lend themselves to certain retail distribution strategies. For example, socks, underwear, and other packaged merchandise lend themselves to retailers that include self-service fixtures in the retail venues.

- *Brand—national/international and private label including specialty store retailer of private label apparel (SPA) and fast fashion brands:* National/international brands are generally found in many different retail stores, whereas private label merchandise, SPA brands, and fast fashion brands are unique to particular stores or groups of stores.

- *Level of customization of merchandise:* Mass-produced merchandise that requires no alternations or customization can be distributed through both bricks-and-mortar, online, and other non-store retailers. Because of the level of service required, merchandise that requires alterations or customization (e.g., tailored suits, wedding dresses) is more often distributed through bricks-and-mortar boutiques or specialty stores than through other types of retailers.

Classifications of Distribution Strategies

Distribution strategies are classified as mass distribution, selective distribution, or exclusive distribution.

- *Mass distribution:* With **mass distribution** (also called **intensive distribution**), products are made available to as many consumers as possible through a variety of retail outlets, including supermarkets, convenience stores, and mass merchandisers or discount stores (both bricks-and-mortar and online). The Hanes hosiery, Jockey underwear, and Champion and Russell activewear brands use this distribution strategy.

- *Selective distribution:* With **selective distribution**, manufacturers allow their merchandise to be distributed only through certain retailers. Some manufacturers require a minimum quantity to be purchased; others limit their products' distribution to retailers in noncompeting geographic areas. Some manufacturers also set criteria for the image of both bricks-and-mortar and online stores and the location of bricks-and-mortar stores where their merchandise can be sold. Most luxury/designer and national/international brands use this type of distribution strategy. For example, 7 for All Mankind premium denim is distributed through selected specialty and department stores based on criteria set by the manufacturer.

- *Exclusive distribution:* With **exclusive distribution**, manufacturers limit the stores to which their merchandise is distributed in order to create an image of exclusiveness. Companies that produce merchandise in the designer or luxury price zone (e.g., Chanel, Armani, Vera Wang) often use an exclusive distribution strategy by selling goods only through a few stores or boutiques. Other examples of exclusive distribution include private label merchandise (e.g., JCPenney's Arizona brand, Kmart's Jaclyn Smith brand, Target's xhilaration® brand, Macy's INC International Concepts brand), exclusive licensing brands (e.g., Target's Mossimo® and Kohl's Simply Vera Vera Wang), SPA brands (e.g., Gap, Hollister, Victoria's Secret), and fast fashion SPA brands (e.g., Uniqlo, Zara, H&M, Forever 21) that are specific to a particular retailer (both bricks-and-mortar and online).

Distribution Territories

Retailers must also determine how broad their distribution territories will be. Some retailers focus on a local target customer with retail establishments in a single community; others distribute more broadly, either regionally or nationally; and still others are global retailers, distributing merchandise in more than one country. Some of the world's largest discount and superstores have retail operations in multiple countries. For example, Walmart, the world's largest retailer, headquartered in the United States, has retail operations in 28 countries; Carrefour S.A., headquartered in France, has retail operations in 33 countries; and Schwarz Unternehmens Treuhand KG, headquartered in Germany, has retail operations in 26 countries. In addition, with non-store retailing, such as electronic retailing—**e-tailing**, for short—companies have expanded their distribution beyond local or even national markets. Before retailers expand their operations into other countries, understanding the demographics, decision-making orientation, and cultural norms of the consumers in the country is imperative.

DISTRIBUTION CENTERS

Some fashion companies ship finished merchandise to their retail accounts directly from the production facility. Other fashion companies use **distribution centers (DCs)** to ensure the flow of goods from production facilities to retailers. Both manufacturers and retailers may use distribution centers as part of their distribution processes. Their decision to use distribution centers in their distribution processes is based on these factors:

- size of the company
- number of products being distributed
- existence of bricks-and-mortar retail stores to be serviced
- number of retail stores being serviced
- distance between where the merchandise was produced and where the retail accounts are located

The larger the company and the more products and retailers involved, the more likely it is to use distribution centers.

Manufacturers' Distribution Centers

Fashion brand companies use distribution centers when shipments to retailers consist of goods produced in more than one location (especially when contractors are used). In these cases, merchandise from the various locations is brought to a central location for quality assurance, **picking** (selecting the appropriate assortment of goods to fill a specific retailer's order), packing the merchandise, and distributing it to the retail store accounts (Figure 13.1). Technology has become important in increasing the efficiencies of distribution centers. Many distribution center processes now incorporate robotics for picking orders and conveyor systems for moving orders from one area to the next.

No longer do distribution centers serve the purpose of warehousing inventory; in fact, merchandise is typically stored at a distribution center for only short periods. Instead, **flow-through** facilities move merchandise from receiving to shipping with little or no time in storage. For example, Nike, Inc. has opened a 2.8 million-square-foot distribution center in Memphis, Tennessee, that "holds all three product lines—footwear, apparel, and equipment—under one roof and distributes Nike and Jordan Brand products to individual consumers, wholesale customers and Nike's own retail channels" (Nike 2015).

In addition to being a centralized destination for merchandise flow-through, distribution centers also focus on adding value (changing the product in some way to make it worth more to the manufacturer, retailer, or consumer) to the merchandise by affixing

Figure 13.1
The distribution process includes inspecting, packing, and shipping merchandise to retail accounts. HOANG DINH NAM/AFP/Getty Images.

hangtags, labels, and price information to make the goods floor ready. When manufacturers pre-ticket merchandise, retailers do not have to spend extra time ticketing the items before the apparel hits the selling floor. This process, known as **vendor marking**, results in **floor-ready merchandise**.

Even with greater efficiencies in distribution center operations, to speed up the process even more, some companies forgo distribution centers and ship merchandise to retailers directly from the production facility. In these cases, merchandise becomes floor-ready at the either the production facility or at the retail store.

Retailers' Distribution Centers

Retailers also use distribution centers to facilitate distribution of merchandise from a variety of apparel, accessory, and home fashions companies (vendors) to a number of stores. Goods are shipped from the manufacturers to a centralized retail distribution center, where merchandise for the retailer's stores is picked, combined, and shipped to the individual stores. If merchandise has not been vendor marked, hangtags, including **stock-keeping unit (SKU)** codes and price information, are affixed to the merchandise at the retailer's distribution center.

Retail distribution centers are often at geographical locations chosen to speed delivery to stores. For example, as of 2015, Target operated 37 distribution centers located in 22 states throughout the United States; Walmart operated 42 regional U.S. distribution centers. A regional Walmart distribution center (2015) can have "twelve miles of conveyor belts, which can move 5.5 billion cases of merchandise" (Walmart 2015).

The productivity of distribution centers is reliant on technologies such as warehouse management system (WMS) computer software programs, along with the use of bar coding and radio-frequency identification (RFID) tagging of pallets and cartons. These software programs and tracking devices assist retailers by integrating data throughout the supply chain, improving shipping accuracy, and improving communications with vendors (manufacturers).

COMMUNICATIONS AMONG COMPANIES: PLM AND SCM

The primary goals of product life cycle management (PLM) and supply chain management (SCM) strategies are (1) to increase the speed of getting merchandise to the consumer; and (2) to lower the costs of manufacturing and distributing merchandise by sharing of data among companies throughout the production and distribution of the goods.

The Foundations: UPC Bar Coding, Vendor Marking, EDI, and RFID

Communications among companies depend on several basic operation strategies that have been adopted by all companies in the supply chain. These include

- UPC bar coding on products and shipping containers
- vendor marking of merchandise
- electronic data interchange (EDI)
- radio-frequency identification (RFID) tagging

UPC Bar Coding and Vendor Marking

The **Universal Product Code (UPC)** system is one of several bar-code symbologies used for electronically identifying merchandise. Bar coding with UPCs is considered the foundation of many supply chain management (SCM) strategies because it is considered necessary for electronic communications along the supply chain. A UPC is a twelve-digit number (represented by a bar code made up of a pattern of dark bars and white spaces of varying widths) that identifies manufacturer and merchandise items by stock-keeping unit: vendor, style, color, and size. UPC bar codes are electronically scanned and read by scanning equipment connected to the company's electronic database (Figure 13.2).

Benefits of UPC bar coding and point-of-sale (POS) scanning include reducing the time needed to complete a transaction at the point of sale and to retrieve accurate SKU information at the point of sale. This means that product sales and retail inventory are automatically tracked. With this accurate and timely sales information, fashion companies (retailers and manufacturers) can plan inventory needs to match sales or projected consumer demand more closely. This approach helps retailers avoid overstocking merchandise and thus reduces markdowns. Correct POS information can also be used to reorder merchandise more efficiently and thereby reduce the possibility of a retailer being out of stock in a particular style, size, or color of merchandise. In addition, **replenishment**—automatic reordering of merchandise—depends on the use of point-of-sale information provided by UPC bar codes. Replenishment strategies will be discussed later in this chapter.

Besides using bar codes for these POS benefits, retailers also use them to scan inventory in their distribution centers and to facilitate the movement of shipping cartons in distribution centers. The bar codes identify each shipping container's contents and are used for tracking and sorting merchandise at the distribution centers. While the UPC bar code is made up of only numbers, two other bar-code formats—code 39 or code 128—can include both numbers and letters and are often used on shipping cartons.

Figure 13.2
Benefits of UPC bar codes on merchandise hangtags include retrieval of accurate SKU information at the point of sale. Dimas Ardian/Getty Images.

Electronic Data Interchange

Electronic data interchange (EDI) makes possible computer-to-computer communications among companies (Figure 13.3). With EDI technology, business data are transmitted electronically directly to another company; through a third party's computer system, called a **value-added network (VAN)**; or through cloud computing technologies. The most common EDI transactions in the fashion industry include

- purchase orders, invoices, packing slips, and advance shipping notices (ASN)
- reports of inventory counts and changes in inventory, such as sales and returns data
- price/sales catalogs

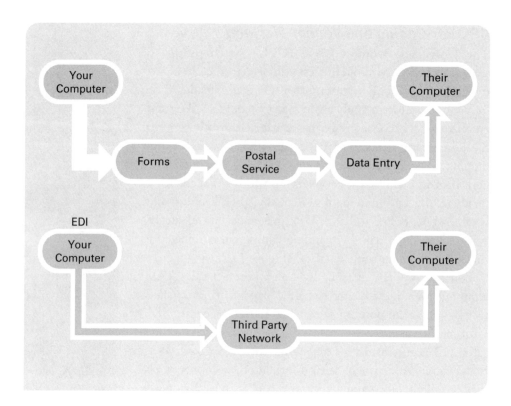

Figure 13.3
Electronic data interchange (EDI) improves efficiency and accuracy of shared data among companies.

In addition, through EDI, retail distribution centers can accommodate **cross-dockable shipments**. This means that goods are received from the manufacturer as floor-ready merchandise, so they can be sorted for store distribution without the need for additional processing. For cross-docking to happen, the retailer must request and receive advance shipping notices from the manufacturer, and the goods must arrive in floor-ready condition. This process would not be possible without EDI technology.

The EDI capabilities of the manufacturer are the backbone of supply chain management. Through EDI, retailer POS data feeds directly into fashion brand companies' manufacturing systems and directly links manufacturers to the suppliers of fabric, trims, and findings.

Replenishment Strategies

A primary goal of all retailers is to have the right style of merchandise, in the right size and color, at the right time for the customer. If a retailer is out of stock of a style, size, or color, a sale is lost. To help alleviate out-of-stock situations, the retailer must be able to replenish merchandise quickly and accurately. Following are some of the replenishment methods used by manufacturers and retailers:

- The retailer initiates an electronic (EDI) order when it determines that the stock level warrants a reorder.
- Information about stock levels is automatically communicated to the manufacturer through EDI, and the manufacturer (vendor) automatically ships reorders when the merchandise stock at the retail store reaches a certain level.

- A specified percentage of the retail buyer's order is delivered before the start of the fashion season, and the balance of the order is delivered either throughout the fashion season or as a single reorder. The mix of styles, colors, and sizes in the reorder(s) is based on POS data from the retailer.

Replenishment strategies vary with the type of merchandise and size of retailer. For basic (staple) items, such as hosiery and jeans, replenishment may be an ongoing activity. For seasonal goods such as turtleneck sweaters and outerwear, replenishment may occur only within a particular fashion season. For fashion goods, merchandise may not be replenished during the fashion season. For companies engaged in fast fashion, replenishment rarely occurs because new merchandise is delivered on a regular basis.

Fashion brand companies may use a variety of replenishment strategies depending on their retail customers, and retailers may use a variety of replenishment strategies depending on the capabilities of their vendors (manufacturers). One of the strategies most beneficial to improving efficiency in the apparel supply pipeline between the manufacturer and retailer has been to establish programs by which the manufacturer reviews sales and **stockout data** (data on out-of-stock goods) and orders replenishments as often as required. The strategy of having the manufacturer (vendor) automatically ship merchandise to the retail store based on POS data from the retailer is known as **vendor-managed inventory (VMI)** or vendor-managed replenishment. In some cases, data are reviewed daily rather than monthly or bimonthly, as was done in the past. Obviously, this type of strategy is not possible unless the retailer sends POS data to the manufacturer.

VMI strategies are most commonly used with merchandise such as lingerie, hosiery, T-shirts, and basic jeans, whose styles change little from season to season and for which retailers want to have desired sizes and colors in stock (Figure 13.4). For example, the hosiery industry is a low-margin business. This means that the

Figure 13.4
Vendor-managed replenishment strategies are typical for products such as lingerie that are delivered to the retailer floor ready. WWD/© Conde Nast.

dollar amount of profit per item sold that the producer earns from the sale to the retailer is small. Similarly, the dollar amount of profit that the retailer garners from the sale to the customer is also small. Thus, the manufacturer and the retailer need high sales volume to compensate for the low margin. VMI assures the retailer that stock is automatically replenished and consumers have a complete selection of styles, sizes, and colors.

Technologies are providing retailers with an array of stock replenishment capabilities. For example, increased use of RFID to streamline inventory management is allowing sales associates to receive alerts when merchandise is delivered, so that top-selling items are always in stock. **Data mining technology** can also be used to examine sales of products by style, size, and color. Data mining technology analyzes data information, searching for selling patterns or trends in the data and identifying correlations among data characteristics. When trends or patterns are found, producers can tailor assortment or replenishments for specific retailers or retail venues. For example, a company may discover that the selling season for shorts was longer in retail locations with higher median incomes and thus adjust assortment and replenishment accordingly.

Implementing Product Life Cycle Management and Supply Chain Management

This book focuses on product life cycle management (PLM) and supply chain management (SCM) strategies implemented throughout the design, manufacturing, and retailing of apparel, accessory, and home fashions products. With SCM and PLM, either an order from a retailer or a retail sale electronically triggers the manufacturing process. Orders or sales data are tied to the fashion brand company's PDM/PLM systems and fabric and findings suppliers. At the retail level, the retailer's financial and merchandise plans are integrated. That is, the retailer's assortment plan is integrated with how much space each retail department will be allocated at each store, thus optimizing the store's merchandise mix. Integrated processes include

- integrating a fashion brand company's patternmaking systems (PDS) with other product information through product information management (PIM) software
- integrating a fashion brand company's various CAD/CAM systems, resulting in PDM/PLM
- providing communications among companies, resulting in vendor-managed retail inventory
- integrating a retailer's merchandise assortment planning, financial planning, distribution processes, and store layout

RETAILING AND CATEGORIES OF RETAILERS

By definition, **retailing** is the process or business activity of selling goods or services to the ultimate consumer, and a **retailer** is the company or business that makes a profit by selling goods and services to the ultimate consumer (Figure 13.5). Retailers range in size from small sole proprietorships that cater to a local market to large corporate store ownership groups. Table 13.1 lists some of the primary retail corporations and the stores owned and operated by these corporations.

Figure 13.5
The evolution of retail. Borgman
© 1999 The Cincinnati Enquirer.
Reprinted by permission of
Universal Press Syndicate.
All Rights Reserved.

Table 13.1 Selected Major Retail Corporations[1]		
Corporation Name	**Web Address**	**Stores Owned**
Abercrombie & Fitch	www.abercrombie.com	Abercrombie & Fitch Abercrombie kids Hollister
Ascena Retail Group Inc.	www.charmingshoppes.com	Ann Taylor Catherines Dress Barn Justice Lane Bryant Loft Lou & Grey Maurices
Bed Bath & Beyond Inc.	www.bedbathandbeyond.com	Bed Bath & Beyond Christmas Tree Shops andThat! Harmon and Harmon Face Values buybuy BABY World Market Cost Plus World Market Cost Plus Linen Holdings
Burlington Coat Factory Warehouse Corporation	www.burlingtoncoatfactory.com	Burlington Coat Factory Stores BabyDepot Cohoes Fashions
Dillard's	www.dillards.com	

(continued)

Table 13.1 Selected Major Retail Corporations[1]		
Corporation Name	**Web Address**	**Stores Owned**
Foot Locker Inc.	www.footlocker-inc.com	Foot Locker Lady Foot Locker Kids Foot Locker Champs Sports Footaction Eastbay Six:02 Sidestep Runners Point
Gap Inc.	www.gap.com	Gap Banana Republic Old Navy Athleta Intermix
Hudson's Bay Company	http://www3.hbc.com/	*North America* Hudson's Bay Lord & Taylor Find @ Lord & Taylor Saks Fifth Avenue Saks Fifth Avenue OFF 5th Home Outfitters *Europe* Galeria Kaufhof Galeria INNO Sportarena
JCPenney Company, Inc.	www.jcpenney.com	
Kohl's Department Stores	www.kohls.com	
L Brands	www.lb.com	Victoria's Secret Henri Bendel Bath and Body Works La Senza Pink
Macy's Inc.	www.macysinc.com	Macy's Bloomingdale's Bloomingdale's Outlet Macy's Backstage Bluemercury
Neiman Marcus Group	www.neimanmarcus.com	Neiman Marcus Bergdorf Goodman Horchow CUSP by Neiman Marcus Neiman Marcus Last Call mytheresa and THERESA

Table 13.1 Selected Major Retail Corporations[1]

Corporation Name	Web Address	Stores Owned
Nordstrom	www.nordstrom.com	Nordstrom Nordstom Rack Trunk Club Jeffrey HauteLook
Sears Holdings Corporation	www.searsholdings.com	Sears Sears Auto Center Sears Home Services Kmart Shop Your Way Kenmore Craftsman DieHard ServiceLive
Target Corporation	www.target.com	Target CityTarget TargetExpress
The TJX Companies, Inc.	www.tjx.com	*North America* T.J. Maxx Marshalls HomeGoods Sierra Trading Post Winners *Europe* T.K. Maxx HomeSense
Urban Outfitters Inc.	www.urbanoutfittersinc.com	Urban Outfitters Anthropologie Free People Terrain BHLDN
Wal-Mart Stores, Inc.	corporate.walmart.com	Walmart Supercenter Walmart Discount Store Walmart Neighborhood Market Sam's Club Walmart eCommerce
Williams-Sonoma, Inc.	www.williams-sonomainc.com	Williams-Sonoma Williams-Sonoma Home Pottery Barn Pottery Barn Kids PBteen West Elm Mark Graham Rejuvenation

[1]North American based unless noted otherwise.

Retailers can be classified according to many of their characteristics, including whether they sell new merchandise or previously owned merchandise, whether they have physical facilities (bricks-and-mortar and/or non-store retailing), type of ownership, merchandise mix, size, location, and organizational and operational characteristics. Table 13.2 lists the number of retail firms and establishments in the United States along with employment statistics.

One overarching way of classifying fashion retailers is according to whether they sell new merchandise or previously owned merchandise. Most retailers sell new fashion merchandise; however, with the growth of **re-commerce**, consumers are reintroducing usable fashion products into the marketplace through consignment stores, thrift shops, online auction sites, and a number of other retail distribution methods for previously owned fashions. In some cases, the retailer has purchased the used merchandise for purposes of resale. In other situations, merchandise is donated to a charity organization that then sells it. For example, Goodwill Industries International has over 3,000 bricks-and-mortar retail stores as well as an online auction site comprised of merchandise donated to the organization.

Another way of classifying fashion retailers is on the basis of their merchandising and operating strategies, which results in the following categories:

- department store retailers
- specialty retailers
- discount retailers
- off-price retailers
- supermarkets and hypermarkets
- warehouse retailers
- convenience store retailers
- contractual retailers
- chain store retailers

Table 13.2 Number of U.S. Retail Establishments and Employment by Category

	Number of Firms[1]	Number of Establishments[2]	Total U.S. Employment
Furniture and home furnishings stores	34,789	51.645	422,595
Clothing stores	36,136	97,566	1,299,149
Clothing accessory stores	3,936	8,564	62,270
Shoe stores	5,909	25,455	201,974
Jewelry stores	16,847	23,413	123,520
Luggage and leather goods stores	484	1,002	5,932
Department stores (not discount)	36	3,507	466,383
Other general merchandise stores	8,007	40,676	1,786,833
Discount department stores	41	4,689	689,847

Source: U.S. Census Bureau. 2012 Statistics of U.S. Businesses.

[1]Firm—a business organization consisting of one or more domestic establishments in the same state and industry under common ownership or control.

[2]Establishment—a single physical location where business is conducted or where services or industrial operations are performed.

Because of the diversity found among retailers, these categories are not mutually exclusive. For example, a retailer may be both a specialty store retailer and a chain store retailer (e.g., Gap).

Department Store Retailers

Department store retailers (or department stores) are large retailers that divide their functions and their merchandise into sections or departments (Figure 13.6). Department stores have the following features:

- a fashion-oriented merchandise assortment
- a variety of services for customers (e.g., purchase online–return to the store, credit cards, wedding registry)
- merchandise offered at full markup price with seasonal sales
- at least 50 employees
- operate bricks-and-mortar stores large enough to be shopping center anchors

The category includes full-line department stores (offering apparel, home fashions, housewares, and furniture), such as Macy's, JCPenney, Kohl's, and Dillard's, as well as limited-line department stores such as Nordstrom and Neiman Marcus. Multiunit department stores include department store chains as well as those that may have a flagship or primary store. For example, Macy's, Inc. includes 885 stores in 45 states, the District of Columbia, Guam, and Puerto Rico. Operations include

Figure 13.6
JCPenney is a good example of a full-line multiunit department store. Ericksen /WWD/© Conde Nast.

Table 13.3 Top Department Stores by Retail Sales			
Company	2014 Worldwide Retail Sales $US (000)	U.S. % of Worldwide Sales	2014 Stores
Macy's	$28,105,000	99.7%	821
JCPenney	$12,257,000	99.4%	1,063
Kohl's	$19,023,000	100%	1,162
Sears Holdings*	$26,792,000	96.2%	1,659
Nordstrom	$13,280,000	99.8%	283
Hudson's Bay*	$7,937,000	65.2%	165
Dillard's	$6,490,000	100%	297
Neiman Marcus	$4,823,000	100%	87
Belk	$4,110,000	100%	297

Source: *STORES*. (2015, July). Top 100 Retailers.
*Includes all retail operations.

Macy's, Bloomingdale's, Bloomingdale's Outlet, Bluemercury, macys.com, bloom ingdales.com, and bluemercury.com. Macy's flagship store is considered to be its Herald Square store in New York City. Table 13.3 is a list of the top nine department store based on retail sales.

With the goal of catering to a broad range of consumers, department stores carry a wide variety of merchandise lines with a reasonably wide selection in each category. Department stores usually carry national brands and private label merchandise. Depending on the store, price zones can range from moderate to designer.

Because of the fierce competition among department stores, strategies for success have been necessary: visually appealing merchandise presentation, strong customer service, and offering private label and exclusive merchandise. Private label and exclusive brand merchandise have become important ways for department store retailers to distinguish themselves from the competition. For example, in addition to its many private label brands, Macy's has a leased department relationship with Destination Maternity offering exclusive lines of A Pea in the Pod® and Motherhood® Maternity brand maternity wear brands. Kohl's offers exclusive lines by Dana Buchman and Simply Vera by Vera Wang; JCPenney has an exclusive line of apparel by Liz Claiborne.

Many department store retailers also have **in-store shops** of designers and national/international brands. These in-store shops are merchandised according to the fashion brand's specifications and carry only the merchandise of the fashion brand company. Fashion brand companies/brands such as Polo Ralph Lauren, Nautica, Tommy Hilfiger, Calvin Klein, Free People, and BCBG Max Azria have all had successful in-store shops. In-store shops benefit both the fashion brand and the retailer. For the fashion brand company, they create brand awareness and make shopping easy for their customers. For department store retailers, in-store shops create a specialty retailer "feel" within the department store retail environment. For example, in September 2015 Ellen DeGeneres opened a temporary in-store shop (called a **pop-up shop**) in Bergdorf Goodman for her ED by Ellen collection of apparel.

Specialty Retailers

A **specialty retailer** (or specialty store) focuses on a specific type of merchandise in one or more of the following ways:

- by carrying one category of merchandise or a few closely related categories of merchandise (e.g., jewelry, footwear, eyeglasses, intimate apparel, housewares)
- by focusing on merchandise for a well-defined target market (e.g., men, women, bicyclists, plus-size consumers, individuals with small children)
- by carrying the merchandise of one fashion brand or fashion brand company (e.g., Polo Ralph Lauren, Guess Kids, Banana Republic)

Specialty retailers typically carry a limited but deep assortment (i.e., excellent selection of brands, styles, sizes) of merchandise. They may carry designer/luxury brands or national/international brands, or they may be a **SPA (specialty store retailer of private label apparel)**. Most specialty stores will carry merchandise in only one or two price zones. Specialty retailers that concentrate on designer/luxury price zone merchandise or unique merchandise with an exclusive distribution strategy are typically referred to as **boutiques**.

Specialty retailers that focus on relatively inexpensive and trendy private label items with a very short lead time from concept to consumer are known as **fast fashion** specialty retailers (Figure 13.7). Examples of fast fashion retailers are Zara (Spain), Mango (Spain), H&M (Sweden), Topshop (UK), Uniqlo (Japan), and Forever 21 (US).

Specialty retailers that are temporary or mobile in nature, focus on a new brand, and/or associated with a live event are typically referred to as **pop-up shops** or stores. For example, during the 2012 Olympic Games, H&M opened two pop-up stores in London with a focus on active sportswear.

Two of the largest apparel specialty store chains in the United States are Gap Inc. (includes Gap, Old Navy, Banana Republic, INTERMIX, and Athleta) and L Brands (includes Victoria's Secret, Pink, Bath & Body Works, La Senza, and Henri Bendel). Table 13.4 presents U.S. apparel specialty chains.

Figure 13.7
Headquartered in Spain, Mango is an international fast fashion retailer. Leslie Burns.

Table 13.4 Top Fashion Specialty Chains by Retail Sales

Company	2014 Worldwide Retail Sales $US (000)	U.S. % of Worldwide Sales	2014 Stores
TJX	$29,061,000	76.4%	2,569
Gap	$16,956,000	77.1%	2,465
L Brands	$10,966,000	94%	2,685
Foot Locker	$7,267,000	72.1%	2,369
Signet Jewelers	$6,312,000	83.2%	2,868
Ascena Retail Group	$4,850,000	97.2%	3,834
Burlington Coat Factory	$4,761,000	98.9%	530

Source: *STORES*. (2015, July). Top 100 Retailers.

Discount Retailers

A **discount retailer** (or discount store) sells brand name merchandise at less than traditional retail prices and includes fashion merchandise at the mass or budget price zone. Examples of discount chain department retailers are Target, Kmart, and Walmart. Examples of discount chain specialty retailers are Old Navy and Bed, Bath & Beyond (Figure13.8). In addition to national brands, **full-line discount retailers** also carry private label merchandise (e.g., Kmart's Jaclyn Smith brand) and exclusive licensed brands (e.g., Liz Lange maternity for Target). When full-line discount retailers also offer grocery items, they are known as **general merchandise discount retailers**.

Figure 13.8
Discount chain specialty retailers, such as Bed Bath & Beyond, include merchandise primarily at the budget and moderate price zones. Stephen Ehlers/Moment Mobile ED /Getty Images.

Table 13.5 Top Large Format Value/Discount/Warehouse Retailers by Retail Sales

Company	2014 $US Worldwide Retail Sales (000)	U.S. % of Worldwide Sales	2014 Stores
Walmart	$508,465,000	67.6%	5,109
The Kroger Co.	$103,033,000	100%	3,730
Costco	$111,530,000	71.5%	464
Target	$74,564,000	97.4%	1,790

Source: *STORES*. (2015, July). Top 100 Retailers.

Through mass merchandising and supply chain management strategies, discount retailers are able to keep prices lower than other retailers. These strategies include

- quantity discounts from manufacturers
- effective replenishment strategies to ensure that the merchandise customers want is in stock
- high turnover rates on products
- limiting brands and styles to only the most popular items
- self-service
- lower overhead costs
- promotions that cater to a broad target market

National and international discount chains such as Walmart, Kmart, Target, and Carrefours buy huge quantities of merchandise from manufacturers and can operate on smaller profit margins than can traditional department store retailers. Target is sometimes referred to as an **upscale discounter** because it has a department store feel and provides more fashion-forward merchandise. Table 13.5 lists the top discount retailers.

Off-Price Retailers

Off-price retailers specialize in selling national brands, designer collections, or promotional goods at discount prices. Off-price retailers are those that buy merchandise at low prices, carry well-established (including designer) brands, and sell merchandise assortments that change quickly and have inconsistent sizes and styles (sometimes referred to as broken assortments). The following subsections describe these types of off-price retailers: factory outlet retailers, independent off-price retailers, retailer-owned off-price retailers, closeout retailers, and sample stores.

Factory Outlet Retailers

Factory outlet retailers sell the seconds, irregulars, samples, or overruns (merchandise produced in excess of their orders) of a fashion brand company, as well as merchandise produced specifically for the outlet retail stores. In some cases, fashion brand companies use their outlet stores as test markets for styles, colors, or sizes of merchandise. Once located primarily near production or distribution centers, factory outlet stores now commonly comprise entire shopping centers. They are typically located at a distance from full-price retailers that carry their merchandise (based on agreements with local full-price retailers).

Independent Off-Price Retailers

Independent off-price retail stores buy irregulars, seconds, overruns, or leftovers from manufacturers or other retailers. Ross (Figure 13.9), T.J. Maxx, and Burlington Coat Factory are examples of independent off-price retailers.

Retailer-Owned Off-Price Retailers

Some retailers operate their own off-price stores (e.g., Off 5th, Nordstrom Rack). In these off-price stores, retailers sell merchandise from their regular stores that did not sell within a specified time period, private label merchandise, or special orders purchased specifically for the off-price store.

Closeout Retailer

Closeout retailers specialize in buying a variety of merchandise through retail liquidations, bankruptcies, and closeouts. Then they sell this merchandise at bargain prices. An example of a closeout retailer is Tuesday Morning, which includes nearly 800 stores "specializing in both domestic and international closeouts of medium to high end name brand gifts, soft home, home furnishings, housewares, luggage, toys, seasonal items, gourmet food and fashion accessories for men, women and children" (Tuesday Morning 2015).

Sample Retail Stores

Sample retail stores specialize in selling fashion brand companies' sample merchandise at the end of the market selling period. These stores may be pop-up stores during market weeks or are located near major marts, such as the California Market Center in downtown Los Angeles.

Figure 13.9
Independent off-price retailers such as Ross sell national brands and promotional goods at discount prices. David McNew /Getty Images.

Supermarkets and Hypermarkets

Conventional **supermarkets** are large self-service grocery stores that carry a full line of foods and related products. **Superstores**, or **hypermarkets**, are upgraded supermarkets that combine the elements of a supermarket and a department store by offering a wide range of merchandise, including food, electronics, clothing and accessories, furniture, and garden items. These **big-box stores** can be as large as 150,000 to 250,000 square feet.

Large discount retailer superstores/hypermarkets (e.g., Walmart, Kmart, Target, Carrefour) have large departments for apparel, home fashions, and accessories. Items sold through supermarkets and superstores must accommodate a self-service merchandising strategy, so visual displays that assist consumers in selecting the right style and size are common. These items are also most likely to use an extended marketing channel that facilitates the supermarkets' buying of these goods.

Warehouse Retailers

Warehouse retailers offer goods at discount prices by reducing operating expenses and combining their warehouse and retail operations. In some cases, merchandise is obtained through an extended marketing channel. This category of retailers includes stores such as big-box home improvement centers (e.g., The Home Depot, Lowe's) and warehouse clubs (e.g., Costco, Sam's Club).

Traditionally, fashion products were not the primary merchandise sold through warehouse retailers. However, home improvement centers are now offering a larger array of home fashions goods (e.g., towels, bedding, carpets, rugs), and warehouse clubs are offering more styles and types of apparel and home fashions products. For example, both Sam's Club and Costco offer a variety of apparel, footwear, accessory, jewelry, and home fashion brands. Generally, at warehouse retailers, fashion merchandise is sold through self-service strategies with limited services (e.g., there may be no fitting rooms).

Convenience Stores

Convenience stores are small stores that offer fast service at a convenient location (on a busy street or combined with a gas station), but they carry only a limited assortment of food and related items. One of the most famous and largest international convenience store chains is 7-Eleven®, which operates, franchises, or licenses approximately 8,600 stores in the United States and Canada and another 47,800 stores in more than 13 other countries. The most typical fashion products carried by convenience stores are basic items such as mass-merchandised socks or hosiery, inexpensive novelty T-shirts or baseball caps, and inexpensive sunglasses, as well as fashion magazines.

Contractual Retailers

Retailers may enter into contractual agreements with manufacturers, wholesalers, or other retailers to integrate operations and increase market impact. Such contractual agreements include the following:

- retailer-sponsored cooperatives that take the form of an organization of small independent retailers

- wholesaler-sponsored voluntary chains, in which a wholesaler develops a program for small independent retailers
- franchises
- leased departments

The term **contractual retailers** covers all such arrangements. Franchises and leased departments are the most typical of the contractual retailers for the distribution of apparel.

Franchises

In a **franchise** agreement, the parent company gives the franchisee the exclusive right to distribute a well-recognized brand name in a specific market area, as well as assistance with organization, visual merchandising, training, and management. In return, the franchisee pays the parent company a franchise payment. The franchisee agrees to adhere to standards regarding in-store design, visual presentation, pricing, and promotions specified by the parent company. Examples of franchises include Flip Flop Shops®, Apricot Lane® Boutiques, and Kid to Kid children's franchise.

Leased Departments

Some retailers will lease space within a larger retail store to a company that operates a specialty department. The larger retail store provides space, utilities, and basic in-store services. The specialty department operator provides the stock and expertise to run the department, which adds to the service or product mix of the larger store. The lease or commission for these departments is typically based on square footage and sales.

Typical **leased departments** include beauty salons and spas; vision care and eyewear; florists and garden shops; books; restaurants; ticket offices; and fine jewelry, fur, and shoe shops. However, retailers may also offer leased departments for specialty merchandise. For example, Destination Maternity Corporation operates leased departments within retailers such as Macy's, Gordmans, and buybuy Baby under the brands Motherhood® Maternity and A Pea in the Pod®. With this arrangement, the primary advantage for the larger retailer is that it can offer its customers products and services that it might not be able to offer otherwise. The primary advantage for the specialty department is its association with the larger retailer and a convenient location for consumers to purchase their goods or services.

Footwear retailing requires an immense inventory (stock-keeping units or SKUs) due to the many combinations of shoe widths and lengths. When the range of seasonal colors is added to the size inventory, footwear retailers have a challenging task to meet the consumer's need for the right product in the specific color and size. Footwear retailers must make a significant capital outlay and have large inventory space. This is one reason for some large department store retailers to lease their shoe departments to companies that specialize in footwear retailing.

Chain Stores

Chain store organizations own and operate several retail store units that sell similar lines of merchandise with a standard method and function under a centralized organizational structure. Chain stores are characterized by the following features:

Figure 13.10
As an international chain retailer, Walmart is the largest retailer in the world. WWD /© Conde Nast.

- centralized buying
- centralized distribution
- shared brands
- standardized store decor and layout

All management and merchandising decisions and policies are made by managers at a central headquarters or home office. Chain stores include:

- large chains (defined as eleven or more units) that may be national or international in scope and include department store retailers (e.g., JCPenney, Kohl's), discount retailers (e.g., Kmart, Walmart, Target), and specialty retailers (Aéropostale, Urban Outfitters, Victoria's Secret; Figure 13.10)
- small chains (two to ten retail units) within a local or regional area

Private label merchandise (e.g., JCPenney's Arizona, Worthington, and Stafford labels), exclusive brands (e.g., Kohl's Simply Vera by Vera Wang), and SPA/store brands (e.g., Gap, Victoria's Secret, Zara) are important parts of the merchandise mix for large chain store retailers. Franchises are always chain store operations. Although large chain stores benefit from the economies of scale that come with purchasing merchandise for a number of stores, they may carry merchandise that caters to the wants and needs of the local target markets. For example, a Kmart store in Athens, Georgia, may carry University of Georgia licensed merchandise.

BRICKS-AND-MORTAR AND NON-STORE RETAILERS

Across operational strategies, retailers can also be classified according to distribution channel:

- Bricks-and-mortar retailers have physical facilities.
- Non-store retailers use catalog, web, and/or mobile technologies.

Many retailers are involved with a combination of bricks-and-mortar and non-store retailing operations. For example, a specialty store retailer may also be a chain store operation; a department store may have bricks-and-mortar stores as well as a retail website (form of non-store retailing). Indeed, **multichannel distribution** or **multichannel retailing** strategies involve offering merchandise through more than one distribution channel.

Bricks-and-Mortar Retailers

Bricks-and-mortar retailers (also referred to as brick-and-mortar retailers) are by far the most prevalent form of retail strategy for fashion merchandise. From downtown shopping districts to small strip malls and large suburban shopping malls, bricks-and-mortar stores offer consumers the opportunity to touch, feel, and try on fashion merchandise. The social atmosphere of shopping areas also provides consumers with destinations for recreation and entertainment. It is often said that the success of bricks-and-mortar stores depends on three things: location, location, and location. The success of bricks-and-mortar stores also depends on:

- effective design and management of facilities including merchandise display areas as well as fitting rooms, restrooms, storage, and business offices
- effective brand identity created through storefront design and visual merchandising including window and in-store displays
- convenience for the customer in locating the store, getting to the store, and parking, if needed

Non-store Retailers

A **non-store retailer** distributes products to consumers through means other than traditional bricks-and-mortar retail stores. For apparel, accessories, and home fashions, the most prevalent forms of non-store retailing include **electronic/internet (e-tailing)** including mobile applications, catalog, and television selling. Other forms of non-store retailing include at-home selling and vending machines. In the past 20 years, non-store retailing, particularly e-tailing and mobile applications, has grown tremendously.

Along with selling merchandise, non-store retailing is used by fashion brand companies for other purposes, such as:

- educating customers about the company and its product lines
- providing customers with fashion direction and style advice
- obtaining information from customers regarding product preferences
- offering specialized promotions
- giving customers a more convenient and/or more recreational form of shopping
- building relationships with customers through personalized customer service

Retailers selling fashion merchandise through non-store retailing methods are facing a unique set of challenges. Because the customer cannot physically evaluate the product, feel the fabric, or try on the merchandise, customer service and information about sizing, fabric, styling details, and color are important. Online strategies—zooming in on photographs to see the details of products, viewing the product from all sides, seeing the product in multiple colors, and online product reviews of previous customers—attempt to address these challenges. Many non-store fashion retailers also offer online "chat rooms" or video chat, so customers can connect with customer service representatives. Non-store retailers are also experimenting with virtual fitting room technologies to allow customers to "try on" merchandise.

Electronic/Internet Retailers

Electronic/Internet retailers use **e-commerce**, the selling of goods over the internet, to reach customers. Since the 1990s, many fashion retailers have included e-commerce in their distribution strategy. They offer goods only over the internet or use the internet as an addition to their stores and/or catalog retailing business as another aspect of their multichannel and omnichannel distribution strategy. With e-tailing, customers can access the retailer through desktop or laptop computers, tablets, and smartphones. Although online shopping will continue to grow, it still comprises less than 15 percent of all apparel retail sales. However, the use of web-influenced bricks-and-mortar shopping is expected to grow to over 60 percent of apparel shopping; bricks-and-mortar shopping will account for the remainder. Indeed, for fashion products, consumers appear to prefer the combination of online and bricks-and-mortar experiences.

E-retailers generally fall into one or more of the following categories:

- exclusive e-retailers
- catalog or TV retailers that have added websites
- bricks-and-mortar department and specialty stores that have added websites
- apparel, accessory, and home fashions manufacturers' websites
- online fashion malls
- online auction/trade websites

Exclusive E-retailers

Some companies sell exclusively on the Web. They include retailers whose target customer prefers the convenience of online shopping; designers of and merchants for specialized or niche products, such as organic cotton merchandise; and/or small retailers that may not be able to afford other forms of retail distribution. For example, Backcountry.com is an exclusive online retailer specializing in active sportswear and outdoor gear. Headquartered outside of Park City, Utah, but with customers all over the world, backcountry.com is well known for its wide range of products, customer service, and online communities. For small fashion brand companies, websites such as etsy.com and ebay.com provide assistance and opportunities to sell merchandise exclusively online.

Catalog Retailers That Have Added Websites

Fashion brand companies that had been successful selling fashion merchandise through catalogs, such as L.L. Bean, Lands' End, and Talbots, found they could make the transition to the Web fairly easily. Both paper and online catalogs are now used to augment the bricks-and-mortar and online experiences for customers.

Department Stores and Stores That Have Added Websites

Most large department stores and specialty stores have incorporated a multichannel or omnichannel distribution strategy by adding e-commerce to their businesses. Customers often use a retailer's website or mobile applications for information and comparison purposes and then go to the bricks-and-mortar retail store to try on the merchandise. Customers might also purchase online and then want to return merchandise to the bricks-and-mortar store. Thus, effective omnichannel strategies by the retailer are important.

Fashion Brand Company/Manufacturer Websites

Today most national/international brands have websites that sell merchandise directly to the consumer through online retail stores. For example, Nike.com offers a wide assortment of Nike, Jordan, and Hurley brand merchandise. In addition, customized footwear through NikeiD is available online. Table 13.6 presents the top mass merchant, apparel, and accessory internet retailers.

Online Fashion Mall

Since the mid-1990s, online fashion malls have served as destination websites that offer merchandise from a number of online stores. Thus consumers can go to a single website and shop for products from multiple companies. Examples of online fashion malls include Lyst.com, yahoo.com, and amazon.com.

Online Auction/Trade Websites

Websites such as ebay.com offer opportunities for anyone worldwide to sell apparel, accessories, and home fashions online. Started in 1995 as an online auction website, eBay has grown into one of the largest websites. Multitudes of new and previously worn apparel and accessories are offered for sale by individuals and companies throughout the world.

Catalog Retailers

Catalog (or mail-order) retailers sell to the consumer through catalogs, brochures, or advertisements and deliver merchandise by mail or other carriers. Apparel is one of the top-selling items bought through catalogs. Customers can order by mail, phone, internet, or fax. All types of retailers may operate catalog businesses. With

Table 13.6 Top U.S. E-retailers Whose Sales Include Fashion Merchandise, in Order of Online Sales

Company	Category
Amazon.com	Online only
Walmart.com	Discount retailer
Costco.com	Warehouse retailer
Target.com	Discount retailer
Macy's.com	Department store

Source: PCTechguide.com (2014). Top American E-Commerce Stores as of 2014.

the growth of e-tailing, virtually all large catalog companies now have internet websites in addition to their catalogs. Consumers frequently use catalogs for browsing and evaluating merchandise and then order and purchase the items online.

Television/Live Video Retailers

Some retailers use television shopping channels and/or live video to sell apparel, accessories, and home fashions products. With these formats, merchandise is presented on the television (and on accompanying websites and mobile applications), and customers order it over the telephone (usually using a toll-free number), online, or on their mobile device. Merchandise is delivered through the mail or by another carrier.

Home shopping has become big business. QVC (Figure 13.11), Home Shopping Network (HSN), and Shop at Home are three of the largest of these television shopping channels. TV shopping has expanded its merchandise assortment to include designer lines and a variety of product categories.

As with other retailers, the movement to omnichannel strategies has also been found to be successful for companies that started as non-store retailers. For example, in addition to the television channel, QVC has a successful website, mobile applications, the QVC Studio Store (in West Chester, Pennsylvania), and three QVC Outlet Stores in Pennsylvania and Delaware. In 2014 QVC's sales revenue was US$8.8 billion, of which US$3.5 billion came from ecommerce.

Direct Sales Retailers

Direct sales retailers use the marketing strategy of making personal contacts and sales in consumers' homes or local pop-up retail venue. Direct sales includes using home party plan selling or private "trunk show" methods. The party plan method involves a salesperson presenting merchandise at the home of a host or hostess who has invited potential customers to a "party." Accessories (e.g., handbags,

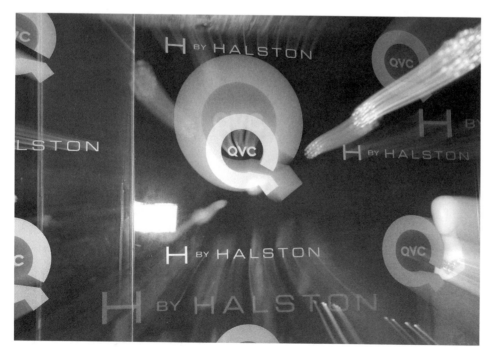

Figure 13.11
In 2015 QVC launched the H by Halston exclusive fashion brand. David M. Benett/Dave Benett /Getty Images for QVC.

jewelry), novelty items, and lingerie are typical fashion products sold using this retail method. In the trunk show method, collections are shown to customers through private invitations at the stylist's home or through a pop-up retail studio. The retailer Doncaster uses the trunk show method by showing collections four times per year and offering customers personalized attention and customer service through trained consultants called stylists. Online parties and trunk shows, as well as direct sales through social media, have also become popular.

Vending Machines

Vending machines operate by accepting coins or credit/debit cards from consumers. The machines are used when other retailing formats are unavailable, or when space is limited for selling merchandise. Although vending machines are seldom used for the distribution of apparel products, they have been used to sell socks /hosiery, T-shirts, undergarments, women's flat shoes, sunglasses, and even men's dress shirts. Such vending machines are most likely found in locations such as airports, train stations, or tourist areas.

Omnichannel Distribution Strategies: Bricks-and-Clicks

Retailers have the opportunity to connect with consumers through multiple channels (referred to as **customer touchpoints**): bricks-and-mortar stores, websites, catalogs, social media platforms, mobile devices, and digital advertisements. In accessing these multiple channels, consumers are now expecting seamless retail experiences that might include viewing in-store inventory online, viewing online product information in the bricks-and-mortar store, calling a customer service representative for assistance with both store and online purchases, or purchasing online and either picking up merchandise or returning merchandise at a store.

This approach of integrating bricks-and-mortar and non-store strategies has become the norm for many fashion brand companies and retailers. Using multiple channels allows retailers to overcome limitations inherent in any of the channels by themselves. For example, the convenience factors offered through online shopping augment retailers' bricks-and-mortar operations. Retailers can also gain insights into their customers' shopping behavior to better meet their needs. Disadvantages of using multiple channels include the efforts of maintaining a consistent and effective brand identity across channels, providing consistent merchandise assortments, and supporting the information technology infrastructure necessary for integrated systems.

Mobile Retailing

Mobile devices and smartphone technologies offer both retailers and consumers opportunities for connecting multiple shopping channels. For retailers, mobile shopping assistance tools with smartphones and/or tablets enable sales associates to find product information and availability, access consumer information, and process customers' purchases without leaving the customer.

For customers, their ability to access product information, receive promotions, connect with social media, and purchase merchandise from their smartphones integrates the shopping experience and increases convenience and enjoyment.

Shopping apps for smartphones provide consumers with coupons, as well as opportunities to comparison shop, connect with social media, and obtain wayfinding maps of shopping malls or large stores.

Virtual Displays, Magic Mirrors, and Smart Fitting Rooms

In the bricks-and-mortar environment, a number of technologies are now connecting consumers to the virtual world. "Smart" mirrors and fitting rooms allow customers to obtain product information, virtually try on merchandise in a variety of colors, and purchase merchandise through the company website while having the benefit of seeing, touching, and trying on the merchandise in the store. For example, a number of fashion brands now attach RFID technologies on their products. Consumers can place the product on a scanner in the store and see the online product information on a screen next to the scanner.

Cross-merchandising Strategies

In the omnichannel context, **cross-merchandising** strategies allow fashion brands to display total fashion images and demonstrate to consumers how their many product categories work together. For example, visual displays at the Uniqlo store in Paris and on its website include apparel, footwear, and other accessories (Figure 13.12).

Figure 13.12
In-store displays allow fashion brands to effectively cross-merchandise assortments and build a brand image.
Leslie Burns.

Behavioral Targeting and Personalized Advertising

Behavioral targeting is the practice of collecting and analyzing customers' online consumer behavior activities to allow fashion brand companies to personalize advertising and promotions. Automated integration of marketing research of online consumer behavior, use of retailer social media sites, and use of promotions will continue to facilitate the creation of these personalized marketing tools. Consumers are becoming more aware of privacy issues with this marketing practice, which may lead to changes in the legal aspects of this practice.

TRADE ASSOCIATIONS AND TRADE PUBLICATIONS

Various trade associations and trade publications serve those involved in distributing fashion merchandise. Table 13.7 provides a list of selected retail trade associations. The National Retail Federation (NRF), the largest trade association for retailers both within the United States and globally, represents retailers in more than 45 countries (see https://nrf.com). The NRF offers a variety of resources to both large and small retailers related to store operations, omnichannel strategies, social responsibility, technology, human resources, and loss prevention, just to name a few.

The NRF publishes *STORES* magazine, a monthly trade publication (paper and digital) as well as a weekly newsletter that addresses the interests of those in the retailing industry. A number of other trade publications cater to those involved with distribution and retailing. Table 13.8 lists some of these publications.

Table 13.7 Selected Retail Trade Associations

Trade Association	Description
A.R.E. | POPAI	Dedicated to enhancing the total shopper experience through research, training programs, industry events, conferences, and awards recognizing the best and most creative stores and displays
Electronic Retailing Association (www.retailing.org)	Leaders in direct-to-consumer commerce
International Council of Shopping Centers (www.icsc.org)	Serving the global retail real estate industry
National Retail Federation (https://nrf.com)	World's largest retail trade association and voice of retail worldwide
Shop.org of the NRF (www.shop.org)	National Retail Federation's digital division
National Shoe Retailers Association (www.nsra.org)	Represents independent footwear retailers
Retail Industry Leaders Association (www.rila.org/Pages/default.aspx)	Trade association of leaders within the retail industry with a focus on continuing education, collaboration, and advocacy

Table 13.8 Selected Trade Publications Related to Business, Distribution, and Retailing

Publication	Focus
Advertising Age (www.adage.com)	Focuses on advertising, marketing, and media news and information.
Bloomberg Business Week (businessweek.com)	Focuses on business news on Wall Street, media and advertising, international business, banking, interest rates, the stock market, and currencies and funds.
Chain Store Age (www.chainstoreage.com)	Focuses on information of interest to retail headquarters management, including trends and strategies in areas such as retail technology, store construction, marketing, physical support systems, finance, security, store design and visual merchandising, electronic retailing, payment systems, human resources, and supply chain.
Multichannel Merchant (multichannelmerchant.com)	Reaches key decision makers responsible for e-commerce, management, marketing, and operations at companies that sell merchandise through multiple channels—including e-commerce, mobile, social, and catalog.
Retail Merchandiser (www.retail-merchandiser.com)	For executives and managers in the mass-merchandise, drug, club, and specialty retailing industries. Topics focus on merchandising and marketing issues, providing ideas and concepts that work within a retail environment.
Retailing Today.com (www.retailingtoday.com)	Focuses on mass-market retailing business news, trends, and research analysis.
STORES (https://nrf.com/connect-us /stores-magazine)	Publication of the National Retail Federation with a focus on information of interest to retailers in general. Topics include retail technology, supply chain and logistics, credit and payment systems, online retailing, customer service, loss prevention, human resources, and other store operations.
Supermarket News (www.supermarketnews.com)	Trade magazine for the food distribution industry. Executives use it as their information source for industry news, trends, and product features. Many large food retailers sell selected apparel, accessory, and home fashions products.
VM+SD (Visual Merchandising and Store Design) (www.vmsd.com)	For retail designers and store display professionals with information on trends in store design and visual presentations, new products, merchandising strategies, and industry news.

TRENDS IN FASHION RETAILING

Change has become the norm in the fashion industries. Faced with increased global competition, fashion companies continually strive to design, manufacture, market, and distribute the best fashion product to their target customer. How, when, and where consumers are shopping and paying for merchandise has changed dramatically over the past five years and will continue to change. Some trends affecting the next steps for fashion retailing include

- brand and lifestyle experiences
- pop-up shops
- sustainability
- technology

Fashion brands are making connections with their customers through social media, experiential marketing, and brand communities. These strategies provide opportunities for customers to create connections with others who share their lifestyle, to receive promotional materials from the brand, and to engage in activities that are supported and/or promoted by the brand. For example, Nudie Jeans Co (www.nudiejeans.com) offers multiple ways for customers to connect with the brand and each other; to learn about their production; to learn how to repair, reuse, and recycle jeans; and to be part of activities such as T-shirt design challenges for human rights. Customer collaborations such as co-design and customization also connect customers with the fashion brand in effectively personal ways.

Pop-up retail stores will continue to emerge as an important trend for established brands that want to have temporary stores at events, during certain times of the year, or in unique locations (Figure 13.13). For example, during the summer of 2014, before opening permanent stores in the Los Angeles area, Uniqlo opened three small pop-up stores to provide customers unfamiliar with Uniqlo a preview of what the permanent stores would offer. Pop-up retail can also be an advantage to new brands or brands that have been primarily online and want to test a bricks-and-mortar retail strategy without investing in a permanent bricks-and-mortar store. Fashion brands opening a pop-up retail store must consider location, lease amount, inventory needs, visual merchandising, and technologies needed to process sales. Still, for many fashion brands, operating a pop-up store for a month or less is an ideal way of determining market demand and feasibility of a permanent store.

As with all other areas of the fashion supply chain, an important trend in retailing is addressing sustainability issues. Beyond the sustainability of the merchandise, from the retail perspective, sustainability issues include the bricks-and-mortar store design and footprint, the store's energy use, and the sustainability of the fixtures, mannequins, and other props used by the store. Non-store retailers also have sustainability issues in terms of office design and operations, paper use associated with mailing catalogs, and/or environmental impact of shipping merchandise to individual customers.

Figure 13.13
Pop-up stores are used by brands to build brand recognition. Kathy Mullet.

With the continued growth of omnichannel retail strategies, integration of technologies into the retail experience will also remain an important trend. Consumers will expect fashion brands to provide them with ever more convenient ways of purchasing merchandise through the multiple channels available to them. Understanding trends in customer shopping behavior (including the need for customer service and returns) will be imperative for success. Basics of effective omnichannel strategies include store associates with tablets to assist customers, mobile POS systems, and synchronizing e-coupons, gift cards, and promotions across all channels. The next level of omnichannel strategies includes integrating inventory management systems across channels and tracking the impact of online marketing on traffic in bricks-and-mortar stores. More advanced omnichannel strategies include creating smart fitting rooms and providing technologies for customers to track purchases across channels. Fashion brand companies such as Burberry, Uniqlo, and Nike will continue to lead the way with innovations designed to create unique and effective shopping experiences for their target customers.

SUMMARY

Fashion brand companies have a number of options for distributing their merchandise to the ultimate consumer. Factors affecting this decision include type of marketing channel(s) used by the company, buying characteristics of the target customer, product and brand type, and level of customization. Companies must decide how widely their merchandise will be distributed; some will choose mass distribution while others will decide on a selective or exclusive distribution strategy. Fashion brand companies will distribute their goods either directly to their retail accounts or through distribution centers. Retailers with many stores may also use distribution centers as central locations for merchandise.

Product life cycle management, and supply chain management strategies are important in the distribution process, and communications among companies contribute greatly to the success of these strategies. The foundations for these strategies are to use Universal Product Code (UPC) bar coding on product labels and shipping cartons as well as RFID tagging on shipping cartons, to have vendors (manufacturers) assume responsibility for affixing labels and price information on products, and to use electronic data interchange for transmission of invoices, advance shipping notices, and other information. Replenishment of goods at the retail level is based on these operations.

Retailing involves the selling of merchandise to the final consumer. Retailers are classified according to whether they sell new merchandise or previously owned merchandise. They are also classified according to merchandising and operating strategies into the following categories, which are not mutually exclusive: department store retailers, specialty retailers, discount retailers, off-price retailers, supermarkets and hypermarkets, convenience store retailers, contractual retailers, warehouse retailers, and chain store retailers. Fashion brands can be found at a variety of retailers; although department store retailers, specialty retailers, and discount retailers are the most common.

Across operational strategies, retailers can also be classified as bricks-and-mortar and/or non-store retailers. Multichannel retailers offer merchandise through more than one distribution channel (e.g., distributing merchandise through both bricks-and-mortar stores and non-store retailing venues). Non-store retailing includes electronic/internet retailers, catalog retailers, television/live video retailers, direct sales retailers, and vending machines. Omnichannel retail strategies provide seamless shopping experiences for consumers across distribution channels. Increased use of mobile and other technologies allow retailers to effectively integrate multiple distribution strategies to best meet their customers' needs.

Numerous retailing trade associations offer their members a variety of resources for improving the retailers' operations. Trends in retailing include brand and lifestyle experiences, pop-up shops, sustainability, and technology integration.

KEY TERMS

big-box store
boutique
bricks-and-mortar retailer
catalog retailer
chain store retailer
closeout retailer
contractual retailer
convenience store retailer
cross-dockable shipments
cross-merchandising
customer touchpoints
data mining technology
department store retailer
direct marketing channel
discount retailer
distribution center (DC)
e-commerce
e-tailing
electronic data interchange
    (EDI)
electronic/internet retailer
exclusive distribution

extended marketing channel
factory outlet retailer
fast fashion
floor-ready merchandise (FRM)
flow-through
franchise
full-line discount retailer
general merchandise discount
    retailer
hypermarket
in-store shop
intensive distribution
leased department
limited marketing channel
mail order retailer
mass distribution
multichannel distribution
multichannel retailing
non-store retailer
off-price retailer
omnichannel distribution
omnichannel retailing

picking
pop-up shop
re-commerce
replenishment
retailer
retailing
selective distribution
SPA (specialty store retailer of
    private label apparel)
specialty retailer
stock-keeping unit (SKU)
stockout data
supermarket
superstore
Universal Product Code (UPC)
upscale discounter
value-added network (VAN)
vendor-managed inventory
    (VMI)
vendor marking
warehouse retailer

DISCUSSION QUESTIONS AND ACTIVITIES

1. Describe the roles of distribution centers for fashion brand companies. How is valued added to the merchandise through these distribution centers?

2. Name and describe three of your favorite retailers. What category does each retailer fit into? What are the characteristics of the categories of retailers you named? How does the retailer engage in multichannel/omnichannel distribution? What are the advantages and disadvantages of these multichannel/omnichannel strategies for these retailers?

3. Explore the websites of three retailers of fashion brands. What are the common features of these sites? What strategies do these retailers use to inform customers about product characteristics? How does each fashion brand use social media in connecting with customers?

Creating an Effective Omnichannel Experience

Omnichannel retailing strategies are designed to provide customers with "integrated, transparent shopping experiences regardless of where shoppers begin or end their journey. The omnichannel business model often requires the adoption of in-store and digital customer touchpoints, both virtual and physical tools" (Naik and Venkatesan 2015).

1. Find and read three articles on omnichannel retailing from trade publications within the past year. Be sure to cite all references.
   a. Summarize the facts surrounding the opportunities and the risks associated with omnichannel retailing.
   b. In what ways do customers expect omnichannel retailing strategies to work?
   c. Summarize the facts surrounding the opportunities and risks associated with social media as part of a retailer's overall omnichannel strategy.

2. Select two of your favorite fashion brand companies (apparel, accessories, home fashions) with retail operations.
   a. Who are the target customers for each of the companies?
   b. Describe the multiple channels that these companies are using to create customer touchpoints.
   c. How are the two companies currently using social media? Print out a page from one of their current social media sites. How is social media being used to connect with customers?

3. Evaluate the effectiveness of the omnichannel experience and social media utilization for each of the companies you selected.

4. Identify a minimum of three new omnichannel and/or social media strategies for each company you chose, and explain why each strategy would create a better shopping experience for the companies' customers.

5. Include a list of all references used for your analysis, evaluation, and recommendations.

Fashion brand retailing offers many career opportunities, including

- Divisional merchandise manager
- Retail store manager: assistant manager, department manager, store manager
- Retail buyer/merchandising manager: retail planner, assistant buyer, buyer
- Visual merchandiser
- Retail event manager
- Retail product developer for pri

REFERENCES

Amazon.com. (2015). "Shop by Department: Clothing, Shoes, and Jewelry." http://www.amazon.com. (accessed March 17, 2016).

Deloitte Touche Tohmatsu Ltd. (2015). "Global Powers of Retailing 2015: Embracing Innovation." http://www2.deloitte.com/global/en/pages/consumer-business/articles/global-powers-of-retailing.html (accessed March 17, 2016).

eBay. (2015). "About eBay: Company Info." http://www.ebay.com (accessed March 17, 2016).

Home Shopping Network. (2015). Company Overview. http://www.hsn.com (accessed March 17, 2016).

JCPenney. (2015). "About Us." http://www.jcpenney.com (accessed March 17, 2016).

Macy's Inc. (2015). "About Us." http://macysinc.com (accessed March 17, 2016).

Naik, Sundip, and Balaji R. Venkatesan. (2015, July 1). "Beyond Technology: 5 New Areas of Focus for Omnichannel Readiness." *Apparel*, http://apparel.edgl.com/news/Beyond-Technology—5-New-Areas-of-Focus-for-Omnichannel-Readiness101049 (accessed March 17, 2016).

National Retail Federation. (2015). "Who We Are." http://www.nrf.com (accessed March 17, 2016).

Nike, Inc. (2015, June 26). "Nike Opens Its Largest Distribution Center Worldwide in Tennessee." http://news.nike.com/news/nike-opens-its-largest-distribution-center-worldwide-in-tennessee (accessed March 17, 2016).

QVC. (2015). "About Us." http://www.qvc.com (accessed March 17, 2016).

Schulz, David P. (2015, July). "Top 100 Retailers 2015." *STORES* https://nrf.com/news/top-100-retailers-2015 (accessed March 17, 2016).

7-Eleven (2015). "About Us." http://corp.7-eleven.com/corp/about (accessed March 17, 2016).

Target. (2015). "About Target." http://www.target.com (accessed March 17, 2016).

Tuesday Morning. (2015). "Tuesday Morning Corporate Information." http://www.tuesdaymorning.com/corporate-information (accessed March 17, 2016).

Walmart Corporation. (2015). "Distribution Center." http://careers.walmart.com/career-areas/transportation-logistics-group/distribution-center/ (accessed March 17, 2016).

glossary

A

acquisition When company A purchases company B and assumes ownership of company B's assets and liability for all of company B's debts.

advertising Strategy by which companies buy space or time in print, broadcast, or electronic media to promote their lines to retailers and consumers.

agile manufacturing Use of a combination of technologies that form an integrated, seamless exchange of information linking retailers and suppliers to the manufacturing facility.

articles of association See *articles of incorporation*.

articles of incorporation or **articles of organization** or **articles of association** Legal document that outlines the nature and scope of ownership and operations of a corporation.

articles of organization See *articles of incorporation*.

articles of partnership Written contracts to form a partnership between two individuals or among three or more individuals.

atelier de couture Workrooms of haute couture designers and staff.

audit fatigue A challenge faced by factories of being audited multiple times with only slight differences in the standards being addressed.

B

B corporation Benefit corporations are those that include a purpose of general public benefit such as social or environmental benefit.

bar codes A series of black-and-white bars that encodes a universal product code (UPC), which enables a retailer or manufacturer to track products.

base pattern or **block** or **sloper** Basic pattern in the company's sample size, without any style features, used as the starting point for creating a pattern for a new style.

bespoke Fashion merchandise custom-made to an individual's specifications; typically suits or specialty items.

big-box stores Stores as large as 150,000 to 250,000 square feet, usually containing elements of a supermarket and a department store and offering a wide range of merchandise, including food, electronics, clothing and accessories, furniture, and garden items such as outdoor furniture and accessories, equipment, and gardening tools.

bilateral trade agreement Trade agreements between two countries.

block See *base pattern*.

board of directors Chief governing body of a corporation elected by the corporation's stockholders.

boutique Specialty store that concentrates on merchandise in the designer price zone or unique merchandise distributed to only a few stores.

brand A feature (e.g., name, logo, symbol) that identifies the products of a company and creates an image in the consumer's mind about the qualities and characteristics of the products.

brand community A community formed on the basis of attachment to a product brand. For example, owners and social media followers of Burberry merchandise.

brand differentiation Marketing process that results in creating distinct brand images in the minds of consumers.

brand extension Expanding the use of a well-known brand name to a variety of merchandise (e.g., decorative pillows and throw rugs bearing the Harley-Davidson logo, manufactured by WestPoint Stevens).

brand identity All means by which a company portrays the brand and communications with the consumer.

brand image Characteristics and image created in the minds of consumers about a particular brand.

brand merchandise Apparel, accessories, or home fashions whose brand or label is well recognized by the public.

brand name or **trade name** Distinctive name given to a product or service for the purpose of making the product or service readily identifiable to consumers.

brand positioning How the company positions its brand on key characteristics as compared to its competitors.

brand tier Strategy by which a manufacturer or retailer offers brands in two or more price zones, with each brand focusing on a specific price zone.

bricks-and-mortar retailer Retailer with a physical store in which customers can see, touch, and feel merchandise.

bridge jewelry Umbrella term for several types of jewelry, including those made from silver, gold (14K, 12K, 10K), and less expensive stones; jewelry designed by artists using a variety of materials.

bundling The process of disassembling stacked, cut fabric pieces and reassembling them grouped by garment size, color dye lot, and quantity of units ready for production.

business-to-business (B2B) Business operations that are conducted between companies through web-based technologies.

C

C corporation or **regular corporation** Type of corporation whereby profits of the corporation are distributed to shareholders in the form of dividends.

capital Funds or resources needed to start or expand a business.

carryover Item in a line or collection that is carried over from one season to the next.

cashmere A soft, luxury fiber that comes from the undercoat wool of the cashmere or Kashmir goat, mainly from China, Mongolia, and Tibet.

catalog retailer Retail company that sells merchandise to consumers through catalogs, brochures, or advertisements and delivers the merchandise by mail or other carrier.

chain store retailer Retail organization that owns and operates several retail outlets that sell similar lines of merchandise in a standardized method and that function under a centralized form of organizational structure.

classification The process by which fashion brand companies are categorized: by the type of merchandise produced, by the wholesale prices of the products or brands, or by an industry classification system for government tracking.

close corporation See *private corporation*.

closely held corporation See *private corporation*.

closeout retailer Retailer that specializes in buying a variety of merchandise through retail liquidations, bankruptcies, and closeouts and then selling this merchandise at discount prices.

code of conduct Guidelines for contractors and subcontractors regarding workplace environment and operations; generally focus on safeguards for workers' health and rights.

collection A group of apparel items presented together to the buying public, usually by high-fashion designers.

color control Color-matching requirement for all like garments in a line and for all their components, such as knit collars and cuffs, buttons, thread, and zippers.

color forecasting Process of predicting consumers' future color preferences for merchandise for a specific fashion season. Predictions are based on research conducted by color forecasters for companies and trade associations.

color forecasting service A company that predicts consumers' future color and trend preferences in textiles, apparel, accessories, and home fashions.

color management Process of maintaining an acceptable color match for all like garments in a line, including all their components, such as knit collars and cuffs, buttons, thread, and zippers.

color palette A selected group of colors, often represented by color chips. Each new line will be composed of a group of selected colors.

color story Color palette identified for each group's fashion season.

colorway The variety of three or four seasonal color choices for the same solid or print fabric available for each garment style.

commercial match Contractor-provided acceptable match of color for fabric, trim, or finding to a control color chip or fabric provided by the apparel company.

computer-aided design (CAD) The hardware and software computer systems used to assist with the design phase of the fabric design or garment design.

computer grading and marker making (CGMM) The computer hardware and software systems that process the pattern grading and marker making segments of the pattern for production.

concept garment End-use garment created by a textile company to promote its new fibers to textile mills.

conglomerate Diversified company involved with significantly different lines of business.

consolidation The combining of two companies to form a new company.

consumer research Information gathered about consumer characteristics and consumer behavior, including broad trends in the marketplace as well as more specific information about a target group of consumers.

contractor Company that specializes in the constructing, sewing, and finishing of goods or that specializes in a specific part of the production process (such as pleating piece goods).

contractual retailer Retailer that has entered into a contractual agreement with a manufacturer, wholesaler, or other retailers with a goal of integrating operations and increasing market impact.

controlled brand name program or **licensed brand name program** Marketing strategy whereby minimum standards of fabric performance for trademarked fibers are determined and promoted.

convenience store retailer Retailer that offers fast service and convenient location.

conventional marketing channel Independent companies that separately perform the manufacturing, distribution, and retailing functions.

converted goods or **finished goods** Fabrics that have been dyed, printed, or finished.

converter or **textile converter** Company that specializes in finishing fabrics (including printing).

co-op advertising A type of advertising strategy whereby companies share the cost of the advertisement that features all of the companies.

cooperative advertising See *co-op advertising*.

copyright The exclusive right of the copyright holder to use, perform, or reproduce written, pictorial, and performed work.

corporate social responsibility (CSR) A philosophy whereby a company takes into consideration human rights, labor conditions, and environmental implications when making business decisions.

corporate selling Strategy by which fashion brand companies sell their merchandise directly to retailers without the use of sales representatives.

corporate showroom Showroom owned and operated by a single company to market its lines of merchandise; generally managed by company sales representatives.

corporation Company established by a legal charter that outlines the scope and activity of the company. Corporations are legal entities regardless of who owns stock in the company.

cost or **cost to manufacture** or **wholesale cost** The total cost to manufacture a style, including materials, findings, labor, and auxiliary costs such as freight, duty, and packaging.

cost to manufacture See *cost*.

costume jewelry Mass-produced jewelry made from plastic, wood, brass, glass, Lucite, and other less expensive materials.

cotton Natural fiber obtained from the fibers surrounding the seeds of the cotton plant.

counterfeit goods Products that incorporate unauthorized use of registered trade names or trademarks.

counter sample or **sew by** A sample garment sewn by a contractor and submitted to the apparel manufacturer for approval. This sample is then used as a benchmark to compare the sewn production goods.

country of origin The country where the last step that added value (i.e., substantial change) to the product happened.

couture A French term that literally means "sewing," it refers to the highest-priced apparel produced in small quantities, made of high-quality fabrics using considerable hand-sewing techniques, and sized to fit individual clients' bodies.

couture house Name for each designer's business; thus, there is the House of Dior, the House of Givenchy, and the House of Chanel.

couturier (couturière) Designer of haute couture (couturier = masculine; couturière = feminine).

croquis or **lay figure** A French term referring to a figure outline used as a basis to sketch garment design ideas.

cross-dockable shipments Goods that are received from the manufacturer as floor-ready merchandise, so they can be sorted for store distribution without the need for additional processing.

cross-merchandising Strategy by which fashion brand companies combine apparel and accessories in their product offerings.

customer touchpoints All of the methods/technologies by which a retailer can connect with its customers (e.g., bricks-and-mortar stores, websites, social media, mobile devices, etc.).

customs broker A person in the United States, licensed by the Office of Customs and Border Protection, to assist fashion brand companies in gaining customs clearance to import goods produced offshore.

cut, make, and trim (CMT) Contractors who cut, make, and trim the garments/products for the fashion brand company.

cut order Instructions for production cutting that include the specific number of items in each color and each size that will be included in the production run.

cut-up trade Belt manufacturers who produce belts for fashion brands to add to their coats, pants, skirts, and dresses.

D

data mining technology Technology used by companies to analyze purchasing data to determine selling patterns or trends and identify correlations among data characteristics.

decorative fabric converter Company that designs and sells finished textiles to jobbers, designers, and manufacturers who use the textiles in home fashions end-use products.

decorative fabric jobber Company involved in the marketing and distribution of home textile piece goods, particularly upholstery and drapery fabrics.

demographics Information about consumers that focuses on understanding characteristics of consumer groups, such as age, gender, marital status, income, occupation, ethnicity, and geographic location.

department store retailer Large retailer that departmentalizes its functions and merchandise.

design and product development The process by which a new style moves from concept sketch to prototype.

design brief Document that guides designers and includes the business aspects of the company in order to develop a unified brand identity and strategy. A brief often includes information related to target customers, target theme or inspiration, deliverables, timeline, and budget.

designer brand Brand classification associated with name designers, high prices, high quality, and distinct prestige.

die cutting Process by which a piece of metal with a sharp edge, similar to a cookie cutter, is first tooled to the exact dimensions of the shape of the pattern piece (the die). Next, the die is positioned over the fabric/material to be cut; then a pressurized plate is applied to the die to cut through the fabric/material layers.

diffusion line A designer's less expensive line (e.g., A/X Armani Exchange; DKNY).

digital printing Method of direct fabric printing that uses digital artwork.

digitizer A table embedded with sensors that relate to the X and Y coordinates (horizontal and vertical directions) that allow the shape of the pattern piece to be traced and converted to a drawing of the pattern in the computer.

direct market brand See *store brand*.

direct marketing channel Marketing channel by which manufacturers sell directly to the ultimate consumer.

discount retailer Retailer that sells brand name merchandise at below traditional retail prices, including merchandise at the budget/mass wholesale price zone.

distribution center Centralized location used by manufacturers and retailers for quality assurance, tagging, picking, packing of merchandise, and distribution to retail stores.

distribution strategy Business strategy to assure that merchandise is sold in stores that cater to the target market for whom the merchandise was designed and manufactured.

dividend Corporate profits paid to its stockholders; dividends are taxed as personal income.

domestic production Production occurring in the country where the merchandise will be sold at retail.

double taxation Situation with a C or regular corporation whereby earnings of the corporation are taxed twice— once at the corporate level and again at the individual level.

drafting Patternmaking process whereby pattern shapes are drawn based on body measurements plus ease allowances.

draping A process of creating the initial garment style by molding, cutting, and pinning fabric to a mannequin.

dual distribution Distribution strategy whereby fashion brand companies sell their merchandise through their own stores as well as through other retailers.

duplicate or **sample** A copy of the prototype or sample style used by the sales representatives to show and sell styles in the line to retail buyers.

duty or **tariff** Tax assessed by governments on imports.

E

e-commerce Buying and selling of goods and services conducted over the internet.

electronic data interchange (EDI) Computer-to-computer communications between companies.

electronic/internet retailer Company that offers goods and/or services over the internet or uses the internet in addition to its stores and/or catalog retailing business.

entrepreneur Individual who starts his or her own business as either a sole proprietorship, partnership, or a limited liability company.

e-tailing Term for electronic retailing.

exclusive distribution Strategy manufacturers use to limit the stores in which their merchandise is distributed and thus create an image of exclusiveness.

export agent A person located in the country that produced the goods who assists the (U.S.) manufacturer with exporting the products.

extended marketing channel Marketing channel in which wholesalers acquire products from manufacturers and sell them to retailers, or jobbers buy products from wholesalers and sell them to retailers.

F

fabrication See *fabric construction*.

fabric construction Methods used to make fabrics from solutions, directly from fibers, and from yarns; weaving and knitting are the most common methods.

factor An agency that provides protection against bad debt losses, manages accounts receivable, and provides credit analysis in the apparel industry.

factoring The business of purchasing and collecting accounts receivable or of advancing cash on the basis of accounts receivable.

factory auditing program Evaluation process of factories including efficiency, working conditions, worker compensation, freedom of association, labor laws, compliance with environmental law, quality assurance, security, and subcontractor arrangements.

factory outlet retailer A type of off-price retailer that sells its own seconds, irregulars, or overruns (merchandise produced in excess of its orders), as well as merchandise produced specifically for the outlet stores.

fair trade International trade networks that provide fair and equitable wages, transparency, and attention to human rights and environmental impact.

fallout The fabric that remains in the spaces between pattern pieces on the marker; thus, the amount of fabric that is wasted.

fashion "Style of consumer product or way of behaving that is temporarily adopted by a discernible proportion of members of a social group because that chosen style or behavior is perceived to be socially appropriate for time and situation." (G. B. Sproles and L. D. Burns, *Changing Appearances: Understanding Dress in Contemporary Society.* New York: Fairchild Books, 1994, p. 4.)

fashion brand Brand associated with fashion merchandise.

fashion color Color used in a seasonal line that reflects the current color trends, determined by the fashion brand company for the target customer.

fashion forecasting service A company that predicts consumers' future style preferences and trends in textiles and apparel. Predictions are based on research conducted by its staff and other associations.

fashion magazine Magazine (print and/or digital) sold by individual issue, as well as by subscription, whose primary focus is on the latest fashion trends.

fashion season Name given to lines or collections that correspond to seasons of the year when consumers would most likely wear the merchandise (e.g., Spring, Summer, Pre-Fall, Fall, Holiday, and Resort).

fast fashion Ultra-fast supply chain operations that focus on consumer demand of fashion goods.

fast fashion production Manufacturing of fast fashions in which products go from concept to retail store in less than three weeks.

fiber The basic unit in making textile yarns and fabrics.

filament yarn Yarn created by spinning together long, continuous fibers.

findings Also called notions or sundries, the garment components other than fabrics, such as fasteners, elastic, stay tape, and hem tape.

fine jewelry Jewelry made from precious metals alone, and with precious and semiprecious stones.

finish Application to a fiber, yarn, or fabric that changes the appearance, hand, or performance of the fiber, yarn, or fabric.

finished goods See *converted goods.*

finishing Process used on fibers, yarns, or fabrics to change or improve the performance or appearance of the material.

first adoption meeting Gathering when a new line is presented (often as sketches and fabric swatches), and the design team reviews each style in the line.

fit model The live model whose body dimensions match the company's sample size and who is used to assess the fit, styling, and overall look of new prototypes.

flat or **flat sketch** Also called a tech drawing, this technical sketch of a garment style represents how the garment would look lying flat, as on a table. Garment details are clearly depicted.

flat pattern The patternmaking process used to make a pattern for a new style from the base pattern (or block or sloper).

flat sketch See *flat.*

flexible manufacturing (FM) Production that focuses on optimizing equipment, flow of goods, and teams of workers to produce the product as efficiently as possible.

flexible manufacturing system Using fast, small, flexible production units that depend on the coordinated efforts of minimally supervised teams of workers.

floor-ready merchandise (FRM) Merchandise shipped by the manufacturer or distribution center affixed with hangtags, labels, and price information so that the retailer can place the goods immediately on the selling floor.

flow-through Facilities that move merchandise from receiving to shipping with little or no time in storage.

FP See *full-package contractor.*

franchise A type of contractual retail organization; in return for a franchise payment, the parent company provides the franchisee with the exclusive distribution of a well-recognized brand name in a specific market area, as well as assistance in running the business.

free trade agreement (FTA) Trade alliance that results in reciprocal reductions in tariffs among member countries.

freight forwarding company A company that moves a shipment of goods from the country where the goods were produced to the country in which they are sold.

full-line discount retailer Large discount chain retailers that carry private label merchandise and exclusive licensed brands (e.g., Target).

full-package contractor (FP) A type of service option whereby the apparel contractor provides preproduction services, fabrics, trims, supplies, and labor.

G

garment dyed Apparel produced as white or colorless goods and then dyed during the finishing process.

garment/product specifications or **garment/product spec sheet** A listing of vital information for the garment style including garment sketch, fabric swatches and/or specifications, and specifications for findings, sizes, construction, and finished garment measurements.

general merchandise discount retailer Full-line discount retailer that also offers grocery items.

general partner Co-owner of a company who shares responsibilities with other owners in the running of a company under a partnership agreement.

general partnership Form of ownership in which co-owners of a company share in the liability as well as the profits of the company according to the conditions of the partnership contract.

generic family Classification of fibers according to chemical composition and characteristics.

globalization Process whereby the economies of nation-states become integrated.

grade rules The amounts and locations of growth or reduction for pattern pieces to create the various sizes.

grading or pattern grading Using the production pattern pieces made in the sample size for a style to develop a set of pattern pieces for each of the sizes listed on the garment spec sheet.

greige goods Fabrics that have not received finishing treatments, such as bleaching, shearing, brushing, embossing, or dyeing; unfinished fabrics.

group Coordinated fashion items using several colors and fabrics within a line of fashion merchandise.

H

haute couture Also sometimes referred to as *couture*; fashion merchandise that is produced in small quantities, uses hand-sewing techniques, is sized to fit an individual's body dimensions, and uses expensive materials, fabrics, and trims.

hide An animal pelt weighing more than 25 pounds when shipped to the tannery.

home fashions Textile products designed for end uses in the home—towels, bedding, upholstery fabrics, area floor coverings, draperies, and table linens.

horizontally integrated Business strategy whereby a company focuses on a single stage of production/distribution but with varying products or services.

hypermarket See *superstore*.

I

information flow Communication among companies within the marketing channel pipeline.

initial cost estimate The preliminary estimate of the cost of a new style based on materials, trims, findings, labor, and other components such as duty and freight.

initial public offering (IPO) When a company wants to become a publicly traded corporation, or "go public," it sells shares to public investors in an initial public offering.

in-store shop Area within a department store that is merchandised according to fashion brand company's specifications and carries only the merchandise of the fashion brand.

intellectual property Creative work such as designs, inventions, or symbols/images for which you may copyright or apply for trademarks or patents.

intelligent textile Optical fiber with integrated electronics that allow the fiber to sense, process, and store data, and that can be woven into fabric; applications include medical devices, high-performance and protective fabrics, and military uniforms.

intensive distribution or **mass distribution** Strategy whereby products are made available to as many consumers as possible through a variety of retail venues.

internal selling Process used for private label merchandise whereby a company's design team presents seasonal lines to in-house merchandisers who will select specific pieces of the line for production.

item house Contractor that specializes in the production of one type of product, such as baseball caps.

J

jobber An intermediary in the fashion industry who carries inventories of merchandise for ready shipment to contractors or retailers.

K

kip Animal pelt weighing 15 to 25 pounds when shipped to the tannery.

knockoff A facsimile of an existing garment/product that sells at a lower price than the original. The copy might be made in a less expensive fabric and might have some design details modified or eliminated.

L

lab dip The vendor-supplied sample of the dyed-to-match product such as fabric, zipper, button, knit collar or cuff, or thread.

lay figure See *croquis*.

lean manufacturing A manufacturing approach designed to achieve the shortest possible cycle time by eliminating process waste.

leased department Contractual retail agreement whereby a retailer leases space within a large department store to run a specialty department. Typical leased departments are fine jewelry, furs, and shoes.

licensed brand name program See *controlled brand name program*.

licensing An agreement whereby the owner (licensor) of a particular image or design sells the right to use the image or design to another party, typically a manufacturer (licensee), for payment of royalties to the licensor.

licensor Company that has developed a well-known image (property) and sells manufacturers the right to use the image on their merchandise.

lifestyle brand A term used to describe brands that are associated with a particular target customer's activities and way of life.

lifestyle merchandising Using the appeal of the target customer's lifestyle choices, especially in product advertising.

limited liability Arrangement whereby owners of a company are liable only for the amount of capital they invested in the company but are not personally liable beyond that for debts incurred by the business.

limited liability company (LLC) Form of company ownership that provides business owners with tax advantages (as with partnerships) along with limited liability (as with corporations).

limited marketing channel Marketing channel in which manufacturers sell their merchandise to consumers through retailers.

limited partnership A specialized type of partnership in which a partner is liable only for the amount of capital invested in the business, and any profits are shared according to the conditions of the limited partnership contract.

line One large group or several small groups of fashion items developed with a theme that links them together.

line catalog or **line sheet** A brochure or catalog of all the styles and colorways available in the line, used to market the line to retail buyers.

line-for-line copy A garment made as an exact replica of an existing garment style, produced in a similar fabric.

line sheet See *line catalog*.

logistics Coordination of the purchasing and movement of materials and components to factories and from factories to distribution centers and to the retailer.

long-range forecasting Research focusing on general economic and social trends related to consumer spending patterns and the business climate.

luxury brand Brand classification associated with high prices, high quality, and distinct prestige.

M

made-to-measure A customized design and production process whereby a garment/product is made specifically for one individual based on his or her measurements and preferences.

mail order retailer See *catalog retailer*.

manufacturer A company that performs all functions of continually creating, marketing, and distributing fashion lines. These companies may use outside contractors to perform the manufacturing function.

manufacturing environment Production circumstances including choice of production facility, location of production, production process, and cycle time to produce goods.

margin The difference between the cost to manufacture a style and the wholesale price the retailer will pay the manufacturer for the style. Margin can also refer to the difference between the cost the retailer paid the manufacturer for the goods and the selling price for the goods.

marker A master cutting plan for all the pattern pieces in the sizes specified on the cut order to manufacture the style.

market (1) consumer demand for a product or service; (2) location where the buying and selling of merchandise takes place; (3) to promote a product or service through media or public relations efforts.

market analysis Information about general market trends.

market center Name given to cities that not only house marts and showrooms but also have important manufacturing and retailing industries (e.g., New York, Los Angeles, London, Paris).

marketing Process of identifying a target market and developing appropriate strategies for product development, pricing, promotion, and distribution.

marketing channel Sequence of companies that perform the manufacturing, wholesaling, and retailing functions to get merchandise to the ultimate consumer.

marketing channel integration Process of connecting the various levels of the marketing channel so that they work together in getting the right product to the right customer at the right price and in the right place.

market niche Specific segment of the retail trade determined by a combination of product type and target customer.

market research Process of providing information to determine what the customer will need and want, and when and where the customer will want to make purchases.

market week Time of the year when retail buyers come to showrooms or exhibit halls to see the seasonal fashion lines offered by apparel companies.

mart Building or group of buildings that house showrooms in which sales representatives show merchandise lines to retail buyers.

mass customization The use of computer technology to customize a garment style for the individual customer, by individualizing the fit to the customer's measurements, by offering individualized combinations of fabric, garment style, and size options, or by personalizing a finished product.

mass distribution See *intensive distribution*.

mass fashion Fashion merchandise characterized by simplified styling and sizing, mass production sewing in large factories, with distribution through retail chain stores.

master calendar A calendar that indicates when each step of the design and distribution of a season's line must be completed.

measurement specification The actual garment measurements at specific locations on the finished goods for each of the sizes specified for a style.

merchandiser (1) A fashion brand company employee who is responsible for planning and coordinating several lines presented by the company; (2) a visual merchandiser creates visual displays of merchandise within a retail store.

merchandising (1) The process of buying and selling goods and services; (2) area of a fashion brand company that develops strategies to have the right merchandise, at the right price, at the right time, at the right locations to meet the target consumers' wants and needs.

merger Blending of one company into another company.

millinery Women's hats, and especially hat making that requires handwork.

modular manufacturing See *flexible manufacturing*.

mohair Natural fiber obtained from the wool of the Angora goat.

monopolistic competition Competitive situation in which many companies compete in terms of product type, but the specific products of any one company are perceived as unique by consumers.

monopoly Competitive situation in which there is typically one company that dominates the market and can thus price its goods and/or services at whatever scale its management wishes.

multichannel distribution Distribution strategy whereby a manufacturer offers merchandise through varying retail venues: bricks-and-mortar stores, catalogs, and/or websites.

multichannel retailing Retail strategy whereby merchandise is offered through bricks-and-mortar stores, catalogs, and/or websites.

multilateral trade agreement Trade agreements among multiple countries.

multiline sales representative Individual who sells lines from several noncompeting but related companies to retail buyers.

multinational corporation Private or publicly traded corporation that operates in several countries.

muslin An inexpensive fabric, usually unbleached cotton, often used to develop the first trial of a new garment style.

N

national/designer brand Brand name that is distributed nationally and to which consumers attach a specific image, quality level, and price.

nearshoring Contracting production in nearby countries.

non-store retailer Distributor of products to consumers through means other than bricks-and-mortar retail stores.

North American Industry Classification System (NAICS) U.S. Department of Commerce categories and subcategories based on the company's chief industrial activity.

O

off-price retailer Retailer that specializes in selling national brands or designer apparel and home fashions lines at discount prices.

offshore production Production outside the country where the merchandise will be sold at retail.

oligopoly Competitive situation in which a few companies dominate and essentially have control of the market, making it difficult for other companies to enter.

oligopsony Competitive situation that involves a large number of sellers offering goods and services to a small number of buyers.

omnichannel distribution Distribution strategy whereby multiple channels of distribution are seamlessly integrated.

omnichannel retailing Retailing strategy resulting in the seamless integration of bricks-and-mortar and online retail operations.

onshoring Contracting production domestically in an area of the home country with lower costs of production.

open-distribution policy Policy by which a company will sell to any retailer that meets basic characteristics.

open-to-buy The process of planning merchandise sales and purchases. Merchandise is budgeted for purchase during a certain time period.

ownership flow or **title flow** Transfer of ownership or title of merchandise from one company to the next.

P

partnership Company owned by two or more persons; operation of partnerships is outlined in a written contract or "articles of partnership."

partner-shoring Contracting production in countries with which your country has free trade agreements.

patent Government authorization granting legal exclusive right to make, use, or sell an invention for a set period of time.

pattern design system (PDS) A computer hardware and software system that the patternmaker uses to create and store new garment (pattern) styles.

pattern grading See *grading*.

payment flow Transfer of monies among companies as payment for merchandise or services rendered.

sell their product without the expense of maintaining their own website or store.

PDM/PLM A term used when combining product data management and product life cycle management. This approach requires all computer systems in the pipeline to be compatible for sharing product data.

peer-to-peer (P2P) Online retail platform for individual crafters to

pelt The unshorn skin of an animal, used in making leather and fur.

perfect competition See *pure competition*.

physical flow Movement of merchandise from the manufacturer to the ultimate consumer.

picking The process of selecting the appropriate assortment of goods to fill a specific retailer's order.

piece-rate wage Method of compensation whereby each production operator's pay is based on individual productivity—that is, specified task completed by the operator on the total number of units in a given time period.

point of measurement (POM) See *measurement specification*.

popular fashion magazine Magazine available for individual purchase or by subscription to consumers and typically read by the target customer.

pop-up shop Specialty stores that are temporary or mobile in nature, focus on new fads, or are associated with a live event.

precosting See *initial cost estimate*.

preline A preview of the line shown to key retail buyers before its introduction at market. These accounts may place orders in advance of market.

prêt-à-porter French term for ready-to-wear; in the United Kingdom, this merchandise is called *off-the-peg*; and in Italy, it is called *moda pronto*.

price averaging A price strategy of pricing one style to sell for less than the company's typical profit margin while pricing another style in the same line to sell for more than the typical profit margin. The margin gain and loss of the two styles are averaged.

price point A price range of merchandise: designer, bridge, better, moderate, or mass.

price zone See *price point*.

private corporation Type of corporation whereby there is not a public market for the stock in the corporation and stock has not been issued for public purchase.

private label brand Brand name that is owned and marketed by a specific retailer for use in its stores. Private label merchandise bears the retailer's label; the retailer has partial or full control over manufacture of the product.

private label product development or **store brand product development** Development of new styles by retailers to sell in their retail stores under a store brand label or private label.

privately held corporation See *private corporation*.

product data management (PDM) or **product development management (PDM)** The integration of computer systems that link style information among departments within a company, and/or among external contacts such as vendors and contractors.

product development management (PDM) See *product data management (PDM)*.

production The construction process by which the materials, trims, findings, and garment pieces are merged into a finished apparel product, accessory, or home fashion.

production cutting Process in which the production fabric, laid open across its entire width and many feet in length, is stacked in multiple layers with the marker resting on the top and then cut by computer or with hand-cutting machines.

production engineer A specialist who is responsible for the production pattern and/or for planning the production process, facilities, and final costing.

production marker The full-size master cutting layout for all the pattern pieces for a specific style, for all the sizes specified for production.

product life cycle management (PLM) Electronic access to style information throughout the design, development, production, and distribution processes within a company and by external contacts such as vendors and contractors.

product research Information gathered by a company regarding preferred product design and product characteristics desired by a specific customer group.

product turn The frequency rate at which a product is sold and replaced at the retail store.

product type The specific category or categories of goods the company specializes in producing.

progressive bundle system Groups of a dozen (usually) garment pieces placed in bundles and moved from one sewing operator to the next. Each operator performs one or several construction steps on each garment in the bundle and then passes the bundle on to the next operator.

promotion flow Flow of communication to promote merchandise either to other companies or to consumers in order to influence sales.

proprietary A contractual agreement between two parties (such as a textile company and an apparel manufacturer) that allows exclusive rights to the use of a product or process for a specified period of time.

prototype The sample garment/product for a new style in the company's base size, made in the intended fashion fabric/material or a facsimile fabric/material. If made in muslin, the prototype is usually called a toile.

psychographics Information gathered about a target group's buying habits, attitudes, values, motives, preferences, personality, and leisure activities.

publicity Promotional strategy whereby the company or the company's fashion brand merchandise is viewed as newsworthy and thus receives coverage in print, broadcast, and/or digital media (including social media).

publicly held corporation Type of corporation whereby stock has been issued for public purchase and at least some of the shares of stock are owned by the general public.

publicly traded corporation See *publicly held corporation*.

pure competition or **perfect competition** Competitive situation in which there are many producers and consumers of similar products, so that price is determined by market demand.

pull system Demand-side strategies that are based on the flow of timely and accurate information about consumers' wants and needs from consumers to the manufacturers.

push system Supply-side strategies used to push the products produced on the consumer.

Q

quality assurance Area of a company that focuses on quality control issues but also takes into consideration the satisfaction of consumer needs for a specific end use;

standards of acceptance set forth by the contracting party for the product being produced.

quality control Area of a company that focuses on inspecting finished products and making sure they adhere to specific quality standards.

Quick Response (QR) Comprehensive business strategy that promotes responsiveness to consumer demand, encourages business partnerships, and shortens the business cycle from raw materials to the consumer.

quota Limits on the number of units, kilograms, or square meters equivalent in specific categories that can be imported from specific countries.

R

rack trade Belt manufacturers who design, produce, and market belts to retailers.

radio-frequency identification (RFID) Tagging technology that uses a silicon computer chip. The chip is incorporated into containers, pallets, merchandise packaging, or individual items and is used to accurately track merchandise through production processes and the supply chain or to deter counterfeiting and shoplifting.

ready-to-wear (RTW) Fashion merchandise made with mass production techniques using standardized sizing; sometimes referred to as "off-the-rack."

re-commerce Reintroducing usable fashion products into the marketplace through consignment stores, thrift shops, online auction sites, and a number of other retail distribution methods for previously owned fashions.

regional sales territory Geographic area assigned to be covered by a corporate or multiline sales representative.

registration For printed textiles with more than one color screen, specified placement for each of the screens to produce the multicolor print.

regular corporation See *C corporation*.

regular tannery or tannery Tannery that buys skins and hides, performs tanning methods, and sells finished leather.

relationship merchandising An emphasis by retail stores on presentation, personal customer service, and having the right products for their target market that are different from the merchandise carried by other stores.

replenishment Reordering of merchandise. Automatic replenishment is the automatic reordering of merchandise.

reshoring Moving production back to the domestic market.

retailer A company that sells merchandise and associated services to the ultimate consumer.

retailing The activities of companies in selling merchandise and associated services to the ultimate consumer.

retail relations program Programs run by merchandising marts, which include a number of services designed to assist retail buyers during market weeks and trade shows.

retail store/direct market brand A retail store whose merchandise carries the retail store name as its exclusive label.

S

S corporation Type of corporation that is given special status by the Internal Revenue Service in that earnings of the corporation are taxed only at the individual level.

sales representative Individual who serves as the intermediary between the manufacturer and the retailer, selling the apparel, accessories, or home fashions lines to retail buyers.

sales volume The level of sales, expressed as either the total number of units of a style that sold at retail or the total number of dollars consumers spent on the style.

salon de couture Haute couture designer's showroom.

sample See *duplicate*.

sample cut A small length of fabric or material ordered from a textile mill or material manufacturer by the fashion brand company for use in making a prototype.

sample sewer A highly skilled technician who sews the entire prototype (sample) garment using a variety of sewing equipment and production processes similar to those used in factories.

selected-distribution policy Policy by which a company establishes detailed criteria that its stores must meet in order to carry the company's merchandise.

selective distribution Strategy whereby manufacturers allow their merchandise to be distributed only through certain stores.

sell-through Percentage of the number of items in the line the retailer purchased or acquired from the fashion brand company that were ultimately sold at retail.

service mark Trade name, symbol, or design used to identify a service that is offered for sale.

sew by See *counter sample*.

shopping the market Looking for new fashion trends in the retail markets that may influence the direction of an upcoming line.

short-cycle production Mass production of goods that can be produced quickly. It is especially suited to high-fashion products that are produced close to the site of their market demand.

short-range forecasting Researching specific fashion trends and new styles for an upcoming season and determining the level of demand and timing for these styles (also referred to as what, when, and how much to manufacture).

showroom Facility used by sales representatives to show samples of a line to retail buyers; may be permanent or temporary.

single-hand system A garment production method in which an individual sewer is responsible for sewing an entire garment. It is used primarily for couture or very high-priced, limited-production apparel and for sewing prototypes.

size standards Proportional increase or decrease in garment measurements for each size produced by a ready-to-wear fashion brand company.

skin Animal pelt weighing 15 pounds or less when shipped to the tannery.

SKU (stock-keeping unit) A number or code used to identify each distinct product and service that can be purchased, thus enabling the company to systematically track its inventory or product availability,

sloper See *base pattern*.

slops Less expensive clothes from scrap material left over from sewing custom-made suits. The term later became a standard term for cheap, ready-made clothing.

smart fiber or smart textile Material or textile that has been engineered to have aesthetic or performance-enhancing properties.

social media Internet-based applications that allow communication among users.

socially responsible design Achieved through inclusive design (i.e., inclusive based on age, physical ability, or socioeconomic status), physically and psychologically healthy design, design that promotes fair trade, and design decisions that facilitate efficient factory operations.

socially responsible distribution The intermediaries responsible for bringing goods to market. These intermediaries deliver goods from producers to end users in a manner that takes into consideration human rights, labor conditions, and environmental implications.

socially responsible marketing An organization shows concern for the people and environment in which it transacts business.

socially responsible production Production that balances the environmental, ethical, and community needs with costs needed to produce a product.

socially responsible supply chain management Supply chain management (SCM) is the oversight of materials, information, and finances as they move in a process from supplier to manufacturer to wholesaler to retailer to consumer. Socially responsible companies consider employee training, philanthropy, environment, workplace diversity, health and safety, and community issues as part of this management.

social responsibility See *corporate social responsibility*.

sole proprietorship Company owned by a single individual.

source or **supplier** or **vendor** Company from which textile producers, apparel manufacturers, or retailers purchase components or products necessary in their production and distribution operations (e.g., fiber sources, fabric sources, apparel product sources).

sourcing Decision process of determining how and where a company's products or their components will be produced.

sourcing fair Trade shows that bring contractors and companies together. At these fairs, contractors have booths with samples of their merchandise and information about their expertise and capacities.

SPA Specialty store retailer of private label apparel (e.g., Zara, Uniqlo, Banana Republic).

specialty retailer Retailer that focuses on a specific type of merchandise.

specification buying Retailer-initiated design and manufacturing of apparel goods in which the retailer may work directly with the sewing contractors (or their agents) to produce store brand or private label goods. Sometimes the retailer works with an apparel manufacturer to produce store brand or private label goods.

spreading The process of unwinding the large rolls of fabric onto long, wide cutting tables, stacked layer upon layer, in preparation for cutting.

spreading machine Equipment designed to carry the large rolls of fabric, guided on tracks along the side edges of the cutting table or rolled along the floor next to one side of the cutting table, to spread the fabric smoothly and quickly onto the cutting table.

spun yarn Yarn created by the spinning together of short staple fibers.

staple color Color such as black, navy, white, gray, or tan that is used in a line that appears frequently, season after season.

stockholder Owner of stock or shares in a corporation; each share of stock owned by a stockholder represents a percentage of the company.

stock-keeping unit See *SKU*.

stockout data Data on out-of-stock goods that is reviewed by the manufacturer, so that replenishments are ordered as often as required. The strategy of having the manufacturer (vendor) automatically ship merchandise to the retail store based on stock data.

store brand or **store-is-brand** Concept whereby the store offers only merchandise with the store name as its brand—for example, The Limited, Gap, Banana Republic, and Old Navy.

store brand product development See *private label product development*.

strike off A length of sample yardage of a printed fabric, used to test the colors and quality of the print.

style number A number (usually four to six digits) assigned to each garment style that is coded to indicate the season/year for the style and other style information.

subcontractor A subcontractor is hired by a main contractor to perform a specific task as part of the overall project.

supermarket Retailer that carries a full line of foods and related products using a self-service strategy.

superstore or **hypermarket** Upgraded large supermarkets that offer a wide range of merchandise including food, electronics, clothing and accessories, furniture, sporting goods, and garden items.

supplier See *source*.

supply chain management (SCM) Planning and management of the business actions necessary to coordinate procurement of materials, production, marketing, and distribution of finished merchandise to the retailer.

supply chain networks All of the interconnected individuals, businesses, and processes that are necessary to get a fashion product to the ultimate consumer; value is added to the product throughout the processes.

supply chain transparency Effective communication of where, how, and by whom all aspects of a fashion product are made and distributed.

swatch A small sample of the material/fabric intended to be used for a style.

sweatshop Originally referred to the system of contractors and subcontractors whereby work was "sweated off." Later became associated with the long hours, unclean and unsafe working conditions, and low pay of contract sewing factories, as well as with the dismal conditions of home factories, where contract workers sewed clothing. Currently used to refer to a company that violates labor, safety and health, and/or worker compensation laws, or that has work environments that are unsafe, inhumane, or abusive without providing opportunities for workers to organize or negotiate better terms of work.

T

tagboard A heavy-weight paper (also called oaktag or hard paper) used for pattern pieces instead of pattern paper.

tagless label Printed information such as care instructions, fiber content, and size, heat-sealed directly onto the product.

takeover The result of one company or individual gaining control of another company by buying a large enough portion of the company's shares.

tannery See *regular tannery*.

tanning The process of finishing leather, making the skins and hides pliable and water resistant.

target costing A pricing strategy of manipulating the fabric cost and styling features to provide a new style for a predetermined cost.

target customer Description of the gender, age range, lifestyle, geographic location, and price zone for most of the company's customers for a specific line.

tariff Tax assessed by governments on imports.

tawning The process of finishing furs, making the pelts pliable and water resistant.

tech drawing An abbreviation of the term *technical drawing*; a drawing of the garment style as viewed flat rather than seen three-dimensionally on a fashion figure. It could include close-up drawings of garment details. A tech drawing might also be called a flat or a flat sketch.

tech pac or tech package See *garment specifications*.

terms of sale Negotiated agreements between the manufacturer and retailer regarding the sale of merchandise; may include discounts, terms of delivery, availability of cooperative advertisements, and other promotional tools.

textile "Any product made from fibers" (Joseph 1988, p. 347).

textile converter See *converter*.

textile jobber Company that buys fabrics from textile mills, converters, and large manufacturers and then sells to smaller manufacturers and retailers.

textile mill Company that specializes in the fabric construction stage of production (e.g., weaving, knitting).

textile stylist Individual who has expertise in the design and manufacturing of textiles as well as an understanding of the textile market and works directly with manufacturers and retailers in creating textile designs.

textile testing "Process of inspecting, measuring and evaluating characteristics and properties of textile materials" (Cohen 1989, p. 165).

throwster Company that modifies filament yarns for specific end uses.

title flow See *ownership flow*.

toile A French term whose literal translation is "cloth"; refers to the muslin trial or sample garment.

tolerance The stated range of acceptable dimensional measurements, expressed as a (+) or (–) in inches (or metric dimensions) of the size specifications.

trade association Nonprofit association made up of member companies designed to research, promote, or provide educational services regarding an industry or a specific aspect of an industry.

trade dress Subset of trademark law; protects the overall look or image of a product or the packaging of a product.

trademark Word, name, symbol, mark, or image used by a company to legally differentiate its products from those of other companies.

trademark infringement Illegal use of a trademark or service mark; use without the permission of the owner of the trademark or service mark.

trade name See *brand name*.

trade preference program Trade agreements that provide incentives for companies to source in these regions of the world through investments and infrastructure enhancements.

trade publication A publication such as a newspaper or magazine that is targeted to the trade, such as retailers, manufacturers, or textile producers.

trade show Event sponsored by trade associations, merchandise marts, and/or promotional companies, to allow companies to promote their newest products to prospective buyers who have the opportunity to review new products of a number of companies under one roof.

trend research Information on future directions of consumer behavior, color, fabrics, and fashion styling obtained by reading trade publications and/or fashion magazines, making observations, or other data collection methods.

triple bottom line For companies, in addition to costs and profits associated with sourcing decisions, the decisions must also consider human rights, labor conditions, and environmental implications. For sourcing decisions, people, planet, and profit factors are all considered.

trunk show Marketing strategy by which a company brings an entire line to a retail store as a special event to show and sell to customers.

U

unit production system (UPS) Production system whereby the parts for each garment are transported as a unit on a conveyor track, one garment at a time, to the sewing operator, who performs one or several sewing operations and then releases the garment for transport to the next workstation.

Universal Product Code (UPC) One of several bar-coding systems used to electronically identify merchandise. A UPC is a 12-digit number that identifies the manufacturer and merchandise item by stock-keeping unit.

unlimited liability Situation in which owners of a company are personally liable for debts incurred by the business; often the case in sole proprietorships and in some partnerships.

upscale discounter Discount retail store with department store feel but offering more fashion-forward merchandise (e.g., Target).

usage The number of yards (yardage) of fabric(s) required to make the garment style. It usually denotes the most economical layout to use the least amount of fabric.

V

value-added network (VAN) Third-party computer system that allows business data to be transmitted electronically from one company to another.

value chain networks See *supply chain networks*.

VAN See *value-added network*.

vendor See *source*.

vendor-managed inventory (VMI) Programs whereby the manufacturer reviews retail sales/stockout data and orders replenishments as often as required.

vendor marking Affixing hangtags, labels, and price information to merchandise by the vendor (manufacturer).

vertical integration Business strategy whereby a company handles several steps in production and/or distribution.

vertically integrated See *vertical integration*.

vertical marketing channel See *vertical integration*.

virtual draping Computer-created simulation of a fabric draped three-dimensionally over an image of a garment as shown on a body or mannequin.

virtual sample Digital images of merchandise samples that are viewed on the computer screen.

W

warehouse retailer Retailer that reduces operating expenses and offers goods at discount prices by combining showroom, warehouse, and retail operations.

wholesale cost See *cost*.

wholesale price The price of the style that the retailer will pay the apparel manufacturer for the goods. The price is based on the manufacturer's cost to produce the style plus the manufacturer's profit.

wool Natural fiber derived from the fleece of sheep, goats, alpacas, and llamas.

work-in-process (WIP) The quantity of goods in the process of being assembled in the sewing factory at a given time.

Y

yarn Collection of fibers or filaments laid or twisted together to form a continuous strand strong enough for use in fabrics.

yarn forward rule of origin Stipulation to a trade agreement that requires yarn production and all operations "forward"—fabrics and production—of merchandise to be in one of the member countries or the trade agreement.

Z

zeitgeist The general social spirit and popular culture of a given time period.

index

Pull system, 14
Pure competition, 56
Push system, 14

Q

Quality assurance, 92–93, 260, 304–305
Quality control, 92–93
Quant, Mary, 15
Quick Response (QR), 14–16
Quotas, 262
QVC, 335

R

Rack trade, 113
Ready-to-wear (RTW), 4–11, 103–107, 203
Re-commerce, 322
Reebok, 56
Registration, 239
Regular corporation, 48
Regular tannery, 78
Relations programs, 202
Replenishment, 315, 316–318
Research
    in brand companies, 118
    color, 138–140
    consumer, 131–132
    fabric, 140–142
    fashion, 135–142
    market, 130–135
    product, 131, 132–133
    trend, 135–138
    trim, 140–142
Reshoring, 284
Resource Conservation and Recovery Act, 65
Retailer, 318
Retailing, 318–331
Retail relations programs, 202
Review of line, 164–166
R. H. Macy & Co., 6
Rich's, 6
Robinson-Patman Act, 63
Roots, 31
Rowley, Cynthia, 193
Rural free delivery (RFD), 6

S

Sachse, Peter, 132
Sale, terms of, 219
Sales, 119
Sales promotion, 120
Sales promotion strategies, 221–225
Sales representatives, 213–218
Sales volume, 154
Salon de couture, 105
Sample cuts, 142, 173, 179–181
Sample garment, 179–182
Sample lines, 216
Sample retail stores, 328
Samples
    making, 188

ordering, 188
    in preparation for market, 188
    virtual, 216
Sample sewer, 179–181
San Francisco, California, 210
Sao Paulo, Brazil, 211
S corporations, 48
Sean John, 33
Sears, Roebuck & Co., 6, 11, 209, 321
Season, 103, 203
Seattle, Washington, 210
Selected-distribution policy, 220
Selective distribution, 312
Selling
    corporate, 213
    internal, 212–213
Selling function, 212–219
Sell-through, 154
Service mark, 59
7 For All Mankind, 56
Seventeen, 136
Sew by, 293
Sewing factories, 7
Sewing machines, 5, 6
Sherman Antitrust Act, 63
Shopping mall, 9, 13
Shopping the market, 138
Short-cycle production, 294
Short-range forecasting, 133
Showrooms, 213–218
Silk, 8
Single-hand system, 299
Size range, in preproduction, 244, 252
Sketch, design, 158–162
Skins, 72
Sloper, 174–178
Slops, 4
Smart fitting rooms, 337
Smart materials, 96
Socially responsible design, 20
Socially responsible distribution, 20
Socially responsible marketing, 20
Socially responsible production, 20
Socially responsible supply chain management, 20
Social media, 222–223
Social responsibility, 258. *See also* Corporate social responsibility (CSR)
Sole proprietorship, 43–45
Sources, 236
Sourcing
    codes of conduct in, 279–283
    company criteria in, 257–262
    control standards and, 260

costs in, 258–259
criteria in, 257–265
decisions, 256–265
definition of, 256
design criteria in, 257–262
domestic production in, 266–268, 269
economic conditions and, 265
environmental impact and, 261–262
equipment and, 261
fabric/materials quality availability in, 259–260
factory considerations in, 261
fairs, 278
geographical criteria in, 262–265
global, 269–277, 278–283
infrastructure and, 264
labor requirements and, 258–259
natural disasters and, 265
offshore production in, 268–269
options, 265–269
philosophy, 258
political criteria in, 262–265
quality assurance and, 260
shipping distance and, 264
skill requirements in, 261
social responsibility and, 258, 261–262
strategies, 278–283
supply train transparency and, 262
trade agreements and, 262–264
trends in, 284
turnaround time and, 264
and yarn forward rule of origin, 260
South America, 211, 273
South Korea, 212, 276
Spain, 211
Specialty retailers, 325
Specialty store retailer of private label apparel (SPA), 28, 32, 57, 108, 190–194, 325
Specification buying, 190
Specifications, in design development, 196
Spinning machine, 3
Spinning mills, 3
Sports licensing, 35
Sportswear, 9, 10
Spreading machines, 247
Spun yarns, 73
Staple colors, 138
Stockholders, 48
Stock-keeping unit (SKU), 314
Stockout data, 317

Store brand, 14, 31, 108
Store brand development, 190–194
Store-is-brand, 194
Stores (magazine), 124
Strike off, 162, 239
Stuart, Jill, 207
Style, in design brief, 151–152
Style number, 172
Style selection, 186–187
Style testing, 225
Stylist, textile, 90–91
Subcontractors, 9
Sui, Anna, 121
Supermarkets, 329
Superstore, 329
Suppliers, 236
Supply, in history of fashion industry, 5
Supply chain management (SCM), 16–18, 20, 26, 96, 314–318
Supply chain networks, 26
Supply train transparency, 262
Sustainability issues, 97, 284
Swatch, 157
Sweatshop, 7, 279

T

Tagless labels, 298
Taiwan, 212, 276
Takeover, 53
Talbots, 194
Tanning, 78
Target, 13, 15, 16, 21, 31, 191, 193, 314, 321, 326, 327, 329
Target costing, 155, 185–186
Target customer, 135, 150–151
Tariffs, 262
Tawning, 79
Taylor, Ann, 103
Team, design, 152–153, 164–166
Tech drawing, 158
Technological advances, 95–97
Teenage fashion, 12
Television retailers, 335
Terms of sale, 219
Textile, definition of, 72
Textile brokers, 91
Textile converters, 73, 91, 238
Textile design, 90–91
Textile design, with computers, 162
Textile industry organization, 73–75
Textile jobbers, 91
Textile mills, 3–4, 73, 88–89, 117
Textile product mills, 117
Textile stylist, 90–91
Textile testing, 82–83, 92–93
Textile trade associations, 85